JADOOWALLAHS, JUGGLERS AND JINNS

John Zubrzycki is an Australian author who has been studying Indian history for more than forty years. He has worked in India as a diplomat and foreign correspondent, taught Indian studies and written extensively on Indian society, culture and politics. He is also the author of four other books – *The Shortest History of India*, *The House of Jaipur: The Inside Story of India's Most Glamorous Royal Family*, *The Mysterious Mr Jacob: Diamond Merchant, Magician and Spy* and *The Last Nizam: The Rise and Fall of India's Greatest Princely State*. He majored in South Asian history and Hindi at the Australian National University and has a PhD in Indian history from the University of New South Wales. John was the deputy foreign editor at *The Australian* before becoming a full-time writer.

Also by John Zubrzycki

The Last Nizam: The Rise and Fall of India's Greatest Princely State
The Mysterious Mr Jacob: Diamond Merchant, Magician and Spy
The House of Jaipur: The Inside Story of India's Most Glamorous Royal Family
The Shortest History of India

Praise for *Jadoowallahs, Jugglers and Jinns*

'John Zubrzycki has found the most wonderful story ... and told it brilliantly. This is – quite literally – a book of marvels'
William Dalrymple

'Enjoyable, authoritative and unexpected ... a wonderfully restrained commentary'
John Keay

'A terrific read ... [John Zubrzycki] paints a vivid picture'
Manu S. Pillai

'Indian magic and its rich history cannot be fully explained only by placing together pieces of a mosaic of experiences and interpretations collected from various parts. You need to be an artiste first to realize and explain an art form as intriguing as Indian magic ... I have really enjoyed reading this new book. I admire Zubrzycki's intent, patience and dedication'
Magician P. C. Sorcar Jr

'Exceptionally well-crafted and brilliantly told, *Jadoowallahs, Jugglers and Jinns* brings alive the most enchanting tales and traditions from the history of Indian magic'
Shashi Tharoor

'Deliciously rich in detail, both historical and contemporary, from the heydays of Indian magic to its current moment of crisis'
Outlook Traveller

'A definitive history of magic in India'
Scroll.in

JADOOWALLAHS, JUGGLERS AND JINNS

A MAGICAL HISTORY OF INDIA

JOHN ZUBRZYCKI

PICADOR INDIA

First published 2018 by Picador India
First published in paperback 2023 by Picador India
an imprint of Pan Macmillan Publishing India Private Limited
707 Kailash Building
26 K. G. Marg, New Delhi 110001
www.panmacmillan.co.in

Pan Macmillan, The Smithson, 6 Briset Street, Farringdon, London EC1M 5NR
Associated companies throughout the world
www.panmacmillan.com

ISBN 978-93-95624-73-2

1 3 5 7 9 8 6 4 2

Typeset by Manmohan Kumar
Printed and bound in India by Gopsons Papers Pvt. Ltd., Noida.

To my children Adele, Alexander,
Jonathon and Nicolas

‘Of the jugglers alone, a whole book might be written’
James Inglis, *Tent Life in Tigerland*, p. 234

CONTENTS

INTRODUCTION

'SO WONDERFULLY STRANGE'

DILSHAD Garden, on the eastern outskirts of New Delhi, is an unlikely location to be probing the veracity of a four-century-old account of Indian magic. To use the appellation 'Garden' was a town planner's clever sleight of hand. There are few open spaces in this congested warren of low-rise seventies-style government housing. The grit and fumes of the Grand Trunk Road make it even harder to imagine how northern India might have looked in the Mughal period. My destination was a small park surrounded on three sides by ochre-coloured flats. My guide was the infectiously enthusiastic Raj Kumar, General Secretary of the Society of Indian Magicians, winner of the International Merlin Award, master of the Rope Trick and levitation act, team leader at the Delhi School of Magic, and founder of MAZMA, the Society for Uplifting Traditional Magic & Performing Arts. It was late November, the middle of the marriage season – the busiest period of Delhi's always-hectic social calendar. Raj Kumar was negotiating the maze of traffic, while fielding bookings for magic shows on his super-sized smartphone. Talent scout and teacher, he had dozens of semi-pro mystifiers on his books, ready to dazzle guests at weddings, corporate gigs and birthday parties.

Waiting at the park were a dozen-or-so jadoowallahs, traditional street magicians, who had come from Ghaziabad, just across the Uttar Pradesh border. Raj Kumar proudly told me how he had pulled them out of poverty by buying each a motorbike. Without their own transport, getting to the small towns and villages where they can still perform is difficult. Making a living as a street magician in New Delhi is tough. Begging is officially banned in the Indian capital and under the law, street magicians are lumped together with beggars and other vagrants, making them easy targets for the bribe-taking police. But this was very much Raj Kumar's territory and over the next two hours his rag-tag magical assemblage performed unmolested, presenting a repertoire of tricks that bore a striking similarity to what the Mughal emperor Jahangir had witnessed in the early seventeenth century.

Jahangir presided over an empire at the height of its power and decadence. He never went near a battlefield and rarely drew a sword, though in his memoirs he admits to ordering one of his grooms to be killed on the spot and two palanquin bearers hamstrung and paraded around his camp on a donkey, for disturbing a nilgai during a hunting trip. The peace and stability his father, Akbar, had left behind allowed Jahangir to indulge in shikari, sensual pursuits, poetry and drinking – the latter being an addiction he spoke of with pride:

> Encompassed as I was with youthful associates of congenial minds, breathing the air of a delicious climate – ranging through

> lofty and splendid saloons, every part of which decorated with all the graces of painting and sculpture, and the floors bespread with the richest carpets of silk and gold, would it not have been a species of folly to have rejected the aid of an exhilarating cordial – and what cordial can surpass the juice of the grape?[1]

He was also a connoisseur of all things exotic: Zebras, turkeys and other strange animals including a creature brought to his court by a dervish from Ceylon with the face of a bat and the body of a monkey, minus the tail. His garden bloomed with 'the apricots of Suliman and Abbas'. It was scented with sandalwood 'peculiar to the islands of Zeir, or Zubberbad'.[2] He owned the finest elephants to transport the imperial assemblage – wives, almirahs, carpets, silver utensils and a canopy of velvet wrought with gold, said to weigh several tonnes that protected his peripatetic court from the rays of the meridian sun.[3] He was also fascinated by magic – once halting his convoy to watch the performance of a Carnatic juggler who could swallow a chain three yards long. His obsession with necromancy interfered with the day-to-day running of the court to such an extent that a group of complainants wishing to report abuses of power by the Governor of Bengal, had to dress up as magicians to get his attention.

Midway through his memoirs, as he contemplates a life well lived, a life of 'gold, and jewels, and sumptuous wardrobes, and in the choicest beauties the sun ever shone upon',[4] Jahangir digresses to 'matters of less serious importance'. There can be found in Bengal, he informs his readers, 'performers in sleight of hand, or jugglers, of such unrivalled skill in their art, that I have thought a few instances of their extraordinary dexterity not unworthy of a

Group of Indian jugglers from Zigzag Journeys in India, *1887. Library of Congress.*

place in these memorials.' He goes on to describe how a troupe of seven came to his court boasting of 'producing effects so strange as far to surpass the scope of the human understanding'. Not only did they keep their word, 'they exhibited in their performances things of so extraordinary a nature, as without the actual demonstration the world would not have conceived possible'.[5] Over the course of what would have been several days and nights, they effected no fewer than twenty-eight tricks, a compendium of marvels that encompassed many of the legendary feats of Indian magic – all executed with such skill and consisting of such marvels, that the loquacious Mughal would often be lost for words.

The chief juggler began by promising to produce any tree in an instance, merely by placing a seed in the earth. Khaun-e-Jahaun, one of Jahangir's nobles, ordered a mulberry tree. 'The men arose without hesitation, and having in ten separate spots set some seed in the ground, they recited among themselves, in cabalistical language unintelligible to the standers-by, when instantly a plant was seen springing from each of the ten places, and each proved the tree required by Khaun-e-Jahaun.' In front of their bewildered audience, they produced other trees in the same manner – mango, apple, cypress, fig, almond, walnut and so on. Fruit was picked and distributed for tasting. 'Before the trees were removed there appeared among the foliage birds of such surprising beauty, in colour, and shape, and melody of song, as the world never saw before,' continues Jahangir. The foliage turned to variegated autumnal tints, before the trees slowly sank into the earth. Stated the emperor: 'I can only further observe, that if the circumstances which I have now described had not happened in my own presence, I could never have believed that they had any existence in reality.'[6]

That evening, one of the jugglers came before Jahangir and spun in a circle, clothed in nothing but a sheet. From beneath it he took a magnificent mirror that produced a light so powerful 'it illuminated the hemisphere to an incredible distance round'. Travellers would later report that on that very same night, at a distance of ten days' journey, the sky was so floodlit it exceeded 'the brightness of the brightest day that they had ever seen'.[7] In the following days, feats of ventriloquism were followed by demonstrations of fireworks that were launched into the air without being touched. A cauldron produced cooked rice and stewed fowl without a fire being lit. A flower turned into a fountain that burst forth with showers of rose petals. A hole dug in the ground and filled with water turned into a sheet of ice so thick, an elephant could walk across it. In quick succession, arrows were shot into the sky where they somehow remained suspended, successive arrows attaching themselves to the ones fired before, forming a heavenly archway. A red rose dipped into a vessel of water changed colour 'a hundred times'. The magicians created the same effect using a length of white thread and later used a mirror that altered the tint of anything put behind it. From sleight of hand, they progressed to acrobatics. Seven men formed a column, head to head and feet to feet. The man supporting the other six then lifted one foot as high as his shoulder. Standing thus, Jahangir stated, he exhibited 'a degree of strength and steadiness not exactly within the scope of my comprehension'.[8]

From an empty bag emerged two cocks that 'fought with such force and fury, that their wings emitted sparks of fire at every stroke'. Two partridges of the 'most beautiful and brilliant plumage' appeared, followed by two frightful black snakes that attacked each other until they were too exhausted

these seven jugglers'. He dismissed the troupe with a donation of fifty thousand rupees and ordered each of his amirs to give upwards of one thousand rupees in appreciation of their performance.

Was Jahangir's description a fantasy of his alcohol-addled mind? Had the passage of time blurred his memory? Did the translator embellish the text? Reflecting on the performance of the Bengali jugglers, Milbourne Christopher, the magic historian, warned: 'Always remember that what a layman thinks he sees and what the magician actually does, are not necessarily the same. Further, many spectators, in telling about tricks, invent considerably to make their accounts more interesting.'[13]

Like their Bengali ancestors, the members of Raj Kumar's troupe carried few props – a couple of baskets, some sheets, a few sticks and some lengths of rope – anything that could fit on the back of a two-wheeler. And of course, there was no stage, just compacted dirt with a hint of grass. My impresario had promised authentic Indian street magic. I was not disappointed.

Dressed in a brightly embroidered black shirt and matching felt cap, and sporting a well-hennaed beard, Farukh Shah went first, I suspect because he was the most senior of the troupe. The Indian way of executing a trick is to start off with plenty of patter. Not a lot happens initially, but great care is taken to convince the audience that the props, in this case two empty baskets and a couple of pieces of cloth, are what they are – not cleverly concealed receptacles for what comes next. With some masterly misdirection and skilful sleight of hand, Shah produced a small tree with red blossoms, seemingly out of nowhere. It looked more like a shrub than the fruit-laden, bird-filled orchard Jahangir was granted, but its provenance was clear. He then pulled out a

Ghaziabad juggler Farukh Shah prepares to do a version of the Mango Tree Trick. Photo © John Zubrzycki.

thick quarto-sized book with a bright red glossy cover. Each time he flipped through the pages a different set of images appeared. Birds, animals, Hindi and English letters, currency notes, flowers and trees. The Mughal would have been impressed.

Next came a levitation trick. Shamin Khan covered his brother Asim with a blue sheet, tapped his stick on the ground and watched his lithe frame slowly rise above the ground, his head and legs clearly visible. Though I had been told the secret to the trick, it was impressive nonetheless. It was followed by a rope-tying feat, where two members of the audience were invited to tie ropes around one of the jugglers, checking the knots as they went. Other members of the troupe then held the ends of the two longest ropes and pulled them tightly. Spinning in a circle, the juggler loosened the bindings without touching them, the ropes falling like leftover spaghetti on the ground. In place of a cauldron that produced rice and stewed fowl without a fire being lit, another of the jadoowallahs, Aas Mohammed, took out a wicker plate and tossed some uncooked rice on it. As he shook the plate, the raw grains magically turned into puffed rice, which was then passed around like a plate of prasad, the holy food offered at temples. Instead of producing snakes from his mouth, Mohammed disgorged marbles and brass balls, before spitting out a jaw full of rusty nails. Ashik Ali's turn came next. Muttering incantations, he covered his son, Shahrukh, with a blanket. With the boy's outline clearly visible, he dismembered the body, pulling legs, arms and head away from his torso. Once the blanket was removed, the boy was whole again.

The members of Raj Kumar's troupe carry smartphones, post images of their shows on Facebook, connect with each other via WhatsApp and pull out laminated testimonials and faded photographs of performances they have given. They are hired by government agencies to promote HIV-awareness and impress on poor people the need to put their savings in the bank (think vanishing coin tricks). But much of their repertoire has changed little over the centuries. All have learned their trade from their fathers, who were taught by their fathers and so on, going back many generations. Although it is getting harder to make ends meet by being a street magician, they know no other life.

India's pantheon of magicians – jadoowallahs, tamashawallahs, jadugars, madaris, mayakaris, maslets, qalandars, sanpwallahs, sanperas, katputliwallahs, bahurupis, peep-showwallahs, the list goes on – ranges across creed and caste. Stronger than religious ties, is their association with the *barah pal*, the brotherhood of twelve, an ancient collective of strolling players that includes jugglers, snake charmers, animal handlers, puppeteers, ventriloquists, storytellers, impersonators and acrobats. Regardless of their backgrounds, members of this peripatetic brotherhood can share a cooking hearth made out of three stones whenever their wanderings bring them together. Economic changes are breaking down what were once strong bonds between these communities. But their arts of legerdemain live on as an integral part of the social, cultural and religious fabric of India as they have for millennia.

For something so enduring, there has been very little scholarship on Indian magic in recent decades aside from Lee Siegel's masterly account *Net of Magic* and Peter Lamont's lucid and entertaining *The Rise of the Indian Rope Trick*. More recently, Chris Goto-Jones has charted the influence of Indian, Japanese and Chinese conjurers during the 'Golden Age of Magic' in his book *Conjuring Asia*.[14] Until the early twentieth century, much of the writing comprised anecdotal accounts of travellers, merchants, pilgrims and missionaries, as well as the memoirs of Western magicians whose texts were often little more than an extension of their showmanship. In flamboyant prose, they fired up the public's expectations about the miracles and marvels of the East. Most were drawn to India because it was considered the birthplace of magic and therefore the source of all that was truly inexplicable. As Nevil Maskelyne, son of the great nineteenth-century English magician and inventor John Nevil Maskelyne, once wrote: 'The difficulty of producing a new magical effect, is about equivalent to that of inventing a new proposition in Euclid.'[15] India promised a cornucopia of undiscovered treasures, tricks and routines whose secrets could be easily stolen and appropriated. By adopting oxymoronic names such as the Fakir of Shiva and dressing in shimmering sherwanis and triumphantly plumed turbans, these Western conjurers tried to give the public what they craved: a glimpse of the mysterious Orient that was out of reach to all but a few. By doing so, they were forgetting one of the cardinal rules of magic: skilful presentation is always more important than technique – and when it came to display, jadoowallahs took line honours. Their poverty, the primitiveness of their surroundings, the use of common articles such as baskets, clay pots and pieces of cloth to execute the most extraordinary of feats, only accentuated their exotic allure, much to the consternation of their Occidental cousins.

My first encounter with Indian street magic was in December 1979. I was on a train from Calcutta to Guwahati in Assam, but a twenty-four-hour *bandh*, or strike, over illegal immigrants from Bangladesh, led to a lengthy unscheduled stop in Alipurduar. Tired of waiting in my third-class compartment, I wandered into the square outside the station where a crowd of curious onlookers had encircled an old man and a young boy who were preparing to do the Basket Trick. The boy climbed into a round cane basket just big enough to fit into. After putting on the lid, the man started chanting incantations that grew louder and louder. Without warning he picked up a large steel sword and started plunging it into the basket. Blood covered the sword and the boy's screams were terrifying. There seemed no way he could have avoided the thrusts of the three-foot long blade. I could sense the crowd getting edgy. If this was theatre, then the performance was utterly convincing. Suddenly everything went silent. In went the sword one last time. A blanket was thrown over the basket.

After a few moments, the blanket and the lid of the basket were removed and the boy appeared with the sword through his neck. Grasping the hilt in one hand and the tip of the blade in the other, the magician lifted the boy off the ground and presented him to the now completely astonished crowd. The boy showed no signs of discomfort, there were no obvious wounds and no trickery involved. I was sure there was no hidden brace. When sufficient *baksheesh* had been collected, the boy was lowered back into the basket, a blanket was thrown over it and a few minutes later he emerged completely unscathed.

The Basket Trick is one of the oldest and most mystifying feats of magic in the world. Expertly executed by an ancient looking wizard on a dirt-covered square without trapdoors, mirrors or curtains, it is a spectacular illusion. If magic is defined as 'the artful performance of impossible effects',[16] then the Basket Trick falls squarely in this category. But defining the wider meaning of magic in an Indian context is as elusive as finding evidence of the Rope Trick. In 1982, the social anthropologist Edmund Leach, whose field work took him to Taiwan, the highlands of Burma, Kurdistan and Ceylon, concluded: 'After a lifetime's career as a professional anthropologist, I have almost reached the conclusion that the word [magic] has no meaning whatsoever'.[17] Few contemporary social anthropologists, he added, could 'confidently distinguish magical from non-magical acts'.[18] Writing a decade earlier, the Dutch cultural anthropologist Jan van Baal warned: 'Magic is a dangerous word, more dangerous than magic itself, because it is such a handsome term to cover everything that we fail to understand. The term is used far too often as a vague kind of explanation, but in fact it explains nothing.'[19]

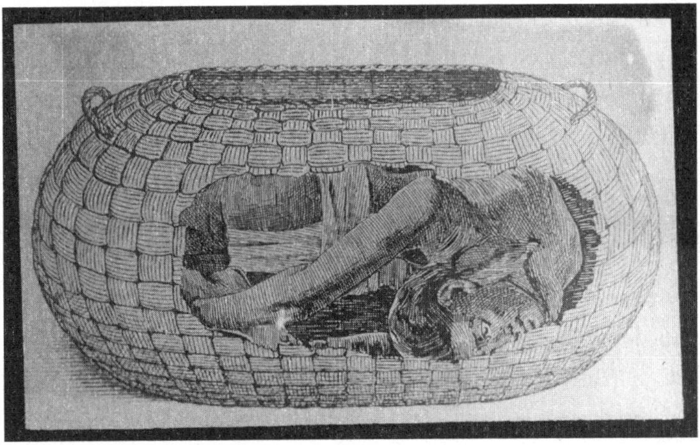

The great Indian Basket Trick. Harry Price Collection, University of London.

Both Leach and Van Baal were referring to ritual or sympathetic magic rooted in religion, nature rites and belief in the supernatural, rather than magic for the sake of entertainment. In India, the lines between these two types have been deliberately – and very effectively – blurred. A Hindu or a Muslim holy man will vanish objects, pass skewers through his body or walk on hot coals to convince alms givers of his spiritual powers. The street magician will copy those feats or add similar ones such as being buried underground or lying on a bed of nails, for the same pecuniary ends. P. C. Sorcar's 1960s two-and-a-half-hour showbiz extravaganza started with the ritualistic drawing of a mandala on the stage and the lighting of an oil lamp before a portrait of Goddess Durga. Dressed as a mock maharajah, India's most famous magician then presented a programme that had more bling than a Bollywood movie but was as authentically Indian as chicken tikka masala.

In this book, the boundaries for what constitutes magic are also deliberately blurred. The most commonly used Sanskrit word for magic, *indrajal*, can refer to the net of the god Indra, sleight of hand, jugglery, illusions, the appearance of things, as well as traps, stratagems and deceptions employed in warfare to confuse one's enemies. Similarly *sihr*, the Koranic term for magic or sorcery, can refer to juggling and conjuring tricks, astrology, the production of spectacular effects through the help of spirits and demons, the use of drugs or perfumes to confuse people, the charismatic seduction of crowds, as well as sowing dissent.[20] Rather than trying to separate magic, religion and science as Western theorists such as James Frazer have done, a more suitable approach is to consider the jadoowallah's craft as the core around which other forms of popular entertainment and ritual practices occur.[21] Traditionally, a typical troupe of street entertainers would comprise men, women and children in often overlapping roles. Music is used to attract the attention of passers-by. When a sufficiently large crowd has gathered, acrobatics, balancing acts and juggling displays warm the audience up. There may be a puppet show, some clowning or a comedy routine. Live cobras dart at spectators, before being lured back into their baskets by the sonorous sounds of the *pungi*. A goat balances on a cylinder no wider that a Coke bottle, a monkey dressed like a groom at a wedding does somersaults to the beating of the *damru* and then carries around a begging bowl. Coin tricks, Cups and Balls, Diving Ducks and Egg Bag routines, lull onlookers into a false sense of security ahead of a series of more complex and often gruesome feats. Chickens are decapitated and restored to life, a man's tongue is severed, swords are swallowed, a child trapped in a basket screams as it is stabbed by a knife. What was sleight of hand begins to look like real magic. If the audience is mainly Hindu, Indra, the god whose net of magic created the world, will be invoked, if Muslim, the same magician's patter will be sprinkled with Koranic references. After the performance, women read palms, dispense herbal remedies and divine answers newly married girls ask about how best to ensure the birth of a male child.

Trying to define what constitutes a magical act in this context runs the risk of becoming meaningless even before considering that other blurred boundary between magic and religion. At one extreme are feats that to many would be classified as being purely physical and associated with circus routines such as clowning and tightrope walking. At the other are deceptions that might be classified by some as black magic or witchcraft. Nor are individual performers specialists in one art. Among the Qalandars, a nomadic tribe found in parts of the Punjab and Sindh, children are taught singing and dancing, tumbling, rope walking and other acrobatic feats, as well as sleight-of-hand tricks and working with performing animals such as bears, goats and monkeys.[22] The term juggler became the widely used word for an Indian magician in nineteenth-century England, because of the public's exposure to troupes that combined a range of physical acts alongside straight conjuring. The Oriental Troupe, which entertained English audiences in the late-1860s and was billed as coming directly from the Kingdom of Oude, included a contortionist who could thread a needle with her toes while blindfolded, an acrobat who could walk on tight-rope with buffalo horns tied to his feet, a gymnast who could somersault atop a twenty-foot-high pole, as well as a magician who made cats and pigeons appear out of nowhere. At

London's Crystal Palace, they appeared alongside a Norwegian giant and a hippopotamus posing as a 'Blue Hairless Horse'.

I am acutely aware that as a Westerner my perception of what is magical in India's performing arts, literature, society, religion and culture will differ from an Indian's. Similarly, in a country as large and as ethnically, religiously and linguistically diverse as India, and where populations coexist at vastly different stages of development, there will be multiple takes on what is magical. Though the boundaries are blurred, I needed to draw the line somewhere, but not before considering whether I should examine the miraculous powers of god-men such as Sai Baba, the story of milk-drinking Ganesh statues, and Sachin Tendulkar's success at the crease after taking the advice of Parsi astrologer, Bejan Daruwalla, and changing the number on his jersey to thirty-three. Although the apparently supernatural powers of religious ascetics, the place of magic in Hinduism and even the predictions of soothsayers, diviners and astrologers are mentioned, I mostly steer clear of Sai Babas and Daruwallas. The core of this book is the role of the magician as an entertainer, whether on the street, in the court or on a conventional stage.

In researching this book, I found evidence of magic almost everywhere I looked: in the verses of the *Atharva Veda*, the stories of Somadeva and Dandin's descriptions of Pallava society with its statues of Kama, the god of love and his consort, Rati, making erotic sounds – to name just a few. Archival material in New Delhi, Bombay, London, Cambridge and other libraries revealed the wonderful Professor Ahmad, court conjurer of the princely state of Charkhari who entertained the Amir of Afghanistan at a state dinner in Agra with his Marvellous Sphinx trick. The archives often illuminated the darker side of India's magical history. After being recruited by corrupt or incompetent impresarios, hundreds of jugglers, acrobats, dancers and musicians were abandoned in cities such as London, Brussels and Berlin, forcing the India Office to arrange for their repatriation. One of those was Amar Nath Dutt, who was duped into going to New York by a curry cook posing as a prince from Baluchistan. After being dumped on the streets of Queens, he joined a revolutionary cell in Paris bent on the overthrow of the British Raj and trained as a bomb maker. He ended up using his pyrotechnic skills to bring dazzling Indian deceptions to the Western stage as Linga Singh. In the 1930s, a Kashmiri who called himself Kuda Bux, created a media storm by staging the first fire walk in England. His fame helped pave the way for other Indians such as Gogia Pasha and P. C. Sorcar to bring their blend of Western and Eastern marvels to the world stage.

Magical menageries from India, such as the Oriental Troupe, became a staple of world fairs and international exhibitions and were seen by millions of people. By the end of the nineteenth century, the wonder-workers of Madras, Delhi, Lucknow and Lahore were synonymous with the greatest possession of the largest empire in the world. Accounts of ropes being thrown in the air and remaining upright without any visible support, yet strong enough for an animal or even a man to climb up and disappear; of fakirs being buried alive for months and brought back to life; of conjurors instantaneously raising mango trees laden with fruit from the bare earth, filled the pages of newspapers and journals. In December 1899, London's *Strand Magazine* declared in its typically unequivocal tone: 'Ask the average man for what India is most celebrated, and chances are ten-to-one that he will ignore the glories of the Taj Mahal, the beneficence of British rule, even Mr Kipling, and will unhesitatingly reply in one word, "Jugglers".'[23]

This book tells the story of how India's jugglers achieved this accolade and what has happened since. To tell the story of Indian magic is to hold a mirror to India's religious traditions, its society and culture. Magic permeated the Vedic period, Sufis and yogis staged miracle contests to see whose *jadoo* was more powerful, Buddhists and Jains resorted to spells and incantations to win philosophical debates. Indian fortune-tellers were in great demand in ancient Rome. The Tang emperors of China employed Indian alchemists who peddled secret formulas that promised longevity and sexual prowess. After watching the tricks of conjurers, the eighth-century sage, Sankara, used their principles to explain the concept of *maya* or illusion. During the Abbasid caliphate, the booksellers of Baghdad sold Indian conjuring manuals translated into Arabic. In the late eighteenth century, Muscovites were startled by the appearance of a yogi who kept his arms raised above his head as a penance. He was midway through a decades-long pilgrimage that took him through Ceylon, Malaya, Afghanistan, Persia, Mesopotamia and back down the Silk Road to Tibet.

The story of Indian magic cannot be told without examining its place in the globalization of popular culture and the interplay between Eastern and Western traditions of performance magic. In 1813, the enterprising captain of an East Indiaman docked on the Thames with a troupe of jugglers. Their appearance at Pall Mall would change the face of Western conjuring forever. Other troupes quickly followed and, in the late 1810s, a South Indian named Ramo Samee started performing in America, Europe and England, becoming one of the most famous magicians of his day.

Within a few decades, continental conjurers were blackening their faces and performing the Basket Trick and levitation acts. By the time professional Indian magicians, with their Western-style routines and matching outfits, began travelling to Europe and America in the early 1900s, they found the market flooded with the likes of Samri S. Baldwin, 'The White Mahatma', Gustave Fasola, 'The Famous Indian Fakir', and Howard Thurston, who strutted the stage looking like a Tartar chieftain while presenting routines he claimed holy men on the banks of the Ganges had taught him the secrets to. Even Harry Houdini started his career posing as a 'Hindu fakir'.

Thurston's show included a version of the Great Indian Rope Trick. With a provenance stretching back to the sixth century BCE, it remains one of the most legendary feats in the world. In the early 1900s, it was being presented as proof that India was a land where real magic was still possible. Determined to bury that notion and take down the legend of the Rope Trick, the Magic Circle, the most prestigious society of prestidigitators in Britain, offered a 500-guinea reward to the first person who could perform the feat without props. The prize was never claimed.

Poster for Howard Thurston's East Indian Rope Trick, c. 1914. Wikimedia Commons.

Unlike most people who have written on this topic, I

am not a magician, though I have tried rather unsuccessfully to pick up a few sleights of hand during my encounters with India's wonder-workers. Barring a couple of exceptions, the reader will not discover the secrets to any of the tricks described in this book – many of which, in any case, seem inexplicable, even to a hardened sceptic such as myself. There is enough disenchantment in the world and I don't intend to add to it. Nor is this a comprehensive account of the jadoowallah's craft. Hidden in back issues of Bengali-language magic journals jealously guarded by collectors, in the arcane manuals of tantrics and occultists, in yet-to-be discovered manuscripts gathering dust in libraries and archives, are any number of stories of India's magical lore and of encounters with mystifiers waiting to be told. My hope is that this overview of India's magical traditions will encourage more scholarship on how the worlds of jadoowallahs, jugglers and jinns shaped its society, culture and religion – and enriched the rest of the world.

A Note on Place Names

WHEN I started writing this book, Gurugram was still Gurgaon. Several other cities probably changed their spelling in the interim that I am not aware of. Since the overwhelming majority of this book is concerned with the period up until the early 1970s, the names appear as they were used when the events described took place, or the documents cited were produced. For the sake of consistency (and personal nostalgia) place names such as Calcutta remain so, even when the story moves closer to the present.

ONE

OF LEVITATING BRAHMINS AND PROPHESIZING APES

BRAHMIN priests strike the ground with their magic staves causing the temple floor to rise and fall like waves on an ocean. A traveller from the Maghreb faints as a magician assumes the shape of a cube and rises above the ground. In the court of Jahangir, a century-old clairvoyant ape outwits the Mughal emperor and his courtiers by divining from jumbled up pieces of paper the one inscribed with the name Jesus as the true prophet. A monastery in the desert of Makran floats between heaven and earth. The rain never touches its walls and those who pray there are cured of any disease. A Jesuit missionary witnesses a procession staged for the pleasure of Aurangzeb with beautifully robed monkeys encircling a dog-king seated on a throne. On the Malabar coast, conjurers recite secret charms to protect pearl divers from man-eating crocodiles. Automatons serve wine to sages dwelling in cloud-shrouded citadels. Alchemists mix Himalayan herbs and precious metals into elixirs that can extend their lives for hundreds of years.

Beginning with Herodotus, in the sixth century BCE, the accounts of historians, geographers, merchants, missionaries, pilgrims, adventurers, storytellers and royal chroniclers presented India as a land of strange beasts and fantastical races, ascetics and saints, soothsayers and snake charmers, wonder-workers and necromancers. Many of these stories were works of imagination. Some borrowed from earlier writings, embellishing details as they vied for the attention of a reading public hungry for stories from the mystical East. Others referred to inexplicable feats that are still being debated in magic and scholarly circles. Among the tomes stored in the libraries of ancient Greece and Rome, the reliquaries of the Tang dynasty, the houses of learning of the Abbasid Caliphate and the monasteries of Medieval and Renaissance Europe, were found secret spells from Vedic texts, strange woodcuts of one-eyed men and giant griffins as well as tales of terrible austerities practiced by yogis in their quest for salvation. By the eighteenth century, many of these works began being translated into French, Italian, German and English, firing the Western imagination and providing more evidence – if any was needed – of the timeless and enduring links between India and all things magical.

The earliest descriptions in Western literature of this mysterious land were those Herodotus incorporated into his *Histories*. The Greek geographer portrays India as a continent of marvels and monstrosities located at the extremity of the known world, or as he put it 'nearest to the east and the place of the rising sun'.[1] Among the Indians are cannibals who eat their dead rather than waste their meat, and those who never kill a living creature. They are black-skinned like the Ethiopians and have sex in the open.

Men produce semen that is also black. Besides these tribes, there are Indians of another race who dwell to the north and follow nearly the same mode of life as the Bactrians. They are more warlike and from among them go men to procure gold dug out of the ground by ants when they make their burrows. 'In colour they resemble cats, and are as large as the wolves of Egypt. This gold, which they throw up in the winter, the Indians contrive to steal in the summer, when the ants, on account of the heat, hide themselves under ground.' Mounted on camels that are as swift as horses, men raid the piles of gold, then flee. If the ants wake up, they can outrun the fastest camel. The gold collected is offered as a tribute to their king.[2]

Writing in about 400 BCE, the Greek physician Ctesias of Cnidus also located India at the eastern extremity of the known world. He lists races of pygmies and *sciapodes*, a people with a single large foot they use as a sort of umbrella against the burning sun. He also mentions *cynocephali*, men with canine heads 'who do not use articulate speech but bark like dogs' and live by hunting. Another race has ears so large they cover their arms to the elbows and their entire back. In some parts of India can be found giants, in others, men with extraordinarily long tails 'like those of satyrs in pictures'. There are fabulous animals such as the *martikhora,* that had the face of a man, the body of a lion and the tail of a scorpion,

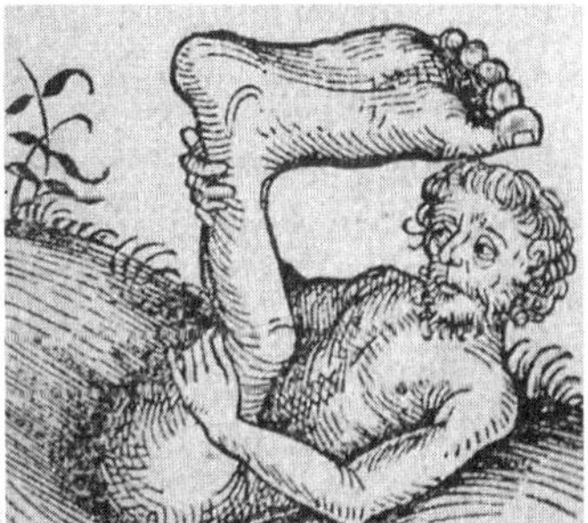

Sciapode or umbrella-foot man. Illustration from the Nuremberg Chronicle, *late fifteenth century.*

as well as unicorns and griffins that guarded treasures of gold.[3] Other tales tell of a fountain from which was drawn hundreds of pitchers full of fluid gold that then solidified. The iron found at the bottom of this fountain could be made into swords and if fixed in the earth, prevented 'clouds and hail and thunderstorms'.[4] The sun appeared ten times larger in India than in other lands, and the sea, just four fingers in depth, was so hot that fish never came to the surface. Ctesias also describes a race of pygmies less than two cubits high with hair so long it flows down their backs to their knees and beards that touch the ground. 'Their privates are thick, and so large that they descend even to their ankles.' Three thousand of this race attend the king on account of their skills in archery.[5]

The earliest first-hand account of India was written by Megasthenes, who was sent by the Macedonian king Seleucus I as ambassador to the court of Chandragupta Maurya at Pataliputra – modern-day Patna – around 320 BCE. Portions of this monumental work, *Indica,* describing his travels in 'this mystical and magical land', have been preserved in the writings of Strabo, Pliny, Arrian and others. Though he repeats fragments of older tales, Megasthenes adds accounts of men without mouths who can survive on nothing but the smell of roasted meat and the perfume of fruits and flowers, and of Hyperboreans who live for a thousand years. Strabo's version of Megasthenes' travels includes a description of a tribe of religious ascetics and wonder-workers called Garamanes, who he divides into three groups. At the top of a rudimentary caste hierarchy are the Hylobioi, forest dwellers who eat leaves and wild fruit, abstain from sex and wine, communicate with the king through messengers and supervise his religious rituals. A second group, the Latrikoi, are sorcerers and mendicant healers, who administer drugs and display great powers of endurance such as remaining in the same position for an entire day. Finally, there are the Mantikoi, soothsayers and necromancers, who go from village to village begging. Strabo also describes the Pramnai, who are the opponents of the sages or Brahmins. Like the Garamanes, they are divided into three groups including the naked Pramnai who spend their life in the open air doing austerities.[6] Megasthenes also recounted the story of Alexander the Great's meeting with gymnosophists in the ancient Buddhist capital of Taxila. Alexander was particularly impressed by the sufferance of these naked ascetics, noting how they could stand motionless on one leg for many hours holding a heavy weight. But when the Greek king asked one of them to join his court as an adviser, Dandamis, their leader, refused, telling him he was also a son of Zeus 'and that he wanted nothing that was Alexander's for he was content with what he had'.[7]

In 43 BCE, another Greek set out for India, but unlike Alexander, he was motivated not by conquest but the desire to learn about this strange land's 'rites, discipline, and doctrines'. Apollonius of Tyana was a Pythagorean and a reputed wonder-worker who had consorted with magi of Babylon and the sages of Egypt and Ethiopia. The Antiochian historian Malalas even gave him the power to repel mosquitoes, which he did by waving magic wands and chanting spells in front of an effigy of the god Ares.[8] Just over a hundred years after his death in 94 AD, Julia Domna, the wife of Septimius Severus, was given the lost memoirs of Damis of Nineveh who had been a disciple of Apollonius and had accompanied him on many of his travels. In

217, Philostratus published the *Life of Apollonius of Tyana* based on Damis's account. Philostratus played down accusations that Apollonius was a wizard, presenting him as an intellectual and moral teacher, a religious ascetic and reformer, as well as being a prophet of divine and superhuman nature.

In Philostratus's narrative, Apollonius, Damis and his two servants travel to India by way of Babylon, reaching Taxila after a long and arduous march. His account of the marvels of India exceeds even those of Ctesias and Megasthenes. On reaching the Hyphasis river, he finds a giant white worm producing an oil that burns forever and is used by the king to set his enemy's defences on fire. There are griffins the size of lions that quarry gold with their powerful beaks and swans that sing themselves to death. And there are dragons. 'The whole of India is wreathed with dragons of immense length; the marshes are full of them, the mountains are full of them, and not a ridge is free from them,' Philostratus writes.[9] The ones living in the hills and plains are hunted for the pupils of their eyes, which are made of a fiery stone with wonderful and mystical properties. The mountain dragons are the fiercest of all. 'They glide on the earth with a sound as of brass; their fiery crests throw out a light brighter than that of a torch.' To capture them, people spread out a magic carpet embossed with golden charms that lulls the dragon to sleep. Using spells, they wake the dragon from its slumber, then rush at it, cutting off its head from which is extracted 'bright-coloured stones, flashing with every hue, and of powers as wonderful as those of Gyges' ring'.[10] The inhabitants of Paraka, Apollonius is told, eat the hearts and livers of the dragons in order to learn their language and thoughts.

Apollonius of Tyana. Engraving by F. Cleyn, 1659. Wellcome Library.

Apollonius finds traces of India's Hellenic past everywhere he goes. In Taxila, which reminds him of Athens, there is a temple with pictures embossed on copper plates using orichalcum, silver, gold and tinted copper, depicting the horses, elephants and weaponry of Alexander's army. Taxila's king shows him a stadium where he practises javelin and discus throwing. A lavish dinner is organized in his honour consisting of fish, birds, whole lions, gazelles and swine. The main delicacy is the side of a tiger.

Entertainment is provided by tumblers and acrobats. A boy, performing 'like a theatrical dancer', does somersaults through the air, skilfully avoiding the javelins being thrown at him. Another man uses a sling-shot to aim darts at his son standing against a board. The darts come so close that when the boy steps away, his outline is clearly visible.[11]

As they prepare to leave Taxila, Apollonius and his party are provided with a set of fresh camels, gifts, a letter of introduction and a guide who takes them to the land of the Brahmins. After a journey of several days they reach their abode, a mountain that rises steeply from the plains and is as high as the Acropolis. On top is a castle surrounded by a cloud no rain can penetrate and that renders the Brahmins and their defences invisible. 'I saw Indian Brahmans [Brahmins] living upon the earth and yet not on it, and fortified without fortifications, and possessing nothing, yet having the riches of all men,' Apollonius remarks.[12] The rocks along the path that leads to their abode are marked by the cloven feet, beards, faces, and backs of the Pans who had tried to scale the height under the leadership of Dionysus and Heracles, but had been tossed down the cliff. There is a well for testing oaths from which a dark vapour rises and a crater that throws up a 'lead-coloured flame'.[13]

Apollonius spends four months with the Brahmins, conversing with them in Greek and observing their magical rituals. Each carries a staff and wears a ring, both containing powerful magic that enables them to accomplish anything they wish. Their most notable feat is to levitate two cubits above the ground. Apollonius insists they do this 'not for the sake of miraculous display, for they disdain any such ambition', but as an act of homage 'acceptable to the God'. The Brahmins also keep a fire extracted from the sun's rays that could be seen 'raised aloft in the air and dancing in the ether'.[14] Their chief, Iarchus, shows Apollonius and Damis a rare and marvellous stone called a Pantarhe. Although it is only the size of his finger-nail, it is powerful enough to break open the earth. 'It is of a fiery colour and of extraordinary brilliancy, and of such power, that thrown into a stream, it draws to it and clusters round it, all precious stones within a considerable range.'[15]

The daily ritual of the Brahmins includes bathing in a spring, after which they anoint their heads with an amber-like drug. This raises their temperature so much that steam rises from their bodies and sweat runs off them 'as profusely as if they were washing themselves with fire'. Led by Iarchus, the sages walk with Apollonius towards the temple of their god, marching in solemn procession and singing sacred hymns. 'Occasionally they would strike the earth in cadence with their staves, whereupon the ground moved like a sea in turmoil rising with them to the height of almost two feet, then subsiding to its regular level.' When the king orders food and wine to be brought, 'four tripods, like those in Homer's Olympus, rolled themselves in, followed by bronze cup-bearers. The earth strewed itself with grass, softer than any couch; and sweets and bread, fruits and vegetables, all excellently well prepared, moved up and down in order before the guests. Of the tripods, two flowed with wine, two with water, hot and cold.'[16]

For all the florid prose and depth of detail, there is little evidence Apollonius witnessed any of these marvels. Though some scholars accept he visited India, his descriptions of its geography, the presence of Greek-speaking Brahmins and their feats of magic, were most probably culled from existing books and travellers' tales. As Osmond de Beauvoir Priaulx concluded after examining Philostratus's work, similar stories, both real and imaginary, could be 'easily collected at that great mart for Indian commodities and resort for Indian merchants – Alexandria'.[17]

◈

PHILOSTRATUS did not have to travel to Alexandria for inspiration. By the third century AD, Indian magicians and jugglers could be encountered in many parts of the Mediterranean and the Near East. References to illusionists, magical contrivances, acrobats, astrologers and fortune tellers from the lands of the East date back to the time of ancient Egypt. The *Ghayat al-Hakim*, a twelfth-century book of magic and astrology, probably written by an Arab scholar in Spain and translated into Latin under the title *Picatrix*, refers to an Indian king who gifted an Egyptian pharaoh a magic vessel. Once this vessel was filled with water, the whole army could drink from it without it running empty. 'The vessel was constructed by [a combination of] man-made artifices, properties of nature and the knowledge of the strengths of the spirits of the planets and the fixed stars.' The *Ghayat al-Hakim* also refers to another Indian king named Acaym who constructed a ball made out of black marble at the city gate of Nubia. By 'the most subtle geometric artifices and magical sciences', moisture from the air was purified and descended into the ball that never lacked water.[18]

Indian jugglers entertained guests at the five-day long banquet that followed Alexander's wedding to Statira, the eldest daughter of the Persian king Darius at Susa, in 324 BCE. Greek traders returning from India carried texts on mathematics, medicine and magic. One trader, Scythianus, returned so convinced of his occult powers, he attempted to fly, perishing in the process. Before then he had composed four magical texts that his slave Terbinthus inherited. When he heard the son of the Persian king was seriously ill, Terbinthus set out for the Persian capital and offered to cure him with his books of Eastern spells. Unfortunately, the king's son died. Terbinthus was thrown in jail, but managed to escape by bribing a guard.[19]

The two-way trade that flourished between India and Rome from the first century BCE onwards, included goods and people. Indian pearls were being exchanged for Sardinian coral. Singing slave girls were gifted to the harems of Rajahs. According to the tariff list of Coptus, Indian prostitutes imported into Rome attracted a heavy duty. Exotic animals were shipped from India for circuses or kept as pets. The first Indian tiger was exhibited by Augustus in Rome around 13 BCE and mahouts were employed to train elephants that later formed part of Hannibal's army. The langur monkeys of India made fashionable additions to the households of the rich and powerful. Colourfully plumed parrots were popular with children and taught to utter words in Latin. They were imported in such quantities that one Roman nobleman decorated his table with the heads of the birds and fed the rest to his lions.[20] The historian Mathew Dickie adds magic workers to this exotic mix, speculating that they were former slaves who dabbled in sleight of hand, as well as actors and prostitutes.[21] Indian astrologers were also in great demand. The late first-century satirist Juvenal describes how wealthy women would pay for answers from a Phrygian or Indian augur 'skilled in astronomy and in the world'. [22]

With the establishment of maritime links between India and China in the second century BCE, jugglers and mendicants began appearing at Chinese courts. Zhang Hua's *Bowu zhi* or *Treatise on Curiosities* mentions an Indian traveller presenting the Han emperor Wu with three perfume balls that could prevent epidemics and resurrect the dead. Wu also received a magic mirror from India that could protect the person carrying it from evil spirits.[23] Early in the first century AD, Indian necromancers were recorded performing feats of 'severing limbs' and 'opening stomachs'. Eyewitness accounts speak of them cutting off their tongues, spitting fire, swallowing swords and rejoining pieces of broken cloth.[24] The lion dance, still synonymous with many Chinese festivities, has been traced back to itinerant magicians and animal trainers who were popular during the Tang dynasty (618–907). Jugglers together with Syrian singers, Afghan actors and camel stunt riders from Central Asia were employed as royal entertainers. Ceramic figures depicting Indian conjurers have been found in tombs in several Tang dynasty cities.

The Tang capital Chang-an, the largest city of its time, attracted traders, pilgrims and scholars from all over Asia. An Indian, Gautama Rahula, held the highest position in the Tang Bureau of Astronomy between 665 and 698 and was responsible for the construction of the Celestial Hall as an astronomical clock.[25] Indian alchemists were in demand because of their supposed ability to prolong life. In 648, the Tang envoy Wang Xuance returned to China with a Brahmin physician named Narayanasvamin, who presented himself as an expert in preparing longevity drugs and claimed to be over two hundred years old. The Tang emperor, Taizong, housed Narayanasvamin in the

Office of Precious Metals and assigned his war minister to look after his every need. Strenuous efforts were made to provide the doctor with ingredients required to manufacture the drugs for the emperor. 'Envoys were sent in from four directions to find strange herbs and rare stones. Embassies were also sent to the Indian kingdoms to procure [longevity] drugs,' the *Zizhi tongjian* records.[26] Narayanasvamin, however, turned out to be more of a quack than a doctor. Taizong died at the age of forty-nine. The alchemist joined him in celestial heaven a few years later. Indian magicians fell out of favour during the rule of Taizong's son, Gaozong (649–683), after he witnessed the stomach-curdling act of Brahmins cutting themselves open as he was enjoying an evening feast. The performers were sent home and border guards were instructed to ban entry of others.

Buddhist monks from India began arriving in China in the third century AD, sometimes employed as military advisers, but mainly as scholars and translators of canonical works. They quickly gained a reputation for their magical powers including rainmaking, healing and the prognostication of fate. The supernatural aspects of Buddhism were harnessed for political and social ends to counter the influence of Daoist priests and local cults. The traffic went both ways. Chinese pilgrims first reached India in the fourth century, visiting places associated with the life of Buddha and obtaining sacred texts. The most important of these was Hsuan-tsang who travelled to India between 671 and 695, and left behind one of the most extensive accounts of the land and its people since Megasthenes seven centuries earlier. In his classic text, *Great Tang Records of the Western Regions*, Hsuan-tsang describes India as 'the homeland of faith and magic, and a link of some sort, the closer the better, with the person of the historic Sakyamuni [Buddha]'.[27] He visited the great monastic centre of Nalanda, where he found several thousand monks learning the Buddhist canon. Magic was one of the many subjects taught at Nalanda as well as logic, grammar, philology, medicine and philosophy. Elsewhere, though, Buddhism was clearly in decline. In the valley of Swat, once a great centre of learning, he found that remaining monks were incapable of understanding the meaning of their sacred texts 'cultivating instead the science of magic formulas'.[28] The Chinese pilgrim also translated several important Buddhist sutras including the *Ekadasamukha*, an esoteric scripture containing a full ritual programme involving 'spells, mudras, a special altar and the use of the process of magic'.[29]

As Chinese interest in India began to wane with the decline of Buddhism, a new religion appeared in the deserts of Arabia. The spread of Islam eastwards to Sind in the early eighth century was accompanied by the rise of fantastical tales of India, its marvels and magical lore. These tales can be found in the genre of '*aja'ib* literature, which dealt with the wonders of the world based on first-hand or collected tales of travellers, merchants and geographers. 'Aj'aib stories would find their apotheosis in the *Alf Layla wa-Layla*, the *Tales of a Thousand and One Nights.* Initially, however, the genre reflected an obsession with India and its wonder-workers. One of the most remarkable texts from this period was entitled *Akbar al-Sin wa-l-Hind,* or *Accounts of China and India*, a maritime Silk Road saga, compiled by Abu Zayd as-Sirafi, himself a noted traveller, and published in 851. Only one of the informants is mentioned by name – Sulayman al-Tajir or Sulayman the Merchant, though most scholars believe he is not the sole author of the text. In Abu Zayd's 'aja'ib-infused world, a mendicant slices open his abdomen, pulls out his innards and cuts off a piece of his own liver that he hands to his brother, before leaping into a funeral pyre and being burned to ashes. The courts of India's kings are frequented by 'astrologers, philosophers, soothsayers, and those who take auguries from the flight of crows and other birds'. Conjurers and illusionists, he insists, are masters of their art: 'they are particularly to be found at Qannawj [Kannauj], a large city in the kingdom of al-Jurz'.[30] Abu Zayd also provides one of the earliest descriptions of India's ascetics in an Islamic text.

> There are some in India whose habit is to wander the jungles and hills, seldom mixing with other people. Sometimes they live on leaves and jungle fruits and insert iron rings into the heads of their penises to stop them having sexual intercourse with women. There are some among them who are naked, and others who stand upright all day facing the sun, naked too but for a scrap of tiger or leopard skin. I once saw one of these men, just as I have described; I went away and did not return until sixteen years, and there I saw him, still in the same position. I was amazed at how his eyes had not melted from the heat of the sun.[31]

Another work from this period is the *Ajā'ib al-Hind,* or *The Book of the Marvels of India,* compiled by Buzurg ibn Shahriyar in about 953. The only known copy of Buzurg's manuscript lay untouched in the vaults of the Aya Sofia mosque in Istanbul for nearly 900 years before it came to the attention of Charles Schefer, the principal dragoman at the French Embassy in

Istanbul in 1878. Schefer translated the book into French and published it in 1883. The 136 tales and anecdotes were compiled by Buzurg after sitting for many hours in tea houses and listening to sailors and storytellers in the ports of Siraf, and Suhar in the Gulf of Oman – the 'Land of Incense' as it was referred to then. Buzurg's rag-bag of salty tales contain second and even third-hand stories from places as far away as Sumatra and Malaya. There are descriptions of shipwrecks and starvation, fish with human faces, men whose beards turn from white to black, cannibals and dwarfs, prophesizing lizards and, of course, the spell-casters of India. So skilled are India's illusionists that they can make a circle on the ground and draw into it any birds that fly above, one of Buzurg's informants tells him.[32] Another repeats stories of invisible jinns who can be heard bartering and haggling in a garden in Kashmir, and of seers who can cure snakebites using special spells.[33] One tale related by Abu Yusuf b. Muslim, who heard it from Abu Bakr al-Fasi, whose source was Mus al-Sindaburi, concerned the crocodile charmers of Sarira Bay. According to the story, a Hindu magician arrived at the bay promising to bewitch the flesh-eating crocodiles that infested its waters. After reciting some spells, he stepped into the bay without being attacked. After releasing the crocodiles from his spell, a dog was thrown in the water and torn to pieces. When the king heard about the magician's powers, he demanded a demonstration. Two men who had been condemned to death were put into the water. The first was unharmed, but when the spell was lifted, the second was immediately killed by the crocodiles. Recognizing the magician's powers, the king called his strongest servant and told him to cut off the sorcerer's head. But first he made the Hindu cast his spell again. This time the condemned man who had escaped unharmed was led into the water. Again, the crocodiles refused to touch him, no matter where in the bay he swam. Only once the king realized the spell covered the whole expanse of water, did he order his servant to decapitate the magician. Since then there had been no more crocodile attacks, Buzurg narrated.[34]

Abu Dulaf al-Yanbu was another master of the 'aja'ib tradition. Described by the great Arab bibliophile, Ibn al-Nadim, as a *jawwala* or globetrotter, Abu Dulaf is thought to have travelled to India in 942. In his *Risala*, he speaks of a magical floating temple known as the House of Gold, situated in the 'wild parts of India, in the territories of Markran and Kandahar'. Built in the shape of a square with sides measuring seven cubits and walls of solid gold, it was populated with idols made of red rubies and other precious stones and 'adorned with glorious pearls each one of which is like a bird's egg or even larger'. The rain did not touch it. Seeing it cured anyone afflicted with any disease. 'Some of the Brahmins stated to me that it is hanging between Heaven and earth without support or suspension.' Abu Dulaf describes another house of worship in the city of al-Sanf, 'an ancient temple in which all of its idols speak with the worshippers, answering everything about which they were questioned'.[35]

IN 1296, three-and-a-half centuries after Abu-Dulaf's journey to India, Marco Polo, a Venetian traveller was captured in a skirmish between rival merchant ships off the Italian coast and imprisoned in Genoa. One of Marco Polo's fellow prisoners was a writer of medieval romances from Pisa named Rustichello. With little else to do, Polo started recounting stories of his adventures to Rustichello, who quickly recognized how extraordinary they were. Polo asked his father to send the notebooks he had compiled, and by 1298 the pair had completed all 233 chapters of *A Description of the World.* Polo's narrative describes the two extensive journeys he made to Asia with his uncle Maffeo. The first, which lasted from 1260 to 1269, took them through the Caucuses and Central Asia to Xanadu, the summer capital of the Mongol ruler Kublai Khan. The second, which started in 1271, followed a more southerly route to China, travelling via Baghdad, Khorasan and Kashmir. Their return journey went via Indo-China and the southern and western coasts of India. They returned to their home in Acre in 1295.

Like his predecessors, Polo embellished his accounts with second-hand stories and marvellous legends of monstrous people, fantastical animals, the austerities of gymnosophists and feats of wonder-workers. He describes how the great Kublai Khan employed Basci, or enchanters, and astrologers from Kashmir and Tibet, 'who are such adepts in necromancy and the diabolic arts that they are able to prevent any cloud or storm from passing over the spot on which the Emperor's Palace stands'.[36] Their magic powers were the work of the Devil, but they made 'people believe that it is compassed by dint of their own sanctity and the help of God'. They went around 'in a state of dirt and uncleanness' and followed a custom of eating the flesh of a man lawfully condemned to death and executed. When dining in his Hall of State, the Basci 'by the power of their enchantments' caused the flagons of wine, spiced liquor, or any other drink to fill cups spontaneously and make them move through the air until they reached the hand of the Grand Khan. 'This every one present may witness, and there are oft times more than 10,000 persons thus present. 'Tis a truth and no lie! And so will tell you the sages of our own country who understand necromancy for they also can perform it.'[37] Tibetan necromancers, Polo continued, 'perform the most extraordinary and delusive enchantments that were ever seen or heard of. They cause tempests to arise, accompanied with flashes of lightning and thunderbolts, and produce many other miraculous effects.' He was equally impressed with the 'idolaters' of Kashmir who 'have an astonishing acquaintance with the devilries of enchantment; insomuch that they make their idols to speak. They can also by their sorceries bring on changes of weather and produce darkness, and do a number of things so extraordinary that no one without seeing them would believe them.'[38] India's ascetics, who he referred to as '*chughis*', a mispronunciation of yogis, lived up to two hundred years 'and yet were so hale of body that they can go and come wheresoever they please, and do all the service needed for their monastery or their idols and do it just as well as if they were younger'. Polo attributed their longevity to eating only small quantities of food and drinking a mixture of mercury and sulphur twice a month.[39]

Polo was not the only Westerner to encounter Indian magicians at the Mongol court. Colonel Henry Yule, who published a two-volume edition of Polo's travels in 1873, added a footnote that throws light on the spread of Indian magic into China and Central Asia. Yule quotes the Franciscan missionary Friar Ricold (1242–1320) as saying:

> There are certain men whom the Tartars honour above all in the world, viz., the *Baxitae* (i.e. *Bakhshis*), who are a kind of idol-priests. These are men from India, persons of deep wisdom, well-conducted, and of the gravest morals. They are usually acquainted with magic arts, and depend on the counsel and aid of demons; they exhibit many illusions, and predict some future events. For instance, one of eminence among them was said to fly; the truth, however, was (as it proved), that he did not fly, but did walk close to the surface of the ground without touching it; and would seem to sit down without having any substance to support him.[40]

Polo died aged sixty-nine in 1324, just as a Muslim from Tangier was preparing to embark on a pilgrimage to Mecca and Medina. This man was Ibn Battuta and he did not return home after visiting the holiest sites of Islam, instead spending the next twenty-seven years travelling as far east as Ceylon, and if we are to take him at his word, mainland China. *A Gift to Those Who Contemplate the Wonders of Cities and the Marvels of Travelling*, better known as the *Rihla*, or *The Journey*, was composed with the help of a ghost writer from memory when Battuta returned to Fez in 1354. Referring to India, Battuta noted that both Hindus and Muslims 'believed in magic, astrology, witchcraft and miracles, and the performance of the yogis were witnessed even by the Sultan (Muhammad bin Tughluq)'.[41] Among Battuta's two most quoted passages are one that describes the Rope Trick (which will be dealt with in a subsequent chapter), and a levitation feat performed by a pair of yogis in the court of the emperor of Hindustan sometime between 1332 and 1347. Addressing them, the emperor said:

'This is a stranger, shew him what he has never seen.' The yogis agreed. 'One of them assumed the form of a cube and arose from the earth,' Battuta later related, 'and in this cubic shape he occupied a place in the air over our heads. I was so much astonished and terrified at this that I fainted and fell to the earth.' The delicate Tunisian was soon administered a tonic and slowly sat up, no doubt relieved that he had imagined it all. But it was no illusion for 'this cubic figure still [remained] in the air, just as it had been'.

A Hindu ascetic garlanded with a metal frame. Etching, c. 1890. Wellcome Library.

Next, another juggler took out a sandal that rose from the ground, until it reached the same height as the cube. It then struck the cube, which descended back to the earth. This again was too much for Battuta, who suffered 'palpitation of the heart, until the Emperor ordered me medicine, which restored me'. What further wonders might have been witnessed we shall never know, as the emperor took pity on the dazed visitor, telling him, 'had I not entertained fears for the safety of thy intellect, I should have ordered them to show thee greater things than these'.[42]

India's ascetics were a constant source of wonder for Battuta. He was among the first travellers to describe the practice of being buried alive, citing the case of a yogi who was placed in a specially dug cave for a year with only a small hole left open to provide air. In Mangalore, a yogi remained on top of a platform without eating or drinking for twenty-eight days. 'I left him so, and I do not know how long he remained after my departure. The people say that they fashion balls that they eat for a certain number of days or months, during which period they need neither food nor drink. They tell of hidden affairs (i.e., predict the future). The Sultan reveres them and admits them to his presence.' Some were so powerful that they could kill another person merely by looking at them. 'The people say that if a man is killed by a look, and the chest of the corpse is split open, it is found to lack a heart. They say that his heart has been eaten. This is prevalent among women, and the woman who does that is called a hyena.'[43]

The Chinese journeyer, Ma Huan, whose travels have been compared to Polo and Battuta's, accompanied the great mariner and explorer Zheng He on his voyages to India in the early fifteenth century. On reaching Bengal, he declared there was nothing unusual about the feats of Indian jugglers, barring a performance involving a man and woman with a tiger they paraded on an iron chain. After untying the chain, the tiger was made to sit down on the ground. 'The man, with bare body and holding only a switch, dances in front of the tiger; he hits it with his fists; he takes hold of the tiger and kicks and beats it; the tiger's temper rises to a terrible pitch; it roars and makes a show of attacking the man; [then] both the man and the tiger fall down in front of each other, and the engagement is finished.' After the mock fight, the man put his arm in the tiger's throat without being bitten. The tiger lay down and begged for food. The audience fed the animal and gave money to the man.[44]

◈

BY the middle of the second millennium, the lands of the East – a blank sheet to most Europeans – took on new textures, forms and meanings. Much of this information was still tinged with fantasy. Gone were the dragons and one-eyed monsters, but not the marvellous, the mystical and the magical. A new empire, led by the descendants of the all-conquering Mongols of Central Asia, implanted itself over much of India. The rule of the great Mughals, which began with Babur's conquest of India in 1526 and ended with the death of Aurangzeb in 1707, produced highly orientalized descriptions of a world that was both exotic and despotic. From the hidden confines of the harem, to the pomp to the ceremonial splendour of the court, magic infused the literary accounts of missionaries, emissaries, travellers and traders.

Arguably the most prolific chroniclers of Mughal India were the Jesuits. In 1667, the polymath Athanasius Kircher, one of the leading Jesuit intellectuals of the time, published *China Illustrata*, the most important work on China and its neighbours for the next two hundred years. Kircher never visited Asia, drawing instead on Jesuit writings, oral accounts by returning missionaries and on a variety of Western sources including Polo, whose work he sought to correct. India features in Kircher's accounts, both as a springboard for the spread of Christianity in Asia and a source of wonders. In one passage, he describes a carnival-like show that took place in the court of Aurangzeb in 1660. To return a favour, the king of Bengal sent the Mughal a delegation bearing priceless gifts. The delegation arrived in a procession led by a triumphal carriage 'gleaming with gold and all types of gems and precious stones'. Two beautiful and elaborately decorated horses pulled the carriage. But instead of a human, it was being driven by a huge dog that sat high on the carriage as if on a royal throne. Adorned with a precious necklace, the dog 'had incredible dignity, and with a bow of the head showed the reverence due to the nobles along the way'. A splendid retinue of beautifully clothed monkeys circled his throne. 'When the dog-king bowed his head, they did the same. A large monkey drove the team. He was clad with a golden garment but had a little hat on his head covered with gold and gems. In his left hand, he held the reins of the bridle. In his right hand, he held a whip with which he guided the horse so skilfully so that you would think a trained groom and not an animal was in charge.'[45]

The triumphal procession does not appear in the otherwise extensive writings of Niccolao Manucci, a Venetian stowaway who left home at the age of fourteen in 1653 and landed in Surat three years later. Manucci was initially employed by Shah Jahan's eldest son and nominated successor, Dara Shikoh, as an artilleryman and remained in the service of the Mughal court for the next thirty years. His multi-volume history of the Mughals, *Storia do Mogor,* was written over the course of his stay in India and parts were published in French during his lifetime. But it was not until the Royal Asiatic Society commissioned a translation in the early twentieth century, that the English-speaking world had access to his work.

Manucci posed as a doctor, developing a reputation for exorcising and controlling demons. Among his many patients were women who pretended to be possessed, giving them an excuse to leave their homes and be with their lovers. 'My usual treatment was bullying, tricks, emetics, evil-smelling fumigations with filthy things,' the Italian recounted. *Storia do Mogor* also contained numerous references to witchcraft, sorcery and magic, ranging from improbable stories of making a cock crow in the belly of the man who stole and ate it, to the use of hair and fingernails to make voodoo dolls. Manucci also claimed extensive knowledge of philtres or love charms, which he probably derived from his unique access to the harem in his role as a quack physician. Sexual longing and promiscuity were rampant behind its walls, he claimed. When putting his hand inside the curtain in order to examine his female patients, some would kiss and gently bite it, some would even apply it to their breast. 'As for the spells practised by the women to bring young men under their control, they are infinite,' Manucci noted. 'Of such a nature are they that any such youth becomes mad, nor is he given any respite to think of anything else.' Europeans travelling to India, he warned, should not succumb to such spells 'for afterwards they will weep over their unhappy irremediable state. It happens often to one so bound by spells that after his lady-love has died he cannot endure the approach of any other woman, remaining ever overcome by sorrow for the defunct.'[46] Even Christian friars were not immune, Manucci added, citing the example of one victim at Sao Thome near Madras, whose female servant cast such a strong spell over him he could not bear to see anyone other than her, even as he lay dying after a bout of diarrhoea. Fortunately, he was found by some friars from Goa. Realizing he was bewitched, they seized the servant and tortured her until she broke the spell.[47]

In contrast to the conman Manucci, François Bernier was an aristocrat and qualified doctor who arrived in India in 1658 and spent a decade attending to medical needs of Mughal royalty. The fakirs of India, he noted, were well acquainted with the art of making gold. When two 'good *jauguis* [yogis]' met, they could put on such as display of the 'power of *Jauguism*, that it might be doubted if Simon Magus with all his sorceries ever performed more surprising feats'. They could 'tell any person his thoughts, cause the branch of a tree to blossom and to bear fruit within an hour, hatch an egg in their bosom in less than five minutes, producing whatever bird may be demanded, and made to fly about the room; and execute many other prodigies that need not be enumerated'.[48]

By the time *Travels in the Mughal Empire* was published in 1670, the prophesizing powers of Indian magicians was well known. In 1622, a thirteen-page booklet appeared in London with the grandiose title *A True Relation without all Exception, of Strange and Admirable Accidents, which Lately Happened in the Kingdome of the Great Magor, or, Magull, Who is the Greatest Monarch of the Indies*. The booklet purported to be an accurate account of the manners and commodities of his Indian empire 'written and certified by Persons of good Import who were Eye witnesses of what is here reported'. Jahangir's portrayal is rather unflattering, dwelling on such details as the thousand women who served his 'lustful desires', and the two hundred boys he kept for his 'unnatural and beastly uses'. The Mughal emperor, the booklet's anonymous author noted, was also 'much delighted with Astrologers, Magicians, and Witches, of which his Country is replenished'.[49]

The most curious tale – and one that occupies a disproportionally large part of the booklet – concerns an ape said to be over one hundred years old brought to the court by a Bengali juggler. Keen to witness the primate's 'strange and admirable tricks', Jahangir hid his finger ring with one of his boys. The primate had no trouble in divining its location. His curiosity aroused, Jahangir told one of his scribes to write on pieces of paper the names of twelve prophets including Moses, Jesus and Mohammed. These were then mixed up and placed on a table. The ape was summoned and immediately chose the one with the name of Jesus as the 'true' faith. Growing increasingly suspicious, Jahangir ordered the operation be repeated, but this time kept the magician and ape under guard to ensure no trickery was involved. Again, the ape selected the paper inscribed with the name of Jesus. More names were added, now written in a code known only to the king, but the result was the same. Finally, one of Jahangir's senior courtiers, convinced this was a ruse to convert the emperor to Christianity, left out Jesus's name. The enraged animal refused to touch any of the pieces of paper and instead leapt upon the offending courtier, drawing out the missing sheet and bringing it 'hastily to Magor'.[50]

The story of the Bengali juggler's prophesizing ape might be dismissed as yet another figment of the febrile imagination of a European who had spent too long under the unforgiving Indian sun, had it not been echoed by the Muslim traveller Mahmud b. Amir Wali. Described by the Canadian scholar Richard C. Folz as a 'seventeenth century predecessor to the rucksack-toting overlanders of the 1970s',[51] Mahmud spent several years roughing it around India, visiting pilgrimage places – and taking every opportunity he could to watch women bathing in their saris. While in Bengal he visited a river port on the Ganges known as 'Monkey Town', where thousands of simians surrounded boats as they came ashore begging for food. Watching from a distance, the biggest ape, dubbed the 'Monkey King', settled disputes by pointing his finger at his clamouring subjects. In Orissa, Mahmud described two highly intelligent apes that were used to find thieves. Names were written on scraps of paper, from which the apes would determine who was guilty, though they often disagreed on the verdict. Bar Khan, the Mughal governor, sent the apes to Jahangir, but in the meantime, Shah Jahan had ascended the throne and, in a snub, sent them back.[52] The prophesizing ape episode was also endorsed by the most senior official England had sent to India, Sir Thomas Roe, the ambassador of James I to the court of Jahangir. Roe said he had 'heard it credibly reported'.[53] His chaplain, Edward Terry, seconded the story, insisting the facts had been vouched for by 'diverse persons who knew not one another and were differing in religion, yet all believe in the story, and in the diverse circumstances thereof'.[54] In 1899, the apish tale reappeared in an edited version of Roe's journals and correspondence, modified slightly from the original contained in *Strange and Admirable Accidents*, but losing none of its mystique.

By then the narrative would have seemed rather tame when compared with stories of Indian necromancy, spell-casting and apparent miracles penned not by accidental travellers, but by Western magicians who had been scouring the subcontinent hoping to discover the secrets behind the mysteries of Oriental conjuring. Seldom did their searches uncover more than what was already known about the basic mechanics of illusion-making. What they did reveal, however, were the blurred boundaries between magic, mythology and religion that continue to be the defining feature of Indian enchantment, the origins of which go back to the start of the Harappan civilization nearly five thousand years ago.

TWO

CASTING INDRA'S NET

ANCIENT India was a land where magical knowledge was controlled through sacrificial rituals. Hindu gods employed the essence of maya as a cosmic sleight of hand to project illusions and materialize them in the world of marvels. The Buddhist *Jataka* tales contained accounts of ropes rising in the air and snake charmers. Jaina monks used magic carpets to carry their congregations to safety. In the *Rig Veda*, the warrior god Indra, the first great magician, employed *indrajala* – a net of magic – to ensnare the world, save it from demonic forces and give mankind a reason to live. Since ancient times street magicians have begun their performances by invoking Indra's blessing. As Teun Goudriaan writes, 'By associating with Indra's mighty deeds, the human performer becomes an imitator of the god.'[1]

In these ancient and cosmic worlds, magic was evoked through prayer and meditation. This was not the sleight of hand of the nearly naked jadoowallah, but something mystical, miraculous and, above all, spiritual. In an incomprehensible universe, the Brahmin priest-magician was revered for his powers and ability to execute spells and sacrifices, even if the desired result did not

The warrior god Indra, the first great magician. Wikimedia Commons.

always eventuate. On a more mundane level, he also served as the court magician, defending the king from demons, diseases and the black magic of his enemies, while at the same time performing wizardry that would make the ruler supreme.[2] In the blurred lines between spirituality and superstition, there was room for conjurers and tricksters, mendicants and wonder-workers.

Miracles described in Hindu myths and Buddhist *Jataka* tales would become part of the jadoowallah's earthly repertoire.

Evidence of magical rites can be found in Harappan culture that thrived for half a millennium beginning in about 2600 BCE. Seals found throughout the Indus Valley and as far west as Oman, show that the mysterious inhabitants of this lost civilization worshipped the Earth Mother goddess, revered plants and practised asceticism. Representations of ascetics with their elaborate ritual costumes and horned headdresses suggest the presence of shamans or medicine men. Kenneth Zysk argues that if the Indus ascetics were shamans, then as with all such practitioners around the world, they would have engaged in ritualistic magic. 'In their healing rituals, such practitioners probably used, among other things, plants (worshipped to ensure their healing efficacy), recitation of powerful incantations (mantras), and the performance of ritualistic dances and other activities in order to exorcise diseases believed to result from demonic possession.'[3] Figures wearing horns and worshipping the peepul tree appear in a number of seals. Others show beings with human faces and the bodies of tigers, crocodiles and buffalos. One seal has a human face, the horns of a goat and the legs of a bird. The presence of amulets worn on the body points to a belief in their supernatural powers. None of this is surprising. Most ancient societies resorted to rituals, spells, sacrifices and other means to alter the outcomes of hunts, ensure bountiful harvests and protect against malevolent beings.

The migration of Aryan people from central Asia starting in around 2000 BCE, brought them into contact, and sometimes conflict, with India's indigenous inhabitants. The Aryans were a nomadic people made up of numerous tribes. Their gods were heroic male deities such as Indra, Varuna and Mitra. Hymns composed by Brahmin priests in praise of these gods and sung at sacrifices were handed down by word of mouth over generations. The greatest collection of these hymns is in the four Vedas: *Rig Veda* (Knowledge of the Verses), *Sama Veda* (Knowledge of Songs); *Yajur Veda* (Knowledge of Sacrifices); and *Atharva Veda* (Knowledge of the Fire-Priest). From the time of their appearance in written form until today – a span of some three thousand years – they have remained largely unchanged. The mantras recited at a local shrine overshadowed by the glass and steel skyscrapers of modern cities such as Gurgaon, belong to an unbroken, living tradition that stretches back to antiquity.

In Vedic times lived sages skilled in the interpretation of omens, and prophets who based their predictions on signs such as the shape of smoke rising from a piece of burning dung. Making a charm with the herb Sadampuspa would reveal sorcerers disguised as animals or birds that flew in the night sky. Ritual sacrifices overcame matrimonial strife and ensured a monarch in exile regained his throne. Many of the earliest references to magicians, mendicants and ascetics placed them outside Aryan society. The *Rig Veda* describes non-Aryans called *munis* that were associated with the god Rudra and were capable of magic feats. Respected and feared, they had long hair, were clad in 'brown filth' and 'girdled by the wind', a reference to their nakedness. Munis could fly through the air. They dwelt by the oceans of the rising and setting suns, followed the tracks of the Apsarases and Gandharvas and understood the thoughts of wild beasts.[4] The *Atharva Veda* refers to *vratyas*, a class of heterodox nomadic holy men who practised sympathetic magic, exorcism, ritual dancing, breath control and could place curses on their opponents. Some scholars believe they were prototypes of gypsies who wandered from place to place presenting magical rituals. Others label them as mendicants, peripatetic madmen, fire-eaters, poison-swallowers and libidinous pleasure-seekers. Like other forms of ritual, magic practices were codified. Though the lists vary, the *sat-karman* or six kinds of *abhicaras* or magical rites were: pacification (*santi*), subjugation (*vasikarana*), immobilization (*stambhana*), extirpation (*uccatana*), sowing dissension (*vidvesana*) and killing (*marana*).[5]

As descendants of the composers of the Vedas and custodians of their knowledge, the Brahmins held enormous power. The sacred words of Vedic hymns were capable of swaying the gods for good or evil purposes. A single syllable or word in a hymn falsely intoned would render it valueless. Brahmins were essential in performing sacrifices to ensure the sun rose in the morning, animals and crops flourished, people led long and healthy lives and ancestors were properly worshipped after death. For this, they were rewarded with grain, cattle or gold. As custodians of the correct chant and inner meaning of the Vedic hymn, Brahmin families rose to supreme influence and importance.[6] Perfectly recited by the *hotr*, the priest of sacrifice, the mantra gave the gods immense pleasure and Indra the strength to slay the demon Vritra. 'Here as everywhere the tendency of the sacrifice to pass into magic is illustrated; the prayer which is essentially free from magic is at last turned by the pride of its composers into nothing but a spell.'[7]

Of the four *Vedas*, the *Atharva Veda* was the most closely associated with the rites, superstitions and spells of the inhabitants of pre-Aryan India. Mainly tribal communities, they practised sorcery and witchcraft and believed in the efficacy of charms and incantations through which men could achieve powers greater than the gods. Rather than trying to suppress these beliefs, the Aryans absorbed them. In the *Atharva Veda*, writes D. A. Pai: 'The old hymns [were] inextricably confused, the deities confounded and merged into a new pantheon, strange gods introduced with demons and goblins, incantations for evil purposes and charms to gain worldly ends composed, formulas of maledictions to be directed against enemies and magical verses to obtain children and to prolong life invented; hymns to snakes, to diseases, to pronounce curses, composed.'[8]

The *Atharva Veda* was the work of Atharvans, fire priests skilled in the performance of magical rites. Composed in around 1400 BCE, it was originally known as the *Atharvashirsha*, formed from the names of two ancient families of mythical priests. The Atharvans, were concerned with 'sacred auspicious magic' used for such ends as curing disease, whereas the Angiras were associated with sorcery practices or black magic.[9] Because of its contentious focus on magical practice and belief in the world of supernatural phenomena and malaise, the *Atharva Veda* was originally excluded from the canon of Vedic scriptures.

Atharvanic magic was deeply rooted in all aspects of life, including medicine, eroticism, statecraft and sacrificial rites. 'In these various Atharvanic practices, the priest occupies a prominent part,' writes N. J. Shende, a former professor of Sanskrit at Elphinstone College in Bombay. 'He acts like a physician, mediator in love affairs, a Purohita [pandit] with the dignity of statesman, minister and director of the technique of war, an officiating priest in the domestic and sacrificial ritual and finally as a magician controlling the divine and demonic agencies for the benefit of his clients.'[10] What the American Sanskrit scholar Edward Hopkins calls the Atharvan religion, 'shows a world of religious and mystical ideas. ... Here magic eclipses Soma and reigns supreme. The wizard is greater than the gods; his herbs and amulets are sovereign remedies. Religion is seen on its lowest side.'[11]

The 730 hymns of the *Atharva Veda* contain a plethora of magical charms, spells and incantations for curing diseases, immortality, fecundity, prosperity, defence against demons, sorcerers and witches and for succeeding in battle against one's enemies. Cures for leprosy, rheumatism, snakebite and even baldness involved a mixture of rituals, the use of special plants, salves and ointments, amulets, purification ceremonies and sacrifices. Fever was transferred to a frog by pouring water over the patient and putting the reptile under the bed. Longevity, a lifespan of one hundred autumns being the Vedic ideal, necessitated propitiating a number of gods, including Yama, the ruler of the dead, Mrtyu, the personification of death and Nirrti, the goddess of misery and decay. One way of achieving longevity was by wearing an amulet made of gold, which symbolized immortality, incorruptibility and light. So detailed are the spells regarding love and sex in the *Atharva Veda,* that the *Kamasutra* refers to the text as the sole authority on certain erotic rites. There are charms to make rival wives barren, for holding the flickering love of a man or woman, restoring the affection of a mistress whose passion has grown cold and ensuring the privacy of lovers by putting the other householders to sleep. To make a man's penis like that of an elephant, ass or horse – another Vedic ideal – an amulet made out of *arka* wood, or one fashioned from the skin of a black antelope and fastened with hairs from the animal's tail was used.[12] With the proper magical rites, the Atharvan priest could make a woman look more beautiful by removing blemishes and excess body hair. The same spell could ensure her feet were no longer like an antelope's, her teeth were not like a bull's, her movements no longer resembled a cow's and she stopped snorting – all of which were considered great hindrances to matrimonial happiness.[13] Wide-ranging as the powers of the magician-priest were, the *Manu-Smriti* or *Laws of Manu,* drew the line at witchcraft, as well as sorcery by means of sacrifices, magic using roots, fortune telling and astrology. Practitioners could be fined 200 *panas.*[14]

FIRST mentioned in the *Rig Veda*, the concept of maya is essential to understanding the place of magic in Hinduism. The word comes from the Sanskrit root *ma*, which means 'to measure, to form, to build'. It denotes the power of god to produce illusory effects, change form and appear under different masks.[15] Magic in this sense is the production of an illusion by supernatural means – a sort of cosmic sleight of hand. It is also the force by which the magician – celestial and earthly – achieves his effects. Maya becomes an extremely effective weapon when employed by the warrior god Indra, who tricks his enemies into using their own weapons. The most celebrated and important god of the Vedas, Indra is called the first great magician. He dwells in the city of Amravati situated on the summit of Mount Meru, the centre of the earth, somewhere to the north of the Himalayas and close to the heavens of other deities. 'It has beautiful houses for its happy inhabitants to occupy, and its splendour is unequalled in the universe. Its gardens are stocked with trees, which afford a grateful shade, yield the most luscious fruits, and are adorned with beautiful and fragrant flowers. Beautiful nymphs charm the inhabitants; whilst choristers and musicians, unrivalled in the universe, discourse the sweetest music.'[16] Built by Visvakarma, the city is 800 miles in circumference and forty miles high. Its pillars are made of diamonds and its palaces, thrones and furniture of pure gold.

Indra can change himself into different beings, human and animal. In certain Rig Vedic hymns, he appears as a bull, in others as a rutting buffalo in search of *soma*, the magical elixir without which he is powerless. In the *Ramayana,* he adds to his marvellous feats by becoming a peacock. He can murder his enemies, seduce women and win riches and glory.[17] Indra's use of illusion is so commonplace that in classical Sanskrit the usual word for jugglery is *indrajala*.[18] The word can also refer to a stratagem or trick in warfare, such as creating a line of fortifications manned by dummies. It also involves the spreading of false information and beliefs against one's enemies.[19] In the *Rig Veda* (1.32), Indra uses his net of magic against his equally magical enemy the snake demon, Vritra. Indra magically turns himself into the hair of one of his horses' tails, and Vritra conjures up a storm. He is defeated when Indra splits a mountain to release the terrestrial waters Vritra has swallowed.[20]

Sankara, the celebrated early eighth-century Hindu sage from Kerala and founder of the school of Advaita Vedanta, developed the meaning of maya to embrace the illusion superimposed upon reality as an effect of ignorance. To illustrate this concept, he used the example of a wonder show. A conjurer throws a rope up into the sky, climbs it, engages in a battle with demons, is dismembered, falls and rises again. Though verified by the senses, this is only an illusion, explains Sankara. The power of illusion or ignorance traps the individual in a world of magic. 'The magician himself is in no way affected in past, present or future by the magic display he has spread forth by his hypnotic power (maya), as it is nothing real. And in just the same way, the supreme Self is unaffected by the magic display of the world of transmigratory experience (*samsara-maya*).'[21] Elsewhere, he compares the real world to a reflection. 'Seeing the reflection of the sun mirrored in the water in a pot, the fool thinks it is the sun.'[22]

According to the Indologist Robert Watson Frazer, these analogies suggest that Sankara's commentary on the doctrine of maya, and of the world being illusively conjured forth by a magician, may have originated from observing the very believable tricks of earthly conjurors that excited as much wonder then as they do today. Aside from the Rope Trick, the Mango Tree Trick – still part of the repertoire of many street magicians – is a seen as metaphor for maya. 'The conjuror's object is not to perform the trick as one of sleight-of-hand, but to arouse the idea that the whole appearance of the mango tree is an illusion,' writes Frazer. For this purpose, the trick is best performed where mango trees are not blossoming or bearing fruit. 'The conjuror, however, manages somehow to produce from distant places the flower and fruit of the mango tree.' [23]

The concept of magic as illusion is artfully illustrated in the Sanskrit play *Ratnavali* (*The Lady of the Jewelled Necklace*) by the accomplished seventh-century dramatist Harsha. The plot centres on the love intrigue of King Udayan and Sagarika, a woman of unknown descent from Ceylon, who is employed as the queen's attendant after surviving a shipwreck. Udayan falls in love with Sagarika, whose real name is Ratnavali. A magician from Ujjain, Samvara Siddhi, arrives in the court carrying a bunch of peacock feathers. Invoking Indra 'who lends our art his name', he asks the king: 'Would you see the moon brought down upon earth, a mountain in mid-air, a fire in the ocean, or night at noon? I will produce them – command!' Udayan calls for the queen to come and witness the spectacle. Waving his plume of peacock feathers, the magician calls on the gods to appear in the heavens. As the king and queen look skyward, they can see Brahma seated on his lotus throne, Sankara with the crescent moon as his glittering crest, and Hari, the destroyer of the demon race, holding in his four hands the bow, sword, mace and disc. Mounted on his stately elephant is the king of Swarga, around whom celestial beings and 'countless spirits dance merrily in mid-air, sporting with the lovely nymphs of heaven, whose anklets ring responsive to the measure'.[24] All this, of course, is an illusion. Soon afterwards, the magician offers to show the king another play. This 'play' begins with the announcement that a fire has broken out in the women's apartments. The queen, jealous of Sagarika, has shackled her in an inner room. The king rushes to her rescue, followed by the queen, a jester, a visiting minister from Ceylon and the chamberlain. As they plunge into the fire, the flames suddenly disappear. The apparent conflagration is an illusion, another piece of magic as promised by the magician. But this trick has served to bring Ratnavali before the Ceylon minister, who was convinced she had drowned. Recognizing her, he announces that she is the queen's cousin. As the queen has no objections to her cousin as a rival wife, King Udayan is allowed to marry her.[25]

BRIMMING with tales of beautiful maidens and their fearless lovers, of statecraft and intrigue, of magicians and their spells, the eleventh-century *Katha Saritsagar*, or *The Ocean of Story*, by the Kashmiri Brahmin Somadeva, rivals the tales of the *Arabian Nights* in its imaginative fables and is nearly twice as long as the *Iliad* and *Odyssey* put together. Charles Henry Tawney, the principal of Presidency College in Calcutta, translated the work into English and published it in two volumes in 1880 and 1884. In his introduction to the expanded 1924 edition, N. M. Penzer writes that Somadeva felt 'his great work united in itself all stories'. As every stream of myth and mystery flowing from the sacred Himalaya sooner or later reached the ocean, so did other streams from other mountains until they created 'an ocean full of stories of every conceivable description'.[26] Its 124 chapters are called *tarangas*, meaning 'waves' or 'billows'. Like the *Arabian Nights*, there are stories of adventures at sea and shipwrecks, smiling fish, unfaithful and devoted wives, princesses and thieves, treachery and tricksters, goblins and ghouls, and of beggars, ascetics, drunkards, gamblers, prostitutes and bawds.[27]

In the *Story of Vararuchi*, one of the earliest works in the collection, a Brahmin prince named Putraka is wandering through the wild jungles of the Vindhya Mountains after escaping an assassination plot by his father-in-law and uncles, when he stumbles across two men fighting over a pair of shoes, a staff and a vessel. The shoes, the men explain, give their owner the power of flying through the air and whatever is written on the staff turns out to be true. If a man wishes for food, the vessel provides it immediately.[28] Putraka takes possession of all three. They come to his rescue when his secret marriage to Patali, the daughter of the king, is discovered. To escape, he puts on the magic shoes, takes Patali in his arms and flies through the air, landing on the banks of the Ganges. There he refreshes his weary bride with cakes produced by the magic vessel. In accordance with Patali's request, he uses the magic staff to sketch out a city and establishes himself as king. 'His great power having attained full development, he subdued that father-in-law of his, and became ruler of the sea-engirdled earth. This is that same divine city, produced by magic, together with its citizens; hence it bears the name of Pataliputra, and is the home of wealth and learning.'[29] Elsewhere in the *Katha Saritsagar,* appear Vidyadharas, or 'those possessing spells or witchcraft', as well as Yakshas with their magical powers, and the demonic Rakshasas. Known as the harmers or destroyers, the Rakshasas 'delight in disturbing sacrifices, worrying devout men when engaged in prayer, animating dead bodies and generally living up to the meaning of their name', writes Penzer. 'Their eyes, like those of the Arabian *jinn*, are long slits up and down, their finger-nails are poisonous, and their touch most dangerous. They eat human flesh and also that of horses.' They are most powerful at night when they prowl about the burning-ghats in search of corpses or humans. They are also 'possessors of remarkable riches, which they bestow on those they favour'.[30]

Shri Ram shooting a magical arrow at Ravana, the ten-headed demon. Wellcome Library.

Rakshasas also feature in Valmiki's *Ramayana*, composed in about 400 AD. In this great epic, Ravana, the king of the Rakshasas, rules over the kingdom of Lanka. He is immortal, thanks to a boon he received from the creator-god Brahma. When Rama and his wife Sita travel south to the banks of the Godavari river, Ravana, disguised as an ascetic, catches Sita, pulls her into his flying chariot, Pushpak, and takes her back to Lanka. The monkey god Hanuman helps Rama by using his simian army to create a magic bridge linking India and Lanka. During the ensuing battle, Rama's brother Lakshmana is badly wounded by an arrow shot by Ravana's son, Indrajit. Hanuman, now a giant, leaps over the ocean and across the whole of India, to the Himalayas to collect a healing herb. Because he doesn't know which of the herbs growing there to pick, he uproots a whole mountain, lifts it onto the palm of his hand and flies with it back to Lanka. Later Ravana sends Indrajit to kill Hanuman by shooting at him with a magic snake arrow that pierces his thigh. Indrajit's conjuring is so powerful he can make himself invisible and therefore undefeatable in battle. He conjures up an illusory Sita and hacks her to pieces in front of Hanuman who conveys the news to Rama. The only person who knows about Indrajit's powers is the Rakshasa Vibhisana, who tells Rama that her death was maya, an illusion. Armed with this knowledge, Rama and Lakshmana are able to block Indrajit's magic and defeat him and Ravana.

❖

Recent scholarship has tended to view the Buddha primarily as a teacher and Buddhism as a rational religion devoid of belief in divinities or any faith in the supernatural. But as Susanne Mrozic points out, in pre-modern times the Buddha was represented 'as an extraordinary being with vast miraculous powers who could barely take a step without the earth quaking, gods raining down flowers from the heavens, and divine music sounding in the air'.[31] Miracles played an important role in the dissemination of Buddhism by convincing non-believers of the greatness of the Buddhist doctrine and, just as importantly, to defeat heretics. They included making a mango tree grow instantly from a planted seed; levitating in the air while emitting fire and water from various parts of his body; magically creating a double with whom the Buddha engages in dialogues about the *dharma*; cutting and restoring limbs and the multiplication miracle in which the sky becomes filled with 'an array of Buddhas'.[32] Of these, the mango tree miracle and restoring a cut-up body have entered the jadoowallah's repertory as masterpieces of sleight of hand. In the Pali version of the Buddha's sayings known as the *Dhammapada Commentary*, he announces that he will meet the heretics for a competition of magical powers at the foot of a mango tree. Fearing they would lose such a competition, the heretics chop down all the trees in the area. The king's gardener Ganda gives the Buddha an offering of a mango. When he finishes eating it, he gives the seed back to Ganda and asks him to plant it. The Buddha then sprinkles some water over the seed and instantly a mango tree, fifty cubits high, shoots up laden with fruit and flowers. Known as Ganda's mango, the tree marks the place where the Buddha rises into the air and performs a miracle where water and flames erupt from his body.[33]

The Buddhist *Jataka* stories dating back to 600 BCE contain references to *maykara* (magicians), *nata* (actors), *langhika* (acrobats), and *vaitalika* (bards), who performed at fairs and religious festivals attended by thousands of spectators, as well as in more exclusive settings such as the courts of kings. The *Dubbaca Jataka* mentions an acrobat who could jump over a row of half a dozen lances sunk in the ground. In the *Salaka Jataka,* a snake charmer gives an ape an antidote that allows the animal to play with a serpent. The *Dasannaka Jataka* contains what is probably the first reference to a sword swallower, who performs the feat at the Samajja festival.

In the *Suruchi Jataka,* the Mango Trick is combined with the earliest account we have of the Rope Trick. The tale describes a young prince named Mahapanda who is perfect in every way except that he never laughs. Even a seven-year-long festival that combines the consecration of his palace, his ascendency to the throne and his marriage, fails to elicit the faintest smirk. In exasperation, his father King Suruchi sends for two magicians, Bhandukarana and Pandukarana (Shaved Ears and Pale Ears), and their troupe of acrobats. Promising to make the prince laugh, Bhandukarana conjures up a great mango tree from a seed, throws up a rope, climbs up followed by his assistants and disappears. This tree represents the god Vessavana, one of the four guardian kings, who orders his servants to grab Bhandukarana. They take him away and chop up his body before throwing his severed limbs to the ground. Pandukarana rejoins the limbs by sprinkling water on them. He then lights a fire and, followed by the rest of the troupe, walks into it and is reduced to ashes. When water is poured on the smouldering embers, Pandukarana and his troupe emerge dancing and wearing colourful garments of flowers. Still unable to make the prince smile, Suruchi summons a divine dancer who, while levitating, performs a strange gyrating dance using only half of his body – one hand, foot, eye, tooth, etc. As the rest of the audience bursts out laughing, Mahapanda manages an almost imperceptible grin. After seven long years, everyone can finally go home.

The *Jataka* tales also contain references to *ahigunthika* (snake charmers). In the *Campaka Jataka*, a Brahmin who has learned serpent lore from a renowned teacher at Taxila, earns his living as a snake charmer in villages, market towns and the residences of kings. Unbeknown to him, the cobra he has captured, that now dances to the sound of his flute, is the Bodhisattva reborn as the Naga King Campaka. The story of the wonderful dancing serpent reaches King Ugrasena of Benaras, who sends for the conjurer and his captive. The king arranges a magnificent show in his palace attended by thousands of people. The Bodhisattva's wife, Suman, who is searching for him, reaches Benares, where preparations are being made for the snake's performance. When the Naga raises himself into the air, he sees his wife and struck by shame, crawls back into the basket. Suman asks Ugrasena to release her husband. Touched by her devotion, he orders the snake set free. The Naga creeps into a flower where he transforms himself into a young man magnificently arrayed. To thank the king, he invites him to share the divine food, drink and luxuries of his kingdom.[34]

◈

MAGIC, divination and fortune telling featured in the Ajivika school of ancient philosophy. Referred to as the 'vanished religion' of ancient India, it was founded in the fifth century BCE by Makkhali Gosala, a reputed wonder-worker and a former disciple – and then adversary – of Mahavira, the twenty-fourth Tirthankara of Jainism. Gosala achieved his magical powers after a six-month-long penance that consisted of sitting next to a lake, facing the sun, raising both hands above his head and eating only a handful of beans every three days. His followers were known as 'bald recluses' after the practice of pulling out rather than shaving their hair. Buddhist sources and Kautilya's book of statecraft, the *Arthasastra*, mention Ajivika mendicants engaged in spying. The taciturn Gosala once reduced to ashes a follower who dared to remonstrate him. After this incident, he challenged Mahavira to a magic tournament, but the Jain's asceticism was so perfect that Gosala's powers were ineffectual. The stream of supernatural forces he unleashed recoiled into his own body. Mahavira told him the force of this rebounded magic would cause him to die within seven nights from bilious fever, whereas he would live for another sixteen years. The prophecy came true and, according to the late Indologist, A. L. Basham, may have had a historical underpinning, as the two men did engage in a violent quarrel shortly before Gosala's death in around 485 BCE.[35]

The school's fatalistic teachings, encompassed in the doctrine of Niyati, placed it in opposition to Hinduism, Buddhism and Jainism. It also led to the parallel rise of belief in the efficiency of magic, spells, sacrifice and prayers to counter the effects of fate.[36] Ajivikas were frequently astrologers and fortune tellers. One of their primary texts was the *Mahanimitta,* or *Books of Great Omens,* a collection of eight canonical works on divination.[37] Mahavira condemned divination as an evil and warned against other aspects of Ajivika philosophy such as 'the art to bring about madness, magical incantations, conjuring [and] magical sacrifices of substances'. [38]

This condemnation was directed at the Ajivikas and their heretical ideas per se, rather than against magic, divination and fortune telling.[39] Jaina texts such as the *Vijjanuvada Puvva* and *Anga-vijja* condoned the use of spells and charms and the science of divination from bodily signs. Conjuring (*vijjapinda*), incantations (*manta*) and tricks (*joga*) were used by Jaina monks to obtain alms. Some were endowed with supernatural powers and could cure diseases simply by touching their patients with their hands. Using special charms, they could assume any form at will, rise through the air and make their speech as sweet as milk.[40] By anointing the feet with a consecrated paste, a practitioner could walk on water. Other spells were used for making a person miserable or bewildered, the latter being particularly useful for kidnapping.[41] *Vijjas,* magical powers, could be acquired only in barren places such as deserts and burial grounds and monks were warned to use them only as a last resort. When Vajra, the last Jaina elder with knowledge of all ten *Purvas* (*Original Texts*), went to northern India, he discovered his congregation was starving because of a famine. After the monks assured him it was not sinful to use magic to save them, Vajra made a carpet, large enough to accommodate everyone. At his command, it 'flew up into the sky as if it were being wafted up by the wind' before landing in the city of Puri.[42] A more contemporary legend concerns the fifteenth-century Digamber mystic and miracle worker, Taran Svami, who founded a sect in Malwa. Acquainted with the art of *indrajala*, Taran Svami went to fairs where he used sleight of hand to convert people. He could make his sacred texts float in the air and come back to earth. One of his chief disciples was a juggler and he competed with other magicians for the patronage of the local king. His status as a wonder-worker attracted followers from Gypsy communities, as well as Muslims and Hindus.[43]

Not all disagreements between religious leaders ended as violently as Gosala's confrontation with Mahavira. Philosophical debates were a feature of the Vedanta tradition. Often these debates would transcend the mundane as both sides invoked the supernatural. This could take the form of enlisting the help of a benign deity or summoning up evil forces to gain the upper hand. Recourse to the supernatural was based on a debater's fears that human effort alone would not defeat a superior opponent. 'At times, it is the hero of a story who turns to the Gods for help in his moment of adversity, feeling that his own position is correct but fearing that it will be defeated in the debate at hand. At other times, it is a villain who is described as resorting to trickery and magic, convinced that his doctrine is wrong and that it could otherwise never triumph, or perhaps with even baser motives in mind than the simple propagation of heresies,' writes Phyllis Granoff, in her study of Vedanta hagiographies.[44]

Granoff refers to a debate between Sankara and Mandana Misra. The monk Sankara is determined to triumph because if he does he must accept his opponent's life-station. Misra is a householder married to Ubhayabharati, the incarnation of Sarasvati, with whom Sankara is having a secret dalliance. Winning the debate means he can continue the affair without the interference of her husband. In a shameful exercise of black magic in pursuit of unsavoury ambitions, Sankara uses Tantric mantras to defeat the unsuspecting Misra. 'That a debate could be manipulated by the use of spells or mantras was widely acknowledged in medieval India,' writes Granoff, noting that Buddhists used spells as a last resort against their Jain opponents. Details of the black magic rites that would ensure victory in a debate were listed in the *Indrajalavidyasamgraha*, a compilation of magical texts.[45]

◈

TRANSCENDING religious boundaries in the medieval period was the Tantra, a body of unorthodox theories, techniques and rituals teaching mystical and magical formulas originating in Shaivism, Jainism and Buddhism between the sixth and eighth centuries. Magical powers were appropriated through intense meditation assisted by mantras that evoked the desired deities. Those who mastered *siddhis,* or supernatural forces, could cause rain to fall, see far distances, fly through the air and generate living beings out of ashes. The interaction of these theories and practices with indigenous traditions of shamanism and magical cults, resulted in potent hybrids that employed mantras, *yantras* (magical devices), *mandalas* (ritualistic circles), *mudras* (gestures), *maithuna* (sexual play) and the physical and psychological discipline of yoga. These were combined with elaborate forms of worship and ritual, magical sorcery, necromancy, astrology, alchemy, the harnessing of female sexual energy and a monistic philosophy.[46]

Transgressive Tantric techniques and rituals to gain access to the divine energy of the Creator such as indulging in orgies in burial grounds, eating flesh and using ceremonial bowls made from human skulls, attracted much criticism. Monier Monier-Williams, the leading Sanskritist of the late nineteenth century, described the Tantra as 'mere manuals of mystics, magic and superstition of the worst and most silly kind'.[47] Western scholars weren't the only ones voicing their disapproval. Swami Vivekananda called Buddhist Tantra a degraded form of the religion: 'The most hideous ceremonies, the most horrible, the most obscene books that human hands ever wrote or the human brain ever conceived, the most bestial forms that ever passed under the name of religion, have all been the creation of degraded Buddhism.'[48] Others, such as the Italian scholar Giuseppe Tucci, saw in the Tantras 'one of the highest expressions of Indian mysticism which may appear to us rather strange in its outward form, chiefly because we do not always understand the symbolical language in which they were written'.[49]

The siddhas were a diverse group of practitioners who sought by 'tantric, ascetic and alchemical means - to acquire the powers and accede to the stations of various immortal demigods (also known as siddhas) and magicians (vidyadharas) residing in heaven'.[50] These medieval Tantric ascetics, asserts Ronald Davidson, frequented 'both cemeteries and the palaces of the new lords of the land, [where] they practiced every form of magic,

Tantric Feast, Himachal Pradesh, c. 1790. Los Angeles County Museum of Art.

from love potions to ritual slaughter. With a political awareness as to the prerequisites of royal patronage, siddhas acted as the kings' agents, engaged in secret signs and elaborate disguises, and provided their royal patrons with sacred entertainment through sophisticated temple song and dance.'[51] Based on the teachings of Patanjali's *Yoga-Sutra*, yogins, through their ascetic practices could attain supernatural powers such as *animan*, the ability to become minute; *mahinam*, the ability to become large and to have the power to touch any object including the moon and *gariman*, the ability to become heavy.[52]

The emphasis on transmutation and bodily immortality features throughout the Tantric period. India's alchemic tradition was initially bound up in religious and spiritual pursuits rather than the transmutation of base metals into gold. In the *History of Hindu Chemistry*, published in 1902, the Bengali *bhadralok* and intellectual, Praphulla Chandra Ray, traces its origins back to references to the *rasa* or juice of the *soma* plant in the *Rig Veda*. Like the Greek ambrosia, the *soma rasa* was said to confer immortality on the gods and could be used as a medicine to cure diseases in humans.[53] David Gordon White, however, attributes beginnings of Indian alchemy to the spread of Buddhism into China where Taoist speculative alchemic practices had been developing since the second century AD. At first, its aims were magical, namely transmutation and bodily immortality. 'These were powers to be won or wrested from gods, demigods or demons rather than produced in a laboratory', but that did not stop 'Hindu alchemical heroes and buffoons' from trying, says White.[54] Tantric alchemy burst on the Indian scene in the tenth century, displaying a remarkable breadth of botanical, mineralogical, chemical, geographic, religious and technical knowledge that set it apart from magical alchemy. Rooted in the powerful impact of Tantrism on Indian mystical and metaphysical speculation together with development in medical science, it lasted until the fourteenth century.[55]

Abu al-Rayhan Muhammad ibn Ahmad al-Biruni, known in the West as Alberuni, refers to Tantric alchemy in his writings. One of the most prominent figures from the Golden Age of Islamic Science, Alberuni was born in 973 in the district of Kath, in what was then Persia. In 1017, he was forced to accompany the Muslim iconoclast Mahmud Ghazni on one of his raids into India. He stayed for twelve years in the Punjab, learning Sanskrit and gathering material on Indian life, society, religion, science and mathematics that was published as the *Kitab al-Hind* or *The Book of India*. Alberuni was sceptical of India's magical practices particularly alchemy, which he compared to witchcraft. He lashed out at 'the greediness of the ignorant Hindu princes', who would do anything to make gold, even if it meant having to kill children and throw them in a fire.[56] One of his stories described a door made of pure silver on which the outlines of the limbs of a man were clearly visible. The shape was of a magician who had promised the king of Dhara in central India an alchemic formula that would make him 'immortal, victorious, invincible, and capable of doing everything he desired'. Anxious that the promise be fulfilled, the king ordered all that the magician needed. The man boiled oil for several days until it achieved the proper consistency and then told the king to jump into it. Not surprisingly, he refused. Undaunted, the magician offered to throw himself in and instructed the king on what drugs and compounds to add for the elixir to be effective. Stepping onto the edge of the cauldron, the man jumped into the mass of oil and immediately turned to pulp. Frightened the magician would emerge invincible and immortal, the king did not add the last compound to the mix. When the cauldron cooled, all that was left was a silver ingot in the shape of a man.[57]

Elsewhere, Alberuni mentions the alchemist Nagarjuna who lived about a century before his arrival in India. 'He excelled in it, and composed a book which contains the substance of the whole literature on this subject, and is very rare.'[58] The Chinese Buddhist pilgrim Hsuan-tsang also records meeting a sage at the court of King Harsha named Nagarjuna, who was 'so skilled in the art of compounding medicines that he produced a pill with which he had extended his own life and as well as that of his companions for hundreds of years'.[59] Whether Nagarjuna was a historical figure is still being debated – a debate complicated by numerous references to persons with the same name, many of whom were connected in some way with the Indian alchemic tradition. Hsuan-tsang writes that when Harsha ran out of funds to build a monastery for Nagarjuna, one of the monks 'scattered some drops of numinous and wonderful pharmakon over certain large stones, whereupon they all turned to gold'.[60] He also describes a meeting with a Brahmin disciple of Nagarjuna who was seven hundred years old, but looked only thirty.

The most important work of the Indian alchemic tradition is the thirteenth-century *Rasaratnikara*, or *Ocean of Mercury*, attributed to Nityanatha Siddha, who was most likely a practitioner of the Nath Siddha tradition. 'Whatever can be found elsewhere is here; what is here cannot be found elsewhere. This is an Ocean of Mercury,' the opening verse declares, before ascribing the work to Nityanatha. 'This discipline, beneficial and dear to aspirants, has five sections. It gives fame to doctors, it is beneficial to the sick.

It is of great interest to theoreticians, and it perfects the bodies of the old. It makes the spells of magicians successful, causing many wonders.'[61] The Siddha or mantra section was a collection of purely magical spells, incantations and practices divided into seven chapters. These included *Sarvavasyadipativasyam:* 'From the subjugation of all creatures to the subjugation of one's husband'; *Kautuhalani:* 'Conjuring tricks'; and *Anjanadipadukasadhanam*: 'From [magic] ointments to acquiring [magic] shoes.'[62]

The extent of magical lore in Hinduism, Buddhism, Jainism and their offshoots is as wide as the scope of Somadeva's *Ocean of Story*. As the contents of the *Atharva Veda* and the Tantras show, belief in the efficacy of spells and rituals ran deep in pre-modern India. There was hardly a poem, a work of drama or an epic tale that was not infused with supra-normal events driven by magical forces. In this vast jungle of teachings, symbolism and ancient myths, there was much that could be appropriated by the jadoowallah, the fortune teller, the purveyor of magical herbs and remedies, the actor and the storyteller. But Indian magic would evolve into a body of sacred and secular practices that was much more than the sum of its pre-Aryan heritage, its Vedic traditions, its earliest religions and schools of philosophy. As Islam spread eastward, so did new forms of magic and mysticism – and so did those elusive spirits of the ether known as jinns.

THREE

THE LOVERS OF JINNS

BY the light of flickering oil lamps, Baghdad's literati gather in homes, libraries, coffee houses and bazaars. When dusk descends on the Abbasid capital and it becomes too dark to read, the *rawis*, or professional storytellers, entertain their audiences with tales of Arab adventurers, the monsters of the sea, the lovers of jinns and the magic lore of India. As a centre for literature and learning, Baghdad in the ninth and tenth centuries had no rivals. While the city owed its prosperity to the legendary Abbasid Caliph, Haroun al-Rashid, it was his son and successor, Abdallah al-Ma'mun, who promoted the arts and sciences by attracting philosophers, poets, astronomers, mathematicians and doctors. One of his greatest achievements was establishing the Bayt al-Hikmah, the House of Wisdom, which doubled as a vast library and translation centre and was a meeting place of poets and writers. By the end of the ninth century, almost every available work of Greek science and philosophy had been translated into Arabic.

Al-Ma'mun's other great achievement was ordering the construction of a factory that produced paper of such high quality and consistency that it gradually replaced parchment and vellum. The ready supply of paper, the superior artistry of Baghdad's calligraphers and the skill of its copyists, created a flourishing publishing industry. There were auction houses that dealt with rare books and collectors willing to pay high prices for manuscripts. Scholars and collectors assembled vast private libraries larger than the combined monastic collections of Europe at the time. Passing through Baghdad in the late ninth century, the geographer Ahmad ibn Abi Ya'qub counted more than one hundred booksellers whose shops were located on the upper floors of houses that lined the narrow by-lanes of the bazaars. By the middle of the tenth century, the largest and most visited of these shops belonged to al-Faraj Muhammad al-Nadim.

Little is known about al-Nadim other than he was a Shi'ite and had taken over the shop from his father. He would later be referred to as a *katib*, a writer, and it is likely that he worked in one of the many libraries in the city, perhaps even in the House of Wisdom itself.[1] From an early age al-Nadim compiled catalogues of the books in his father's shop to help buyers find what they were looking for. He also visited numerous libraries – royal, private and public – as well as bookshops in different parts of the country, gradually amassing a vast list of titles. Around 987, al-Nadim published the *Fihrist al-Ulum* or *Catalog of the Sciences*. Its ten chapters contain an annotated listing of more than three centuries of Arab literature and translations into Arabic from numerous languages, including Persian, Greek and Sanskrit. What began as the wide-ranging literary interests of one man, became the reflection of an entire civilization. As al-Nadim writes in his prelude:

> This is a catalogue of the books of all peoples, Arab and foreign, existing in the language of the Arabs, as well as their scripts, dealing with various sciences with accounts of those who composed them and the categories of their authors, together with their relationships and records of their times of birth, lengths of life, and times of death, and also of the localities of their cities, their virtues and faults, from the beginnings of the formation of each science to this our own time, which is the year 377 after the Hijrah.[2]

The *Fihrist* contains al-Nadim's commentaries on sacred scriptures, including the Koran and the holy books of Jews and Christians. There are descriptions of the works of the great jurists of Islam and the Greek sciences of philosophy, mathematics, astronomy and medicine. There is a listing of storytellers and their trade, a section on 'passionate lovers whose names enter evening stories', and another on 'humans in love with the *jinns* and *jinns* in love with the humans'.[3] The first part of chapter eight deals with 'accounts of those who converse in the evenings and tellers of fables'. Al-Nadim refers to an early and incomplete version of the *One Thousand and One Nights*. He also lists an Indian collection of stories known as the *Fables of Bidpai*, which were translated into Persian and then into Arabic. At one point, he draws on information about China and Korea from a Nestorian missionary returning from the Far East. Other sources provided him with knowledge about India, Transoxania, Russia and other countries, and about people both in and outside of the Islamic Empire.

Indian magic features in a section entitled: 'Accounts of scholars and the names of the books which they composed, including accounts of the exorcists, jugglers, magicians, and those who use incantations, tricks and talismans.'[4] 'The art of illusion is a speciality of India where there are books on the subject, some of which have been translated into Arabic,' writes al-Nadim. Its magicians use talismans based on astronomical observations to produce things connected with 'wonderful actions, excitements, favour and forms of authority'. They can perform miracles for routing armies, killing enemies, walking on water and transporting themselves over vast distances in a matter of seconds.[5] He also refers to an Indian named Babbah whose books on incantations and illusion were known throughout the Arab world.[6] He then lists the names of more than a dozen magicians who wrote books about their craft including Qutb al-Rahha, the author of *Swallowing the Sword, the Rod, Pebbles and Shells and Eating Soap and Glass with the Trick for That*, as well as Ubayd al-Kayyis, whose work was simply entitled *Juggling*. Al-Nadim also mentions a sleight-of-hand artist named Mansu Abu al-'Ajab, who was 150 years old when he died, and the conjurer Qalishtanus, who wrote on incantations and talismans.[7]

Al-Nadim's references to Indian magic reflected the deep interest among Arab scholars and practitioners in the mysterious lands to the East. The titles of the works also reveal a degree of cross-fertilization in the magical practices of India and Arabia, Asia Minor and the Euphrates Valley. Sword swallowing was practiced in Buddhist India, the pebbles and shells referred to in the title of al-Rahha's book is most probably the Cups and Balls trick that was familiar to Indian as well as Egyptian and Persian magi. The exchange in magical methodology accompanied the wider trade in ideas that so enriched the land of al-Hind, as Arab geographers referred to India, and the Near East. During the tenure of the first Barmakid vizier, Khalid ibn Barmak, envoys were sent to India to bring back medicines, texts and scholars. As well as translations of Sanskrit medical works into Arabic, there was a strong focus on Indian astronomical literature and mathematics, algebra and algorithms.[8] The vizier sent Yayha ibn Khalid to India to bring back medicinal plants and write about its religions. Ibn Khalid's original report on his travels is lost, but parts of it were copied by the savant Yaqub Ishaq al-Kindi, and these in turn made it into the ninth chapter of the *Fihrist*, providing some of the earliest descriptions of India in Arabic. Ibn Khalid begins with a description of a Hindu temple in central India with 20,000 idols made from 'gold, silver, iron, copper, brass, and ivory, as well as crushed stones adorned with precious jewels. The king, who has 60,000 elephants in his stables, visits the temple once a year and worships an idol twelve-cubits high and made of solid gold.'[9] He also describes the Buddhist cave temples of Bamiyan in present day Afghanistan, where one eyewitness tells him up to 50,000 pilgrims offer themselves as human sacrifices every year.

The fascination with Indian religious practices embraced the occult sciences, yoga and Tantra. In 1718, the Vatican library received an unusual donation from Rinaldo de Bufalo, a member of the Roman Senate. The book, forgotten until recently, was the *Kamru Bijaksa*, or *The Kamarupa Seed Syllables*. Discovered in Persia, then carried through India before finally reaching Rome, this 'recipe book for occultists'[10] contained information on the 'Arts of Divination, Secrets of Herbs and other natural things, and also in Magick and Inchantments, whereunto they are much addicted, and boast of doing great wonders'.[11] According to its anonymous translator, the book contained two types of science. The first was the science of magical imagination (*wahm*) and discipline (*riyadat*), of which there was in India nothing greater or more powerful. 'On the basis of this science they affirm things that intellect does not accept, but they believe in it, and among them it is customary.'[12] The second was the science of divination, also known as the science of reading thought (*damir*), which was attained through breath control.

> This book is known throughout India, and among the Hindus no book is nobler than this. Whoever learns this book and knows its explanation is counted as a great scholar and wise man. They serve him, and whoever is occupied with the theory and practice of this they call a *jogi* [yogi] and respect him greatly. They serve him just like we respect the saints and the masters of struggle and discipline.[13]

The book's chapters include information on teachings of Hatha Yoga according to the tradition of the Nath yogis, breath control and the rites of the yogini temple cult associated with Kaula Tantrism. Inscribed in large letters was a major section entitled *The Book of Magical Imagination*. The term 'seed syllables' alluded to the recitation of mantras.

The book's journey to the Vatican was as unusual as its contents. It was given to De Bufalo's relative, Pietro della Valle, while he was travelling through Persia in 1622. Born into an aristocratic Roman family that counted two cardinals in its ranks, Della Valle was a member of the Accademia di Umoristi, a select circle of scholars, literati and scientists interested in recovering lost ancient texts that might offer cures for diseases. In 1614, to escape a failed love affair, he embarked on a journey that took him through the Levant, Asia Minor and Mesopotamia. While visiting some ruins near Baghdad, he met an eighteen-year-old Nestorian woman, Maani Gioerida, who he married a few weeks later. Together, they travelled to Persia, but in 1622, after they had been married just six years, Maani contracted fever and died. Grief-stricken, he had her body embalmed, hid it under his clothing in a large leather trunk and carried her with him until his return to Rome, where he arranged a grand funeral. After spending several years in Isfahan, toying with founding a Christian colony and building a replica of a Saint Peter's basilica, he journeyed south to Lar, a small but vibrant centre of Persian learning. It was in Lar that *The Kamarupa Seed Syllables* was copied out for him. By the time he reached India in 1623, he was fully versed on the Indian practices of yogic breathing and divination techniques and the conjuring of female spirits.

First translated into Persian in the fourteenth century, the contents of this Indian text on magic and the occult would have been considered heretical by the conservative religious teachers of the time. The book's portrait of Indian wisdom rests on the authority of Kamakhya Devi, a goddess from Assam (Kamarupa). She was the leader of a cult of sixty-four yoginis (female followers of yoga). Her temple, which stands on a hill overlooking the Brahmaputra river, contained a cave only accessible to magicians: 'When someone enters that cave, he goes in darkness until he reaches the end of that cave. He sees lamps and a clean, fragrant, beautiful place.' The translator gathers information from a Brahmin priest on how to summon the goddess Lakshmi for sexual relations and testifies to his own success in employing these techniques.[14] The scholar Carl W. Ernst of the University of North Carolina, who rediscovered *The Kamarupa Seed Syllables,* writes that such a reference to a Hindu goddess in a text circulating in orthodox Muslim circles, 'confounds one's expectations'.[15] One magical recipe uses a nail fashioned from bone that is employed nefariously with a voodoo-type doll's comb made from the right paw of a mad dog killed with an iron stake. There are also descriptions of rituals performed at cremation grounds. The text employs standard Arabic terms for astral magic (*tanjim*), the summoning of spirits (*ihdar*) and the subjugation of demons, fairies and magicians (*taskhir*). The chants or mantras of the yogis are repeatedly referred to as spells (*afsun*), a term of magical significance.[16]

The cosmopolitan Persian culture Della Valle encountered in Lar and that fostered the translation of works such as *The Kamarupa Seed Syllables* and *The Pool of Nectar*, also flourished in India creating fertile ground for the syncretic blending of magic, mysticism and astrology from Occidental, Oriental and local sources. The most remarkable reflection of this was the *Nujum al-Ulum* or *Stars of Science,* composed in 1570 by Ali Adil Shah. The ruler of the Deccani Sultanate of Bijapur, Adil Shah developed a reputation for tolerance, banning the slaughter of animals at his court and holding religious discussion with Hindus, Muslims and Jesuits. He was such a just ruler that Hindus believed he must have been reincarnated as a king seventy times.[17] Adil Shah took an interest in a range of esoteric knowledge and practices. Described as 'of one of the most mysterious, eclectic and syncretic texts to survive from medieval India',[18] the *Nujum* draws openly on a whole spectrum of traditions rooted in varying Indic, Persianate, Turkic and Semitic cultures. Its various talismans and spells are attributed to a range of scholars from ancient Greece and the Middle East, including Apollonius of Tyana and Plato. It includes a Sanskrit text on astrology that it claims was translated in its entirety.[19] Conceived as a compendium of courtly life, the *Nujum's* fifty-two chapters covered everything from recognizing and repelling rare events to Persian and Indian systems of spells and a description of their benefits and nature. The *Nujum* also dealt with prognosticating by the stars, emitting smoke signals, the science of alchemy, methods for making someone act against his nature, conquering planetary forces, enslaving jinns and the art of geomancy. By collating the most effective and powerful practical techniques available for bringing both mundane and cosmic forces under the ruler's control, the *Nujum* was a valuable tool for consolidating power in the fluid political circumstances of mid-sixteenth century Deccan, writes Emma Flatt, the text's leading scholar. 'The gathering together of diverse strands of ancient knowledge in chapters on the signs of weapons, horses, and elephants, and the astrological charts that plot out the influence of planets on territorial conquest, should underline the fact that the *Nujum* was a corollary of this military revolution – which in itself was part of a broader process of state building – not a distraction from it.'[20] The *Nujum* also details 140 spiritual beings, some of which share the names of yoginis. This interest in Tantric goddesses appears to be confirmed by Della Valle, who refers to a Deccani Muslim ruler who held 'enormous feasts and sacrifices in honour of one of these women' who lived in a cave high in the mountains. According to Flatt, Adil Shah is the most likely candidate for this ruler.[21]

ONE legacy of Muslim rule in India was the influence of Islamic beliefs and storytelling traditions on Indian religious life and folklore. This interplay is particularly pronounced in the Punjab, where there are still thousands of shrines of Muslim pirs or saints and Sufis. Denzel Ibbertson, who supervised the 1881 census in the province, noted that the Hindu god of water was named after a Khwaja Khizr, a Muslim saint who was tasked with the care of travellers. The other legacy is the belief in semi-divine beings known as jinns. In Indian folklore, they appear as beings 'of gigantic stature, sometimes resplendently handsome, sometimes horribly hideous. They can become invisible and move on earth where they please. They ride the whirlwind like Indian demons, and direct the storm. Their chief home is the mountains of Qaf, which encompass the earth.'[22] The heretical or evil jinns roam at night, heard but rarely seen, haunting houses and bringing misfortune, sickness and death to all but the most devoted. Jinns could be found almost anywhere. Ploughing virgin soil, digging wells or setting a thicket on fire disturbs jinns who fly out in the form of white snakes.[23] Farmers believe they are entitled to a share of their crops. To deny jinns their due will cause a crop to fail or make it so abundant that it will be valueless. In parts of Sindh, Hindu demons known as rakshas were interchangeable with jinns. 'The Gin [jinns] of the Beelooch hills is wayward and often morose, but not necessarily malignant,' wrote Mary Frere in *Old*

Deccan Days; or, Hindoo Fairy Legends, Current in Southern India. 'His usual form is that of a dwarfish human being, with large eyes and covered with long hair, and apt to breathe with a heavy snoring kind of noise.'[24] Frere travelled extensively through India with her father, Sir John Arthur, collecting local folktales with the help of her half-Portuguese ayah. Jinns, she recounts, do not always retain their own shape, and can assume the form of a camel, goat or any other animal. 'If a Gin [jinn] be accidentally met, it is recommended that the traveller should show no sign of fear, and above all, keep a civil tongue in his head, for the demon has a special aversion to bad language.' Once attached to a man, a jinn will work hard and remain faithful, sometimes revealing to him 'great subterranean caverns under the hills, where there is perpetual spring, and trees laden with fruits of gold and precious stones; but the mortal once admitted to such a Paradise is never allowed to leave it'.[25]

Six animal-headed jinns from Marvels of Things Created and Miraculous Aspects of Things Existing, *National Library of Medicine.*

Belief in the magical powers of jinns – supernatural beings that predate the creation of Adam – was incorporated into Islam by the Prophet Muhammad. According to legend, they were the first inhabitants of the earth, but were forced underground by an army of angels sent by God. The Koran says that jinns were created out of smokeless flame. Muhammad divided them into three categories: Those that have wings and can fly; those that appear as serpents, scorpions, lions, wolves, or jackals; and those that move from place to place like men. The Koran further divides jinns into the pious, who flocked to the Prophet's side whenever he disclosed his revelations, and heretics, who served Iblis (Satan). Though they are presented as a pagan throwback to pre-Islamic times, the Koran's references to them ensured they became an integral part of the Islamic world view, notes Michael W. Dols. 'Even the legal status of the *jinn* was worked out by medieval Muslim jurists in all respects and in astonishing detail, especially with regard to marriage between *jinn* and human beings.'[26]

Theological references to jinns varied according to time, place and popular superstition. In Arabia, they were created from flame or smoke and were said to be like air. In Egypt, they were described as having flaming eyes and could disappear by turning into fire. Another common belief was that their eyes were perpendicular, not horizontal as in humans.[27] One type of jinn known as a *ghul*, could be either male or female. One blow would kill a ghul, but a second would bring it back to life. Among some Indian Muslims, jinns are believed to be the souls of Hindus who were compelled to live a wandering life because they never accepted Islam as their true faith. 'The Mahomedans firmly believe in their agency,' wrote James Forbes in his *Oriental Memoirs* published in 1813. 'The Hindoos are taught that two of these genii [jinns] attend upon every mortal, from the moment of his existence until his death; that to the one is committed the record of his good actions; to the other the report of his transgressions, at the tribunal appointed for judgment.'[28]

Jinns are also said to take the form of columns of dust crossing the plains in hot weather and can appear without warning from under the expanded hood of a cobra. Another belief states that they can be recognized by their inability to wink. This, however, was compensated by having extremely elastic arms and legs. A jinn would not think twice of suddenly stretching out his arm and picking a sparrow off a roof, or extending his leg and using his foot to crush a black beetle ten or twenty paces away.[29] The future can be foretold by consulting Hazirat, the king of the jinns. A young boy is hypnotized after his hand is placed on a betel leaf smeared with *kajal* or lamp-black. The medium, looking on the lamp-black, sees the Hazirat appear as in a mirror. The king of jinns then answers questions put to him through the medium.[30]

In Rohilkhand and the western districts of Oude, phantom armies were said to appear at the burial-grounds of soldiers slain in battle. 'Tents are pitched, horses tethered, and *nautches* held which the deceased heroes and *jinns* attend. One occasionally hears of an ordinary mortal who, attracted by the lights, went and witnessed such a spectacle, the sequel in such cases being that the unwary person had to pay for his temerity with death or loss of reason.'[31] A folktale from Bijnor tells the story of a travelling fakir who came across the ruins of a great city where people lived in huts on its outskirts. They told him they could not live there because the city was infested with jinns. The fakir went into one of the deserted palaces, killed two goats and cooked their meat in a couple of cauldrons with some rice for himself and his companions.

> When he opened the cauldrons, he found naught therein, because the *Jinn* had eaten the food. Three times he did the same and each time the *Jinn* devoured the food. Then he filled the cauldrons with oil and when it was boiled by the force of his spells, he consumed the *Jinn* therein. Only the leader of their host escaped and he came and kneeling before the fakir asked for mercy. The fakir pardoned him on condition that he left the city in peace. Then he called to the people of the city to return to their homes. But they refused to come unless the fakir remained to guard them. So he stayed in the city as long as he lived and thenceforth the people lived in safety.[32]

When compiling his glossary of the castes and tribes of the Punjab in the first decade of the twentieth century, the British civil servant Horace Arthur Rose found that Jats and Baluchis were reluctant to talk about jinns. 'The more intelligent profess a disbelief which they do not really feel, while the poorer and more ignorant will not say much, either from fear of ridicule or to avoid being questioned.' The jinns dwelt in ruined wells, abandoned dargahs, graveyards and desolate tracts. They often used a woman's voice to call men back by name. 'Two men have told me that this has happened to them. Safety lies in going on without turning around.'[33]

JINNS were firmly established in folklore and legend by the time northern India came under the control of the Mughals in the early sixteenth century. The Empire's founder, Babur, was largely preoccupied with conquest and consolidating his administration. Though he admired the skills of Indian acrobats, who he considered were far more accomplished than their Central Asian counterparts, he made little attempt to learn about Hinduism and only had negligible encounters with Hindu ascetics. An illustrated version of the *Baburnama* (*Memoirs of Babur*), commissioned by Akbar in the late sixteenth century, depicts Babur with the yogis of Gorkhatri, an important Hindu pilgrimage centre located where the city of Peshawar now stands. The first painting shows Babur's failed attempt to reach Gorkhatri in 1505. The second shows him seated on a horse and being greeted by two ascetics, one with a shaven head, the other with matted hair and a long beard. Like all Turkish rulers and his successors, Babur believed in miracle shrines, magic springs, astrology and mastery over the weather. He employed three servants specifically for their skill in bringing down great thunderstorms with lightning and hail, which could disorientate an enemy army on the field of battle or put out a fire.[34] When the noted Persian astrologer, Muhammad Sharif, made a dire prediction on the eve of an important battle against a Rajput king, Babur negated the prophecy by declaring his intention to give up drinking wine. Three hundred of his commanders joined him in his pledge and Babur ordered jars of wine brought from Kabul to be poured into a specially dug step-well. He also announced that if the battle was won, he would repeal an un-Islamic tax on trade. Finally, he made his commanders swear on the Koran that they would not abandon him on the battlefield.[35]

Babur died in 1530 within four years of seizing Hindustan, bequeathing his son Humayun what the historian Bamber

Gascoigne called a 'shaky inheritance'. Humayun had been a brave soldier on the battlefield, but as a ruler lacked long-term strategy. He found the fruits of victory more appealing than consolidating his gains and would settle down for months enjoying his favourite pastimes, which consisted of drinking wine, taking opium and reading poetry. 'He was superstitious to a point ludicrous even in his own age,' Gascoigne writes.[36] Anyone who entered the court left foot first was summarily dismissed. He believed in the efficacy of necromancy, the influence of the stars, the mysterious qualities of precious stones and the importance of signs and omens. Hours would be spent shooting arrows into the air, some marked with his own name, others with that of the Shah of Persia in the belief that the way they fell would reveal which nation would become more powerful. One day he summoned his nobles, soothsayers and astrologers and told them he had seen in a dream the moon, the sun and the stars come down to the foot of his throne. Those assembled said the position of the heavenly bodies confirmed the purport of his dreams and that the rulers of Turkey, Persia and other kingdoms would soon present themselves at his court and pledge their loyalty. In fact, the opposite happened. His spiritual waywardness and obsession with magic was blamed for the loss of much of northern India to the Afghans.

To lighten the mood of the court, Humayun ordered a magical carpet for the imperial audience hall large enough for 1400 people to sit on. The carpet was patterned in concentric circles, with each circle matching a planetary sphere or one of the four elements. Humayun sat in the sixth circle of heaven, golden in colour and spherical like the sun, which governs the fate of rulers and kings. He was surrounded by his officers and courtiers, arranged according to an elaborate astrological scheme. They would throw a dice with figures in different postures painted on each side. A person had to assume the figure that turned up on his throw. If the picture was of a person standing, he stood up, if seated he sat down, if reclining, he lay down and even went to sleep, and so on. The entire exercise was a means of increasing mirth. Humayun also constructed a pavilion where the places of the constellations and the signs of the zodiac were represented. His household was arranged into four branches corresponding to the four elements. Different days were assigned to different matters that bore no resemblance to the efficient running of the court. On each day Humayun wore colours appropriate to the planet of the day. On Sunday, which was set aside for government affairs because it was the day of the sun, he wore yellow. On Monday, designated as a 'day of joy', he wore green. Courtiers were grouped into three different classes that were further divided into twelve grades. Each grade was then divided into three ranks – a system that did little but create confusion in administrative matters.

Humayun died on 24 January 1556, a week after falling down the stairs from the roof of his library where he had been consulting with his astrologers about the hour they expected Venus to rise. Despite being only thirteen at the time, his son Akbar survived challenges to his throne, including from Adil Shah, and became the greatest of the Mughal rulers. The first of the dynasty to be born in India, Akbar's commitment to religious pluralism was one of the defining features of his nearly fifty-year long reign. He was said to walk incognito through bazaars and villages to satisfy his curiosity about the diverse faiths of his people. The Mughals believed that their rule was legitimized through God's sanction.

Religious power and political power were synonymous. For Akbar and his successors, it was perfectly acceptable to seek political counsel from religious figures. The more spiritual insight the emperor gained, the more successful his reign.[37] Translating the great Hindu epic, the *Mahabharata* into Persian was, as Audrey Truschke of Rutgers University points out, 'a thoroughly political project that was intimately connected to Akbar's kingship'.[38] Renamed the *Razmnamah* (*Book of War*), it remained a seminal work, being shown and read in imperial circles for decades.

Akbar commissioned his head vizier and court poet, Abul Fazl, to compile a record of his reign. A liberal-minded scholar and gifted historian, Fazl produced two monumental works, the *Akbar-nama* or *History of Akbar* and the *Ain-i-Akbari* or *Constitution of Akbar*. A combination of gazetteer, almanac, rule book and statistical digest, the *Ain-i-Akbari* contained information on everything from 'Regulations for Oiling Camels and Injecting Oil into their Nostrils' to mathematical methods for calculating the size of the earth.[39] It also gave the Persian-reading world a description of India's geography and society, manners and beliefs, its various schools of philosophy, its sciences and its music, literature and magic. *Indrajala*, the art of sorcery, magical spells and sleight-of-hand, was listed as one of the eighteen sciences (*arthara-vidya*). 'The wonders performed by these means,' Fazl wrote, 'are beyond the power of expression.' *Rasa-vidya* or alchemy was another of the sciences. By the art of 'fusing of mercury (rasa), gold, silver, copper, and the like … the elixir, or philosopher's stone, is produced'.[40]

For Fazl, Akbar was nothing short of a saint who 'sought for truth amongst the dust-stained denizens of the field of irreflection and consorted with every sort of wearers of patched garments such as [yogis, renouncers, and Sufi mystics], and other solitary sitters in the dust and insouciant recluses'.[41] He credited the great Mughal with the power to end drought by bringing down rain through prayers. 'To prevent too much rain from falling he would breathe on a mirror then throw it into the fire. His breath could also cure the aliments of animals and human beings. Standing close to the king protected a person against bullets.'[42] Not a day passed without people bringing cups of water to him, asking him to breathe on them. Wrote Fazl: 'He who reads the letters of the divine orders in the book of fate, on seeing the tidings of hope, takes the water with his blessed hands, places it in the rays of the world-illuminating sun, and fulfils the desire of the suppliant. Many sick people of broken hopes, whose diseases the most eminent physicians pronounced incurable, have been restored to health by this divine means.'[43]

Akbar's pretensions of his own divinity irked the orthodox Sunnis in his court. One of his most strident critics was the historian Abd-al-Kadir Badauni, who detested being ordered to translate Hindu epics such as the *Mahabharata* and the *Ramayana* into Persian. Badauni also criticized Akbar for allegedly worshiping the sun four times a day with prostrations and recitations of Sanskrit names, holding religious debates and interviewing 'famed holy men of all sects'.[44] In his *Muntakhab Al Tawarikh* (*Selection of Chronicles*), Badauni relates that in 1583 Akbar ordered two places be built to feed poor Hindus and Muslims, Khairpurah and Dharmpurah, and put some of Fazl's officers in charge of them. Because of the immense number of yogis that came, Akbar ordered the building of a third place,

Jogipurah. 'Nightly meetings were held with some of these men (*jogis*) and they used to employ themselves in various follies and extravagances, in contemplations, gestures, addresses, abstractions and reveries, and in alchemy, fascination and magic.'[45] On the night of the Hindu festival of Shivaratri, Akbar ate and drank with the yogis who promised he would live three or four times longer than ordinary men. 'Fawning court doctors, wisely enough, found proofs for the longevity of the emperor,' Baudani recorded. After being told that there could be found in Tibet lamas, Mongolian devotees, recluses, and hermits, who lived for more than 200 years, Akbar restricted the time he spent in the harem, curtailed his consumption of food and alcohol and abstained from meat. He also shaved the hair of the crown of his head (the tenth opening of the body), and let the hairs at the sides grow to allow his soul to escape freely at the moment of death.

Akbar's fascination with the occult was commented on by Thomas Coryat, the eccentric English traveller and former jester in the court of James I, who walked from Aleppo to Ajmer for a cost of three pounds. According to Coryat, Akbar had 'learned all kinds of sorcery' and 'once in a strange humour, to show a spectacle to his nobles, brought forth his eldest queen, with a sword cut off her head, and after the same, perceiving the heaviness and sorrow of them for the death of her (as they thought), by vertue of his exorcismes caused her head to reappear, no signe appearing of any stock with his sword.' [46] Coryat's account was based on hearsay and should be treated with scepticism especially as it comes from a man known for his unpredictability. One of his stunts was to yell out from the minaret of a mosque that the only God was Christ and 'Mahomet was an Imposter'.[47]

Emperor Jahangir receiving a petition from a fakir, c. 1605-27. British Library.

Coryat, who referred to himself as 'the Legge-Stretcher of Odcombe in Somerset', arrived in India in 1613, when it was under the rule of Akbar's son Jahangir. He described the Mughal emperor as 'a sensible, kind-hearted man, very courteous and cultured, with a passion for justice'. This view was not shared by contemporary travellers or subsequent historians, who broadly agreed that his addiction to alcohol and opium exacerbated his sadistic cruelty and vicious temper. There was also a mystical aspect to his personality, which goes some way to explaining why the seven Bengali jugglers who turned night into day, produced a instantaneous forest of trees and sent a pack of animals scurrying up a self-supporting chain to their oblivion were treated like royalty. In his memoir, the *Tuzuk-i-Jahangiri,* the emperor describes encountering Carnatic jugglers who could swallow a chain five-yards long and weighing several pounds.[48] These magicians, he wrote, 'had no rivals or equals'. One juggled ten balls of different sizes without ever dropping one and did so many other tricks 'that one's wits became bewildered'.[49]

Born on the eve of the first Islamic millennium in 1592, Jahangir's son and successor Shah Jahan, took a more orthodox approach to matters of religion and state. The practice of prostration before the sovereign, considered un-Islamic, was banned. He reinstated patronage of the annual Hajj pilgrimage and stopped the building and repair of non-Muslim places of worship. These changes would be consolidated by Aurangzeb, the last of the great Mughals, but not before a bloody war of succession. Shah Jahan backed the free-thinking Dara Shikoh over the austere Aurangzeb, his younger brother. In 1652, he sent Shikoh on an expedition against the Afghan city of Kandahar that Aurangzeb had twice failed to capture. His 70,000-strong army, which included Muslim and Rajput officers as well as hundreds of war elephants, set out from Lahore on what was deemed the astrologically auspicious day of 11 February 1653. To bolster his fortune in the difficult battle ahead, he included pious ulemas and Hindu magicians in his ranks. The combined forces of a strong army, religion and magic, however, proved useless against Kandahar's fortified citadel. Desperate to break a months-long stalemate, Shikoh turned to his miracle workers. A holy man came forward claiming to have forty jinns at his bidding and offered special prayers that he promised would make the garrison fall in twenty days. A group of gurus from the Deccan also submitted their services, promising to build 'a wonderful thing which could carry two or three persons with hand grenades, and fly in the air without wings and feathers'.[50] A fraudster assured the prince he could reduce the fort to ashes if supplied with some wine and a particular woman whose blood would be used to write a special charm. Shikoh provided both. Instead of fulfilling his promise, the fake magician 'enjoyed the company of the woman for some days', then fled before he could be exposed as a fraud. This soon became the talk of the camp.[51]

Let down by these various occultists and illusionists, Shikoh tried to raise the morale of his troops by telling them his dreams and visions of victory. When that failed, he decided to make a direct assault. Despite the reluctance of his commanders, the Mughal army stormed the fort on 21 August 1653. The Persians held their fire until the last moment, then set the Mughal horses and elephants into a stampeding panic. By the end of the day a thousand men were dead and another thousand wounded. A humiliated Dara retreated to his tent while the Persians played victory music from the ramparts and sent out dancing girls to undulate in full view of the demoralized Mughal soldiers.[52]

The failure to seize Kandahar was Shikoh's downfall. While he was in Afghanistan, Aurangzeb had taken Agra in 1658 and imprisoned Shah Jahan in the Red Fort. On his return to India, Shikoh was betrayed by one of his generals, captured and brought back to Delhi, where he was paraded through the city seated on a dirty elephant and in chains. He was then charged with apostasy and sentenced to death. In a violent struggle with his executioners, his head was cut off and carried to Aurangzeb to prove that his rival was finally dead. On Aurangzeb's orders, the corpse was then paraded through the streets on the back of an elephant for a second time, before being buried at Humayun's tomb.

In his later years, Aurangzeb lived like an ascetic, spending his time, even when battles were raging around him, engrossed in reading the Koran. Under his austere rule, women were no longer allowed to visit shrines, Hindu salutations and hunting were forbidden, as was the consumption of *bhang* and alcohol. But his piety did not lessen his belief in the efficacy of spells or his magical powers. Manucci described him as a 'past master in witchcraft', who practiced sorcery in his youth.[53] Every Friday before the midday prayers, he made special incense using pepper to ward off the evil influences of demons. He used every opportunity to nurture his reputation as a miracle worker. In 1672, a revolt by Satnami fanatics rattled the Mughal throne. The Satnamis were mainly traders and farmers who lived in an area southwest of Delhi. Although they numbered only around 5,000 insurgents, they managed to defeat the imperial army at Narnaul. 'It was said that swords, arrows, and musket balls had no effect upon these men, and that every arrow and ball which they discharged against the royal army brought down two or three men,' the court chronicler Khafi Khan wrote. 'They were credited with magic and witchcraft, and stories were currently reported about them which were utterly incredible. They were said to have magic wooden horses like live ones, on which their women rode as an advanced guard.'[54] Led by an old witch who was blamed for sparking the revolt, their numbers boosted by local Rajput clans, the Satnamis marched towards Delhi less than a hundred miles away. 'Great rajas and veteran amirs were sent against them with powerful armies,' but they failed to halt their march, Khafi Khan continued. Aurangzeb wrote out prayers and ordered them to be sewn into the Mogul army banners, telling his men that these would work against the Satnami's magic. Wrote Manucci: 'The spells of Aurangzeb prevailed over those of the old woman.' The Satnami were slaughtered 'nearly all dying, including the old woman herself'.[55]

In 1668, Aurangzeb issued a decree banning musicians from his palace and followed up with a proclamation prohibiting singing and dancing. According to Manucci, a thousand artists protested his ban, confronting the emperor at a mosque as he was going to his Friday prayers 'crying aloud with great grief and many signs of feeling, as if they were escorting to the grave some distinguished defunct'. Aurangzeb responded by saying that the protesters should 'pray for the soul of music, and see that she was thoroughly well buried'.[56] Manucci does not mention the effect of his decrees on the magical arts and recent scholarship has questioned the veracity of the Italian's claims.[57] But if the tenor of his account is true, nobles in the Mughal court would have been forced to reduce or end their patronage of jugglers. Magic was also proscribed by the Koran, which stated: 'Whoever goes to a magician and asks about mysteries and believes what he says, verily is displeased with Muhammad and his religion.'[58] Aurangzeb had memorized the sacred text by heart and copied it out by hand. For a brief period at least, piety triumphed over prestidigitation.

FOUR

IN THE COURT OF THE KINGS

> The juggler swallowed a sword like water, drinking it as a thirsty man would drink sherbet. He also thrust a knife up his nostril. He mounted a little wooden horse and rode in the air. Large bodies were made to issue out of small ones; an elephant was drawn through a window, and a camel through the eye of a needle. … Sometimes they (the jugglers) transformed themselves into angels, sometimes into demons. … They sang enchantingly.[1]

THE fourteenth century writer, mystic, musician, poet – and possible inventor of the sitar – Amir Khusrau was the greatest chronicler of the Delhi Sultanate. He moved 'among the crowd', as one historian noted, his prose and poetry capturing the decadence and depravity of pre-Mughal India. Khusrau's world was populated by turbaned ulemas, saintly and imposter Sufi mystics, quarrelling jurists, gamblers and courtesans.[2] There were mimics, acrobats, jugglers, conjurers, rope dancers and fortune tellers. The jugglers he describes in his poem *Ashiqa* are so dexterous in their use of swords that they can split a hair in two and dissect a fly in mid-air.

Acrobat and musician. Wellcome Library.

In *Nuh-Siphir*, he vouches for enchanters who can bring a man killed by a snake back to life after six months, convert themselves into wolves, dogs and cats, extend their lives by controlling their breath and make themselves invisible by applying a magic paste to their eyes.[3]

Writing in the *Journal of the Asiatic Society of Bengal* in 1935, Khunwar Ashraf combed through the works of Khusrau and other writers of the period to compile a kaleidoscopic portrait of life in the Delhi Sultanate. Bazaars were filled with performing rams and monkeys, snake charmers and puppeteers. Dancing elephants amused the crowds. In princely courts, the most skilful of jugglers executed a version of the Rope Trick where a magician climbed into the air until he disappeared. Soon his limbs rained down and were collected by his wife, who threw them into a funeral pyre and then committed sati by consigning herself into the flames. A short while later, the magician reappeared and demanded to know what had happened to his wife, only to see her emerge from the zenana quarters of the ruler's palace unscathed. Hindu and Muslim nobles employed acrobats, mountebanks, professional jesters, buffoons and clowns to entertain their guests. 'Some of these jesters wore the most comic masks and gave amusing surprises to the party. At other times, they caricatured the popular courtiers and other lackeys and suffered indignities and beating or snubbing, to create an effect.'[4] Further evidence of the importance of magic and other forms of entertainment at this time comes from the writing of the Sufi poet Maulana Daud, who lived during the reign of Firoz Shah Tughluq (1351–1383). Daud is best remembered for his love story *Chandayan*, a narrative poem that contains imagery and mystical idioms appropriated from Nath yogi saints, followers of the legendary Hindu guru Gorakhnath. This made them accessible to diverse audiences.[5] Like many Sufi poets of the Delhi Sultanate, Daud was well versed in astronomy, astrology, Hindu mythology, yogic rituals, Sanskrit, Prakrit and Apabramsha poetry, as well as erotic literature. In *Chandayan*, Daud refers to sects of male and female mendicants, theatrical performers, acrobats and magicians thronging the marketplaces of northern India. Bahurupi (impersonators) would disguise themselves as mythological characters and recite stories, and Nats danced and played on *tala* (cymbals).

Sword swallowers, conjurers, court jesters and other performance artists have been a part of the social fabric of India since the Vedic era. Over the centuries, they would be celebrated and censured. These mostly itinerant show-people occupied the lowest rungs of the caste hierarchy, yet they were indispensable. They were patronized by kings, queens and the nobility for their powers in performing exorcisms and divinations, countering the effects of inauspicious omens, dispensing life-prolonging elixirs and love charms, as well as providing entertainment for the ministers of the court, the women of the harem and ambassadors from distant lands. They were an integral feature of festivals, religious rituals and secular ceremonies – their skills codified in the sacred list of the sixty-four essential arts. Travellers and chroniclers would leave descriptions of extraordinary feats of physical dexterity and talismanic devilry staged in dusty village squares and cool marble courtyards of palaces and havelis. Their wonder-working abilities were celebrated in the literature and poetry. Magicians appeared in Hindu dramas carrying bunches of peacock feathers for casting spells and executed feats of legerdemain. As early as the seventh century BCE, universities such as Taxila offered a curriculum that included the study of magic charms, knowledge of spells for bringing the dead back to life and for understanding animal cries, snake charming and the treatment of snake bites, divination, archery, elephant lore and medicine.

In the third century BCE, India's greatest military and political strategist, Kautilya, sought to regulate professional entertainers. A licence fees of five *panas* was levied on jugglers, dancers, singers, instrument players, buffoons, mime artists, rope-dancers and wandering bards from foreign countries.[6] Kautilya also banned amusements that brought people together in recreation halls. 'Actors, dancers, singers, musicians, professional storytellers or minstrels shall not create obstruction in the work (of the people),' he decreed. Similarly, magicians and jugglers were barred from entering the queen's apartment. But even such outcastes had their uses. The *Arthasastra*, Kautilya's manual of statecraft urged the employment of sleight-of-hand artists, fortune tellers, ascetics, monks, astrologers, vintners, lunatics, deaf and blind persons, the handicapped, brothel keepers and prostitutes, among others, to be used as spies to ascertain the integrity of village officials and heads of departments.[7] Astrologers, soothsayers, horologists, storytellers were to sow confusion among the king's enemies by spreading news abroad 'of gods appearing before the conqueror and of his having received from heaven weapons and treasure'. They should also proclaim that the king 'is a successful expert in explaining the indications of dreams and in understanding the language of beasts and birds'.[8]

The *Arthasastra* contained extensive instructions on the use of the necromantic arts in warfare. Disguised as humpbacks, dwarves, blind men and lunatics, magicians would attack opponents with an armoury of spells and poisons killing enemy soldiers, their animals and crops, spreading diseases such as leprosy, cholera and gonorrhoea and causing deformities. There were secret formulas for potions that could turn a body black, render it impervious to fire, allow someone to walk on hot coals, to see in the dark and achieve invisibility. Swallowing a specially prepared ball turned a magician into a fire breather. A Macbeth-like concoction combining the fingernails of a woman from an outcast tribe, beans from a basket buried in a cremation ground, the hair of a monkey and a human bone wrapped in the garments of a dead man, would rob someone of their wealth. Conjurors were also employed to fight great perils such as fire, flood, famine, rats, tigers, snakes and demons. So crucial was their role, Kautilya declared that those who 'are experts in magical arts, and being endowed with supernatural powers, can ward off providential visitations, shall, therefore, be honoured by the king and made to live in his kingdom'.[9] Sorcerers, fortune tellers and astrologers were given ranks and paid accordingly. Tactically, a king was urged to approach his enemy in the way of the snake charmer (*saman*), lulling him into passivity through a non-aggressive pact or defining spheres of influence. Aside from launching an outright assault, he could consider using deceit and pretence (maya) to entrap his foe.

The Villavati inscription dating back to the sixth century AD points out the importance of magical entertainers in medieval India. The South Indian inscription listed all professions subjected to taxation under the rule of the Pallava king Simhavishnu and included licensed spies, rope-jugglers, dancers, mendicants and *imikhadharakas* or masked actors.[10] *Aindrajalika*, or conjuring, was one of the sixty-four *kalas* or arts mentioned in Vatsyana's fourth-century AD work, the *Kamasutra,* together with *chalitakayoga*, the art of mimicry or impersonation and the art of obtaining another's property by means of mantras or

Three musicians sitting with their instruments. Wellcome Library.

incantations. Other kalas included *sutrakrida*, or magic with the help of threads. The term embraced tricks such as taking out different coloured threads from inside the mouth, as well as cutting a piece of thread into pieces, burning it to ashes and then making it whole again. It also included puppetry, rope walking and rope tying. *Hasta-laghava,* or sleight of hand, referred to making items vanish, as well as palm and card tricks.[11]

Numerous writers compiled their own versions of the sixty-four kalas including the seventh-century novelist, poet and litterateur, Dandin. As well as practising conjuring and mimicry, Dandin's fictional characters were masters of *citrayoga*, the practice of charms and spells; *kaucumarayoga*, the art of making a woman fall in love; and *nimittajnana*, the science of omens and portents.[12] Once compared with the legendary composers of the *Ramayana* and the *Mahabharata*, Dandin was born into a family of priestly scholars about 650 AD and lived at the Pallava capital Kanchi, known today as Kanchipuram. His various works, including the *Dasa Kumar Charitam,* the *Adventures of the Ten Princes,* paint a vivid picture of life in a south Indian medieval kingdom. Actors, magicians and snake charmers frequented the courts of the Pallava kings and gave public performances. Visruta, a skilled actor and impersonator, was also a dancer and acrobat whose feats included moving like a scorpion, leaping like a sea monster and darting like a fish. His tricks with daggers carried evocative names such as the 'sweep of a hawk' and the 'flight of the sea-eagle'.[13] Dandin described the performance of Vidyesvara, a skilled conjurer from southern India: As he waved his wand of peacock feathers, snakes appeared and were devoured by vultures. He then created a cameo where prince Manasara and his bride appeared in magical form.

Elsewhere, Dandin dwelt on the dark side of Pallava society, a world of knavish princes, corrupt officials, sweet-tongued parasites, dexterous magicians capable of defrauding even the wisest men, licentious men-about-town, tricky gamesters and expert thieves, impetuous princesses, avaricious whores and 'cunning nuns acting as bawds', to quote Dandin's biographer, Dharmendra Kumar Gupta.[14] Theft, a crime punishable by death, was often carried out with the help of magic. Dandin refers to the *Steya-castra*, the lost manual of thieves, composed by the master magician Muladeva, also known as Karnisuta. The successful thief employed a variety of contrivances, including using a crab tied to a string to pick locks. A special wick illuminated serpents hiding in the walls of houses and could bring on blindness. Magic powders, ointments and even *tilakas* applied to the eyes or the forehead made a thief invisible and therefore invulnerable.[15] Dandin goes on to mention the use of automatons or magical contrivances known as *yantras*. The architect and magician, Lalitalaya, a contemporary of Dandin, created mechanical figures that staged a mock-duel to entertain the court. An artificial cloud brought down heavy rain. Mounted on the heads of elephants were medieval missile launchers.

Somadeva in his *Katha Saritsagar* tells a tale of two brothers, carpenters by profession, who were skilled in making ingenious automata of wood and other materials 'such as Maya first invented'. The elder bother Pranadhara fell in love with a 'fickle woman' and wanting to lavish wealth on her, decided to raid the king's palace. The brothers built a pair of mechanical swans attached to a rope and fastened it to one end of a window of the king's treasury. Every night the swans were hoisted up the rope and into the treasury. Using their beaks, they pried open the lids of jewel boxes and stole whatever was inside. When the king discovered the theft, he ordered an all-night vigil to catch the culprits. Realizing he was about to be caught, Pranadhara built an aerial escape vehicle large enough to accommodate his family, and so fast that it could travel 800 *yojanas* in an instant.[16]

Not all yantras were mythological in nature. Some resembled sophisticated toys. In Harsha's poem *Naishadha Charita (Adventures of Nala Raja of Naishadha)*, statues of Kama, the god of love and his consort, Rati, make erotic sounds.[17] The tenth-century Jain writer Somadeva Suri, refers to mechanical wind-damsels placed in the royal bedchamber that blew cool breezes from their fly-whisks, cloud-damsels spraying sandalwood-scented water from their breasts and female figures. If the figure's hands were touched, water sprayed through her nails, if her face, through the eyes, and so on.[18] Others had military applications. Kautilya's *Arthasastra* mentions fastening rods built into arches that when withdrawn would crush the enemy, as well as trapdoors built over deep pits studded with spikes. Yantras employed in warfare included catapults, driverless carriages that could be deployed against enemy lines, and an iron elephant that exploded on the battlefield.

The richest source of information on magical automata in ancient India can be found in the *Samarangana Sutradhara*, a classical work on Hindu architecture by Raja Bhoja, the eleventh-century ruler of Dhar. Bhoja's name was closely associated with the popular Sanskrit text, the *Vikramacarita,* in which thirty-two statues holding up King Vikrama's magic throne tell Bhoja a series of fantastical tales. Most of the contrivances Bhoja lists in chapter thirty-one of the *Samarangana sutradhara* are works of fantasy, such as *vimanas* or airships resembling UFOs. Others such as dolls made out of leather and cloth that could perform scenes from popular Hindu myths, were probably real.

Bhoja divided yantras into two categories – those that required a mechanism to propel them and those that worked automatically. Some had magical qualities, including automata that produced fire in water and vice versa, made objects disappear and created them out of thin air. Others were used for pleasure, such as a mattress that rose and fell by the soft action of air, 'like that of a serpent's breathing'. Yantras for entertainment included mechanical birds that spoke, sang and danced by means of air being driven through them by water, as well as dancing elephants, horses and monkeys. Another category of yantras were figures of men and women whose movements were managed by an elaborate system of holes, pins and strings attached to rods controlling each limb. These mechanical figures were capable of looking into a mirror, playing a lute, stretching out their hand, sprinkling water, serving betel to guests and making obeisance. Similar robots, used as palace guards, were armed with batons, swords, iron rods, spears and other weapons to prevent the entry of outsiders and to kill thieves who tried to break in at night.[19] For the king's enjoyment, mechanical figures of dancing peacocks, cuckoos, bees and swans were arranged in water parks, including miniature elephants that closed their eyes when another threw water on their face. The walls of his palace could speak by means of attendants hidden in special cavities.[20] Bhoja also describes various classes of flying vehicles including a *daru-vimana* powered by four pitchers of mercury over iron ovens. When aloft, the boiling ovens produced such a terrible noise that elephants on the battlefield went mad with fear.

Bhoja's yantras were of little help when Someshvara I of the Kalyani Chalukya dynasty invaded his kingdom around 1058. The Kalyani Chalukyas ruled over large parts of southern India from the tenth to the twelfth century, leaving behind ornate temples and a vast corpus of literature on Hindu epics, astrology, mathematics, eroticism and mysticism. In the early twelfth century, King Someshvara III composed one of the earliest encyclopaedic works in Sanskrit. The *Manasollasa (Delight of the Mind)* covered everything from the culinary habits of the royal court, to detailed horticultural notes on how to create the ultimate pleasure garden where the king could play hide-and-seek with his lovers or indulge in more amorous adventures. One chapter described an elaborate game where the king entered a pitch-black cellar full of sixteen-year-old girls who competed for his sexual favours.[21] The king also arranged magic shows in the palace courtyard for his wives, lovers, ministers and foreign guests. During these performances, magicians used special compounds to create illusionary effects. A person looking at the light of a candle with a wick made out of seedlings that sprouted from the skull of a dead dog and were ground with lac and cotton, imagined he saw snakes. Small seeds of a berry ground with dried scorpion and the oil of *sidhva*, enabled a person to hold a flame or walk on water. The meat of a special fish when mixed with oil and butter and applied to the body, protected a person from freezing to death in the snow.[22] The *Manasollasa* also contained alchemic formulas for retaining the king's youth and vitality. If taken in the correct quantities, hair would remain 'jet black like the wings of bees', he could walk one hundred yojana a day and retain the strength of an elephant for 2,000 years. Other formulae gave him the power to see hidden treasures, become invisible and finally, if taken for long enough, become the god of love and bring all men and women under his control.[23]

In January 1442, Shahrukh Mirza, ruler of Transoxiana and son of the great Timurid ruler Tamerlane, despatched an emissary with a caravan full of gifts to the southern Indian kingdom of Vijayanagara. Kamal-ud-Din Abd-ur-Razzaq ibn Ishaq Samarqandi was a reluctant ambassador. By the time he arrived in Muscat, it was so hot that 'rubies would have burned in the mines, marrow boiled in the bones and the metal of their swords melted like wax'.[24] *The Rising of the Auspicious Twin-Stars, and the Confluence of the Ocean*, Abdur Razzaq's chronicle of his journey to India and three-year embassy at Vijayanagara, promised to provide 'the minutest details … [with] all sorts of marvellous facts and wonderful matters worthy of notice'. On reaching the capital he wrote: 'The pupil of the eye has never seen a place like it, and the ear of intelligence has never been informed that there existed anything to equal it in the world.' The jewellery bazaar was stocked with pearls of such quality 'that the field of the moon of the fourteenth day caught fire simply by gazing on them'. Even the courtesans were 'bedecked with priceless pearls and gems and dressed in costly raiment', he added. 'They are all extremely young, and of perfect beauty. Each one of them has by her two young slaves, who give the signal of pleasure, and have the charge of attending to everything which can contribute to amusement.'[25]

During his stay, he witnessed the three-day festival of Mahanadi, where a thousand elephants covered with armour and bearing howdahs filled with jugglers were gathered together. When seen en-masse the elephants resembled 'the wave of a troubled sea, or a stormy cloud'. On their trunks were drawn with cinnabar and other substances extraordinary pictures and figures of wonderful beauty. There were giant automata five-storeys high 'representing everything imaginable including men, wild beasts, birds and animals of every kind, down to flies and gnats'.[26] They rotated and changed their appearance using hidden mechanisms. In front of this assemblage was a magnificently ornamented palace with nine pavilions, where the king sat watching musicians and storytellers as they sang and invented tales. Young girls, 'with cheeks as full as the moon, and with faces more lovely than the spring', emerged from behind a curtain and presented a graceful dance 'calculated to seduce every sense and captivate every mind'. Next, it was the turn of the jugglers to execute their wonderful feats. They began by building a platform out of thick beams of wood, each about half-a-metre in length and roughly a metre high:

> A large elephant, trained to this exercise, stepping upon the first and second pieces of wood ascends the third, the surface of which is scarcely broader than the sole of one of the feet of this animal. While the elephant supports himself with his four feet upon this beam, they raise behind him the other pieces of wood. The animal once placed on the top of this beam, follows with his trunk all the airs which the musicians play, and moving in cadence with the time, raises and lowers his trunk alternately.[27]

The jugglers then erected a giant set of scales with a huge rock positioned at one end of a beam of wood matching the weight of an elephant. This piece of wood – one end of which bore the dancing elephant and the other the stone – turned in a semicircle, making a half-rotation from right to left.[28] For their performance, the magicians, orators and musicians received gold and costly garments.

The Vijayanagara empire's chroniclers also left behind detailed descriptions of palace life. According to the early sixteenth century text, *Shri Krishnadevarayana Dinachari* (*The Diary of Shri Krishnadevarayana*), composed by court poets during the reign of Krishnadevaraya, the king would hold a daily public audience attended by his sons, ruling chieftains, officers of the palace, scholars, priests, religious teachers, sages, astrologers and elephant trainers, as well as magicians, bards, singers and other representatives of all branches of the performing arts.[29] A slightly later text, the *Mohana Tarangini*, written as a romantic poem by Kanakadasa, a spiritual adviser to Krishnadevaraya, described the everyday life of a princess. On being awakened at daybreak by the sound of songs from the Vedas, she would look at her palms and observe their auspicious lines. Flanked by attendants bearing mirrors, drinking water, betel nuts, spittoons, fans and fly whisks, she went to the audience hall and listened to recitals from the Hindu epics and enjoyed displays of singing, music and dancing. Then it was the turn of magicians to perform shows and actors to present dramas, before she retired indoors to play dice games. One of the princess's closest confidantes was the sorceress, Chitralekha, an expert in the art of magic formulas, talismans and astrology. Before every journey, Chitralekha would recite incantations to all the planetary deities, including the god of love, and apply talismans on the princess's forehead and arms with the power to ward off malignant spirits. She could cure love-sickness by making her lie on a bed of leaves under a tree next to a stream of cool running water. It was said that Chitralekha was such an expert in the art of magical spells that hardly any other sorceress could match her skills. She could also fly.[30]

ONE of Akbar's first decrees after inheriting the Mughal throne in 1556 at the age of thirteen, was to commission the *Dastan-e-Amir Hamza* or *The Tale of Amir Hamza*. In real life, Hamza was an uncle of the Prophet who was killed in the battle of Uhud in 625. The fictional Hamza is born in Arabia with the horoscope of a great sovereign. On the day of his birth, the emperor of Iran, Nausherwan, is told by astrologers of a boy

Page from The Tale of Amir Hamza. *Wikimedia Commons.*

who would bring his dominion to an end. Hamza rides out of Arabia on a magical horse to defend Islam and himself against unbelievers, sorcerers, dragons and other monsters. He travels to Persia where he battles Nausherwan and is then trapped in Qaf, the land of jinns and fairies, for fourteen years. In the *Dastan-e-Amir Hamza*, the hero is accompanied and supported in his exploits by his trusty friend Amar Ayyar, or Amar the Artful, the greatest trickster of all time. Amar uses his magical powers, which include being able to run at superhuman speed, change appearance at any time, and speak any language, to reinforce Amir Hamza's valour. His main prop is his magic bag, Zanbil. The bag can make anything put inside disappear and produce whatever anyone desires. In addition to jinns, the heroes encounter sorcerers, giants, demons, fairies, man-eaters and cow-headed creatures. When Hamza returns to Arabia, fiction turns to fact. He defends his nephew, the Prophet, against the kafirs of Mecca only to die a gory death in the battle of Uhud. To bring the tales to life, Akbar also commissioned 1,400 folios of paintings on cloth, each approximately two feet high, which would be unfolded before an audience as each story was narrated. Producing the folio, the most extraordinary collection of art to come out of Mughal India, took fifteen years, with Akbar personally supervising and approving each painting. The emperor became so absorbed in the story of Hamza, he took to narrating it himself in the style of a professional storyteller. The brave hero of the Hamza story may have provided an inspiration for the exploits and adventures of Akbar's reckless teenage years when he was known to jump on the back of rampaging elephants much to the distress of his regents and ministers.[31]

Over time the original tales of Amir Hamza were translated from Persian into Urdu, their content often embellished by professional storytellers. The adventures of his sons and grandsons were added, battles extended, his martyrdom postponed. One edition published in Lucknow in the 1860s, comprised forty-two volumes, 46,000 pages and more than 52 million words. Its size notwithstanding, storytellers in Lucknow had become disenchanted with the content of the tales and decided they needed a stronger dose of magic: fantastic fauna, terrifying tricksters, evil spirits, sorcerers and sorceresses, all of which were in plentiful supply in India. Between the 1840s and 1850s, the *Tilism-e-Hoshruba* (*The Enchantment that Steals Away One's Senses*) took Lucknow by storm. The chief storyteller, Mir Ahmed Ali, became the most sought-after person in the kingdom of Oude. Attending his public and private recitals was an almost sacred ritual and every gathering attracted hundreds of people. Improvising as he went, it took Ali several years to finally finish the tale. And when he did, the people wanted him to start again. 'Mir Ahmed Ali wanted to make *Hoshruba* the most sharp-clawed, shiny-scaled tale in the whole of the Amir Hamza cycle, so he liberally poured in vicious sorceresses, nubile trickster girls, powerful wizards and dreaded monsters and stirred the tale with non-stop action,' writes the work's translator, Musharraf Ali Farooqi. 'In that process, Mir Ahmed Ali transcended the whole business of legend-making and created a fantasy – the first, the longest, and the greatest fantasy of the *dastan* genre.'[32]

To boost the story's appeal, Ali claimed the *Hoshruba* was a sequel to the Amir Hamza stories, but according to Farooqi, that was a massive literary hoax and there was more than enough to inspire the storyteller. 'Islamic history was chock-full of all kinds of occult arts and artists. A thousand camel loads of treatises had been written on the occult arts in Arabic, Persian and Urdu. Many renowned sorcerers were household names.' The storytellers of Lucknow, he writes, felt 'it would be a shame to let that occult heritage go to waste.'[33] Inspired by this heritage, Ali created a magical world called a *tilism*, in which the King of Magic, Afrasiyab Jadoo, together with his queen, ruled over an empire of sorcerers and sorceresses, ranked according to their magical powers. Afrasiyab is a Jupiter-like figure, who can release lightning bolts from the tip of his fingers. Amar Ayyar reappears, but with additional powers and leads an army led by a woman known as Mahrukh Magic-Eye. Amir Hamza also returns to fight the eighty-five-foot tall, pitch-black giant named Laqa: 'His head was full of vanity and resembled the ruins of a palace dome, and his limbs were the size of giant tree branches.'[34] So sought after was Ali, that he was poached by the neighbouring kingdom of Rampur. His legacy, however, lived on. In the late nineteenth century, Lucknow's Naval Kishore Press published the *Hoshruba* in forty-six volumes, totalling more than one thousand pages each.

IMPERSONATORS known as *bhagatiyas*, or bahurupis, were another popular form of entertainment in the Mughal courts. Maulana Ganimat in his *Naurang-e-Ishq* written in 1685, described a performance by one such group: 'They sometimes perform the *nakal* of a man, sometimes of woman, sometimes of a child. Sometimes they become child mendicants, sometimes

Muslims. Sometimes they dress like Kashmiris, sometimes they become Englishmen … Sometimes they make the face of a Mughal and sometimes of a slave.'[35] The disguise of a bahurupi artist who appeared in the court of Akbar dressed as a bull was so perfect it fooled everyone, except for the emperor's storyteller and closest confidante Birbal, who exposed his identity by throwing a stone at him. The next day the bahurupi was told to appear as a tiger. To prove how real he was, he leapt on one of the courtiers and, to everyone's horror, killed him. 'The stunned courtiers wanted to hang the *bahurupi*, but Birbal intervened. He simply asked the artiste to come in the guise of Sati another day. The *bahurupi* accordingly came and burnt himself on the pyre.'[36]

According to Peter Mundy, the British merchant and traveller who visited India in the 1630s, the best court jugglers, tumblers and jesters were from the Deccan. Their dancing 'is full of anticks, Gestures, faces and postures, flinging out their leggs and bestirringe themselves as fast as ever they can, others playing and singing the while, exhibiting their antics in different styles'. Young girls performed acrobatic feats for the entertainment of their royal patrons. 'The dancing wenches doe it with of grace, turnieinge, traceinge and windeinge their bodies, and with it heads. Armes and hands, acte many wanton womanish and some lascivious gestures'.[37] Mundy also described a performance by a group of 'Bazighurres' or Bazigars:

> One takes a pole of about three yards longe, which hee setteth upright upon his head, holdinge it with his hands, while a boye clambers up to the topp of it (where is fastned a board halfe a foote broad) and with his feete stands upon it, when the other,

> lettinge goe his hold, daunceth about with him. More than that, the boye stood with his head on the said board with his heeles bolt upright in the ayer, while the other daunceth with him as aforesaid, not once touching the pole with his hands.[38]

On holy days the shrines of martyrs were so congested with 'jugglers, dancers, players, and such rabble', the Dutch trader Francisco Pelsaert complained, it was impossible to see anything. Mendicants gathered in their thousands, swarming 'like flies, so that no one could walk a yard without molestation'. The greatest nuisances of all were 'secluded ladies' who under pretext of a performing pilgrimage came to see their lovers. 'Assignations were made in the gardens, which are numerous in the neighbourhood, and their passion was given the food for which it hungered, and for which, in the case of many, no opportunity could be found on any other day.'[39]

Inspired by the accounts of travellers such as Mundy and Pelsaert, the Frenchman Jean de Thévenot undertook three long journeys between 1652 and 1667. Thévenot epitomized the Orientalist journeyer. The front piece of *Relation d'un Voyage Fait au Levant* published in 1664 shows him wearing a turban, baboosh-style shoes and a caftan, pointing to a map of Africa and the Near East to illustrate his travels. Two years later, he arrived in Surat. Thévenot devotes almost an entire chapter to a performance by a troupe of acrobats that he chances upon while passing through a village in the province of Daulatabad. The tumblers did everything that the rope dancers of Europe could do and more, he insisted. 'These People are as supple as an Eel. They'll turn their whole body into a Bowl, and then others rowl them with the hand.' The finest tricks he witnessed were by a girl of thirteen or fourteen years, who performed for more than two hours.

> She sat down upon the Ground holding cross-ways in her Mouth a long cutting Sword. With the right Hand she took hold of her left Foot, brought it up to her Breast, then to her left side and without letting go that Foot, she put her Head underneath her right Arm and at the same time brought her Foot down along the small of her Back. Then she made it pass under her sitting, and over the right Leg four or five times without resting, being always in danger of cutting her Arm or Leg with the edge of the Sword. And she did the same thing with the left Hand and right Foot.[40]

Next, she retrieved a nose ring that had been placed in a pool of water without using her hands by bending over backwards. Other feats involved balancing on a pot perched on the head of one of the other performers who ran swiftly around the compound. 'These People shew'd a hundred other tricks of Agility which I shall not describe that I may not be tedious only,' Thévenot continued. 'We gave them at parting three Roupies for which they gave us a thousand Blessings. We sent for them at Night to our Camp where they diverted us again and gained two Roupies more.'[41]

The French doctor François Bernier found Delhi of the 1660s so cosmopolitan and sophisticated, there was much that could be favourably compared to his beloved Paris, including the bazaar near the Great Mosque, which reminded him of the Pont-neuf. The bazaar was a rendezvous point for mountebanks, jugglers and astrologers, both Muslim and Christian. 'These wise doctors remain seated in the sun, on a dusty piece of carpet, handling some old mathematical instruments, and having open before them a large book which represents the signs of the zodiac,' Bernier wrote in *Travels in the Mogul Empire*. 'Silly women, wrapping themselves in a white cloth from head to foot, flock to the astrologers, whisper to them all the transactions of their lives, and disclose every secret with no more reserve than is practised by a scrupulous penitent in the presence of her confessor.' The most ridiculous of these diviners was a half-caste Portuguese fugitive from Goa. 'This fellow sat on his carpet as gravely as the rest, and had many customers notwithstanding he could neither read nor write. His only instrument was an old mariner's compass, and his books of astrology, a couple of old Romish prayer-books in the Portuguese language, the pictures of which he pointed out as the signs of the European zodiac.'[42]

John Fryer, an East India Company surgeon who travelled extensively along the Coromandel and Malabar coasts in the 1670s, considered Bengali jugglers, mountebanks and conjurers the most skilful. 'These are Vagrants, that travel to delude the Mobile by their Hocus Pocus Tricks (living promiscuously like our Gypsies).' Fryer's account reflected his interest in anatomy. One juggler 'swallowed a Chain, such as our Jacks have, and made it clink in his Stomach; but pulling it out, it was not so pleasant to the Spectators (being mostly Ladies, for whose Diversion he was brought), they puking when it was accompanied with a filthy roapy Slaver'. On another occasion Fryer was promised 'a Fellow that cast up his Tripes by his Mouth, Stomach and all, shewing them to the Beholders; but he was excused, having some time allowed him to prepare himself for it. Another drew his breath until his lower belly 'had nothing left to support it, the midriff being forced into the Thorax, and the Muscles of the *Abdomen* as clearly marked out by the stiff Tendons of the *Linea Alba*, as by the most accurate Dissection could be made apparent'.[43] Fryer also saw a conjuror produce 'a mock creation of a mango tree arising from the stone in a short space, with fruit green and ripe; so that a man must stretch his fancy to imagine it witchcraft; though the common sort think no less'.[44]

Another Frenchman travelling in India at this time was Abbe Barthélemy Carré. Fluent in half-a-dozen languages, including Arabic, Persian and Urdu, Carré was despatched to India on the orders of Louis XIV to gather intelligence on the activities of French citizens in India, British military manoeuvres and the machinations of the princely courts. Wonder-workers were everywhere. While staying in Bijapur, he complained of Moors and Portuguese renegades who brought to his house 'courtesans, magicians, and players of instruments, who stayed sometimes two or three days without leaving it, committing the most infamous and disgraceful acts'.[45] While in the town of Athni in Belgaum district, he came across jugglers hurling themselves from cross beams onto a bed made of swords, dagger and knives.

> Every free corner was full of fakirs, conjurors, mountebanks, sorcerers, magicians, and the like – each surrounded by a circle of people. They were crowding one another so much that those at the back, not being able to see anything, snatched the turbans off the heads of the spectators in front and threw them far behind: this obliged their owners to run after them, whereupon

> the vacant front places were immediately filled by those at the back. They could then comfortably watch the dangerous jumps, grotesque postures, miracles, cunning, and skill of these people, who never failed to bring some money into their boxes. This they demanded before showing to the crowd some special trick, 'the like of which had never been seen before'.[46]

◈

IF the accounts of travellers such as Thévenot, Fryer and Carré are any indication, the arts of illusion and deception continued to thrive in the courts, towns and fairgrounds of India even under the austere gaze of Aurangzeb. With his death in 1707, the stability and prosperity of nearly two centuries of Mughal rule came to a messy and chaotic end. Blood-soaked disputes over succession saw the empire slowly disintegrate and with it, Aurangzeb's puritanical strictures. Musicians, dancers and other entertainers found patrons in new centres of power such as Hyderabad, Oude and the Rajput states. In 1864, the French traveller Jean Rousselet found himself in the court of Sikander Begum, the female ruler of Bhopal. The reform-minded queen rejected the purdah and rode around Bhopal dressed as a prince. When Rousselet arrived, she scandalized the kingdom by sharing her three-foot-tall royal hookah, ornamented with precious stones, with the Frenchman. The ritual smoking of the hookah was a precursor to a night's entertainment that included male and female dancers, as well as acrobats and conjurers. 'Of the conjurors who thus passed before us in succession on our evenings at the palace, one of the most singular was an individual who juggled in the most extraordinary manner with sharp-edged tools.' There was no deception, Rousselet insisted, because the swords and sabres used belonged to members of the audience. 'Taking one of those swords he pressed the sharp point against his head and bent the blade into a half circle. He then lay on his back and placed on his chest a betel leaf. His assistant then approached and using a freshly sharpened sabre thrust it down with all his might, cutting the leaf in half, but leaving the man unscathed.'[47] The queen was so impressed that she invited the conjurer to give an exhibition in the square of the palace the next day. His most prodigious feats included 'passing over a narrow circle surrounded with sabre points, and walking upon sharp blades. Then asking for some fresh coconuts, and throwing them into the air, he let them fall upon his skull, whereon they were smashed as upon a rock.' For his final act, one of the guard's lances was fastened to a wagon so heavy that two oxen could scarcely drag it. To make it even heavier audience members were invited to climb into it. The juggler then placed his head against the point of the lance and pushed the wagon forward for about ten paces. 'After this feat, of course, everyone wanted to inspect his iron skull. The man complacently showed his head to each of us, and we were able to assure ourselves that he had no other cuirass than the very thick skin which Nature had given him for his share, but which, nevertheless, was stout enough to resist a pressure that would have pierced through the body of an elephant.'[48]

Passing through India a few years later was the cigar-chomping, free-talking, Republican senator and arch-rival of Abraham Lincoln, William Henry Seward, making what at the time was the first round the-world tour by an American politician. Seward was treated like royalty wherever he went, no more so than in the northern kingdom of Patiala where Maharajah Mahendra Singh provided a coach drawn by six white horses for his arrival. The other members of his party were mounted upon the backs of richly caparisoned elephants. Another sixty elephants, five hundred horsemen and ten thousand troops formed a guard of honour. The following day, the Maharajah organized a 'grand darbar' that began with an elephant fight and was followed by a performance of court jesters whose drolleries and pantomimes, Seward recalled, were worthy of Dan Rice or G. L. Fox, two contemporary American vaudevillians.[49] Next came an acrobat who looked about eighty but managed to turn a double somersault with a long sword in his hand cutting a betel nut in two. He was followed by a company of jugglers including a young man who performed feats with a goat and a monkey, and 'a very old and eccentric Sikh with long white hair and eyes as large and sunken as those of Daniel Webster', whose signature tricks included making 'a pigeon fire a mimic cannon'. Unfortunately, the bird took flight just as the cannon was fired and perched on the roof of the palace. 'The juggler became inconsolable. When he saw his loss, he assumed an attitude as piteous as that of "Rip Van Winkle" when he discovers the absence of his faithful "Schneider",' Seward mused.[50] The entertainment ended with a display of pyrotechnics. 'There were lanterns, transparencies, rockets, serpents, trees, wheels, stars, ribbons, candles, balloons, naval fights and bombardments,' all set off simultaneously, their illuminations reflected in the surface of a clear smooth lake surrounded by cascades and fountains.[51]

Years later, Seward would find himself inadvertently drawn into the controversy over the Rope Trick. Henry Olcott, an associate of Madame Blavatsky, needed evidence to support Theosophical Society's founder's claim to have seen a version of India's most famous magical act performed in Egypt. After poring through Seward's diary of his Indian travels, Olcott claimed he found a description of a man climbing a bare pole sixty-feet high, standing in open and mysteriously disappearing when he reached the top.[52] There is no record of Seward substantiating the claim, but in the 1930s such supposed 'eyewitness' accounts would be pored over by Western magicians desperate to disprove the legend. The average Indian, however, would not have understood what the fuss was all about. The Rope Trick was just another divertissement in a pantheon of wondrous feats as varied as the deities that dwelled in the thousands of temples, stupas and shrines scattered across the plains, mountains and river banks of the subcontinent.

FIVE

A BED OF NAILS

AS the first rays of the rising sun touch the ghats of Benares, pilgrims and Brahmin priests, sadhus and sannyasis gather on the banks of the Ganges and offer their prayers. Hindus believe that Kashi, the Sanskrit name for the City of Light, is the abode of Shiva and the centre of the earth. Its ghats are continuously thronged with beggars and ascetics soliciting alms from devotees as they prepare to plunge into the waters of India's holiest river. In this pantheistic panorama, the miracle worker revered for his austerities and sanctity, competes with the jadoowallah whose magic powers are supposedly derived from the same sacred source. The two are often indistinguishable. The American historian Lee Siegel calls the Indian street conjurer a 'mock holy man'.[1] It's an apt comparison. They share props and symbols. They mirror each other's methods. They move between the secular and profane. The damru, the hour-glass shaped drum the jadoowallah beats to attract attention, also belongs to Shiva, the god of the yogis. Peacock feathers used by priests to absolve worshippers of their sins, are carried by conjurers to affirm their magical skills. The monkey skull that jugglers often display, connects their powers with those of the ash-smeared Aghori sadhus who inhabit cremation grounds. The antecedents of numerous tricks from cutting and restoring the tongue, fire walking, putting a skewer or sword through the neck and restoring severed limbs, derive from the real and mythical practices of Hindu, Muslim, Buddhist and Jain ascetics.

In the late eighteenth century, few Englishmen knew this semi-celestial city and its denizens as well as Jonathan Duncan. Few East India Company officials left such an imprint on their adopted country. The bas-reliefs on his memorial plinth in Bombay Cathedral show two cherubs displaying a scroll with the words: 'Infanticide abolished in Benares and Kattywar.' Above the plinth, a tonsured ascetic watches as a Greek goddess starts to write a eulogy on an urn: 'He was a good man and a just …' A sacred bodhi tree drapes its tendrils over the scene – a tribute to his Orientalist outlook. Born in Forfar, Scotland, in 1756, Duncan went to India as a writer at the age of sixteen, rising quickly through the Company's ranks. In 1788, he was appointed the Resident in Benares. He immediately set about trying to fix the city's almost non-existent sanitation system, traversing its labyrinthine laneways on foot to map out new drains. While undertaking a survey of Jaunpur, he discovered female infanticide was rife in the Rajkumar community. To curb the practice, Duncan invoked an ancient Sanskrit text that condemned anyone killing a foetus to hell where they would be 'gnawed by worms for as many years as there are hairs on a woman's body'.[2] His admirers called him the 'Brahmanized' Scotsman. In 1791, he established the Sanskrit College at Benares for the study of Hindu law, literature, religion and philosophy. Four years later, he was appointed Governor of Bombay where he died in 1811 after a remarkable thirty-seven-year career in India.

In May 1792, news reached Duncan of the presence in the city of two remarkable 'fakeers'. Pran Puri and Prakashanand were in fact yogis, whose extraordinary travels and austerities would colour Western perceptions of India's ascetics for decades to come. Puri's pilgrimages had taken him as far west as Moscow, across the deserts of Central Asia and the high passes of the Himalayas to Lhasa, a journey that took several decades during which he kept both arms raised above his head, an austerity known as *urdhvabahu*. Prakashanand also travelled widely, reaching the Tigris river in today's Iraq. But it was his practice of 'fixing himself on his *ser-seja*, or bed of spikes', that astonished Duncan most

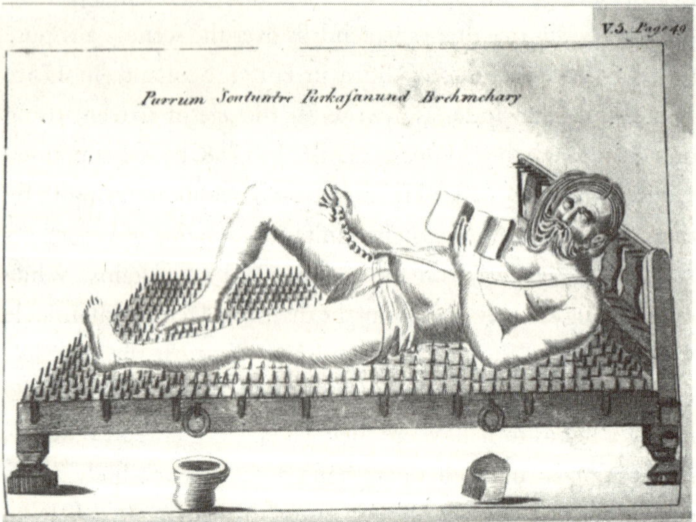

Portrait commissioned by Jonathon Duncan of Prakashanand (Purkasanund), Asiatick Researches, *vol. 5, 1899.*

of all. He assumed it was repentance for a crime. Prakashanand vouched for its antiquity – the warrior Bhishma lay on a bed of arrows in the *Mahabharata*. The feat, he explained, had been practised by yogis since ancient times.

Puri and Prakashanand would have lost themselves in the overflowing ashrams of Benares had it not been for Warren Hastings, the Governor of Calcutta. Puri arrived in Calcutta in 1783 from Lhasa, where he met Tibetan Buddhism's spiritual leader, the Tashi Lama. Samuel Turner, a relative of Hastings who led the second English embassy to Tibet, recalled the yogi riding on 'a piebald Tangun horse from Bootan', and wearing 'a satin embroidered dress, given to him by the Teshoo Lama, of which he was not a little vain'. He was robust and hale, with a florid complexion that contrasted with a long bushy black beard. 'Two Goseins attended him, and assisted him in mounting and alighting from his horse. Indeed, he was indebted to them for the assistance of their hands on every occasion; his own being fixed and immoveable, in the position in which he had placed them, were of course perfectly useless.'[3] The Tashi Lama gave Puri gifts to take to Hastings including a letter, a sealed packet, four large dogs and a magical vessel shaped like a boat and as long as a human hand. 'This boat appeared to me very extraordinary; there were several pictures in the inside of it; and if placed on the ground it whirled round,' Puri later said.[4] After a month in Calcutta, Hastings sent the holy man to Benares where he granted him a parcel of land in a nearby village.

When Duncan met the yogis, he commissioned an artist to draw them and began to document their extraordinary stories. In 1799, he presented his findings in *Asiatick Researches*. Puri is shown sitting cross-legged on a tiger skin. He is naked from the waist upwards, his withered arms forming an arch above his head. Prakashanand is pictured reclining on a wooden bed studded with spikes, holding a sacred text in one hand and holy beads in the other. He told Duncan his life of asceticism began by lying on a bed of thorns and pebbles for ten years, followed by another year locked in a cell where vermin gnawed at his flesh. The scars, Duncan noted, were still visible. 'It is thirty-five years since I made *Tupisa* [penance] upon this *ser seja*. I have been in several countries ... I have been at every place of religious resort and have no longer any inclination to roam, but being desirous of settling in Benares I have come hither.'[5]

Unlike the abridged version of Prakashanand's story in *Asiatick Researches*, Puri's full account, as given to Duncan, was published by *The European Magazine* in 1811. Born in the city of Canouge (Kanuj), he left home at the age of ten and became a 'fakeer' in 1757. Before describing his travels, Puri listed the eighteen *tapasyas* or austerities practised by yogis, many of which have been adapted as tricks by street magicians. They included *pattali*, 'burying oneself underground up to the breast with the head downwards'; *nyas-dheean*, holding one's breath while meditating so 'there appears to be no respiration in the corporeal frame'; *pancha-agni*, 'to be immersed in smoke from fire on all sides'; and *tirbhangi*, 'standing always on one foot'. His own austerity began by abstaining from eating and sleeping for a year, after which he began the *urdhvabahu*. 'For one year, great pain is endured, but during second less, and habit reconciles the party; the pain diminishes in the third year, after which no kind of pain is felt.' As for the merits incurred, 'God alone is thoroughly acquainted therewith; what can I, an ignorant mortal, know,' he told Duncan.[6]

Puri's travels were nothing less than extraordinary. After starting from Allahabad where he attended the Kumbh Mela, he ventured to Kanya Kumari, the southernmost point of India, before proceeding up the east coast to the temple of Jagannath Puri. From there he retraced his journey south to Rameshwaram and took a boat to 'Singal-deep', or Ceylon, to see Rama's footprints on the top of Adam's Peak. From Ceylon, he took another boat 'to the country of the Malays', where he stayed with a Hindu for two months. He then sailed to Cochin before travelling north through Kutch and Sindh to Multan and the holy city of Haridwar. After crossing the Indus at Attock, he joined a party of yogis on their way to Kabul and Bamiyan 'where there are innumerable statues of stone, but no one knows at what time or by whom these statues were erected'. On approaching Ghazni, he watched as Ahmed Shah Abdali, accompanied by an army of 30,000 horsemen, marched across Hindu Kush mountains. Impressed by Puri's piety he provided him with elephants and an escort until he reached Herat. Many of the places the yogi visited such as Basra, Astrakhan and Muscat had substantial Hindu communities, but not Moscow where there was no place of worship and he was forced to stay in an Armenian serai. Though he contemplated proceeding to Britain, he decided to make his way back to India, travelling through the Persian Gulf, the Indus Valley, Kashmir and Nepal. In Kathmandu, he visited the city's numerous temples, including one where a water vessel placed before the deity was always full, so that 'thousands of people may drink without exhausting it'.[7] Despite the deep snow, he traversed the Himalayas to Tibet, stopping at the town of Aini where he was told there were 'five thousand temples, in each of which is a female fakeer ... all of them were maintained at the expense of the Emperor of China'.[8] He also travelled to Lake Manasarovar, noting the rivers flowing from it, and completed a circumambulation of the sacred mountain, Kailash. In a postscript, Duncan regrets not paying more attention to Puri's observations about the sources of India's major rivers, one of the greatest geographical mysteries of the time.

FROM Alexander the Great onwards, visitors to India were struck by its ascetics – those 'extraordinary personages' who 'almost continually perambulate the country, make light of everything, affecting to live without care, and to be possessed of most important secrets'[9]. The practice of magic, sorcery and witchcraft, the belief in the efficacy of charms, spells, and incantations, and the conviction that humans could obtain powers over nature and even over gods, proved to be fertile ground for the development of asceticism. To obtain mastery over nature, ascetics practiced severe penances (*tapas*), such as sitting in the midst of fires and standing on one leg, with the object of subduing the gods and subjecting nature to the will of man.[10]

Sometimes naked, their bodies smeared with ash, at other times wearing saffron robes and the symbols of their sects drawn in sandalwood paste and vermillion on their foreheads, sadhus, yogis, fakirs and other religious mendicants were impossible to

'Various Temples and Penances of the Fakirs,' from Ceremonies and Religious Customs of the Idolatrous Peoples, *1729.*

ignore. The seventeenth-century French Orientalist, Barthélemy D'Heberelot, estimated there were 8,00,000 fakirs and 1.2 million yogis in India. The jeweller and gem trader, Jean Baptiste Tavernier, spoke of 'the infinite multitude of *faquirs* that swarm all over India', generally moving about in large parties and quite naked.[11] The reaction of French physician François Bernier was one of disgust. 'No fury in the infernal regions can be conceived more horrible than the *jauguis* [yogis], with their naked and black skin, long hair, spindle arms, long twisted nails, and fixed in the posture I have mentioned.'[12]

It was not just outsiders who were shocked by their ghoulish rituals. Somadeva's *Yasatilaka* contains a long description of the temple of the goddess Chandamari with its *mahayoginis* – fearsome female spirits who engaged in vile forms of self-torture:

> Certain devotees were burning *guggula* incense on their heads. Extremely ferocious [persons] were burning their arteries like lights; while others, exceedingly bold, were trying to please Shiva by drinking their own blood. In one corner Kapalikas selling their bodies, and at another place certain fanatics were worshipping the Mothers by swinging from their intestines, extracted with their own hands. Elsewhere certain grim men were offering their own flesh as oblation in the sacred fire. Such was the terrible temple of Chandamari.[13]

A century after Duncan documented the lives of Puri and Prakashanand, on the Western flank of the imperium, the British professor of Sociology at the Lahore College, John Campbell Oman, was putting the final touches to his monumental work, *The Mystics, Ascetics, and Saints of India*. Like Duncan, Oman was no stranger to the cremation grounds and sadhu encampments of the Punjab. Though now considered arcane, his book, published in 1905 and replete with Oman's photographs of ascetics suspended upside down from the boughs of trees or dragging iron chains weighing hundreds of pounds, was at the time the most detailed English-language study of India's holy men and women. In his narrative, religious ritual and the conjurer's craft are intertwined. 'As in medieval Europe, the air in India is full of marvels and mysteries, and, if we may believe Hindu apologists, there still live, even in this sinful age, very potent wonder-working sadhus'.[14] He meets one such holy man who puts pieces of live charcoal into his mouth and chews them as if 'they were savoury morsels and his usual food'.[15] They cure ailments, dispense love-philtres and resort to spells 'calculated to influence a cold, impassive heart', skills that 'can easily command a considerable pecuniary reward'.[16] Many mendicants, he observes, obtain alms by practising 'as fortune tellers, palmists, and interpreters of dreams, the hidden things of the future'. One astonished his audience with acrobatic feats 'that would earn him a fortune in England'. One moment he was standing on one leg with the other curled round his waist. A second later, he was on his hands, head downwards, with his legs round his neck. He was last seen 'tied up in some sort of reef knot and clove hitch combined'.[17]

Oman also noted the symbiosis between the jadoowallah and the sadhu, relating the story of how a Hindu holy man taught a Muslim the craft of magic. Hassan Khan was a young boy when a sadhu arrived in his village. Khan soon established a close rapport with the holy man who offered to confer on him a certain secret power if he followed a strict regime of fasting and learned a series of special spells and incantations. He passed his first test by willing a pile of stones to be transported magically from the sadhu's abode to his room. Khan went on to perform before Europeans in Calcutta. One of his most popular tricks was to ask an audience member to name any type of wine. Once the name was called out, the person put their hand under the table or behind a door and 'a bottle of the wished-for wine, with the label of some well-known Calcutta firm, would be thrust into the extended hand'. Khan could also magically produce biscuits, cakes and cigars. As a dare, an audience member asked him to produce a bottle of champagne.

> Much agitated and stammering badly – he always had an impediment in his speech – Hassan Khan went into the verandah, and in angry tones commanded some unseen agent to bring the champagne at once. He had to repeat his orders two or three times, when, hurtling through the air, came the required bottle. It struck the magician on the chest with force, and, falling to the floor, broke into a thousand pieces. 'There,' said Hassan Khan, much excited, 'I have shown my power, but I have enraged my *djinn* by my importunities.'[18]

The East India Company trader John Marshall, who lived in Patna in the 1670s, recounted the story of a yogi whose power of flight was aided by a pellet of quicksilver held in his mouth. One day, while flying to the shrine of Jagannath in Orissa, he stopped to rest on the terrace of the harem of the Mughal emperor Akbar. While sleeping, the pellet of quicksilver slipped from his mouth and was picked up by the emperor. The yogi pleaded for its return. Akbar consented on the condition that he teach him some magic. The yogi agreed and turned himself into a deer. Still unconvinced, the Mughal asked that he also be turned into a deer. The yogi complied. When Akbar was brought back into his own body he was so frightened he ordered the yogi killed. According to Marshall, the act of killing the yogi so affected Akbar's disposition that people began to believe he had exchanged his soul with the emperor's.[19]

Numerous accounts of live burial were published nineteenth century onwards. In 1837, a sadhu named Haridas was interred for forty days at Lahore, then disentombed and resuscitated. The story was recounted by Sir Claude M. Wade, the political resident at Ludhiana and the agent of the British Government at the court of Ranjit Singh. Wade arrived a few hours after the burial, but based on the testimony of the Sikh ruler 'and the most credible witnesses at his court', he was satisfied no deception or collusion was involved.[20] When the forty days were over, Wade accompanied Singh to one of the gardens adjoining the Lahore palace where Haridas was buried. The burial chamber was in a square building with four doors, three of which had been hermetically sealed with brick and mortar, while the fourth had a padlocked door, affixed with the Singh's private emblem. Guards were stationed around the clock to prevent the tomb being tampered with. When the door was opened, Singh and Wade entered accompanied by a servant of the buried sadhu. In a cell below the floor was a wooden box, four-feet long and three-feet wide, securely padlocked. Haridas's body was enclosed in a white linen bag, drawn together at the top, and securely fastened with a string. His servant removed his master's body from the box, placed it against the closed door of the receptacle in a squatting posture, and began to pour warm water over it. 'The legs and arms of the fakir were shrivelled and stiff, but the face was full as in life, the head reclining on the shoulder, like that of a corpse,' Wade noted.[21] A doctor was sent for. Though he could not detect a pulse, he was able to detect warmth about the coronal region of the brain. The body of the sadhu was washed in warm water and Singh assisted in rubbing his lifeless arms and legs. A hot chapatti was placed on the head. The wax and cotton plugs sealing the nose and ears were removed and the rigid jaws opened by inserting a knife between the teeth and prying them apart. Holding the jaws open, the servant drew the sadhu's tongue forward. Ghee was rubbed into the eyelids until they opened, but they remained glazed and motionless. The next process, wrote Wade, was to place another warm chapatti on the top of the head.

> At this instant the body heaved convulsively, the nostrils became violently inflated, respiration was resumed, and the limbs began to assume their natural fullness. The servant, at this stage, placed some clarified butter on the tongue of the fakir, and made him swallow it. A few minutes afterward the eyeballs began to dilate slowly, recovered their natural colour by insensible gradations, and gleamed with intelligence; and recognizing Runjit Singh, who sat facing him, the fakir commenced to articulate in scarcely audible tones, inquiring whether he was now convinced.[22]

Other cases of live burial included a young man in Rajasthan in the 1830s, who allowed himself to be interred for weeks or months at a time. Desiring a male heir to his throne, the ruler of Jaisalmer summoned him to perform the auspicious ritual and had him buried for one month. According to an account by H. M. Twedell published in 1838, the man acquired the art of holding his breath by shutting his mouth and stopping the interior opening of the nostrils with his tongue. 'He also abstains from solid food for some days previous to his interment so that he may not be inconvenienced by the contents of his stomach while put up in his narrow grave,' Twedell wrote. After a month in a sealed tomb-like structure, he was revived in the same way as Haridas. 'He gradually recovered his senses and the use of his limbs and when we went to see him, was sitting up supported by two men and conversed with us in a low gentle tone of voice saying that we might bury him again for a twelve month [period] if we pleased.'[23]

Accounts of live burial were mostly treated with scepticism. In 1721, the Governor of Surat was told that a 'miracle-monger' buried in a grave ten-feet deep, would reappear fifteen days later at the town of Amadabant (Ahmedabad), a distance of 200 miles. When he went to inspect the grave, he noticed a large water jar under the shade of a great banyan tree close by. Suspecting an underground passage led from the grave to a trapdoor beneath the jar, he ordered his soldiers to smash the jar, much to the consternation of a group of yogis gathered there. His hunch proved correct and according to an account by Captain Alexander Hamilton, the soldiers retaliated by killing a number of the yogis, including 'the poor Miracle-monger who lost his head in the fray. That spoiled his journey to Amadabant, and, which was worse, brought great scandal on the whole Order.'[24]

Whether by trickery or breath control, live burial caught the West's imagination. In his novel, *Dracula*, Bram Stoker associated the ability of the vampire to slip out of a locked tomb with the powers of India's wonder-workers. To convince the sceptical Dr John Seward, whose beloved Lucy had become Dracula's latest victim, that there were phenomena that could not be explained, Stoker's vampire hunter Professor Van Helsing asked him: 'Can you tell me how the Indian fakir can make himself to die and have been buried, and his grave sealed, and the corn sowed on it, and the corn reaped and be cut and sown and reaped and cut again, and then the men come and take away the unbroken seal,

Poster for the 'Great Indian Fakir' Blacaman. Circus Museum.

and that there lie the Indian fakir, not dead, but that rise up and walk amongst them as before?'[25]

Houdini performed at least four versions of the trick. On his first attempt in 1915, he was shackled and buried in a six-foot deep pit. Trapped by the sheer weight of dirt, he panicked as he attempted to claw his way to the surface. When his hand finally broke through the top of the dirt, he passed out and had to be extracted by his assistants. In the mid-1920s, he remained in a sealed casket submerged in the pool of New York's Shelton Hotel for ninety minutes, using controlled breathing to stay alive. The feat was a challenge to Rahman Bey, a stuntman who claimed to be an Egyptian, but was probably an Italian and was usually referred to in the American press as a 'Hindoo fakir'. A few weeks prior to Houdini's feat and using what he claimed was a combination of 'yogic power and cataleptic trance', Bey remained submerged in a casket in a swimming pool in Dalton for an hour. He also boasted that he could vary his pulse at will and regularly invited doctors on stage to thrust long pins into whatever part of his body they wanted to.

Rahman Bey, in turn, had a competitor in Tahra Bey, who probably was Egyptian, but was also referred to as being from India. The 'lettuce-eating, champagne-drinking' Bey arrived in the United States in July 1926, after hugely successful seasons in Paris and London. With his piercing black eyes, long thin nose, black pointed beard and picturesque burnoose, he looked more like a handsome sheikh than a mystic with psychic powers. Absolute control of his nerve and blood systems, he claimed, enabled him to be buried alive for a month. His fee was $1000 a night for a two-hour performance, which included lying down on a bed of six-inch nails driven point upward through a wooden door while his 160-pound assistant stood for several minutes on his chest. Writing in *The Spectator* after seeing his Paris show, Francis Yeats-Brown said there was not a shadow of doubt as to the authenticity of his act or the provenance of his powers. 'The Fakir had the same powerful neck, the same deep lungs, the same poised rhythm of walk, the same level eyes as those Brahmins of the Ganges side, our Aryan cousins of a remote antiquity.' However, he considered the performance unsuitable for the stage. 'The public would neither appreciate it nor understand it; indeed, it would do nothing but feed the sadistic instincts of what I hope is a minority.'[26]

Versions of the burial trick are still performed by Indian street magicians – though the deception mostly involves burying the head in the ground and breathing through a hidden straw. In 1950, Swami Ramdasji, a forty-five-year-old yogi from Bombay was dug out of an airtight crypt in which he had been interred in for eighty-seven hours on a bed of nails. According to United Press, his devotees sat by the crypt day and night chanting Vedic prayers, while keeping a sacred fire. His disciples hacked open the cement-lined crypt with picks and lifted Ramdasji, still in a trance, onto a dais where they massaged his arms and body until he opened his eyes and smiled.[27] Not all interments ended successfully. In 1953, Narayan Acharya, a fifty-six-year-old yogi could not be revived after being buried in a wood-lined pit for nine days. Doctors believed he had been dead for up to twenty-four hours when he was taken from the pit. Foreigners fared no better. Pietro Blacaman, an Italian with a mass of frizzy black hair who called himself 'The Great Indian Fakir' and whose signature acts included hypnotizing crocodiles, died in 1929 during a circus act in Argentina. He was buried alive on stage for three hours, while clowns and acrobats entertained the audience. On opening his coffin, it was discovered he had suffocated while trying to escape.

❖

THE blurring of the boundaries between ascetic ritual and street magic was not confined to live burials and chewing on red-hot charcoal. In the early 1930s, Lady Olive Crofton penned an unpublished memoir to counter the myth that there was more to being the wife of an ICS officer than the boredom of 'bridge and club life'.[28] On a visit to Hyderabad, she was entertained by a group of Rafa'i fakirs, who she believed were descendants of the Persian sect of the Assassins. Other scholars such as Duncan MacDonald, trace the sect back to the Rifa'ite fraternity founded in Baghdad in 1158 by Ahmad ar-Rifa'a. The fraternity migrated to Hyderabad in the late sixteenth century and eventually came under the protection of Hyderabad's prime minister, Salar Jung III, 'who often produced them for the entertainment of his guests at his luncheon parties'.[29] Crofton attended one such party at Salar Jung's palace with a group of British sailors. After a sumptuous meal that many would later regret ingesting, they sat in a large circle in one of the palace courtyards. The Rafa'is arrived with an assortment of swords, daggers and other sharp instruments. Standing in the middle of the circle, the first placed the hilt of his sword on the ground, then leaning over it and with considerable force, drove the point of the blade deep into this stomach. He then walked around the circle with the sword embedded in his body, but without any signs of bleeding or discomfort. The next drove a dagger through his neck until the point extended several inches on the other side. A third poked out his tongue and drove a

A 'fuqeer' with skewers through his arms. Wellcome Library.

knife through it, while another walked around with a dagger protruding upright from his skull, which quivered as he walked. Wrote Crofton: 'Horrible as these things were, I could not help watching the faces of the sailors with some amusement. They were hard fighting men who have been through all the horrors of the evacuation of Crete, but now their faces were white. Some hid their eyes and when the last Rafa'i appeared and gouged out one eye and then holding it in the palm of his hand, walked round the circle, before replacing it in its socket apparently uninjured, two of the men fainted dead away.'[30] Doctors had tried but failed to explain how the Rafai's accomplished their feats, Crofton continued. 'Hashish had something to do with it, but that was only the beginning, there was no explanation, and it wasn't a case of delusion, these things really happened.'[31]

The early twentieth-century scholar and author of *Islam in India,* Jafar Sharif, claimed the members of the sect were related to the Howling Dervishes of Turkey and Egypt, famous for their masochistic and bloody rituals. Referring to the Rafa'i, he wrote:

> All sorts of marvels are told and believed about them. They strike the points of their mace against their breasts and eyes, aim sword blows at their backs, thrust a spit through their sides or into their eyes, which they are said to be able to take out and replace. Or they cut out their tongues, which on being put back in their mouths reunite. It is even said that they are able to cut off their heads, and fix them again on their necks with saliva, and what is equally strange, there is no haemorrhage, or if it does occur the performer is said to be inexpert.[32]

Other acts included searing their tongues with a red-hot iron, putting live scorpions into their mouths, making a chain red-hot, pouring oil upon it, and when it was set alight, drawing their hands through it. 'They can cut a living being into two parts and reunite them by means of spittle,' added Sharif. 'They are also said to eat arsenic, glass, and other poisons. They rattle their maces in front of shops till they receive alms, but sometimes they throw away the money they receive, as it is unlawful to take money by extortion.'[33]

In 1932, Edmund Henderson Hunt, Chief Medical Officer of the Nizam's State Railway, delivered a paper to the Royal Anthropological Institute of Great Britain and Ireland in which he described the Rafa'i's headquarters as being in a graveyard where hundreds of their priests and fakirs were buried. Every October or November, they held an Urs in memory of their first priest that consisted of fasting, readings of the Koran, processions and self-mutilation. 'Individual fakeers are also willing to submit to any test, and to perform for the special purpose of photography, including X-ray and the cinema.' Hunt described the passing of skewers through the neck in any direction and the levering out of eyeballs as their most astonishing feats. 'One old man can protrude his eye so far that the lids close behind it and it appears like a teed-up golf ball.' He discounted the use of drugs. Older performers showed no signs of pain, though younger recruits often were distressed. Hunt regretted that the Hyderabad group, long isolated in their 'human backwater', were showing signs of breaking up.[34] Jack Devlin, a member of the prestigious conjuring society, the Magic Circle, accompanied by Edwina Mountbatten, witnessed a performance in the mid-1940s. By then, however, any religious connection to their craft had all but disappeared. 'As far as the Fakirs were concerned, it was to them Show Business with a nice fee attached.' Hyderabad's Resident, Sir Arthur Lothian, told him he had seen a fakir in Hyderabad 'slit his stomach open and spread his bowels on a tray', yet there was no trace of a scar the next morning. Commented Devlin dryly: 'Hardly an appetizing number to include in one's programme at a cocktail party.'[35]

Many of the feats of the Rafa'i fakirs have been taken up by street magicians. Passing a skewer or sword through the neck is included in some versions of the Basket Trick. Cutting off the tongue is a relatively simple deception using a substitute organ taken from a sheep or goat. Chewing on hot charcoal, swallowing scorpions and snakes, as well as handling red hot chains, have been absorbed into the jadoowallah's repository of tricks and in Western stage repertoires. There has also been a degree of fluidity between the practice of performance magic and religious begging. In the early 1800s, it was noted that the Panchpeeree Nats, an itinerant community related to European Gypsies and famous for being 'nimble and adroit every kind of sleight of hand, practicing juggling in all its branches', would also 'wander about as sects of religionists, and calling themselves Moosulman Fuqueers, live on the bounty of the pious followers of the Prophet'.[36]

Indian fire walking, brought to the West by the Kashmiri magician Kuda Bux in the 1930s, is still practised by the Shah Madar fakirs of northern India. After lighting a charcoal fire and sprinkling ground sandalwood on it, they jump on it with their bare feet, shouting 'Dam Madar!' (by the breath of Madar!) – a phrase regarded as a charm against snake bite and scorpion stings. After the fire walk, the feet of the performers are washed and found to be uninjured.[37] Known for their feats of legerdemain and for exhibiting performing monkeys and bears, Shah Madar fakirs, or Madaris as they are commonly referred to, are followers of Zinda Shah Madar, a Syrian Sufi preacher who arrived in India from Aleppo in the fifteenth century and established his headquarters at Madhapur near Kanpur. Shah Madar was portrayed as a pious and learned man known for his constant fasting – up to twelve years at one stretch – his ability to retain his breath for up to forty days and his remarkable beauty and longevity. Estimates of his age when he died in 1436, ranged from 124 to 496 years. He was also gifted with magical powers. When a servant boy was abducted, dismembered and then eaten by a group of evil yogis, Madar confronted the holy men and extracted the boy's reconstituted body through the nostril of the chief yogi and revived him. In the second half of the eighteenth century, Madari fakirs joined with Hindu sannyasis in a series of rebellions against the East India Company over their right to collect religious taxes from zamindars. Jafar Sharif was disparaging about the Madaris, calling them 'one of the disreputable Orders of begging Faqirs'. 'They generally wear dark clothes, and fasten to one of their ankles a chain which they throw out and drag back as they beg at shops,' he wrote. 'Some keep tame tigers, bears, and monkeys, the two last being taught to dance and perform tricks. Some of them are jugglers and make a figure of a man or animal to dance without any apparent mechanical means. Others place an earthen pot without a bottom on their heads and put fire in it, on which they lay a frying-pan and cook cakes.'[38] Other offshoots of Sufism that absorbed anti-

Islamic features included the Jalalis, who took hashish, ate snakes and scorpions and permitted sect leaders to have sexual relations with female members. If they did not receive alms while begging, they branded themselves with hot irons or 'gain their ends by noise and uproar. ... They have little heed to prayer.'[39]

◈

THE growth of Sufi orders in India from the twelfth century onwards, combined with the Arab tradition of intellectual curiosity and analysis of Indian religion and science, translated into a vibrant intermingling between Muslim and Hindu devotional sects. Sufi scholars had ample access to Arabic and Persian translations of works such as the *Yoga Sutras* and the lost Hatha Yoga text, the *Amritakunda* or *Pool of Nectar,* which was translated by Rukn al-din Samarqandi first into Arabic, then Persian. The relationship between Sufism and Hindu mysticism has been described as ranging from 'polemical hostility through missionary zeal to tolerant co-existence'.[40] When it came to miracles, the competition was fierce. One of the earliest examples of magic being used as a weapon in such contests relates to Khwaja Moin-ud-Din Chishti, whose shrine in Ajmer in Rajasthan is one of the most important places of Sufi worship in India. According to legend, Chishti's arrival in Ajmer in 1190s was prophesized by the astrologer mother of its ruler, Rai Pithaura. Border officials tried to prevent his entry to Pithaura's territory, but he managed to reach Ajmer and camped near Ana Sagar lake with a handful of his disciples. When the local Brahmins forbid them from performing ablutions in the lake, Chishti sent a servant to bring water. As soon as the servant's ewer touched the lake, it sucked out water from all the lakes, tanks and wells in the area. He then went to the Ana Sagar temple where he turned the idol into a human being, made it speak and recite the *kalima* (confession of faith), and gave it a new Islamic name, Sadi. Pithaura then asked his minister, Jaipal, who was also a magician, to stop Chishti. Accompanied by 700 disciples, a similar number of dragons and 1,500 magical discs, he attacked the Sufi, but the saint killed them all. Jaipal then challenged Chishti to a competition to see whose magic was the most powerful. When Jaipal flew to heaven sitting on a deer skin, Chishti ordered his slippers to fly. They thrashed Jaipal, forcing him back to earth. Pithaura and Jaipal then begged for Chishti's forgiveness. He agreed and used his prayers to restore water to the lakes, tanks and wells.[41]

A fourteenth-century example of a miracle contest between a Sufi and a yogi appears in the *Fawa'id al-fuwad*, or *Morals of the Heart*. One of the earliest authentic collection of descriptions of Indian Sufi saints, it describes a conversation between the poet Amir Hassan and Shaykh Nizam ud-Din Auliya of Delhi. Nizam ud-Din recalls how a yogi challenged Shaykh Safi al-Din Gazarun, saying he could equal any of his powers. Going first, the yogi rose into the air until his head reached the ceiling before returning to the ground. Turning his gaze towards heaven, the Sufi asked God to bestow on him the same abilities he had given to the yogi. Rising in the air, he flew west towards Mecca, then north and south before finally returning to his palace. Laying his head at the Shaykh's feet, the astonished yogi said: 'I can do no more than rise straight upwards from the ground and come down in the same way. I cannot go to the right and to the left.

You turned whichever way you wished! It is true and from God: my own powers are false.'[42]

Common to all these stories is the power of Sufi miracles over the lesser magic of the yogis. The fourteenth-century historian and thinker, Ibn Khaldun, differentiated between the miracle worker, who 'is supported in his activity by the spirit of God', and the magician, who 'does his work by himself and with the help of his own psychic power, and, under certain conditions, with the support of devils'.[43] Referring to miracles, he explains that: 'No piece of sorcery can match them. One may compare the affair of the sorcerers of the Pharaoh with Moses and the miracle of the staff. Moses' staff devoured the phantoms the sorcerers produced, and their sorcery completely disappeared as if it had never been.'[44]

Even the greatest of India's yogis, Gorakhnath, the eleventh-century founder of the Nath monastic movement, the dominant yogic order in north India, could not compete against the superior powers of the Sufis in hagiographical accounts. As Carl Ernst notes, Sufis and Nath yogis 'shared overlapping interests in psycho-physical techniques of meditation, and which competed to some extent for popular recognition as wonder-workers, healers, and possessors of sanctity'.[45] Oral traditions relating to the poet-saint Kabir, a low caste weaver from Varanasi and a convert to Islam, tell of a confrontation with Gorakhnath, who invites Kabir to a miracle contest in which he plants his iron trident in the ground, rises up and sits on one of its prongs. He challenges Kabir to sit on one of the other prongs. Kabir responds by taking out a ball of thread and throwing one end up into the air. He rises up and sits at the top of the thread and challenges the yogi to do the same. In the next contest, Gorakhnath tells Kabir to find him in a pond. He changes into a frog and dives into the water, but Kabir finds him easily. Kabir then enters the pond and turns himself into water. Gorakhnath is unable to find him. Finally, he sends two poisonous snakes to bite Kabir. But when he passes by his hut to see if he is still alive, he sees him entertaining the snakes as he would his guests. Admitting defeat, he becomes Kabir's disciple.[46]

A number of legends link the powers of yogis with the repertoire of the jadoowallah's tricks. In the *Rasalu* legends, Gorakhnath restores the severed limbs of Prince Puran, the son of Raja Sulwahan of Sialkot.[47] When Puran refuses the advances of his stepmother, Luna, who in reality is a terrible witch, she denounces him, claiming he has tried to seduce her. Sulwahan orders Puran to be beheaded, but the boy prince takes a vow of truth telling his father to plunge him into a vat of boiling oil to prove his innocence. After four hours, Puran emerges unscathed, but Luna gets her way and orders an outcaste to cut off his hands and legs, gouge out his eyes and throw him into a disused well. Twelve years later, Gorakhnath finds Puran and draws him out with a single thread of spun cotton. He puts back his eyes and by sprinkling holy nectar over him, restores his limbs.[48] The legend anticipates later stories of the Indian Rope Trick, which ends with the severed limbs that fall from the sky being reinstated, while placing a hand in boiling oil or water, has long been a mainstay of Indian street magic.

SIX

THE JUGGLER'S CHILD

ON 13 November 1858, Captain D. N. McKinnon, the commanding officer at the isolated outpost of Hingoli in central India, received a disturbing report from one of his peons. A pale-skinned girl had been seen performing as a dancer with a troupe of native jugglers at the weekly market. The peon was certain the child was a European. 'I immediately ordered an enquiry to be made when it was reported they had left the place some days ago,' McKinnon wrote in his report to Colonel Cuthbert Davidson, the British Resident in Hyderabad. 'I sent two Sepoys to search for them who traced them to the village of Peergaun, and brought into the Cantonment the child, a girl of about nine years of age, a pure European child. This I believe without any doubt.' The child had been removed from the troupe and a man and a woman claiming to be her parents had been placed in detention. She had been washed and clothed and was being cared for by the ladies of the cantonment 'where she seems very happy', McKinnon added.[1]

Attached to his report was a statement by the Officiating Surgeon at Hingoli, Dr John Reed. 'The formation of the head, the colour of her eyes (a light grey), the colour of her hair (of a light brown sandy hue), all tend to show that the child is European,' it read. 'Her skin, though much tanned by exposure to the sun, is covered with freckles, an appearance never seen in the natives or half-caste persons. The scalp, after her head was washed, is quite white. The skin behind the ears is also much fairer than the other parts of her body. She has altogether the appearance of a soldier's child who has been much exposed to the influence of a tropical climate for several years, and who has but scanty nourishment.'[2]

Davidson ordered McKinnon to write to the Bombay and Madras governments asking for their help in locating the child's parents. Meanwhile, his agents had discovered another European woman living in the nearby town of Sawargaon. She was aged between twenty-five and twenty-eight and was married to a juggler with whom she had four children, but could not remember how she got there. 'The poor woman has been so long with the natives that she is in the habits as one of themselves,' McKinnon wrote after she was brought to Hingoli. 'But her accent is so different from theirs that anyone hearing her speak would remark on it.' Rumours that more European children had been seen with troupes of jugglers near the town of Mungloor in Nizamabad district proved false. The mystery of how the pair came to live with jugglers only deepened when the child told McKinnon that the woman claiming to be her mother was, in fact, a relative. She had been told to say otherwise. Further enquiries revealed that the girl had a younger sister who died several years earlier.[3]

The discovery at Hingoli of a child who was either abducted or found abandoned and raised to be a dancer in a troupe of jugglers, recalled reports of children being reared by wolves in central India – reports that would become the basis of the story of Mowgli in Rudyard Kipling's *Jungle Book*. News of the juggler's child spread quickly with the *Madras Times* commenting: 'It is to be hoped that this matter will be carefully and fully enquired into. We cannot but hope, that if publicity be given to these facts, the parents of some poor kidnapped children may yet come forward and have the pleasure of welcoming their little ones back to their care and home, thus rescuing them from a fate we cannot contemplate without a shudder.'[4]

Unfortunately, there is no mention in McKinnon's report of what caste or tribe the two groups of jugglers belonged to. While the Hingoli incident appears unique because it involved Europeans, cases of children being stolen from their families by itinerant groups were well documented. Not long after the incident, William Oldham, an officer in the Bengal Civil Service reported how three girls were kidnapped by a gang of Seorees (also known as Sansis), a nomadic group found in Ghazipur district in what is now Uttar Pradesh. They resembled European Gypsies, were nomadic, fond of alcohol and ate pork and beef, Oldham wrote. They were also known to 'procure wives for their young men by kidnapping female children and live principally by jugglery, coining false money and theft'. In 1859, a gang of fifty to sixty Seorees snatched three young girls in Mirzapur district. A few months later, one managed to escape and told Oldham about the other two still being held captive. 'On the following morning at dawn, I surrounded the camp with a large number of men, some of the Seorees escaped to the hills, but most of them were arrested. After much searching, the girls were found in a hole in the ground concealed by leaves,' he related. As the children had no close relatives, they were handed over to the Church Mission Orphanage in Benares.[5]

In 1837, James Stevenson published an article in *The Journal of the Royal Asiatic Society* describing the Shudgarshids, a tribe of jugglers and fortune tellers, who moved about the Deccan. Also known as Garodis, they were notorious for trafficking in children, as well as making charms from sinews extracted from the breasts, wrists and ankles of murdered females who had recently given birth.[6] The Pardhis, who inhabited parts of what is now Maharashtra, were another tribe involved in buying or kidnapping children and using them as slaves or training them to be dacoits. The Bediyas of Bengal, usually denoted in police reports as vagabonds, jugglers, tumblers, hunters and thieves, carried out similar practices. Male Bediyas would marry 'none but a woman of his own caste or perhaps a kidnapped child brought up in his own camp'.[7] Cases of children being abducted and then killed for sacrifices or being deliberately maimed and made to beg for alms were regularly reported around the time of the Hingoli case.

Until Europeanized Indians started taking up magic professionally in the late nineteenth century – often adopting Western dress, tricks and stage techniques – the majority of jadoowallahs came from marginalized communities, including lower castes and nomadic or semi-nomadic tribes. They practised sleight of hand, juggling, snake charming, tumbling, tight-rope walking and other forms of acrobatics, sold magical charms and herbs, played music and trained monkeys, bears and other animals to perform. The women were often fortune tellers, palm readers, dream interpreters, dancers, gymnasts, quack doctors and tattoo artists. The French cleric and Sanskrit scholar, Jean-Antoine Dubois, who travelled in India in the late eighteenth and early twentieth centuries, called these magic makers and entertainers 'among the degraded beings who form the dregs of society in India'. Thanks to the credulous nature of the Hindus, Dubois continued, imposters abound. 'They are regarded as magicians and sorcerers, as men versed in witchcraft and all the occult sciences, and are viewed with fear and distrust; while the hatred in which they are held is much greater than is recorded in Europe to people of the same description.'[8]

In northern India, the main itinerant groups were the Banjaras, Nats, Bazigars and Kanjars, an overlapping amalgam of sub-castes, mostly Muslim, and all believed to be related to the Gypsies of Europe. Just as groups of sadhus, fakirs, monks and other religious sects could be found congregated at religious sites, so too were these nomads. One writer likened their camps somewhat romantically to a 'Lilliput or Fairy Land' – until closer inspection revealed them to be overcrowded with men, women, children and domestic animals.[9] Travelling through northern India in 1800, James Forbes described coming across a group of Vanjarrahs (Banjaras) accompanying a party of mendicants:

> Reposing under contiguous trees, we generally saw *yogees*, *gasannees*, Mahomedan *dervises*, and other religious mendicants who travel all over Hindustan, and often met with large caravans of Banjarrees, or Vanjarrahs, a set of merchants, who do not belong to any particular country. ... The Vanjarrahs are likewise followed by conjurors, astrologers, jugglers, musicians, dancing-bears, dancing-snakes, monkeys, and various entertainments;

> they gain a livelihood by what they receive in the camp, or pick up in the towns and villages through which they pass.[10]

In his three-volume *Hindu Tribes and Castes as Represented in Benares* published in 1872, the protestant missionary Matthew Atmore Sherring devoted a chapter to 'Gipsies, jugglers, rope-dancers, snake-charmers, thimble-riggers and robbers'. It included the Nats, 'a tribe of vagrants, who live by feats of dexterity, sleight of hand, fortune telling, and the like, and correspond in their habits with the Gipsies of Europe'. He divided the Nats into seven clans, including snake and bear exhibitors, jugglers, dancers, rope dancers and monkey trainers. 'The rope dancers are expert gymnasts and perform various clever antics with long bamboos. They make use of only one musical instrument, the drum,' he wrote. A subgroup found in Oude were known as Bazigars and earned their livelihood as conjurers. 'All the Nats are prone to drink to excess. They are for the most part of unclean habits. Many of them practise as doctors and are expert in the use of herbs.'[11] Along with the Madaris, who were conjurers and reared snakes and scorpions, he listed the Chai, 'a class of jugglers, thimble riggers, and adventurers, who attend fairs and other festivals like men of the same profession in England. They are notorious for all kinds of artifices for making money.' The final group were the Badhak, 'a caste of professional robbers and assassins', who committed great havoc in association with Thugs, 'but of late years they have been much broken up and have been compelled to resort to gentler avocations'.[12]

Sherring's inclusion of the criminal Badhaks in his list of groups that otherwise made their living from feats of legerdemain and related activities, was no accident. Magic, murder and thievery were seen as going hand-in-hand in colonial India. The acute stigmatization of itinerant groups in the nineteenth century can be traced back to one man, William Henry Sleeman. Known as 'Thuggee' Sleeman, the Cornwall-born army cadet arrived in India in 1808 and spent ten years as a soldier before becoming a political officer stationed in Jubbulpore (now Jabalpur). He is best known for the persecution of Thugs (literally deceivers), a criminal group that sought the blessings of the goddess Kali before befriending and then strangling innocent travellers, sometimes using a silk scarf wrapped around a silver rupee coin. Sleeman described the Thuggee as a 'pan-Indian fraternity of felons' united by profession, heredity and divine sanction in pursuit of their macabre trade. In Sleeman's view, the system of criminality he had discovered was 'the most extraordinary that has ever been recorded in the history

Engraving showing 'Thugs and Poisoners'. Illustrated London News.

of the human race'.[13] In 1836, he was appointed Superintendent for the Suppression of Thuggee with authority over the whole subcontinent. Four years later, he declared that the scourge had been eliminated. His life would become the stuff of legend, fictionalized in books such as Meadow Taylor's *Confessions of a Thug* and in films such as the 1988 Merchant Ivory production, *The Deceivers*, starring Pierce Brosnan, and, more obliquely, in Steven Spielberg's *Indiana Jones and the Temple of Doom*.

Recent historians have cast doubt on whether the Thugs were a tight-knitted group of marauders as Sleeman claimed, or simply regular bandits, but at the time few challenged either his classification or his methods, which relied on informers and forced confessions. Hundreds were killed at the gallows and thousands more incarcerated. The end of the Thuggee menace was just the first step to a broader crackdown on supposed criminal groups. Sleeman had a particularly poor opinion of traditional holy men declaring: 'There is hardly any species of crime that is not throughout India perpetrated by men in the disguise of these religious mendicants; and almost all such mendicants are really men in disguise.'[14] He claimed the great majority were 'assassins by profession', but in spite of 'abundant proofs of their atrocious character' and the discovery of the most horrible acts, he despaired about never lifting 'the veil from their crimes'.[15]

Sleeman's list of undesirables was eventually broadened to include the Megpunnas, a group related to the Thugs, who murdered their victims, not to steal their money and belongings, but to obtain their children who were sold into slavery. To these were added the Tashma-baz Thugs who, according to Fanny Parks, owed their iniquity to the thimble-riggers of English fairgrounds. Parks claimed they used a sleight-of-hand trick known as Stick-and-Garter to commit their crimes. The trick was taught to them by an Irish soldier named Creagh, who was stationed in Cawnpore in 1802. His pupils became gang leaders 'who traversed the country, gambling with whomsoever they could entrap to try their luck at this game'. If the victim lost, he would go about his business. 'If he won, he was induced to remain with the gamblers or was followed and as opportunity offered, was either stupefied with poisonous drugs, or by any convenient method murdered. Many corpses found from time to time along the vicinity of the Grand Trunk road without any trace of the assassins, are now believed to have been the remains of the Tashma-baz's victims,' Parks noted.[16]

The original source for these Thug subgroupings was a report by D. F. McLeod, the officer in charge of Thuggee operations in Rajputana. More than forty different 'classes' of Thugs originating from seven Muslim clans were alluded to. The predominant groups were Banjaras, Kanjars, Bediyas and Nats – all of whom included members who performed magic routines or related entertainment. These seemingly innocent pursuits did little to quell the suspicion applied to all nomadic groups in India, an impression that mirrored the attitude to itinerants, vagrants and 'idle-classes' in England. Kanjars were described as 'wandering hordes, such as may still be seen among the lowest races of men'.[17] The Bediyas of Bengal were conspicuous for 'their dirty habits and enjoy an evil repute as kidnappers of children and plunderers of burial grounds'.[18] Conveniently forgotten was the critical role Banjaras had played in providing crucial supply lines by transporting men, food and equipment on bullocks during the siege of Seringapatam in 1792, in the war against Tipu Sultan.

Even the most astute observers of Indian society were confounded by this dizzying array of groups, subgroups and clans. Robert Russell, author of *The Tribes and Castes of the Central Provinces*, conceded that Nat, derived from the Sanskrit root *nata*, which connotes drama or performance, could be 'applied indefinitely to a number of groups of vagrant acrobats and showmen, especially those who make it their business to do features on the tight-rope or with poles, and those who train and exhibit snakes'.[19] The Bazigars were another subgroup whose name was based on the Persian word *bazi* – a person who does

Group of snake charmers, c. 1890. Library of Congress.

any sort of game or play. Sir Denzil Ibbetson, one of the foremost authorities on the tribes and castes of northern India in the late nineteenth century, lumped them together with the Nats and dubbed them the 'Gipsy Tribes of the Punjab' – an appellation that has stuck despite being challenged by more recent scholars. 'Some say that the Bazigar is a tumbler and the Nat a rope-dancer; others that the Bazigar is a juggler as well as an acrobat, while the Nat is only the latter, and it is possible that those who reach the higher ranks of the profession may call themselves by the Persian name ... Others again say that among the Nats the males only, but among the Bazigars, both sexes perform,' he somewhat inconclusively concluded.[20]

Almost every description of these so-called Gypsy groups included references to males practicing thievery and the women prostitution. An Archaeological Survey of India report on Gorakhpur District published in 1885, labelled the Doms (another group associated with Gypsy tribes) as 'the most expert and inveterate thieves ... ready to murder at a moment's notice, without the least scruples!' Like Gypsies, they moved around 'with the flitting uncertainty of sprites or demons' and had a 'thieves' language of their own'. The men were tall, lithe and powerfully built, 'having a cunning look, and a sinister but confident and daring expression of countenance; and their women fond of finery, bright colours, and jewellery.'[21] G. J. Nicholls, the Inspector General of Police for the Central Provinces set out what he described as the ten 'ostensible callings' of predatory tribes based on ethnological and anthropometric data built up in police files and intelligence-gathering exercises since the 1840s. His list included religious mendicants, 'carriers of Ganges water', bards and fortune tellers as well as 'snake charmers, tumblers and exhibitors of monkeys and bears, in short, the Oriental representatives of the tent-loving gypsies of Europe'.[22] A wide range of groups engaged in juggling and related occupations found themselves listed in a report commissioned by Lieutenant Governor of the Punjab in 1911 as being 'not professedly criminal' but 'not completely free from suspicion of committing theft and other crimes'. They included Bazigars, fakirs, sapelas (snake charmers), Pernas (dancers) and Ararpopos (astrologers and palmists). It singled out Nats who used magic shows and acrobatic performances by women to lure people out of their houses, while other members of the gang would pick the locks on their empty dwellings, selectively steal valuables that would not immediately be noticed as missing such as jewellery and money, and then move quickly on. The modus operandi was ingenious. 'Nobody has thought of linking his loss with the two pretty women he saw weeks before performing such remarkable feats on a tight rope outside his village.'[23]

While such practices did little to endear these itinerant groups to the police, it was their real or imagined association with far more dangerous castes and tribes that would impact the art of jugglery as the nineteenth century progressed. Among the worst were the *datura* poisoners, worshippers of the goddess Bhawani, who befriended their victims before offering sweetmeats laced with the deadly poison. If death did not come immediately 'the victim might spend the rest of his life in a state of disordered mentality'.[24] Police files are full of cases of malevolent mendicants and tricksters. In 1878, Calcutta Police were tipped off about the imminent arrival in the city of a gang of Nausairees (literally 'nine tricks') headed by Shahzada Khurrum Singh, 'an unworthy descendent of the late Maharajah Runjeet Singh, a gambler and cheat from his youth'. The same report warned of 'swindles by mystic healers and love doctors with powers of healing barrenness in women, impotence in men, of restoring love of unfaithful husbands or paramours, in return for a fee'.[25] The Jadua Brahmins of Patna duped their victims, usually wealthy moneylenders, by pretending to turn silver into gold using their magical powers. Operating in groups they arrived at a village, with one pretending to be a mendicant and the others his followers. The victim is told that the Brahmin possesses alchemic powers and is duped into allowing him and one of his disciples to take up residence in a darkened room with a mud floor. To demonstrate his magical powers, the Brahmin tells his victim to place a rupee on his forehead and look at the sun for five minutes. He is assured that when he returns the Brahmin will have disappeared by magic. When the victim walks back into the room, his eyes cannot adjust to the darkness and it appears as if the mendicant has indeed vanished, before gradually reappearing as the victim's eyes get used to the lack of light. The Brahmin now directs his victim to hand over his silver, which he puts in a cloth bag and pretends to bury in a hole in the mud floor of the hut, while secretly hiding it in his garments. A fire made of ghee, oil and incense is lit over the hole and the duped man is told to wait several hours or days before digging out the bag, by which time the Brahmin and his confederates have long disappeared.[26]

Sleeman's solution to what was perceived as an endemic law-and-order crisis was an India-wide system of control by surveillance. The result, he argued, would be that 'in every district infested by the Criminal classes of "Sansees," "Bouriahs," and "Kunjars" petty crime would be considerably diminished'.[27] The problem was that while peripatetic tribes were considered undesirable, not all wandering tribes were criminal. Similarly, even in the case of criminal tribes, not all their members were engaged in some form of criminality – in other words, not all jugglers were 'addicted' to thievery or fraud. Nevertheless, it was widely felt that 'the existence of a criminal class, living notoriously on robbery, is an outrage on civilized society, and their suppression is urgently called for'.[28] As Martine van Woerkens points out: 'In English eyes, all forms of disorder could be attributed to the dangerous classes, regardless of whether these forms were customary or exceptional.'[29] A variety of ad hoc measures were applied to break up, control, punish and reform the criminal tribes, including registration of tribesmen with the local police, confinement to a specified village, surveillance and relocation in special settlements on waste land, where forced agricultural labour was carried out under police supervision and a system of roll call. These various measures, many of which were originally designed specifically to control the Thuggee menace, were formalized with the passing of the Criminal Tribes Act of 1871.[30]

The Act provided for the registration of any 'tribe, gang or class' a local government official had reason to believe was 'addicted to the systematic commission of non-bailable offences'.[31] Once notified, a whole range of restrictions could be placed upon the group, encompassing simple restrictions of movement to the complete relocation of a village or tribe. In the Punjab, the law was tightened in 1911. Members of notified tribes had to report regularly to the police and were threatened with being placed

THE INDIAN FAKIR AND HIS MODERN IMITATOR—"MAJOR" TUCKER, OF THE SALVATION ARMY, CONVERSING WITH A HINDOO FAKIR

The Salvation Army's Frederick Booth-Tucker, The Graphic, *1884.*

in reformatory settlements, many run by the Salvation Army, if they continued to misbehave. 'In other lands criminals are individuals who may be described as the "rogue elephants" of society. They are branded, boycotted and segregated from the decent law-abiding members of the human race,' Commissioner Booth-Tucker of the Salvation Army wrote in 1900. 'In India, they consist of entire Tribes, Villages, Clans, and Families, all the members of which are devoted from the cradle to the grave to a life of crime. Nor are they ashamed of their profession. Rather do they glory in it, and regard themselves with all the pride of ancestry of warriors engaged in a perfectly legitimate war against society.'[32] Recalcitrants, Booth-Tucker argued, should be sent to a remote Himalayan valley where they would 'soon become absorbed by inter-marriage with hill tribes, many of whom greatly need new blood'.[33] Most castes and tribes that came under this legal net could no longer carry on their traditional means of livelihood. Once cohesive communities disintegrated as targeted groups and individuals, they scattered across the countryside to avoid being press-ganged into sedentary life. Writing in 1918, the ethnologist William Crooke mourned the impact of such policies on an ancient nomadic tradition. 'With the almost complete disappearance of the Banjara *tanda,* or caravan, from the roads of Northern India and the Deccan, the traveller misses one of the most picturesque types of Indian life.'[34] By the time of India's independence, 128 tribes or castes, totalling nearly 3.5 million individuals, were designated as 'criminal tribes'.

Gauging the impact of these draconian government policies on the craft of conjuring is difficult. The freedom of movement was crucial for all varieties of entertainers, whether they were jugglers or bards, snake charmers or animal handlers. Their routes followed the calendar of religious festivals, pilgrimages, fairs and harvest times. An already precarious existence would have worsened by laws restricting their movements. The monsoon left roads impassable reducing access to their means of livelihood, time had to be made up by travelling as widely as possible to reach new audiences during the dry season. Many peripatetic groups never adjusted to settled modes of living or agricultural activities. Land allocated to them was often marginal and the allotments too small. Booth-Tucker, however, insisted all that was missing was a proper chance. 'They need guidance. They need capital. And above all, they need to have the fruits of their labour assured to them.'[35]

ALTHOUGH the conjuring arts were stymied temporarily, the black arts thrived. Writing in the early 1800s, James Mill, the father of John Stuart Mill and the author of the now much maligned *History of British India*, protested that belief in witchcraft and sorcery was universally prevalent in India 'and is every day the cause of the greatest enormities'. Enchantment was being used as an excuse for prisoners breaking out of secure cells and pleading innocent to murder in the courts. 'The villagers themselves assume the right of sitting in judgment on this imaginary offence, and their sole instruments of proof are the most wretched of all incantations.'[36] *Mantra-sastris*, who could include astrologers, diviners or fortune tellers, were another source of aversion for the British, particularly Christian missionaries who became increasingly active from the 1830s. Religious people used prayers, supplications, made offerings or sacrifices to a deity; whereas, those who believed in witchcraft, sorcery and astrology were aided not by divine power, but by demons or evil spirits who they invoked by uttering mantras, which to the ears of Europeans sounded like 'chirp and mutter', K. S. MacDonald, editor of the *Indian Evangelical Review*, complained.[37]

Monier Monier-Williams, who as Professor of Sanskrit at the University of Oxford was far more qualified than Mill, wrote that no magician, sorcerer, wizard or witch in Indian history or fable had ever come close to accomplishing through their incantations and enchantments what the *mantra-sastri* could do with the help of mantras.

> For example, he can prognosticate futurity, work the most startling prodigies, infuse breath into dead bodies, kill or

> humiliate enemies, afflict anyone anywhere with disease or madness, inspire any one with love, charm weapons and give them unerring efficacy, enchant armour and make it impenetrable, turn milk into wine, plants into meat, or invert all such processes at will. He is even superior to the gods, and can make gods, goddesses, imps and demons carry out his most trifling behests.[38]

Monier-Williams recalled one incident where a Sakta Brahmin came to see him in Patna. After examining his hand, he prophesized that his stay in India would be happy and prosperous, aside from meeting with a great disappointment in exactly a fortnight. As the Oxford don later admitted, 'I only met with one unexpected and most mortifying contretemps from the day of my departure from England to the day of my return, and that happened on the very day predicted. It must at least be acknowledged that the coincidence was remarkable.'[39] Monier-Williams also related the story of another Sakta Brahmin, named Bhaskaracharya, well-versed in the mantras, who felt snubbed at not being asked to a dinner party given by a wealthy friend. Having waited until the assembled guests, their appetites stimulated by the aroma of the choice dishes, were about to start their feast, he extracted his revenge. By repeating a special mantra, he 'turned all the viands into foul and fetid excrementitious matter'. Suspecting the cause of this 'disastrous metamorphose', the householder hastily sent a messenger 'to implore the immediate presence of the offended Brahmin, who thereupon becoming mollified, obligingly consented to repeat another mantra, which reconverted all the filth into the most delicious ambrosial food'.[40]

Ojhas, variously described by anthropologists as shamans, magicians, diviners, soothsayers and sorcerers, plied their trade in many parts of India. Healers used mantras and fake medicines to cure diseases. Witches, it was believed, could turn a woman into a tigress or make her lose her hair. They could stop cows from giving milk, steal property from a house and make children disappear. In the Deccan, witches were so powerful they could extract a person's liver from a distance of 150 miles. In the Thana district of Bombay Presidency, they were ascribed with the ability to turn themselves into animals such as bulls, dogs or buffaloes. 'The person once charmed by their spells is said to blindly abide by their orders.'[41] To practice their black arts they went naked to the cremation grounds at midnight holding in their hands hearths containing burning coals. They untied their hair and began reciting incantations. Next, they dug out the bones of buried corpses which they took home and preserved for magical rituals.[42]

In the villages and remote tribal areas of India, sympathetic magic – the belief in charms, omens and possession, as well as the supernatural world of spirits, ghosts and jinns – often intersects with performance magic. Ojhas use simple sleight-of-hand techniques to demonstrate power over nature and animals, such as pretending to kill a chicken and then bringing it back to life. Among the Tharus of the Terai, witches were accused of using their knowledge of black magic to inflict disease and epidemics. Their modus operandi was far more practical, consisting of contaminating water and milk supplies, poisoning livestock and food supplies and using toxins to make crops barren.[43] In Bombay Presidency, sorcerers were employed to use their powers of sleight of hand to detect witches. Small brass cups that appeared to move of their own accord, but were manipulated by invisible threads, were used to locate the houses of witches. Once discovered, the cups would alight on the top of the witch's head.[44]

The Austrian missionary Stephen Fuchs, who studied the Balahi, an untouchable caste living in the Narmada valley in the 1940s, found them to be no strangers to the realm of 'the mysterious, of ghosts and demons'.[45] The Balahi took it for granted that beings of the invisible other world interfered in their lives and were always on the alert to protect themselves 'by charms and spells, by various offerings and magic practices against the harmful and malignant intentions of the evil spirits'.[46] They did not distinguish between the supposed supernatural powers of the *barwa*, the village sorcerer, and the tricks of the sleight-of-hand artist. The *barwas* claimed to be possessed by a *bhoot*, the common term for a ghost, in whose authority they acted and spoke. Some sincerely believed in their magical powers, others admitted their cures and devices 'were a fraud and a deception of credulous people'. It was easier to win the confidence of their clients with a few clever tricks. These, Fuchs observed, 'were handed down from father to son, or from master to disciple, and their secret was carefully kept'. They included the Mango Tree Trick and heating an iron chain in a fire until it was white hot, stepping into the fire and whipping oneself with the chain without getting hurt or leaving a mark. Fuchs's informant had an uncle who could make money appear from nowhere. Had it been genuine magic 'he would certainly have been a rich man, but he had died in poverty', the informant admitted.[47] *Barwas* also had the power to cure snake bites and to transfer the pain of a person stung by a scorpion onto another.[48]

Among the Baigas, a tribal group living in the Satpura mountains of central India, the role of spells, the importance of magical ritual and belief in the supernatural, still govern every aspect of life. 'The Baigas regard themselves as the most powerful magicians in the world, and they are looked upon with awe by other tribes and communities,' wrote the Austrian ethnologist Christoph von Furer Haimendorf, who devoted four decades to studying the tribal cultures of South Asia and the Himalayas.[49] As priest-magicians conversant with all the secrets of Mother Earth, they serve the neighbouring Gonds and other tribes, as well as Brahmins and merchants. They believe their male ancestor, Nanga Baiga, was a great magician. His right shoulder, which contained red blood, was considered the source of white magic. The left shoulder bled black blood and was considered the source of black magic.[50] According to the anthropologist Verrier Elwin, the foremost authority on the Baigas, they had four grades of magicians. The most powerful was the *dewar* who could conjure up rain, stop earthquakes, defend the village from tigers and protect crops. Next was the *barua*, a type of medium through whom god spoke directly. During ceremonies, they threw themselves on the ground in a sort of frenzy, twitching their limbs and shaking their heads, beating themselves with spiked chains and running iron spikes through their tongues and cheeks. The *gunia* had sufficient skills to deal with human and animal diseases, which in practice amounted to a continuous warfare against both witches and invisible beings. The Baigas claimed that in olden times the *gunia* could sit on a pole and fly through the air. The lowest class of magicians, the *jana panda,* were clairvoyants who divined dreams and visions and dealt with deciphering good and bad omens.[51] Elwin documented how the *barua* would run up a wooden ladder, swing or rope studded with iron spikes and scourge himself with chains while divining answers to questions.

Employing magicians to go after thieves was well documented in a report on the state of India's jails commissioned by the Governor General, Lord Wellesley, in the 1790s. One of those interviewed was a man named Sheikh Khyrulla who described himself as a professional detector of thieves. Khyrulla described the case of a quarter-master named Gillespie who reported the theft of 120 gold *mohurs*, which had been locked in a large chest. On reaching Gillespie's bungalow, the magician used a ritual known as the 'ceremony of the enchanted vase' to find the culprit from among more than one hundred suspects. 'I write the names of the four angels Gabriel, Michael, Israfeel, and Azraeel on a new earthen vase and place it with its mouth upwards, on the closed hands of two indifferent persons, and perform certain religious ceremonies over it,' Khyrulla explained. 'The names of all the accused or the suspected, are written on slips of paper and thrown one by one, into the vase. When the name of the thief is put in, the vase will turn around.'[52] The magician identified the thief as a boy named Rowshun, who frequently visited the house. This was angrily denied by his employer who placed Khyrulla in custody for falsely accusing his servant. The magician was given three days to find the missing treasure and prove it was the boy. Khyrulla used a ritual that required reciting a Koranic text 101 times over a piece of paper bearing the name of the thief, which was then thrown into a fire and burnt. 'The guilty person will experience great distress of mind and he will unbosom his secret to somebody,' he explained. When the ceremony was performed over Rowshun's name, he confessed to the theft and revealed where he had hidden the money.[53]

Had the vase ceremony not worked, Khyrulla had other ways of proving a person's guilt. The first method was psychological. Having lined up the suspects, he examined their countenances carefully. 'The eyes of the guilty person become flushed. The vein on his forehead becomes dilated, his pulse irregular, the palpitation at his breast great, and accompanied by a kind of fever. The consciousness of guilt and the dread of detection prevents the offender from looking up.' Hinting that he knew who the guilty party was, he waited until the thief came forward.[54] If this didn't work, he had recourse to more powerful ceremonies involving enchanted arrows, shoes and razors. In the latter case, the accused was forbidden to shave his head. Khyrulla would recite some verses from the Koran, breathe on the razor and shave his thigh with it. This caused the guilty party's hair to fall out.[55] The ceremony of last resort involved reading a certain text from the Koran eleven times and another text three times over raw unhusked rice. 'It is then to be weighed with a rupee bearing the names of Abubekur, Omur, Osman and Alii, and given to each of the accused to chew and spit out. The guilty cannot chew it, the rice becomes dry, the criminal's tongue parched, and if the property be still in his possession, blood flows from his tongue.'[56]

◈

MAGIC and spy craft were closely linked in ancient and medieval India. To deal with seditious ministers who dabbled in sorcery or were addicted to witchcraft, the *Arthashastra* advocated that spies disguise themselves as magicians and trick the offending minister into displaying his powers by promising a great reward. While the minister was engaging in his display, the spy could murder him and blame the death on his proclivity to witchcraft.[57] Magicians, mendicants and soothsayers were also recruited as spies. The importance of intelligence gathering was highly regarded in the *Arthashastra*, which recommended it be undertaken by ambassadors in enemy kingdoms and by spies and enforcers at home. 'The king's cunning knowledge (*rajniti*) was generated by his success in training his spies, his "eyes and ears". His enlightened knowledge (*buddhi*) was then to work on the pool of information created by able sleuths,' notes the historian Christopher Bayly.[58] The duties of ambassadors were laid out in the fifteenth century Hindu treatise, the *Kamandakiya Nitisara* or, *The Elements of Polity*, derived ultimately from the *Arthashastra*:

> An ambassador should secretly communicate with the spies of his own lord stationed in places of pilgrimage, hermitages and temples, in the guise of hermits pretending to study the *sastras* [holy books]. … As in a sacrifice, priests are guided by the Vedic Sutras [chants or hymns], so the king can undertake any action guided by the spies. Spies should be carefully fashioned for their assignments like vessels for a ritual. … Wandering spies may be of reckless type, mendicant or recluse type, sacrificer or black magician type and poisoner type, or in the guise of persons of noble character.[59]

During the reign of Shah Jahan, intelligence gathering relied on fakirs who made assignations and passed on information from the royal courts and the women's quarters of the great households. Astrologers were another source as their clients – described by the Venetian traveller Niccolao Manucci as 'credulous Hindus' – trusted them so much that they told them everything. 'Even the bazaars swarm with these folk [astrologers], and by this means they find out all that passes in the houses.'[60] Groups such as the *unani hakims,* itinerant doctors, of Peshawar travelled extensively, reaching as far as Bokhara and the Deccan, dispensing medicine, spiritual advice and spells.[61] The magical prowess of tribal groups, their skills at hunting and tracking animals and their intimate knowledge of the vast tracts of jungles that once covered much of India, made them valuable additions to armies – a practice that continued until the nineteenth century.

Indian storytellers have delighted in telling tales of mythical thieves and their magical powers. As Ariel Glucklich points out, India in the second and third centuries BCE when the *Laws of Manu* were composed, was a land where 'thieves lurked behind every corner, and anything that wasn't nailed down was fair game'.[62] People were kidnapped for ransom, livestock lifted and foodstuffs pilfered and even cow dung was purloined. The popular fifteenth-century Jaina tale, *Raunhineya Carita* (*The Story of Raunhineya*), describes a thief named Raunhineya who can imitate any voice or assume any form, including that of a deer, peacock or camel. Raunhineya's charms make him immune to injury, render him invisible or turn his attackers against each other. He can even turn water into fire.[63] In one version of the story, Raunhineya is caught by using smoke that makes him shed tears, thereby washing away the collyrium, the magic salve of invisibility. Once captured he is condemned to death and impaled.[64] The story also gives a detailed description of robber dens – places of magic and power, bloodthirsty and barbarous vices. The mountain of Vibhara near the town of Magadha, was said to be a repose of both thieves and ascetics. During the day, the roaring of thousands of lions and tigers could be heard, while by night came the terrifying howls of jackals and the hooting of owls. 'By virtue of magic charms, amulets and simples, the young of the thieves habitually played there with the young of the lions. Many ascetics, who lived on bulbs, roots, and fruit, dwelt in the woods around the mountain and performed manifold penance; and hundreds of families of thieves dwelt in the caves, which, shut in by bamboo network, were in the recesses of the mountain.'[65]

Sanskrit literature makes references to a mythical manual of thievery, the *Steya-sutra,* which contained numerous spells and charms designed specifically for the art of burglary. There were salves and ointments for making thieves invisible or immune to harm, locating underground treasure chambers, vanquishing demons, putting their victims to sleep and even stealing their wives. Collyrium applied to the eyes would make the darkest night 'seem as [though] a *crore* of suns were in the sky'.[66] The only Sanskrit treatise on the art of thieving to have survived is the *Sanmukhakalpa* (*Rules for the Six-Headed Being*) – a reference to Kartikeya, the god of thieves – composed sometime between the seventh and ninth centuries. The Italian scholar Alessandro Passi compares the incomplete and corrupted manuscript to a 'compilation of pages from a badly ruined dictionary'. Nevertheless, the dependence of the subject matter – and the burglar's craft – on magic is clear. 'Potions, poisons, invisibility ointments and sleeping draughts make the [*Sanmukhakalpa]* far more similar to a manual of sorcery, *abhicâra*, than to a treatise on stealing.'[67]

SEVEN

TRICKS OF THE TRADE

ACROBATS vault over five camels standing abreast. Impersonators pretending to be 'broken down gentlemen' beg for alms. Mendicants plunge their hands down their throats and pull out their intestines. Jugglers, tricksters, ventriloquists, funambulists, rope dancers, snake charmers, sword swallowers, astrologers and fortune tellers throng the Esplanade and Bombay's other main roads, alongside ascetics who practice such severities that if listed would 'enumerate almost all forms of torture'.[1] As an editor at the *Bombay Government Gazette*, Krishnanath Raghunathji was a keen observer of what he called the 'obscure members of humanity'. In 1892, he published a unique work of social history. *Bombay Beggars and Criers* painted a vivid picture of the lowest rungs of society in the closing years of the nineteenth century – and of the extraordinary range of street magic and spectacular entertainment on offer. The book would go through three reprints, expanding significantly in size from fifty-five to more than 150 pages in the 1898 edition. Little is known about Raghunathji, but his interest in his city's social outcasts and their obscure beliefs is clear. In 1884, he published an

Cotton label showing fairground amusements. Priya Paul Collection.

article in *Indian Antiquary* on Bombay's dancing girls, most of whom were Goan devadasis. The following year he wrote 'Omens from the Falling of House Lizards'. In the preface to the third edition of *Bombay Beggars and Criers*, Raghunathji regrets he could not produce the book with illustrations as 'the people that had to be photographed could not all be got together for that purpose'. He promised to include them in the next impression, but none was never published.[2]

Even without photographs, the book is encyclopaedic in scope. Its descriptions, though given with a minimum of embellishment, are rich and textured. When it comes to the feats of wonder-workers, almost all means of deception imaginable are described. While Raghunathji dismisses Bombay's beggars, petty criminals, hawkers, mendicants and mages as 'worthless members of society … encouraged in idleness by the ready supply of their wants',[3] he is clearly fascinated by the characters he encounters. There are ventriloquists, Hindu and Muslim, who can 'imitate thunder, the sound of running water, roaring waves, the cries of beasts, the whistling of birds and the speech of men';[4] Pingales, who read fortunes with the aid of a spotted owl and believed in spirits and ghosts; and Bahurupis, 'men of many faces and disguises' who dress up as gods, milkmaids and ascetics.[5] Many of these groups have long since disappeared.

Magic is omnipresent in Raghunathji's throbbing metropolis. Experts in legerdemain swallow pieces of iron an inch-and-a-half wide and an eighth-of-an-inch thick, inserting them deep into their stomachs. Others twirl a small brass pan on the end of a stick balanced on their noses or on their chins. A juggler keeps up to six balls in the air at once, first throwing them straight up, then behind his back, then under his arms and legs. 'Moreover, he keeps up four balls continually in the air, tossing them round his back, hitting them with his elbows, his wrists and his hands, and throwing them in various forms. ... In a like manner he throws up four daggers, in a variety of shapes, catching them all as they descended by their handles.' The next performer takes three flutes of different tones and plays them by placing one in each nostril and the other in his mouth.[6]

Troupes of rope dancers, known for the agility of their bodies and pliability of their limbs, form themselves into almost any kind of animal. 'Several bodies are so interlaced that the different individuals can scarcely be distinguished. They all perform feats of strength, and one man will bear on his shoulders six others,' Raghunathji explains.[7] Stilt walkers execute acrobatics on poles fifteen feet high. A man runs over the edges of two sabres placed parallel on the ground without cutting his feet. A boy fixes a scimitar upright before him and places a piece of cloth on its point. He sits down, then leaps at the sword striking off the cloth with the tip of his nose. Next, he takes a ten-foot high stilt. From a step affixed halfway up, he performs gymnastic feats, while keeping the stilt balanced the whole time. Another takes a length of cord between his teeth, which is attached to a six-foot long log of wood and flips it behind him. Balancing six water pots on his head, a man ascends a rope and with a pole in his hand walks backwards and forwards swinging the rope to its full extent without letting a single pot fall. The same man repeats the stunt with one foot in a slipper and the other in a brass pan, which he uses to slide along the rope. Next, he attaches stilts on his legs made of buffalo horns. 'These encumbrances are no impediments, however, to his walking on the ground, climbing up the spars, nor his proceeding backward and forward upon the rope with his wanted agility.' Men, women and children cut somersaults from the ground 'with as much seeming facility, and apparent ease, as the vaulters on a theatre'. Two boys link arms and legs turning themselves into a human ring, rolling on the ground a dozen times. Bending over backwards, a girl lifts a piece of cloth covering the point of a scimitar with her mouth and then with her eyelid. Three men throw themselves through the arms of ten pairs of men linked together to form a kind of tunnel.[8]

The best performer is an old man who stands on a board eighteen-inches square and does a backwards somersault, his feet landing on the same board. The board is then placed on a pole twenty-five-feet high. The man climbs up the pole and repeats the feat. For the final act, a springboard five-feet long is placed sloping on the ground at an angle of about forty-five degrees. An elephant stands next to it. Two men run at full speed up the board and then do a somersault over the animal's back. 'Five camels were then placed abreast, over which they vaulted in a like manner. They also leap and turn in a similar way, over the point of a sword held by a tall man, as high as he can extend it.' After the performance, the old man, the head of the tumblers' troupe, tells Raghunathji how in his youth he performed the same feat in the presence of Nadir Shah, but age and infirmity had now nearly incapacitated him. [9]

Not all those he encounters earn Raghunathji's praise. He warns against the Dombaris who are 'of bad character, the women prostitutes, and all, when they get the chance, thieves'.[10] Nor is he impressed with Inamdars who impersonate 'broken down gentlemen' by putting a chain around their necks, hands and feet fastened with a padlock and pretending to be in this state because of the debts they owe the government. Worse are the 'bad tempered and ill-behaved' Kabaligars, who, if nothing is given, slash their arms and bodies with a knife until blood flows and threaten to kill themselves.[11] 'Then there is another who has no particular name assigned to him, but who stands abusing the shopkeeper, and at last puts his hand in his mouth and pulls out, as he says, his stomach all bloody.' This, Raghunathji concedes, 'is a horrible sight to look at'.[12] Suspect fortune tellers abound.

Pehelvan or wrestler. Priya Paul Collection.

'Kalonganis pretend to know everything about futurity, what awaits mankind, what is to become of this world and when there will be a deluge.' The Chudbudke Joshis read fortunes by looking at a person's face. 'They have good fortune in store for everyone who asks them. Their usual blessing is, brother thy belly will grow large.'[13] Budlendes resemble the Joshis and induce people to part with their possessions by repeating the line: 'A fortnight hence wilt thou hear of prosperity, and in a palanquin wilt thou sit within a couple of months.' Having raised their victim's expectations, the fortune teller says a Halaki bird has whispered in his ear that danger awaits and can only be averted by offering a token – an old waist coat will do.[14]

Among the Muslim beggars are the Pehelvan or wrestlers, who excel in keeping half a dozen or more knives in the air at once. One witnessed by Raghunathji, took a large stone ball and kept it rolling up and down one of his arms, then with a jerk sent it to his other arm. Next, he flung it into the air and let it fall heavily on his chest and back. Finally, he pulled out a long knife that he clasped with both hands and forced down his throat allowing it to remain there for a few minutes. 'He pulls it out covered with blood, and shows it to each of the spectators, and asks for a *pice*.'[15] Muslim jugglers known as Garudis perform with snakes, swallow and spit out fire. 'They also pull out of their mouths cotton thread several hundred yards long, quite dry, and by a clever trick, apparently change a pinchful of dust into copper, silver, gold coin, &c.'[16]

Raghunathji's ability to delve into Bombay's underworld with its tamashawallahs, impersonators, prostitutes and pimps was rare among India's educated classes. Elitism and caste were partly to blame, but complacency was also a factor. The fakirs who hypnotized deadly cobras, the jadoowallahs who stabbed children with swords and then brought them back to life again, the yogis who stopped their hearts from beating before being buried alive and the conjurers who made objects float in the air, were a normal part of the chaotic and colourful landscape of India. The other great vernacular account of daily life in Bombay, Govind Narayan's *Mumbaiche Varnan* published in 1863, pays scant attention to the city's popular culture as expressed by its wandering minstrels, madaris, folk artists and story tellers. Narayan is mesmerized by the 'sky-chariot' that takes to the air at dusk on 18 January 1853, though he is disappointed, like the thousands of others who witnessed the spectacle, that the imported English balloon sailed aloft without its promised human cargo. Bombay's streets are witness to traditional shows and magical spectacles every day. But he prefers the foreign acts with their magicians and showmen who can do somersaults on horses, to the humdrum of tumblers, rope dancers and bear handlers. Local showmen are lucky to make eight annas a day, whereas Europeans who set up their tents on Camp Maidan can take from ten to twenty thousand rupees in a couple of months. 'Our people are glad to spend their money on such events,' he writes. 'The Europeans are very skilled in all things and as they are very shrewd, they can convert any vocation into money.'[17]

❖

THE tendency among Indian authors and historians during the colonial era to brush aside India's rich magical heritage left the field wide open to European writers who became enthusiastic, though not necessarily objective, chroniclers of the conjurer's craft. The jadoowallah's skills were matchless, executed with a minimum of props. Unlike Western illusionists with their 'ornamental attendants', tables and chairs, the Indian conjuror:

> at the utmost … has a withered old ragged scarecrow like himself to assist in his deceptions. He is all but naked; there is a dirty cloth around his loins and a cotton rag over his shoulders, and his whole stock-in-trade consists of a little stick, an earthenware vessel, and a few baskets. He can hide nothing, for he has no place to put anything in, but he is among the first performers of the art in the world, and it certainly contributes to the effect of his wonders that they are done without any suspicious surroundings.[18]

The sheer range of legerdemain baffled even the most hardened cynic. As anyone who travelled extensively would know, India's necromancers were capable of feats for which there was no explanation, A. A. Cocksedge wrote in the late 1930s.

> There was an old wizard in Kashmir who could de-atomize and re-atomize solid objects hundreds of miles apart. Then there is the man who calls himself Mussaffar (the Traveller) living in the railway colony near Sukkur, who emptied a safe more than a mile away of its cash and account books just to prove to its owner that he could do it. Finally, there is the old story of the Madras jail where a sadhu mystified the warders by being found each morning outside his locked cell.

The only reason more people never talked of such things was for fear of being called liars. Continued Cocksedge: 'An American friend whom I tried to interest remarked: "It is all very strange and yet you have an honest face".'[19]

George Thompson writing in the *Liverpool Mercury* in 1862, described a juggler who could change the nature of his eyes. Putting his hands on his hips he opened his lids and in the place of his natural eyes there were two balls of finely polished steel. Next time he opened them, 'a pair of burnished brass ones shone in their stead .... During the performance of this trick he never took his hand from his hips, and I was the only person near him.'[20] South Indian jugglers were considered superior. 'The quality of iron and brass-ware which they contrived to swallow was truly marvellous,' a witness told the *Manchester Times* in 1851. 'Tenpenny nails, clasp-knives, gimblets, were all treated as so many items of pastry or confectionary, and I could not but picture to myself the havoc a dozen of these cormorants would commit in an ironmonger's shop.'[21] Emily Eden, who travelled across India extensively with her sister Fanny and brother George in the 1830s and 40s, related the following performance by a magician from Madras:

> He did all the tricks the Indian jugglers do with balls and balancing, and swallowing a sword, &c., and then he spit fire in large flames, and put a little rice into the top of a basket or small tray, and shook it, and before our eyes a tiny handful of rice turned into a large quantity of cowrie shells. Then he made a little boy, who is one of my servants, sit down, and he put a small black pebble into his hand and apparently did nothing but wave a little baguette round his head, and forty rupees came tumbling

> out of the boy's little hands. He made him pick them up again, and hold them as tight as he could, and in an instant the rupees were all gone, and a large live frog jumped out.[22]

In his memoir *Quicker than the Eye*, the American magician and historian John Mulholland singled out the beheading of a boy by a Sikh on a street in Rangoon as the most impressive performance of Indian deception he ever saw. The boy was made to lie on the ground as the magician's assistants 'beat drums and sang a song so barbaric that one felt in the mood for a beheading'. The magician, a man with piercing black eyes and a full black beard, unsheathed his sword, toyed with the blade and drew a line in the earth out from the boy's neck. The boy was covered with a cloth to save the spectators from seeing the actual gash. 'With a wild cry, he whipped the sword through the waiting neck. Without so much as a glance at the body, he carefully examined the sword edge and wiped the gore from the blade. He then stepped on the cloth and kicked the head away from the body. It could be seen under the cloth three feet away from the shoulders.' The magician begged for coins, warning the crowd he would not restore boy's head until enough money was collected. Satisfied with his takings, he reached under the cloth, replaced the head in position and walked around the body. 'The cloth was jerked away and the boy jumped up, salaamed and went around rapidly collecting coins on his own account.'[23]

One of the most detailed accounts of Indian legerdemain came from the pen of J. Hobart Caunter. Born in Devon in 1792, he was the second son of George Caunter, governor of Penang. He went to India in about 1810 as a cadet with the 34th Foot, but returned home after spending less a decade 'having discovered, much to his disappointment, nothing on the continent of Asia to interest him'.[24] Caunter's dismissive tone was probably coloured by his later career as a preacher though his writings, particularly his multi-volume work *The Oriental Annual or Scenes in India,* published between 1834 and 1838 and illustrated with the stunning engravings of William Daniell, reveal a deep curiosity about India and its people.

Caunter arrived in Madras just before the monsoon broke in September 1810. Three months later, he set out 'in search of the picturesque', finding it on the first day of his travels in the form of a party of itinerant jugglers. Caunter confines his description to two 'juggles' he claims had never been witnessed by Europeans before. The first of these was executed by a young woman who fixed a device to her head with twenty strings attached to it. At the end of each string was a small noose, while under her arm was a basket holding twenty hens' eggs. Spinning on the spot so fast it became 'painful to look at her' and with the strings forming a horizontal circle, she put an egg into each noose without slowing her gyrations. Next, she removed the eggs one by one, laid them in the basket before stopping in an instant, 'without the movement of a limb, or even the vibration of a muscle, as if she had been suddenly fixed into marble. Her countenance was perfectly calm. She exhibited not the slightest distress from her extraordinary exertion.'[25]

Caunter describes the second trick as 'an instance of visual illusion ... unprecedented in the annals of jugglery'. The juggler, a 'ferocious looking fellow', had a normal wicker basket that was carefully examined and found to be empty. A child of about eight years old 'habited in the only garb which nature had provided for her, perfect of frame and elastic of limb, a model for a cherub and scarcely darker than a child of southern France', climbed into the basket. An argument between the juggler and the girl followed, her voice coming distinctly from inside the basket. Suddenly the juggler screamed and threatened to kill her. 'There was a stern reality in the whole scene which was perfectly dismaying. It was acted to the life, but terrible to see and hear,' Caunter writes. 'As the child begged for mercy, the man seized a sword and to the Englishman's absolute consternation and horror plunged it repeatedly into the basket 'with all the blind ferocity of an excited demon'. By now the juggler's face wore an expression 'indicative of the most frantic of human passions'. The child's shrieks 'were so real and distracting that they almost curdled for a few moments the whole mass of my blood'. Caunter's first urge 'was to rush upon the monster and fell him to the earth, but he was armed and I defenceless. I looked at my companions. They appeared to be pale and paralyzed with terror, and yet these feelings were somewhat neutralized by the consciousness that the man could not dare to commit a deliberate murder in the broad eye of day and before so many witnesses.' Blood poured out from the basket. The child could be heard struggling and crying, her moans growing fainter until she made what sounded like 'the last convulsive gasp which was to set her innocent soul free from the gored body'. After muttering 'a few cabalistic words', the juggler lifted up the basket. To Caunter's shock – and relief – it was empty. Still trying to comprehend what happened, he suddenly saw the child coming towards him from among the crowd unharmed. 'She advanced and saluted us holding out her hand for our donations, which we bestowed with hearty good will. She received them with a most graceful salaam and the party left us well satisfied with our more than expected gratuity.'[26]

Caunter's description of the Basket Trick with its monstrous juggler, the blood-curdling screams of the innocent child and its inexplicable finale, became a yardstick for measuring the marvels of India's jadoowallahs. Before the image of a boy running up a rope, disappearing into the sky, falling back to earth as a mess of dismembered limbs, the illusion was considered one of the greatest conjuring feats in the world. Caunter prefaced his description of the trick by warning people not to be fooled by the supposed 'mildness of the Hindoo'. That mildness, he wrote, was 'mere apathy and that apathy, which would cause us to witness a murder with indifference, is infinitely more detestable and surely a greater moral enormity than the passion which after a desperate conflict with a man's better feelings works him up in the frenzy of its effervescence to take away the life of a fellow creature'.[27]

The version of the Basket Trick described by Caunter was only one of many. In 1876, the *Times* correspondent reported on a display of jugglery put on for the Prince of Wales at Government House in Madras. The juggler took a young girl, bound her hand and foot, and forced her into a shallow basket. He 'proceeded to inveigh against the girl in no measured terms, as if he were a counsel in the Divorce Court, and finally, in a rage, leaped on the basket lid and crushed it in, then trampled on it – mind it rested on the floor – then, raising a sword, thrust it down and through the basket again and again, and pretended to gloat over the blood on the blade.' As the correspondent noted, one of the sharp-eyed members of the audience saw the girl slip like a shadow out of the basked when the attention of the others was diverted by the juggler seizing a child in the crowd and pretending to behead her.[28] In 1902, an Indian showman calling himself 'Prince' performed the trick in New York firing a revolver into the basket as well as using a sword. Another version ends with the assistant lifted out of the basket with the sword or knife pierced through the neck. The feat, according to Colonel Robert Elliot, an ophthalmologist with the Indian Medical Service and an amateur conjurer, is medically possible. Once practiced by the Rafa'i Fakirs of Hyderabad, it requires considerable force – and presumably a high threshold to pain – to execute. 'The handle end is pressed on the ground while the man seizes his windpipe and the other important structures in relation with it, pulls them forward and provides a loose space behind them.' This prevents injuring the vital organs in the neck. Elliot claims to have seen an x-ray photograph showing such a weapon in position and lying just in front of the spine.[29]

Caunter recorded another encounter with jugglers while a guest of the Rajah of Coorg. He found the middle-aged ruler of the south Indian kingdom a handsome man with 'quick penetrating eyes, which occasionally fixed upon you with such ardency of expression that it was painful to encounter their gaze'.[30] The Rajah had a fascination for blood sports involving both animals and humans – occasionally together – and invited the Englishman and his companions to a day-long exhibition of 'animal fights and native gymnastics'. A wild boar stood no chance against a goat with a razor sharp four-inch spur attached to its head; an African buffalo mortally wounded a lion; a man armed with only a knife took on a tiger in a gladiatorial-style clash – and won.[31]

For the weak-stomached Caunter, the most interesting part of the programme was the juggling. After the usual preliminaries of sword swallowing, fire-eating and other common tricks, one of the jugglers took a large earthen vessel, filled it with water, turned it upside down and poured the liquid out. The moment he placed the vessel upwards it mysteriously filled with water. This was done several times. Caunter and his companions were allowed to examine the vessel, fill it and tip it over, but were unable to discover the secret to the trick. The vessel used was an ordinary clay pot and to convince his audience there was nothing special in its construction, the juggler broke it into little pieces and allowed the Rajah and others present to inspect it. Next, a large basket was produced, under which was put a Pariah bitch. After about a minute, the basket was removed, and the dog appeared with a litter of seven puppies. 'These were again covered, and upon raising the magic basket a goat was presented to our view; this was succeeded by a pig in the full vigour of existence, but which, after being covered for the usual time, appeared with its throat cut; it was, however, shortly restored to life under the mystical shade of the wicker covering.'[32]

A man next took a bag full of brass balls and threw them into the air – thirty-five balls altogether – but none appeared to return. After making some motions with his hands while 'grunting forth a kind of barbarous chant', the balls fell from the sky one by one until they were all replaced in the bag. A gaunt-looking man came next and declared he would swallow a snake. Opening a box, he produced five-foot long cobra. He began by putting its tail into his mouth and gradually lowered it into his stomach, until nothing but the head protruded from his lips.

> With a sudden gulp, he seemed to complete the disgusting process of deglutition, and to secure the odious reptile within his body. After the expiration of a few seconds, he opened his mouth and gradually drew forth the snake, which he replaced in the box, making a salaam to the Rajah. This was by no means a pleasing sight, but his Highness laughed heartily, and threw the performer a handful of rupees; thus, clearly showing that his pleasure was no counterfeit, like the juggler's trick.[33]

One of the women in the troupe now took her turn. Taking a twenty-foot-long piece of bamboo, she placed it upright upon a flat stone and without any support, climbed to the top where she balanced on one leg. Round her waist was a girdle, to which was fastened an iron socket. 'Springing from her upright position on the bamboo, she threw herself horizontally forward with such exact precision that the top of the pole entered the socket of her iron zone, and in this position, she spun herself round with a velocity that made me giddy to look at, the bamboo appearing all the while as if it were supported by some supernatural agency.' The next acrobat was a man who balanced himself on his head with his arms crossed over his breast. In this upside-down position, he juggled sixteen balls in the air without dropping a single one. Another man then approached and climbed up the first man's body and stood upright on his inverted feet. He was handed a cup also with sixteen balls and in unison the two men commenced juggling them. 'Thirty-two balls were now in motion, and with the rays of the sun falling upon their polished surfaces, the jugglers appeared in the midst of a shower of gold. The effect was singular, and the dexterity displayed by these men quite amazing.' Next, they did the trick in reverse, with the first man standing on his feet and the second upside-down balanced on the other's head. The balls were again put into their hands, and all thirty-two kept in motion in the air as before. 'It is certain that the manual dexterity of these men is not exceeded; if approached, by the jugglers of any other country in the world.'[34]

Caunter may have been a little promiscuous in describing the abilities of the performers in the troupe, but not the range of the repertoire presented. Traditional Indian juggling was a series of spectacular entertainments, with each member of the troupe – ranging from toddlers to the elderly – being assigned a different role. The blurring of the boundaries between sleight of hand and displays of acrobatics, gymnastics, rope tricks, snake handling and other feats of manual dexterity was part of the jadoowallah's stock in trade. The broader the gamut of tricks, the more profitable the performance. The more skilful the troupe, the more likely they would be patronized by a local ruler, tipped generously by foreigners or recruited to perform overseas.

While travelling from Agra to Surat in 1650, the French physician Jean-Baptiste Tavernier came across a party of tricksters. Planting a stick in the ground, they asked one of the spectators to choose what fruit he liked. He replied a mango, after which one of the performers hid under a sheet placed on the ground and stomped five or six times. Curious to understand what was going on, Tavernier went to an upstairs room where he could see through a fold in the sheet. The juggler was cutting the flesh under his armpits with a razor and rubbing the wood with his blood. 'Each time he rose up the wood grew visibly; on the third occasion, there were branches and buds thereon, on the fourth the tree was covered with leaves, and on the fifth it was bearing flowers.' The performance was interrupted by an English clergyman who was so angered by the heathen display that he grabbed the tree declaring 'he would not give Communion to any person that should stay any longer to see such things'.[35]

Tavernier's account conveys the visual brilliance of the deception that normally culminates with a ripe mango being produced – even out of season. Described as 'the most perfect achievement of the conjurer's art',[36] the Mango Trick was the only feat of juggling to be listed in *Hobson Jobson*, the Anglo-Indian glossary published in 1886. The glossary's authors, Henry Yule and A. C. Burnell, relate the story of a 'traveller of note' who witnessed the trick in the Deccan. 'The narrator, then a young officer, determined with a comrade, at all hazards of fair play or foul, to solve the mystery. In the middle of the trick one suddenly seized the conjuror, whilst the other uncovered and snatched at the mango-plant. But lo! it came from the earth with a root, and the mystery was darker than ever!'[37] The illusion ended with the tree sinking to the ground leaving nothing but the pot, into which the jadoowallah dug and produced the original seed. 'Now, they do this in your own compound on hard earth or stones, on a *chunam* pavement as hard as granite, or anywhere you like,' the *Pall Mall Gazette* explained to an incredulous Victorian public. 'As they are perfectly naked, with the exception of a cummerbund (wrapped like a waist-cloth and bathing-drawers), it is evident that nothing can be concealed.'[38]

IN December 1830, the *Edinburgh Literary Journal* published an extraordinary sketch. Drawn two years earlier by a colonel of the Madras Army, it showed a turbaned Indian sitting cross-legged in the air with his right hand gently resting on what appears to be a stick. Sheshal, the 'Brahmin of the Air', was a slender man 'of considerable age', who had been demonstrating his feat to locals for years. The unnamed Colonel was allowed to examine the different parts of the apparatus that consisted of a stool, a brass nut supporting a forked stick and a thin bar covered with animal skin on which the hand rested. A blanket was held up while Sheshal prepared for his performance. When the blanket was withdrawn, he sat suspended three feet above the ground, with only his hand resting on the cross bar. 'His countenance showed strong marks of great exertion – large drops of perspiration running down his face with his eyes shut, which clearly showed he was anything but at ease.' Many theories were advanced to account for the feat, but none appeared satisfactory, wrote the Colonel. Although a steel brace could have been concealed within the folds of his clothing, this would have overbalanced the stool beneath him. 'When I saw him it was said that he could eat his meals some fathoms under water and remain in that situation for a great length of time.'[39] Sheshal

The 'Brahmin of the Air', Edinburgh Literary Journal, *1830.*

died in 1830 without revealing the secret of his levitation trick. 'A knowing native', claimed it was achieved by 'holding the breath, clearing the tubular organs, and a peculiar mode of respiration'.[40] The reality was somewhat different. As a writer in the *Saturday Magazine* pointed out a few years later, his bench was ornamented with two inlaid brass stars. 'The brass stars conceal a receptacle for a steel bar passing through the hollow bamboo. The antelope skin conceals another steel rod which is screwed into the one in the bamboo. Other machinery of the same kind passes through the man's sleeves and down his body and supports a ring on which he sits.'[41]

Many people, however, refused to accept that levitation was caused by anything other than supernatural means. In October 1884, the letters pages of the *Madras Mail* lit up with a debate over how a Brahmin suspended himself in mid-air with no support except for a few peacock feathers he held in one hand. A writer identified as 'K', responding to a report by 'Supere Aude', claimed the feat was accomplished by mesmerism – the eyes of the spectators were temporarily glued down using a special ointment normally administered to cure hydrophobia.[42] Shortly afterwards, 'Ghost' wrote in refuting 'K's claims and described a common conjuring trick performed by the jugglers of Malabar that sounded suspiciously like a version of the fabled Rope Trick. The deception began with a letter dropping from the sky containing an urgent appeal from the god Indra for help in a deadly contest with Asuras, or giants, taking place in the heavens. 'A thread is now seen slowly coming down, by means of which the performer ascends like a spider. Immediately sounds of tumult are distinctly heard, and there fall upon the stage, heads, arms, bodies, and legs of murdered giants, together with a large quantity of blood. The performer soon afterwards descends by the same thread, and reports that he has gained a complete victory over the Asuras.' The next day, the shattered limbs turn out to be nothing more than logs of wood and the stems of plantain trees.[43]

The debate over levitation coincided with the English translation of *Occult Science in India* by French barrister and judge, Louis Jacolliot, where he recounts meeting a magician named Covindasamy, who was taught by Brahmins 'in the mysterious caves of the pagoda at Trivanderam'.[44] If we take Jacolliot at his word, Covindasamy's powers were considerable. They included making water in a large brass vessel churn like waves on an ocean and moving pieces of furniture without touching them. After asking him to demonstrate how to make objects float in the air, Covindasamy took hold of the Frenchman's ironwood stick, rested his right hand on the knob, cast his eyes downwards, and began his evocations. Still leaning one hand upon the stick and with his legs crossed, he rose about two feet from the ground. 'For more than twenty minutes I tried to see how Covindasamy could thus fly in the face and eyes of all the known laws of gravity, it was entirely beyond my comprehension,' Jacolliot wrote. 'The stick gave him no visible support, and there was no apparent contact between that and his body, except through his right hand.'[45]

IN the pantheon of India's wonders, the powers of those who could charm dangerous animals and serpents were considered among the most extraordinary. Marco Polo spoke of pearl fishers on the island of Ceylon who paid men to 'charm the great fishes, to prevent them from injuring the divers whilst engaged in seeking pearls under water, one-twentieth part of all that they take'. These men were the 'Abraiaman' (Brahmins) who knew how to 'charm beasts and birds and every living thing'. According to the Venetian, their charm held good for one day only. At night, they dissolved the charm so that the fish could 'work mischief at their will'.[46] In the early nineteenth century, the pearl divers of the Malabar Coast refused to enter the water unless shark conjurers performed the proper ceremonies. 'The manner of enchanting consists in a number of prayers learnt by heart that nobody, probably not even the conjurer himself, understands,' wrote James Johnson, a Royal Navy surgeon. 'Standing on the shore [he] continues muttering and grumbling from sunrise till the boats return in the afternoon during this period. They are obliged to abstain from food and sleep otherwise their prayers would have no avail.' When one of the divers lost a leg to shark attack, the chief conjurer explained that a witch had cast a counter spell before he could stop her. 'He afterwards shewed his superiority by enchanting the poor sharks so effectually that though they appeared in the midst of the divers they were unable to open their mouths.'[47]

Found in every town and city in India were the *sanperas,* or snake charmers, who coaxed menacing cobras and other reptiles from their lairs, made them dance and sold remedies to protect against their deadly bites. The depiction of the sanpera with his *pungi,* or flute, pretending to hypnotize a basket full of deadly serpents, would become a stock image of traveller's accounts. While visiting Bengal in 1771, the Dutch Rear Admiral John Splinter Stavorinus was particularly amazed at the 'curious features' of one of its serpent charmers.

> He brought three baskets with him in which there were several snakes. He took out two of them, both Cobras di Capelli, which are esteemed the most venomous of all, and threw them upon the ground, in the grass. They immediately began hissing, and erecting half of their bodies upright, darted upon, and twined round each other, as often as he encouraged them. They sometimes darted at the bystanders, but then he caught them suddenly by the tail, and drew them back. He sometimes excited them against himself, and suffered them to bite his breast, hands, and forehead, till the blood streamed from the wounds. After having made them play their tricks for some time, he took out of a basket, a very large snake, which was at least twelve or thirteen feet in length, and beautifully variegated with tints of green and yellow; he made it bite him so hard in the breast, that it remained hanging by its teeth, without seeming to do him any harm; he then took a smaller one, put its head into his mouth, and made it seize his tongue, to which it likewise cleaved by the teeth, and throwing them round his neck and arms, was encircled in their folds, without suffering any other inconvenience, than the blood flowing from the wounds, along his face and breast. [48]

Many scholars trace snake-worship back to pre-Aryan serpent cults. The snake was regarded as a demonic being endowed with magical power. In the *Mahabharata* and *Jataka* tales, the Nagas were a race of serpent demi-gods usually depicted as half-human and half-serpentine. They were guardians and distributors of wealth, including objects with magical properties such as a gem that granted all wishes. According to the *Bhuridatta Jataka*, as soon as the gem touched the earth, it disappeared and returned to the snake-world from where it came.[49] Nagas lived in the beautiful underground city of Boghavati. The verses of the *Paushya-parvan* of the *Mahabharata* sing the splendours of this mysterious, carefully guarded snake-world – 'palaces glittering with gold and precious stones, gardens rich in flowering and fruit bearing trees, and, above all, crowds of fair damsels, a world of sensual enjoyment, denied to the common mortal and only to be won by special exertions and acts of piety'.[50]

Snake charmers were endowed with the power of recognizing these serpent treasure guardians and would follow them stealthily to their holes. On being given a drop of blood from the little finger of a first-born son, the snakes would point to where the treasure lay.[51] Legends of snakes guarding treasure are also found in Malabar, where snakes breathe on precious stones, diminishing their size but adding to their power and potency. 'The moment their work is finished they are transformed into winged serpents and fly up into the air with the stones lodged in their mouths. It is not known where these stones are carried to, but it is supposed that they are being taken to some vague and unknown land in the ethereal regions.'[52] Such myths inspired treasure hunters including English artist James Forbes who travelled in India between 1765 and 1784. In his *Oriental Memoirs*, Forbes described how he investigated a mysterious chamber in a ruined tower supposed to contain treasure. Finding a hole in the tower he lowered himself down until he reached the top of what appeared to be a deep dungeon. His servants refused to enter it, saying 'wherever money was concealed, there existed one of the Genii [jinn] in the mortal form of a snake to guard it'. He finally convinced them to descend using a rope. No sooner had they reached the bottom than they cried out that they were being encircled by a large snake. 'No language can express my sensations of astonishment and terror when I saw a horrid monster rear his head over an immense length of body coiled in volumes on the ground and working itself into exertion by a sort of sluggish motion. What I felt on seeing two fellow creatures exposed by my orders to this fiend of vengeful nature I must leave to the reader's imagination,' Forbes wrote. The snake was destroyed by fire, but no treasure was found, 'the owner having doubtless already removed it'.[53]

Sarpa-vidya (serpent-lore) was one of the sciences taught in the later Vedic period together with Brahma vidya (philosophy), Naksattra vidya (astronomy) and Daivajana vidya, the lore of supernatural beings. The fatal action of a serpent's poison was like an all-devouring fire. By his fiery bite, Takshaka, one of the kings of the Nagas, reduced a banyan-tree to ashes and set King Parikshit's pillared hall ablaze. A snake's breath or its sight alone was considered powerful enough to harm or even kill. The periodical casting of its skin was taken as evidence of its longevity or even immortality. In Hindu mythology, Vishnu sleeps in the primeval ocean on the coils of the thousand-headed cobra Ananta. While asleep, a lotus grows from his navel and in its petals is born the god Brahma who creates the world. Vishnu then awakens and reigns supreme in Vaikuntha, the highest heaven. In Puranic tradition, the serpent is the ornament of Shiva. Snakes hang from

'Charmers of Serpents', Penny Magazine, *1833.*

his neck in garlands, they stream out of his hair as he executes the cosmic dance. The breast band of Durga, Shiva's divine female aspect, is a serpent, as is the belt that encircles the ample belly of his son, the elephant-headed god Ganesh. Naturally secreted in the heads of cobras and other serpents are snake-stones that if extracted 'are capable of working as astounding miracles for their owners, as the wonderful lamp did for Aladdin'.[54] So powerful were these gems that if placed on a snakebite they could absorb all the poison present in the victim's body.

The fear, fascination and veneration inspired by India's serpents dates back to antiquity. When crossing from Persia to India, Alexander the Great found the frontier guarded by deadly serpents whose mere glance was fatal. Mirrors were erected so that the snakes would stare themselves to death. His admiral, Nearchus, was struck by 'the multitude and malignity of India's reptiles' and how they entered people's homes during floods. 'The minute size of some and the immense size of others are sources of danger; the former because it is difficult to guard against their attacks, the latter by reason of their strength, for snakes are to be seen of sixteen cubits in length.'[55] By the time of the Raj, they were part of the folklore of Hindustan. *The Natural History of Reptiles and Serpents* published in 1821, includes the story of how a cobra glided unobserved into a sahib's dining room while a large company of guests was seated at the table. The snake entwined itself round the frame of a woman's chair until its head and neck were level with hers. Afraid that if they made the slightest attempt to help, the serpent would 'inflict its bite with a quickness greater than they could prevent', the stunned guests sent for a group of snake charmers. 'After half an hour of suspense, the music was at last heard, but so faint from distance that it was the snake itself which gave the first intimation of its arrival. It suddenly erected its head in the attitude of listening, and gradually, as the sounds became more distinct, uncoiled itself, glided down the frame of the chair and out of the room where the musicians were prepared to seize him.'[56]

Often coming from marginalized nomadic communities, sanperas played an important role in village society. In the 1830s, William Adam, a Baptist missionary based in Murshidabad, found no less than 722 snake-conjurors in a single police sub-division in Nattore. There were few villages without one, he noted, and in some there were as many as ten. 'They profess to cure the bites of poisonous snakes by incantations or charms … [They] take nothing for the performance of their rites or for the cures they pretend to have performed.' Instead of pecuniary rewards, they received various privileges and immunities. '[The conjurer] possesses great influence over the inhabitants. If a quarrel takes place, his interference will quell it sooner than that of any one else, and when he requires the aid of his neighbours in cultivating his plot of ground or in reaping its produce, it is always more readily given to him than to others.'[57]

The sanpera's reptile of choice is the cobra. In Hindu mythology, it appears as Kaliya, the great serpent on whose extended hood Krishna danced and trampled underfoot. By his powers the sanpera would come to be regarded 'as the wisest of mankind, as a wizard, and finally as a priest'.[58] Yet, more myths surround the charmer's skills than any other figure in Indian popular culture. Snakes cannot hear music. Cobras do not need to be tamed. No sanpera would handle a reptile that hadn't been rendered harmless. Among the Kalbelia, a semi-nomadic community in Rajasthan, they are usually caught in the jungle or fields by digging into a likely-looking hole. When a snake is found, a line is drawn around it in the dirt. It is then trapped by placing a stick across the back of its head and pressed to the ground. The Kalbelia breaks the cobra's two poison-transmitting fangs by making it bite on a piece of cloth, which is pulled away from its mouth. The two poison sacs inside the cobra's mouth are finally removed with a sharp piece of horn or a large needle.[59] According to Miriam Robertson, whose 1998 ethnographic survey of the Kalbelias remains the most comprehensive study of a snake-catching community in India, neither swallowing the poison sac nor enduring a snake bite in increasing doses, brings about immunity. The length of time a cobra is kept in captivity is quite short as it becomes lazy when confined to a basket. 'A cobra in a basket is like a prisoner. After it has done its time then it should be freed,' a snake-charmer named Bhadra Nath, told Robertson. Nor is any special training required, she writes. 'The snake charmer exploits only the cobra's natural responses, and once its poison is removed there is no danger to the public or to the Kalbelia who takes it to a hotel or round the streets.'[60]

Sanperas are also called on to capture snakes infesting homes. Incidents of jugglers secretly placing a tame snake in a hole, coaxing it out and claiming their reward were common. 'These jugglers frequently contrive to impose upon the superstitious Hindoos by persuading them that their houses are infested with snakes. In order to make this appear, they place one or two of their tame ones in some of the crevices of the building,' noted a writer in the *Saturday Magazine*. 'They then enter the house with all the assumed wisdom of the ancient Sages, begin to pipe such music as would scare any other creature but a snake into the deepest recesses of its retreat, and when the reptile appears they snatch it up, put it immediately into its wicker prison and thus the enchantment ends. These pretended enchanters will sometimes go into every house in a village and practise the same.' [61]

Similar ploys are used by dealers in magical spells known as Mantravadis in southern India. In cases of snake-bite, they wave a cock over the patient's body from the head towards the feet while reciting mantras. The snake charmers belonging to the Dommara tribe put a black stone composed of various drugs over the bite to absorb the poison. Writing in the early 1900s,

Edgar Thurston in *Omens and Superstitions of Southern India* described another much riskier cure. 'As soon as a person has been bitten, a snake charmer is sent for, who allures the same or another cobra whose fangs have not been drawn to the vicinity of the victim, and causes it to bite him at as nearly as possible the same place as before. Should this be fulfilled, the bitten man will as surely recover as the snake will die.'[62] Thurston gives no evidence of the efficacy of the cure. The British surgeon Edward Balfour noted that in 1861, there were 18,670 deaths from snake bites. A century-and-a-half later, the number was closer to 46,000 according to the American Society of Tropical Medicine and Hygiene, giving India the unenviable record of accounting for nearly half of the 1,00,000 snakebite deaths globally.

EIGHT

CROSSING THE *KALA PANI*

ON a sultry Madras evening in 1797, an East India Company officer on his first visit to India, watched as one of the garrison town's famed jugglers prepared for his performance. Dressed in a dhoti and seated on the bare earth, the juggler opened a small phial of oil and rubbed some of it over the surface of a twenty-inch long sword. Throwing his head back, he held the implement in both hands and carefully inserted it into his mouth until only the handle was visible. He then motioned to the surgeon to feel the point of the sword between his breast and navel, bending a little more backwards to

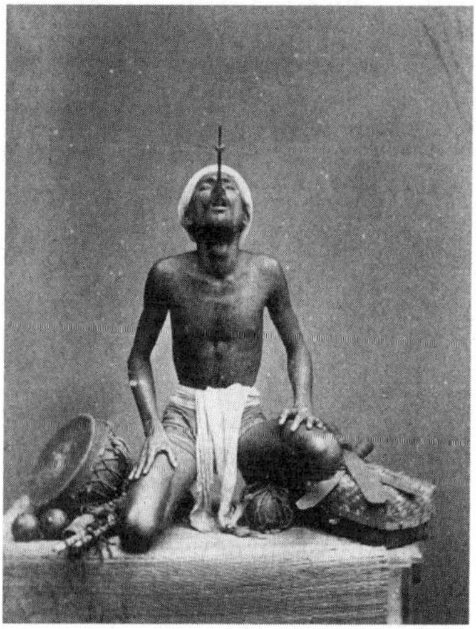

Sword swallower, Madras, Nicholas and Curths, 1870. British Library.

make it easier to locate. The officer asked that the feat be repeated and satisfied beyond all doubt as to its authenticity, made the juggler a proposal. If he went with him to Europe, he would give him 'one thousand *pagodas* on the spot, a like sum on his arrival in England, with the expenses there and all other advantages'. A tenth of that amount would have represented a fortune and guaranteed a comfortable life for the man and his family. But to the officer's disappointment, the juggler refused. He was a Hindu and crossing the *kala pani*, the black sea, was taboo as it would contaminate his soul.[1]

'The whole tribe of sleight-of-hand men in Europe are mere bunglers, when compared with the Jugglers of India,' the writer who witnessed the encounter with the sword swallower declared. 'Their deceptions are so admirably executed, and some of their performances of such a strange nature, that the ignorant and superstitious natives, believing as they do all the enchantments described in such books as *The Arabian Nights Entertainments*, may well ascribe them necromantic powers.'[2]

Jadoowallahs could be found all over the subcontinent, but none rivalled those of the Coromandel Coast. 'The Madras jugglers perform nearly all our legerdemain tricks. They moreover astonish Europeans by swallowing swords; leaping through hot irons and pointed instruments; poising men on long poles, resting on their breasts, chins and noses; tumbling and vaulting on the tight rope; swinging and balancing on the slack rope so that many of them would excite surprise even after the wonders and deceptions of London and Paris,' Robert Grenville Wallace wrote in his 1825 memoir *Forty Years in the World; or, Sketches and Tales of a Soldier's Life*. They excelled as storytellers, buffoons and harlequins, he continued. 'Monsieur Alexandre could scarcely transform himself faster than the heroes of a Hindoo pantomime. They enter in all manner of shapes as tigers, lions, bears, buffaloes, wolves; as gods with monstrous heads of elephants, monkeys, fishes and all the astonishing variety in Hindoo mythology; as old women, old men, lovers, warriors, European drunken sailors &c.'[3] Another early traveller to Madras described the lithe and supple bodies of jugglers as resembling those of serpents rather than men. 'In rope dancing they are not to be outdone by any of the wonders of Sadler's Wells.'[4] Their feats were 'beyond the reach of human power', the region's Catholic missionaries proclaimed, and were proof, if any were needed of their dealings with the devil.[5]

For European passengers arriving at Madras after a long voyage from England, their first face-to-face encounter with Indians occurred even before they set foot on dry land. Scrambling aboard the East Indiaman as it dropped anchor off the coast, were dhobis, cooks and bearers peddling their references, porters, boarding house keepers and nearly naked jugglers with their cups and balls, swords, ropes and cobra-filled baskets. The surgeon James Johnson, who landed in Madras in April 1805, was so impressed by the sword swallower who entertained the passengers on his ship, he invited him to repeat the performance at his bungalow. 'For that purpose [I] ordered him to seat himself on the floor of the verandah and having satisfied myself with respect to the sword by attempting to bend it and by striking it against a stone, I firmly grasped it by the handle and ordered him to proceed.' The juggler's sword resembled a common spit. It was about twenty-six inches long, one-inch wide and a fifth-of-an-inch thick, with a blunt point and edges. After coating the sword with oil, the juggler 'stretched up his neck as much as possible and bending himself backwards he introduced the point of it into his mouth and pushed it gently down his throat until my hand which was on the handle came in contact with his lips.' When Johnson let go of the handle the juggler fixed on it 'a little machine that spun round and disengaged a small firework which encircling his head with a blue flame gave him as he sat a truly diabolical appearance'. When the juggler withdrew the sword, Johnson could see specks of blood on the blade 'which shewed that he was still obliged to use a degree of violence in the introduction'.[6]

Though it seemed improbable, Johnson used his medical training to conclude there was nothing *impossible* about the feat. The flexibility of their joints, the laxness of their fibres and their temperate lifestyles, he surmised, rendered the Madrasis impervious to pain and physical punishment. For a tip, the juggler revealed how he had practiced putting small elastic instruments down his throat and into his stomach since he was a child. Over the years, the instruments became larger until he was able to swallow an entire sword. 'There is, therefore, no great wonder if by long habit and stretching up their necks, they are able to bring the different windings of the passage from the mouth to the stomach into a straight line, or nearly so, and thereby slide down the sword into the latter organ without much difficulty,' Johnson concluded.[7]

With the vast majority of the English public unable to share experiences such as Johnson's first hand, it was only a matter of time before an entrepreneurial employee of the East India Company, recognized the vast profits to be made from bringing Indian magicians to England. In 1812, Peter Campbell, captain of

Her Majesty's ship *Lord Keith*, succeeded where the ship's surgeon had failed fifteen years earlier. While on a visit to Government House in Calcutta, Campbell witnessed a performance by a troupe of South Indian jugglers. On a whim, he offered them a passage to England. Although the terms of the contract were said to be 'very much … to the gallant captain's advantage', they agreed to break the taboos of caste and cross the *kala pani*.[8]

IN early July 1813, playbills started circulating in London advertising the appearance of a troupe of 'Indian jugglers'. The headline act was 'Swallowing a Sword'. This, the handbill promised, was just one of a 'great variety' of tricks, all of them 'perfectly novel in this Country' and guaranteed to 'strike every beholder with astonishment'.[9] For a ship's captain, Campbell had

The first portrait of the Indian jugglers performing at Pall Mall, The Satirist, *1813.*

a knack for garnering the maximum amount of publicity for his unusual and very productive cargo. Before allowing the public to see the jugglers, he arranged a show for the Prince Regent and members of Parliament at Carlton House. By displaying them before the establishment he was not only underlining their exoticism, he was also presenting them as respectable alternative to the 'carnival jugglers' who frequented popular fairgrounds. To see Campbell's company was to get a never-before possible, first-hand glimpse into the mysterious core of Indian culture.

Campbell leased a commodious room at No.37 Pall Mall where the troupe performed four times a day. Tickets cost three shillings each. Within a few weeks of their arrival they were attracting sell-out crowds. 'Their house in Piccadilly is beset from morning to night with carriages of the Nobility and Gentry; and it is supposed they do not take less than 150/- per day,' one newspaper reported.[10] According to the *Times,* 'nearly all the families of distinction' in London had visited their venue. 'The swallowing of the sword, and the novelty of other performances, has attracted the public's attention beyond anything that has appeared in the metropolis for many years past,' the newspaper added.[11] Their popularity was seen as a reflection of the sophistication and cosmopolitanism of British audiences. 'Perhaps there is no other country in the world where every species of curious novelty meets with such certain encouragement as in England. Whatever be the pretensions, whether scientific, athletic, active or droll; sure, are all adventurers to prefer pitching their tents on British soil,' a leading intellectual journal enthused after describing the troupe's performance.[12] Rumours circulating that Campbell paid up to £10,000 to engage the jugglers and that their skills were the far superior to their English counterparts 'whether with cups and balls, or other tricks of legerdemain', only served to enhance their appeal.

In August 1813, *The Satirist* published a detailed account of the troupe's performance, accompanied by a drawing showing two Indians and their assistant seated on a raised platform, wearing striped pants, white blouses and turbans. The main juggler is twirling rings on the ends of his toes while balancing what looks like a parasol on his nose. The second performer is about to swallow a sword, while the assistant is playing a small drum. Although *The Satirist's* review was peppered with snide references to the frequency with which East India Company directors resorted to misdirection, and how the miracles of missionaries paled when compared with the feats of the 'sons of the Ganges', it nevertheless provides the first comprehensive description of Indian magic being performed on stage in Europe.

The performance began with the cups and balls trick, which though similar to that performed by European conjurers, was executed with superior skill. 'The cups seem enchanted; the balls fly; they increase in number; they diminish; now one, now two, now three, now none under the cup: and now the serpent, the cobra de cappella, usurps the place of a small globule of cork, and winds its snaky folds as if from under the puny vessel.' A length of cotton was broken into tiny pieces and made whole again. Sand changed colour when rubbed between the performer's fingers. Four brass balls the size of oranges flew into the air. 'His power over these is almost miraculous,' *The Satirist's* reviewer remarked. 'He causes them to describe every possible circle: horizontally, perpendicularly, obliquely, transversely, round his legs, under his arms, about his head, in small and in large circumferences, with wondrous rapidity and keeping the whole number in motion at the same time.'[13]

Next, the chief juggler placed two four-inch wide rings on his toes and two on his forefingers and rotated them simultaneously 'as if set to work by machinery endowed with the principle of perpetual motion'. Twirling the rings around his toes, he threw himself backwards while balancing a sword on his forehead. A small wooden parasol from which hung a dozen cork tassels was then balanced on his nose. Using his mouth, he inserted into each tassel a twelve-inch quill and then placed them on his tongue. Out came the centre stick from the tip of his nose, leaving the parasol poised on the quills. One at a time they were taken away until only three remained. 'Of these he takes one away, and the top which resembles the roof of a pagoda, swings down and hangs by two, the Indian preserving the astonishing balance even in this motion, which might be deemed sufficient to disconcert any human ingenuity; but even then, he does not stop; the last prop but one is removed, and on that one the erect balance of the machine rests.'[14] Several other tricks followed, including tossing a fourteen-pound ball the size and shape of a Dutch cheese around the juggler's body as if it was weightless, before concluding with a demonstration of sword swallowing.

In September, Campbell took the troupe to Liverpool, then Scotland and Ireland. But his monopoly on presenting Indian magic was short-lived. On 1 August 1815, an advertisement appeared in *The Morning Chronicle* inviting the public to see the 'Wonderful Indian Jugglers Just Arrived from Seringapatam, Far Superior to any before Exhibited in England,' at a venue on

Bond Street. According to a pamphlet printed shortly after their arrival, the troupe consisted of four performers. The entertainment began with one of the jugglers taking a small black ball, holding it between his finger and thumb, and without otherwise touching it, changing its colour instantaneously. The ball 'afterwards assumes the appearance of a fine set of teeth or whatever his fancy might suggest'. The remainder of the repertoire was broadly similar to Campbell's ensemble, aside from a trick where a steel hook was passed through one of the juggler's nostrils and into his mouth. A string was then looped through the eye of the hook, from which a stone weighing twenty pounds was suspended. This was swung to and fro before being 'thrown off at some distance, without the string being either cut or broken'. The swallowing of a twenty-inch sword 'with as much ease as though it were being sheathed in a scabbard' concluded the entertainment.[15]

The identity of the entrepreneur who tried to capitalize on the success of Campbell's troupe is unclear. Nor is there any certainty about where its members were from. Seringapatam was a name still seared in the minds of the English public as the city where the British executed their decisive victory over the ruler of Mysore Tipu Sultan in 1799. Tipu's defeat delivered them control over much of southern India and thwarted France's hope of gaining a permanent foothold in the region. Though the troupe may have come from Seringapatam, it is more likely they were recruited in Madras, where there were ample opportunities to be noticed by Europeans. The names of the jugglers in the second party is also uncertain. Playbills, newspaper advertisements and reviews began mentioning individuals by name only after they started performing in their own right.

Anecdotal evidence suggests that the chief juggler in Campbell's troupe was a man known as Ramo Samee. In 1809, the sports writer and fox hunter, Frederick Peter Delme Radcliffe saw the juggler, whose name was probably a corruption of Ramaswamy, and two others from Madras, performing at Government House in Colombo and at his father's residence. After 'reaping a tolerably good harvest' from their performances, they sailed to Calcutta where they were seen by Campbell. Delme Radcliffe's recollection is contained in an article he wrote for *The Sportsman* in 1842 and is probably out by a year or two, but it roughly tallies with other accounts.[16]

What is certain is that Samee would become a household name and a highly successful performer who toured all over England, the east coast of America and Europe, appearing on stage both on his own or as part of variety performances. Though other Indian jugglers who were brought from India in the 1810s achieved considerable popularity, it was Samee whose name became synonymous with all forms of jugglery, whether on the theatrical or political stage. Now largely forgotten in the land of his birth, he was the most famous Indian magician of the nineteenth century and his legacy would have a profound impact on the evolution of magic in the West.

In July 1819, Samee parted ways with Campbell and the other members of his troupe and sailed to Boston arriving in September of the same year. He spent the next six months touring New England, being lauded for his displays of 'dexterity of hand, quickness of eye, muscular activity and perfection in the art of balancing'.[17] The tour, however, almost ended in disaster. In March 1820, while performing in Concord, Massachusetts, a thief cut through Samee's trunk and stole his earnings of $1720 (around $40,000 in today's currency) and his costumes. Donning the juggler's clothes made the crook easily recognizable. He was apprehended while escaping by coach to New York and Samee's money was returned.

Samee was not the first Indian magician to travel to America. On 5 November 1817, the *Moses Brown* berthed in New York after a four-week voyage from Liverpool. On board the square rigger was Sena Sama, who billed himself as 'the superior East Indian juggler'. Within two weeks of arriving, he grabbed the headlines by staging America's first sword-swallowing act using a blade manufactured by the New York locksmith William Pye 'as a substitute for the one lately stolen from him by some villain'.[18] Despite the initial publicity, Sama had little idea of how to break into the American entertainment circuit, which in the words of one writer for the *Republican Chronicle*, was dominated by '*blow-puffs* and *wind-bladders*'. His shows were poorly attended, and he lacked the experience and the resources to generate publicity. The *Chronicle's* writer, who followed Sama's career in America, noted that although he had 'astonished the princes, nobles and literati of enlightened Britain ... he had yet to learn that in this country, a bladder of wind outweighs a globe of gold'.[19]

After a disappointing season in New York, Sama travelled to Washington and Philadelphia with an expanded repertoire. Audiences in Philadelphia were promised a set of seemingly impossible feats: 'He will balance an artificial tree on his forehead, on the boughs of which are placed eleven birds – and with a tube and balls he will shoot them off with his breath. ... He will balance the skeleton of a Chinese Castle on his nose and complete the building without any other aid than his mouth.'[20] The makeover, coupled with word-of-mouth endorsements, seemed to work. 'Rumour caught a whisper of his wonderful talents' and the public realized they 'had a treasure among them', the *Chronicle* noted. 'His houses are now filled to overflowing – beauty, taste and fashion, flock to his exhibition, and the "white turban'd East Indian" *is all the go*.'[21]

From Philadelphia, Sama travelled south, arriving in Richmond Virginia in the early spring of 1818. There he caught the eye of the portrait painter James Warrell. Born in England, Warrell arrived in America in 1793 with his English parents to join a Philadelphia-based theatrical company. He appeared in numerous shows until 1799, when a leg injury forced him to give up acting and turn to painting instead. Warrell's interest in theatre would have attracted him to the Indian juggler. His portrait, which hangs in the Valentine Museum in Virginia, shows Sama wearing a white turban and blouse, red waistcoat and blue shawl. With his thin moustache that curls around his full lips and shoulder length hair, he resembles a prince rather than a performer.

As in England, the American public's positive response to Indian juggling prompted the arrival of other troupes. In January 1818, a ship carrying 'four Bengalese jugglers – and an elephant' berthed in New York. Advertisements promised a performance of 'various and singular feats, as is usual before their Highnesses, the Rajahs of the East, on their Poojahs, or days of festivity'.[22] The group included Sheiek Withershaw with his 'Herculean powers', Sheiek Cheughie who displayed his 'Wonderful Flexibility in the Exercise of Swords', and Sheiek Khallumbhue who lifted 'fifty pounds weight solely with his eyes'.[23] They were followed by a company of Indians known as the 'Mussulmen and the Hindoos', that appeared in Boston in 1820.[24]

When Ramo Samee returned to England in late 1820, he found the entertainment scene had changed significantly even in his short absence. Dwindling receipts at the box office meant magicians were adopting a more narrative form, adding stories or musical scores to sleight of hand. Theatrical managers found variety acts that combined magic with melodramas, comedies, tragedies, music and even fireworks more profitable. Actors engaged at theatres such as the Olympic in London had to sign contracts binding them to playing on demand any of the following genres: 'Burlettas, Melo-Drames, Afterpieces, Chorusses, Masks, Ballets, Preludes, Interludes, Processions, Spectacles, Pantomimes, Dances and other Performances.' [25] Samee's set pieces rarely had any relation to other acts on the same programme. This occasionally jarred with audiences. On 4 June 1821, he appeared in Bristol sandwiched between the melodrama *Where to Find a Friend* and the burlesque rendition of *Theresa Tomkins*. While the *Bristol Mirror's* reviewer acknowledged Samee to be 'a very extraordinary personage [who] would no doubt rank very high among the itinerant gymnasia of a fair or a revel', what worked for the 'motley' London public was not always suited to the fastidious tastes of country audiences. 'With regard to Ramo Samee's "deceptions", we cannot say that "the doubleness of the benefit defends the deceit from reproof" for the House this evening was miserably attended.'[26]

Samee also found himself competing with another juggler named Khia Khan Khruse. Although he called himself 'The Chief of the Indian Jugglers', Khruse was a Portuguese spell-caster from Lisbon whose real name was Louis Antonio. Within a few years of arriving in England in November 1815, he was making extravagant claims about learning magic in the caves of Salamanca and performing before the royal families of England and Europe 'who were pleased to express their wonderful approbation'. He boasted of his extraordinary physical strength by having 'an immense stone of 1200 weight, broken in pieces on his breast with sledgehammers, with perfect ease to himself, and without deception'.[27] A playbill from 1818 for his *Protean Transformations* show, promised 'Serpentine Posturing' and other contortions. 'He will run on his hands with his foot in his mouth; and will also run on thirty tumbler glasses.' His act included 'juggling with swords, rings, knives, chairs, money etc', as well as catching a marked bullet in his hand. Another segment of his performance saw him turn a small ball into a toad, barley into wheat and a coin into a horseshoe. 'In another instance, he will show his superiority by Performing Blindfold; making Cards march from the Pack, one by one, on the Floor of the Room,' his playbill stated. He will lift a bottle of water by a straw, make a Half a Crown pass from one Cup to another, at ten yards distance'.[28] Khruse later added a sophisticated automaton to his show in the form of 'A New Grotesque Indian Dance by Three Figures', mysteriously operated by him.[29] For all the hype, Khruse's career was short-lived. On 23 July 1822, he was declared an 'insolvent debtor' at Westminster Court.[30]

Around the same time as Khruse's conjuring career was terminated, a real Indian juggler found himself on the wrong side of the law. Mooty Samme was making his way from Poland to Russia when he was arrested under suspicion of being a spy. His unconventional garb probably caught the eye of the Russian border guards, who seized his papers and sent them to Vilnius to be deciphered. Written in Tamil and unable to be translated in Vilnius, the papers were sent to St Petersburg, where they finally reached the desk of Richard Knill of the London Missionary Society, who, fortunately, had spent three years in Travancore. 'It is very probable that I was the only person in the Russian empire who could speak the Tamul [sic] language, and but for my knowledge of it, the poor Indian juggler might have been in prison until this day,' Knill later reminisced.[31] The cryptic papers that aroused so much suspicion turned out to be bank records, an itinerary and an account of costs for lighting, hiring venues, food and other performance-related expenses. A lithograph from Prague printed in 1820, shows Mooty and his brother Medua performing with Chinese devil sticks. Their German playbills list an almost identical repertoire to that of the first troupes of jugglers who arrived in Britain.[32] It is possible the pair were even related to Ramo Samee and left for Europe at the same time he went to America. A review of their appearance in the German daily *Morgenblatt* pokes fun at their 'whimsical gibberish', which even 'the most learned Brahmins would find hard to decipher'.[33] Mooty was last heard of living in Stockholm where he had converted to Christianity, changed his name to Frans and married a Swedish woman.

In March 1822, an etching was published showing Samee about to juggle several balls in the air at the Royal Coburg Theatre. His figure is dwarfed by the sumptuous interior. The venue's 'looking glass curtain' acts as a kind of mirror reflecting the overflowing galleries and stalls, making the interior seem circular. He had been performing at London's most popular theatre since November 1821 in variety shows featuring melodramas such as *El Hyder*, the *Palace of Mystery*, the *Fortress of Pressburg* and *The Two Bears,* the latter billed as 'a laughable farcical Burletta'. Contemporary writers described him as good looking, with an excellent command of English, evoking laughter from the audience as he joked about having to swallow his sword for supper when he preferred eating 'mutton chop', and that the stone he was digesting was indeed a stone and not a 'mosh potato'.[34] 'His dexterity has not been diminished by practice, and he never created more astonishment, or afforded more gratification, than was evinced by those who witnessed his labours yesterday,' declared a review of one of his Royal Coburg performances in August 1822.[35]

Samee continued performing throughout the 1820s and 1830s, his playbills presenting him as the 'original', the 'celebrated' and only 'true Indian juggler' – an artist who appealed to the 'Nobility, the Gentry and the Public'. That Samee's popularity cut across class lines is evident from the range of venues he appeared at. When not playing at popular theatres such as Coburg, the Adelphi and the Olympic, he could be found at the more gentrified Vauxhall Gardens where he performed alongside the greatest magicians, ventriloquists, acrobats, stilt dancers and tight rope-walkers of the era. Attending one of these shows was

Ramo Samee at the Royal Coburg Theatre, 1822. Library of Congress.

the English radical and journalist William Edwin Adams, who described how as a young boy he was plucked out of the audience by Samee's stage assistant to partake in an egg-swallowing act. The juggler threw the egg in the air, caught it as it descended then clapped his hand over Adams's wide-open mouth before shouting in a broad Irish accent: 'Did ye swallow it?' As Adams recalled later: 'Fearing that unutterable things would befall me if I did not give the answer he required, I stuttered out, "Y-e-e-s."' The feat was received with thunderous applause. More applause followed when Samee, fiddling about his nervous assistant's ear, 'feigned to extract from it, not only the egg, but yards and yards of coloured ribbon'.[36]

With his shows in strong demand, he was reputedly earning between £25 and £30 a week, whereas a normal juggler was lucky to bring in £1 a week.[37] He was also able to afford a domestic servant to help his English wife, Ellen, look after his two daughters and a son. In 1833, he appeared in Hull alongside 'a real Mermaid and Merman caught Alive by a Scotch Fisherman, near the Isle of Sandy, one of the Orkney Islands'. Sharing the same bill as these freaks of nature – said to be three feet in length, with curly hair, large fish-like scales, gills and fins – was 'the Grand Caberet of Performing Lilliputians' and 'The Italian Scaramouch, Grimaldi, the noted Clown'.[38] A benefit concert for the Asylum for the Aged and Decayed Freemasons at London's Royal Pavilion Theatre in October 1835 featured one of Samee's daughters, 'a pupil of Mademoiselle Leoni', doing a Scotch Dance.[39] In August 1841, he performed at Vauxhall Gardens, juggling balls and swallowing swords between 'Mr Green's Last Ascent But One in the Nassau Balloon' and an orchestral concert featuring the overture to Rossini's *Barber of Seville*.[40]

By the 1840s, Samee's deteriorating health was affecting his ability to perform, and he was sliding into debt. In early 1849, his son died from internal injuries after attempting the sword-swallowing trick. The tragedy came as shock to Samee, triggering a further deterioration in his health. In early August 1850, he accepted an offer for a season in Paris, but was taken ill and returned to London where he died on 21st August. A few days later *Bell's Life in London* launched an appeal for donations for his funeral and for the maintenance of Ellen and her two daughters. 'There are thousands who have witnessed his performances who would now, I am sure, kindly give a trifle to assist in procuring him a coffin, which we are unable to do,' Ellen wrote in a letter to the newspaper. Her husband's death left the family 'without the slightest mean of procuring him a burial, our all being expended for his illness, and he from the nature of his performances being inadmissible to any theatrical club'.[41] But the donations were slow in coming. By 1st September, the day of his funeral and burial at St Pancras Churchyard, the newspaper had received £1 from William Cooke of the Circus Royal, ten shillings a well-wisher collected from friends in High Holburn, five shillings from 'Two Jews', two shillings and six pence from 'a Bird', one shilling from 'a Bishop', and a 'trifle' from passing the hat around the editorial office. 'Surely the managers of theatres and other establishments, who have derived so much advantage from the talents of the deceased, ought to contribute to lift his widow, a most respectable woman from the severe grip of poverty,' the newspaper's editor pleaded.[42] But his entreaties fell on deaf ears. In 1871, it was reported that Ellen and her and daughters had been reduced to 'a state of complete destitution'.[43]

SAMEE may have been disowned in death by his peers, but his skills and those of other Indian wonder-workers who came to England in the 1810s and onwards, would ensure that the juggler became 'one of the greatest sights of India … almost a trademark of Hindustan'.[44] That legacy extended into the scientific and literary realms. In 1817, three 'nearly nude' Indian jugglers were seen performing yogic feats on stage at the Royal Academy as part of a lecture series on the human anatomy by the scientist Sir Anthony Carlisle. On another occasion, Carlisle, known for his curled and powdered bagwig, cocked hat and lace ruffles that extended to his wrists, introduced eight naked life-guardsmen doing sword exercises so audiences could analyse their musculature. Though hugely popular with the public, such displays were considered highly inappropriate by some. Referring to the Indians, a writer in the *Review and Register of the Fine Arts* complained: 'The only plausible pretext for their introduction is for the purpose of demonstrating the almost unbounded flexibility of the human figure. Until it be proved desirable to represent the form of man in these uncouth attitudes, it is useless to submit them to the inspection of the student.'[45] The writer of a letter to *The Satirist* concurred. 'What could be gathered in the path of science from seeing a black mummer whirl half a dozen of brass knobs round his cranium or project a pebble from his nape to his wrist?' asked the writer. 'Nothing, aside from illustrations of foppery, folly and quackery.' [46] A year later Carlisle's colleague, William Hazlitt, made Samee's compatriots the theme of his groundbreaking commentary on popular entertainment culture. Although Hazlitt ultimately concluded that feats of manual dexterity could never match those of fine art, he described the jugglers' skills as 'something next to miraculous . . . the utmost stretch of human ingenuity'. But his admiration was mixed with shame: 'I ask what is there that I can do as well as this? Nothing. What have I been doing all my life?'[47]

Samee's juggling feats became so well known that cartoonists used him to caricature politicians. In 1834 *Figaro in London* depicted the liberal leader in the House of Commons, Lord Brougham, wearing a turban and using a pea-shooter to take down the government ministers he had demoted. The accompanying text stated that Brougham was the 'Ramo Samee of the Ministry' whose chief trick was 'keeping balls in the air'. During a debate over protectionism versus free trade in 1852, the Tory MP Ralph Bernal Osborne accused Benjamin Disraeli of being a 'great conjurer' unequalled since the days of Samee – 'an Indian gentleman who only swallowed swords, while the Chancellor of the Exchequer had swallowed three amendments in one night'.[48] William Makepeace Thackeray used the Indian's sword swallowing to poke fun at a woman's poor table manners his 1848 novel, *The Book of Snobs*: 'I have seen, I say, the Hereditary Princess of Potztausend-Donnerwetter (that serenely-beautiful woman) use her knife in lieu of a fork or spoon; I have seen her almost swallow it, by Jove! like Ramo Samee, the Indian juggler. And did I blench? Did my estimation for the Princess diminish? No, lovely Amalia!'[49]

Nowhere was the figure of the Indian mystifier used to greater effect than in Wilkie Collins' quasi-detective novel *The Moonstone*. Published in 1868, the novel introduced three 'mahogany coloured' jugglers with 'the patience of cats (and) ... the ferocity of tigers'.[50] They are Brahmins in disguise who appear on the Yorkshire Moors on a sacred mission to reclaim the Moonstone. The priceless yellow diamond was stolen by a British solider named John Herncastle from the forehead of a 'Hindoo' idol in a temple in Seringapatam following the defeat of Tipu Sultan in 1799. The novel is set in 1848 when Indian strolling players 'infest the streets' attempting to enter houses on the 'pretence of charity'.[51] When Herncastle returns to England he becomes addicted to opium and dies leaving the diamond to his niece Rachel Verinder. The Brahmins give a magic performance at Rachel's eighteenth birthday party where she wears the jewel for the first time. But that night the diamond vanishes, as do the Brahmins. Suspicion falls on the 'snaky' Indians, but the thief turns out to be an Englishman named Godfrey Ablewhite. In a final twist to the plot, Ablewhite, disguised as an Indian, goes to the bank where he has pawned the diamond only to be murdered by the Brahmins who take the stone back to Somnath in Gujarat.

The Indian magician is also the central figure in G. A. Henty's mutiny romance, *Rujub the Juggler* (1893). Rujub is indebted to Ralph Bathurst, the British administrator, for saving his daughter, Rabda, from a tiger. Afterwards he comes to his bungalow to demonstrate some of his tricks. 'With us there are two sorts of feats,' Rujub explains.

> There are those that are performed by sleight of hand or by means of assistance. These are the juggler's tricks we show in the verandas and compounds of the white sahibs, and in the streets of the cities. There are others that are known only to the higher order among us that we show only on rare occasions. They have

> come to us from the oldest times, and it is said they were brought by wise men from Egypt; but that I know not.[52]

Sprinkling some powder onto a dish of glowing charcoal, Rujub creates a cloud of white smoke and explains that he will now show a scene from the past. As the smoke grows brighter, flashes of colour turn into the scarlet uniforms of advancing soldiers that Bathurst recognises as the battle of Chillianwalla.[53] The next scene is of the future and reveals a group of Europeans being besieged by sepoys. Bathurst cannot believe that sepoys would rise against their masters, but Rujub assures him that the 'pictures never lie'.[54] When the mutiny erupts, Bathurst's lover, the beautiful Isobel Hannay, is captured and imprisoned in the zenana of the treacherous Nana Sahib who has thrown in his lot with the mutineers. Rujub helps her escape with the aid of some magic philtres smuggled in by Rabda, thereby repaying his debt to Bathurst.

❖

The public's exposure to Indian jugglery prompted a greater interest in magic from the East as numerous Westerners tried to emulate Samee's skills and mystique. Highly stylized and in some cases imaginary tricks, exotic sets and Oriental-style costumes were introduced into performances. This often resulted in a confusing amalgam as in the case of an unarmed 'English-Chinese juggler' whose repertoire, according to a handbill dated 1823, consisted of Indian tricks in the style of Ramo Samee including 'swallowing an Egg, a Stone and a Sword'.[55] The first evidence of Western magicians mimicking their newly arrived Eastern counterparts came in May 1817 when the *Chester Chronicle* announced that a 'young English Juggler' would exhibit his 'unequalled experiments, after the manner of the Indian Juggler'.[56] In August of the following year Louis Comte, a French magician and ventriloquist credited with inventing the trick of pulling a rabbit out of a hat, performed at the Opera House in London accompanied by an assistant who executed juggling tricks while dressed 'in imitation of a Hindoo'. According to reviews of the show, Comte's young 'uncommonly lively' assistant not only imitated but also improved on several Indian deceptions. One of the 'improvements' was the Frenchman's ability to swallow a sword and dance around the stage with the handle extending from his mouth.[57] His juggling was also judged to be superior. 'There is scarcely a figure in mathematics, from the square to the circle, that he did not make them describe, and that with a velocity which the eye could not follow.'[58]

On the other side of the Atlantic an American juggler, gymnast and tumbler named Master Henderson, who performed in the mid-1820s, promised 'wonderful imitations of the celebrated Indian juggler Ramo Samee with a number of BRASS BALLS causing them to describe every possible Circle – horizontal, perpendicular, oval, elliptic &c. &c, with wonderful velocity'.[59] The magician, ventriloquist, juggler and bird handler, Signor Blitz, who was English but found it more profitable to pretend he was from Moravia, included in one of his shows a mechanical Indian juggler who exhibited some 'very laughable acts'. He also for a brief time performed Khruse's bullet catching trick before abandoning it because it was too dangerous.[60]

Writing around the time of Samee's death in 1850, Henry Mayhew, the great nineteenth-century chronicler of London's working classes, interviewed a man who was reputed to be one of the cleverest 'street jugglers' in England. The nameless performer told Mayhew how he began playing as a tumbler, but his life changed after seeing Samee. 'One night I went to the theatre and there I see Ramo Samee doing his juggling, and in a minute, I forgot all about the tumbling, and only wanted to do as he did.'[61] Mayhew's London-born showman soon learned to do all of Samee's tricks and adopted his Indian persona. 'I used to have a bag and bit of carpet, and perform in streets. I had an Indian's dress made, with a long horse-hair tail down my back, and white bag-trousers, trimmed with red, like a Turk's, tied right round at the ankles, and a flesh-coloured skull-cap. My coat was what is called a Turkish fly, in red velvet, cut off like a waist-coat, with a peak before and behind.'[62]

His Indian-themed show proved lucrative. 'I used to perform in the barracks twice a day, morning and evening. I used to make a heap of money. I have taken, in one pitch, more than a pound.' He became so dexterous that when travelling Samee often 'paid him ten shillings not to perform in the same town with him'.[63] As he gained confidence as a juggler, he began devising his own tricks. 'I also do what is called "the birds and bush", which is something of the same, only you knock off the birds with a pea-shooter. The birds are only made of cork, but it's very difficult, because you have to take your balance again as every bird falls; besides, you must be careful the birds don't fall in your eyes, or it would take away your sight and spoil the balance. The birds at the back are hardest to knock off, because you have to bend back, and at the same time mind you don't topple the tree off.' By the time Mayhew interviewed the juggler he was past his prime. He complained he was 'too old … to go out regularly in the streets', but was still earning a respectable income performing at the Temple of Mystery in Old Street Road, where he was billed as 'The Renowned Indian Juggler, performing his extraordinary Feats with Cups, Balls, Daggers, Plates, Knives, Rings, Balancing, etc. etc.'[64]

The story of Mayhew's juggler highlights the ambiguity and confusion over what was authentically Indian. The 'long horse-hair tail' he wore was closer to the style adopted by Chinese conjurors. The white baggy pants trimmed in red and the red velvet waistcoat were, as the juggler himself admits, of Turkish origin. The juggler's repertoire also reveals a blend of European, Indian and Chinese magic. 'I had a drain and pipes, and I used to play them myself. I played any time, anything, just what I could think of, to draw the crowd together; then I'd mount the stilts and do what I called "a drunken frolic," with a bottle in my hand tumbling about and pretending to be drunk. Then I'd chuck the balls about, and the knives, and the rings, and twirl the plate. I wound up with the ball, throwing it in the air and catching it in a cup.'[65] The trick of 'catching a ball in a cup' was something he first saw performed by a juggler in Samee's troupe. The rings and plate twirling were imported by jugglers from China, as was the use of stilts.

Aside from artistic debt expressed by Mayhew's anonymous entertainer, Samee's role remained largely unacknowledged by Western conjurers. His death, however, coincided with a turning point in the globalization of popular culture. On 1 May 1851, the Great Exhibition of the Works of Industry of All Nations opened at the specially built Crystal Palace in London, ushering in the era of world fairs in England, Europe and America. The demand for exotic entertainment at these fairs led to the recruitment of unprecedented numbers of Indian magicians and entertainers. The second half of the nineteenth century saw Western magicians travelling to India for the first time. Some hired Indian assistants. Others presented tricks they learned from Eastern necromancers. Their writings described the intersection of two great magical traditions. At times combative, at others cooperative, but always colourful and dynamic, these interactions would transform the art of necromancy in the East and the West.

NINE

SPELL-CASTERS IN THE STRANGERS' HOME

ON 31 July 1868, an unusual group of passengers disembarked from a train at London's Great Eastern Railway Station in Shoreditch. The men wore turbans and loose fitting white garments, and carried their pitiful belongings in a couple of dirty cloth sacks. The women resembled Gypsies – colourfully attired with heavy silver jewellery, nose rings and bracelets. It was later reported that they were 'strolling players' – a term used loosely to describe magicians, jugglers and acrobats. None of them – four men, three women and four children – spoke English. They had no money, no food and no one to turn to. After sitting on the platform for several hours, two homeless men took them to the Bishopsgate Police Station where the Sergeant 'sent them off declining to take any notice of them'. After spending a night in a barn, they were brought to the Strangers' Home for Asiatics, Africans and South Sea Islanders at West India Dock, the refuge of last resort for the destitute of Britain's imperial colonies.[1]

It was an ignominious ending for a group of artists described as once being attached to the noble 'Court of the King of Oude' at Lucknow. The eleven Indians arrived in England in February 1868 as part of the Oriental Troupe of 'Carnatics, Nuths and Jadoogheers'. They were billed as being the most 'wonderful of their class of performers in India'.[2] The *Bombay Chronicle* described their performances as being 'unique and unrivalled. … Any attempt to give a description of their varied and surprising feats must fall short of reality.'[3]

For English audiences used to second-rate imitations of Eastern conjuring performed by local magicians with boot-polished complexions and ill-fitting turbans, the arrival of the Oriental Troupe was a chance to see a genuine Indian magic show in all its bizarre and splendid other-worldly glory. Not since the appearance of Ramo Samee and the 'Indian jugglers' in the 1810s, had the public been so captivated by artists from India. Combining conjurers, contortionists, gymnasts, rope-walkers, acrobats and vaulters, the troupe was larger and more authentic than anything ever seen in England or the West. There was Lachee, 'the Gum-elastic girl', who could thread a needle with her toes while blindfolded and her body contorted in the shape of a hoop; and Cabotree, who dropped her nose ring into a vessel of water and then, while bending backwards, plunged her head into the vessel and emerged with the ring back through her nose. Another of Cabotree's tricks was spinning on her head with ten razor-sharp sabres almost brushing her face. Among the male performers there was Sumjoo 'who put Blondin to shame by walking the tight-rope on the tips of buffalo horns', and Rajub, who 'balanced himself on the same rope with wonderful impunity' with four huge water bottles on his head.[4] *The Sunday Times* singled out Moulah Bux, the chief juggler, who produced a live cat and two pigeons out of nowhere and performed the Basket Trick 'with a neatness yet unattained by European manipulators'. A boy bound hand and foot was placed into the basket just big enough to hold him. The juggler jumped on it and ran it through repeatedly with his sword. He then showed the empty basket to the audience. When he called out, the boy answered from a distant part of the building. 'Clearly, those who want to have it proved that seeing is not believing must witness the basket trick of Moulah Bux,' the newspaper recommended.[5]

The claim that leading members of the troupe played before the King of Oude had no basis in fact, but it was a convenient narrative. Known for its decadence as much as for its opulence, Oude was annexed by the British in 1856. It seemed logical that displaced artists would now be touring the world. In reality, the group comprised mainly Nats, an itinerant group generally classified as Gypsies and found all over northern India. For the next five months, the Oriental Troupe dazzled the crowds at the Theatre Royal in Covent Garden, the Crystal Palace at Hyde Park and at venues in regional cities. The *Pall Mall Gazette* complimented the troupe for its 'picturesque costumes, quiet grace, and an admirable arrangement of drapery in feats which, if performed by Europeans, would inevitably be accompanied by vulgarity and indelicacy'. But it couldn't resist playing up stereotypes of a passive and primitive India that Britain was duty-bound to rule over and civilize. When executing feats that suggest 'torture or anguish', the performer 'wears either a look of placid resignation, as if the sufferer (so to speak) were

A snake charmer 'tames' a cobra with his pipe, water colour, nineteenth century. Wellcome Library.

Portrait of Sena Sama or the 'Sword Swallower', by James Warrell, c. 1818. Valentine Museum, Richmond, VA.

Engraving of Indian jugglers Mooty and Madua Samme performing the Chinese stick play, Prague, c. 1822. Author's collection.

Jugglers, snake charmers and acrobats were a favourite subject of nineteenth-century photographers, Bourne and Shepherd, c. 1870. India Office Records, British Library.

A troupe of Indian show people, postcard printed by Gobind Ram and Oodey Ram, Jaipur, c. 1900. Priya Paul Collection.

Etching showing Purana Poori (Pran Puri) performing a penance known as urdhvabahu, *Prakashanand (Purkasanund) on his* ser-seja *(bed of nails), and a Yogey (yogi), 1809. Wellcome Library.*

Pair of cotton labels showing street performers, late nineteenth century. Priya Paul collection.

A Hindu ascetic or holy man suspended by a hook and two spikes, gouache painting, c. 1880. Wellcome Library.

Walking on fire as a penance, Tanjore, c. 1800. Wellcome Library.

A group of rope dancers and tumblers, Tanjore, c. 1815. Wellcome Library.

A troupe of jugglers in the gardens of Bombay University, c. 1920. Library of Congress.

Maskelyne and Cooke's 'The Fakirs of Benares', at Egyptian Hall, London, 1884. British Library.

Panoramic view of the Exposition Universelle, 1900. Wikimedia Commons.

Publicity poster for Howard Thurston's version of the Indian Rope Trick 'as performed in India', c. 1914. New York Public Library.

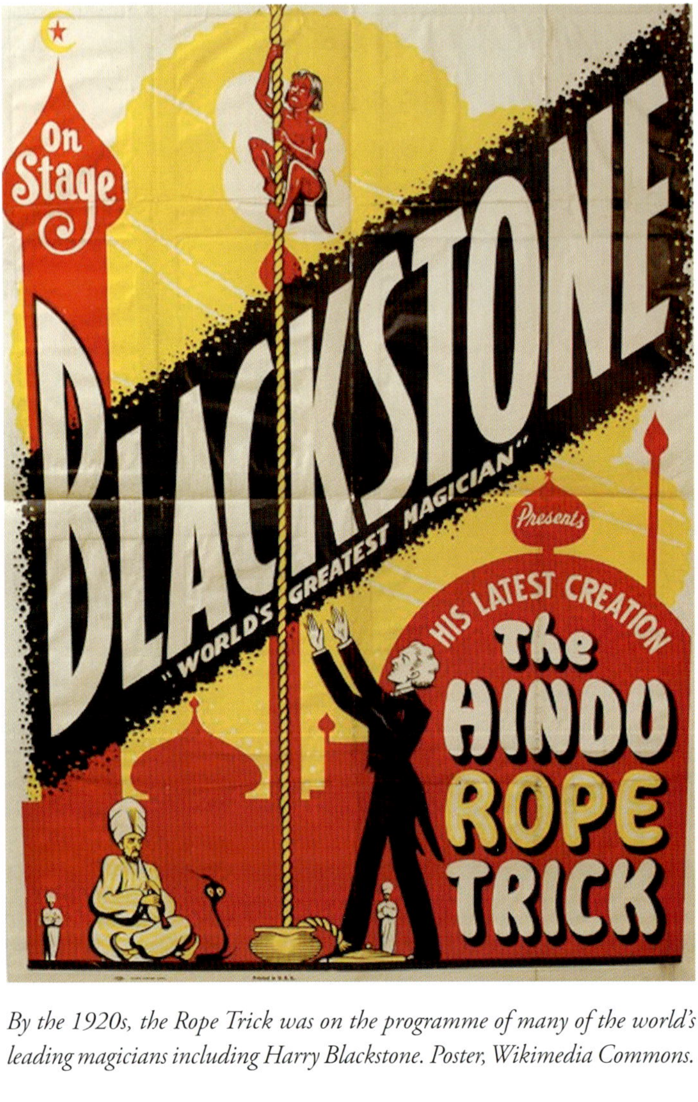

By the 1920s, the Rope Trick was on the programme of many of the world's leading magicians including Harry Blackstone. Poster, Wikimedia Commons.

Publicity calendar for the 1956 Australian tour of Gogia Pasha, 'the last of the great magicians'. Alma Collection, State Library of Victoria.

Souvenir programme of P. C. Sorcar, 'The World's Greatest Magician'. Collection of Saileswar Mukherjee.

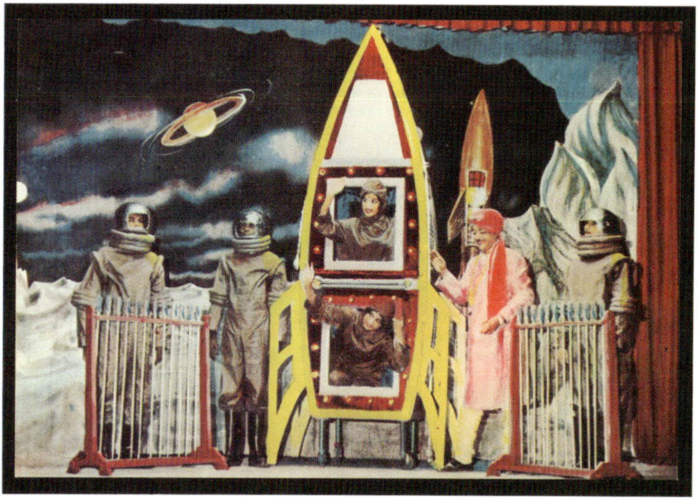

Scene from P. C. Sorcar's Indrajal. *New York Public Library.*

Maneka Sorcar and P. C. Sorcar Jr carry on Sorcar Senior's legacy, Calcutta, June 2016. Photo © John Zubrzycki.

Since the 1940s, Bollywood has largely neglected India's rich magic traditions. Jadoo, *released in 1966 and starring Rajan, was an exception. Author's collection.*

performing a painful vow according to the rites of a peculiar religion, or a gentle smile as if it were quite a pleasure to hold one end of a long bamboo thrust into your abdomen whilst at the other end a man and his brother perform the antics of a chimpanzee, or as if there were something soothing in the sensation of bending back your head until your forehead nearly touches the ground and picking up flowers with your eyelids.' Continued the newspaper: 'Moreover, there is something in the shiny and supple figure and limbs of the "mild Hindoo" which perfectly reconciles the looker-on to the contortions of the performer, who appears to have been ready-oiled and kneaded by nature for the purpose.'[6] In its typically condescending style, the *Times* noted that the members of the troupe possessed 'countenances so intellectual that those of us who are sceptical of the mental capacities of the Hindoos may be furnished with a proof that the inhabitants of northern India – for such they are – could be at one time capable of a high civilization'.[7] Encapsulated in these contrasting descriptions was the duality of the appeal of exotic performers. They are simultaneously

Acrobat balancing on a pole. Wellcome Library.

denigrated and celebrated, but always from the standpoint of the West's racial, cultural and scientific superiority.

After a sell-out season at Covent Garden, the troupe performed at Crystal Palace, where it was the chief attraction during Easter 1868, sharing the stage with a variety of acts including Ethardo, the spiral gymnast; the Italian 'Men in Miniature' Ernesto and Primo Magri; a Norwegian giant; as well as a hippopotamus posing as a 'Blue Hairless Horse'. From London, the troupe travelled to Liverpool and Manchester before arriving in Norwich where they were advertised as the main event at The Oddfellows' Gala on Monday, 6th July. Bolstered by plenty of advance publicity, the Gala was a huge success. The troupe lived up to their reputation. 'The delight of the audience was unbounded,' the *Norfolk Chronicle* enthused. Accompanying the Indians were three English clowns whose 'well-knit English frames contrasted forcibly with the lithe and sinewy forms of the tawny natives of Hindoostan'.[8] The evening ended with ballooning and fireworks displays. A special feature of the show was the use of gas to illuminate the stage.

But behind the sell-out crowds and rapturous reviews, strains were emerging among the members of the troupe. Neighbours of the house where the Indians were lodged reported hearing violent arguments and one of the scheduled shows was nearly cancelled. A few days later, several men and a woman named Perojah went to the local police station alleging they had been assaulted by Moulah Bux and their interpreter, a man named Jeddo. The argument was over the non-payment of wages. The aggrieved Indians told the police they had been engaged by two brothers, Edward and George Hanlon, railway contractors stationed in

Lucknow. The brothers made them sign contracts to sail from Bombay to Suez, where they would perform for three months. They were to be paid twenty rupees a month in addition to food and lodging, and then repatriated back to India. However, the performances in Suez proved so profitable the Hanlons decided to take the troupe overland to Cairo and Alexandria where they were put on a boat to France. After a brief season in Paris they travelled to London. Despite leaving India ten months ago, they had never been paid. Jeddo had also cut their rations. As for the Hanlons, they had not been seen for weeks. The Indians were now demanding they be returned home.

On the following day, Norwich court house and its surrounds were thronged with curious onlookers. 'Most of the members of the troupe were present, and their Oriental costume gave to the Sword Room a most animated and unique appearance,' the *Norfolk Chronicle* noted.[9] Aside from Bux and Jeddo, four other members of the troupe had been summoned and accused of assault. Months of pent up anger and frustration, it seemed, had taken a violent turn. Perojah told the court that Jeddo had pulled her by the hair, slapped her face and nearly strangled her. When another member of the troupe named Byrhee tried to protect her, he was also beaten up. With tears streaming down his face, Byrhee produced before the court the contract he had signed with the Hanlons but was now worthless. A 'Mr. Seal', an agent for the employers, then appeared in the witness stand and told the court he 'had positive orders not to pay them any money, as they were addicted to drinking. If he were to give them money the town would not contain them .... he and those who had charge of them ran the risk of having their throats cut.' This was denied by Byrhee, who said that whatever money he could get would be used to return to India. Weldon, the troupe's manager then gave evidence alleging the Hanlons had spent between £1200 and £1300 to bring the artists to England. They intended to take them back once some 'pecuniary difficulties' were resolved.[10]

To the presiding magistrates the matter before them was complex. Aside from reconciling the conflicting statements of the members of the troupe, there was the question of whether the Hanlons had broken laws governing the emigration of Indian workers to England. One thing, however, was clear. As a magistrate observed, the members of the troupe were English subjects, yet they had been kept as slaves. The agreement they had signed 'was not worth a straw' and 'they were not bound to their so-called masters one atom'.[11] After conferring among themselves, they ordered the release of Bux and Jeddo on condition they did not reoffend. Those accused of assault were to be housed separately from the rest of the troupe and Weldon had to produce sufficient funds to meet their immediate needs. The court also ruled that the performers be paid thirty-five shillings a month in addition to board and lodging. An account for the troupe was to be maintained by the chief prosecutor and once sufficient funds were deposited by the managers, those who wanted to return to India would be able to do so.[12]

There would be no more performances of the Oriental Troupe in Norwich. Nor would the Hanlons reap any more profits from their human cargo. Shortly after the court hearing, they were arrested as debtors and detained at Lancaster Castle awaiting their appearance at the bankruptcy court. With no prospect for finding work, Byhree, Perojah and nine others, pooled whatever little money they had and took the train to London. Now they were waiting in the Strangers' Home, uncertain of what would happen next.

THE case of the Oriental Troupe reflected both the ongoing fascination of the Victorian public with Indian magic and the highly exploitative nature of the trade in show people from the subcontinent. The troupe was the forerunner of an influx of Indian entertainers who were displayed at international exhibitions, theatres, circuses, amusement parks, dime museums, zoos and even aquariums for commercial purposes until well into the twentieth century. Apart from magicians, acrobats and dancers, they included artisans, animal handlers, curry cooks and human freaks. They joined African Negros, Aboriginal Australians, Amazonian tribes, American Indians and other racial groups in ethnographic recreations of distant, exotic and in some cases only recently discovered worlds.

The 'Age of Exhibitions' began with the Great Exhibition of the Works of Industry of All Nations at the Crystal Palace in 1851. From then until the outbreak of the First World War in 1914, international exhibitions and world fairs were held almost every year in Britain or its colonies. Exhibition fever also took hold in America and Europe, peaking in size and grandeur with the Exposition Internationale in Paris in 1900. By the onset of the Second World War, according to historian Paul Greenhalgh, about one billion people had visited international exhibitions.[13] India figured prominently in many of these. Between 1886 and 1924, twenty-five Indian palaces and courts were displayed in foreign exhibitions. These spaces were generally dressed up as bazaars or street scenes populated with jugglers, snake charmers, artisans and other show people. India was the most carefully curated of Britain's colonial possessions. The Indian Court at Crystal Palace in 1851 measured 30,000 square feet. At the Exposition Universelle in 1900, the palace 'was a treasure house full of opulent produce, complete with beautifully dressed Indians serving as exhibition attendants'.[14] The last and most impressive Indian display was at the Wembley exhibition in 1924, where the Indian site covered five acres and the palace itself, three acres.

The Oriental Troupe's case triggered a wider policy debate within the India Office about the best means to protect jugglers, acrobats and dancers from unscrupulous impresarios. Cases of ensembles from India, Ceylon, Burma and even the Straits Settlements being abandoned because their recruiters ran into legal or financial difficulties, resulted in the Indian government being forced to foot the bill for their repatriation. Often itinerant and impoverished, show people were easily lured into believing that by travelling to Europe and performing, they would be richly rewarded. Many were exploited, made to sign contracts that were not legally binding or abandoned in the street when their recruiters went broke. In England, dozens ended up at the Strangers' Home begging for a passage back to India. Located at the West India Docks, the home catered mainly to lascars, or seamen who crewed the vessels sailing from India and other British colonies in Asia and were awaiting return passage. According to a petition published in the *Sailors' Magazine* in 1842, an average of 3,000 lascars were arriving in Britain every year. Although their employers were obligated to provide for them while on shore, hundreds 'were left to sleep in the open air or beneath some defenceless covering, with scarcely an article of clothing; while in every part of the city they be seen engaged in sweeping the crossings of the streets for a few chance pence'. Worst of all, the petition stated, nothing was done to instruct them in the 'saving truths of Christianity'. As a result, many returned 'more corrupt and depraved when they left their native land'.[15] Able to accommodate 220 people, the Strangers' Home promised 'comfortable and respectable lodging with wholesome food'. Those staying were required to pay a minimum of ten shillings a week for 'three meals a day, medical attendance, baths, washing, etc'. According to the Home's records, between its opening in June 1857 and December 1877, 5,709 sailors had registered as lodgers and 1,605 destitute cases had been taken off the street. The India Office contributed £200 annually for temporarily maintaining the lascars. Beyond meeting the material needs of its inmates, the Home openly touted its mission to propagate the Christian faith. Joseph Salter, the Home's founder, made ridding London of its 'plague spots of Oriental vice' his main priority. Those inmates who could read were provided with 'a copy of the Holy Scriptures in their own language' and offered the opportunity 'to be taught in the Truths of the Gospel'.[16]

For Lieutenant Colonel R. M. Hughes (Retd), the secretary of the Strangers' Home, the Indians who had run away from the Oriental Troupe and were now under his care represented a political cause rather than a moral one. On 12 August 1868, he wrote to Sir Stafford Northcote, the Secretary of State for India, outlining their circumstances. After asking for funds to cover their maintenance and repatriation to India, he wrote:

'The infraction of contracts whether drawn up in writing or made verbally by Europeans with Natives of India does great discredit to the British name – and if infractions of similar contracts to this are permitted to be passed over with impunity – it will not be long before the streets of the Metropolis will again ... be inundated with destitute Asiatics and the Jails and Hospitals will again have numerous Asiatic occupants who have been cast adrift unprovided for.'[17]

When Northcote asked for clarification as to the Government's liability in the case, he was referred to a letter dated 7 July 1852 from the Board of the East India Company that stated: 'The East India Company, as the Governors of India, stand in the same relation to Lascars and other East Indian Subjects who may be left destitute in this country, as the Government of this country stands in relation to distressed British subjects who may be left destitute in any foreign country.'[18] Northcote was unimpressed. 'These people should never have been allowed to leave India for Europe without a repost being made by those employing them, sufficient to cover the expense of taking their return passage to India,' he wrote in a memo dated 13 August 1852 and circulated within the India Office. It was 'absurd to expect that can be obtained from the Messrs Hanlon who are in Lancaster Goal, and who will probably be relieved by law from all liabilities'. He recommended that the Government reimburse the Strangers' Home for the cost of looking after the Indians and their passage home and that the amount be debited to the Fort of Bombay. 'A copy of the correspondence should be transmitted to that Fort with instructions to exercise a vigilant watch in future over any such despatch of helpless natives to Europe.'[19]

Despite Northcote's missive, the Government of India paid little heed to the case of the Oriental Troupe or the broader problem of ensuring guarantees so that all 'natives' engaged in India for service out of the country could be returned to their home at the end of their contracts. The Emigration Act of 1846 was considered adequate as it decreed that 'England is not a place to which emigration (for the purpose of labouring for hire) from British India is lawful; consequently any person who takes strolling players or men following similar professions to England violates the law, since these men labour for hire in the full legal sense of the term.'[20] Concerned primarily with plantation labour in colonies such as Mauritius, Jamaica and Fiji, the Act was framed with coolies rather than conjurers in mind. For men like the Hanlons, it was easy to evade the law by passing off magicians as menial servants or seamen, rather than hired labourers. Northcote argued for a legally binding contract and a deposit of Rupees 500 be lodged for every Indian sent to England or its colonies for employment. However, this was ruled out as it placed an unfair burden on British subjects. Instead the Government of India decided it was sufficient for officers at various ports of embarkation explain to the emigrants their position and 'assist them in securing a satisfactory arrangement for their return passage'.[21]

Fortunately for Northcote, the burden of looking after the performers and their children was relatively short-lived. Hearing that the *Lord Warren* was about to sail for Calcutta, Hughes contacted the captain and reserved two cabins. On 11 September 1868, the entire party departed for India. 'The Directors of this Institution trust that all that has been done for these destitute Natives of India in preventing their becoming mendicants on the streets, in attending to their every want during severe sicknesses and in making the necessary arrangements for their return to India may meet with the approval of the Rt. Hon'ble the Secretary of State for India in Council,' Hughes wrote to Northcote on 15 September. Enclosed with the letter was an account of expenses incurred on their behalf. The total, including maintenance for six weeks, suits of warm clothing, cartage, tolls and the passage to India, came to £243, 12s, 5p.[22]

The wider costs of ignoring Northcote's concerns soon became apparent. In September 1868, a further four members from the Oriental Troupe turned up at the Strangers' Home, bringing the number of 'destitute Asiatics' the Home had cared for to fifty-four that year. Hughes was not the only person agitating for firm measures to be taken. On 19 January 1869, Syed Abdoolah, a retired professor of Oriental languages, wrote to the Under Secretary of State claiming there were hundreds of 'half-starved and half-dead' Asiatics on London's streets. The 'jugglers, mountebanks, necromancers' belonging to the Oriental Troupe were a typical case. They were brought out by Hanlons who 'lived upon their earnings, accumulated a considerable fortune, speculated in some sort of money making projects, and finally lost all. They themselves were comfortably lodged in the House of Detention whilst their unhappy victims were turned adrift absolutely starving and their infants crying for a crust of bread.'[23] Abdoolah's letter was dismissed as sensationalizing the situation. But it was only a matter of time before what had been a trickle of magicians and performers from the subcontinent turned into a flood.

ONE of the most popular attractions of the 1851 Crystal Palace exhibition was its collection of miniature ethnographic models of Indians arranged in village and bazaar-like settings. For the 1862 Colonial and Indian Exhibition held in London, each local government area was 'expected to collect into one collection such photographic likenesses of the Races and Classes within its borders as it may obtain and to forward very brief notes on each'.[24] These photographs were forwarded to Calcutta and then to London where a selection was put on display. The Islamic section of the Paris Exposition of 1867 was the first international exhibition to feature living displays. At the Egyptian *okel* 'real natives, varying in shade from light brown to ebony black, work at several trades', including carving, jewellery making and barbering, Eugene Rimmel, the Exposition's Assistant Commissioner wrote. 'In the recess behind the stall,' he added, 'is sometimes seen an Egyptian cooking his dinner.'[25] By the mid-1880s the English public could ogle at 'friendly Zulus, African earthmen, Tartar nomads, and civilized Japanese' at various venues around London. The stay-at-home Englishman could acquire an insight into the habits and customs of faraway regions, the *Morning Post* commented in December 1885. Now, the newspaper noted, it was the turn of the Indian Empire to make its presence felt.[26]

If measured by the numbers of participants and the variety of acts alone, the years 1885 and 1886 signalled the high point of Indian magic and popular culture in England. The public could choose from the 'Indian Village' at the Albert Palace, a performance by the Parsee Victoria Theatre Company at the Gaiety Theatre, or the 'India in London' display at Portland Hall on Regent Street. The 'India in London' and Gaiety spectacles

Poster for India in London Exhibition, Langham Place, 1886. Evanion Collection, British Library.

were put together by the dramatist Coonvarji Sorabji Nazir. One of the pioneers of Parsi theatre in Bombay, Nazir studied drama at Elphinstone College. In 1866, he wrote and staged *The First Parsi Baronet*, probably the earliest Indian English play in verse. With the support of patrons such as L. H. Bayley, the Advocate General of Bombay, and the eminent curator George Birdwood, Nazir announced the formation of a company in 1865 with the purpose of staging 'entertainments of various kinds' in London. The first of these entertainments would be an 'Indian Native Village' at the Langham Exhibition Hall on Regent Street. The village would feature a bazaar 'attended by natives, and in the shops, which will line the street of the village on each, native artificers, such as workers in brass, potters, carpet weavers, shawl makers, gold and silver smiths and jewellery inlayers in ivory, turners, carpenters and wood carvers'.[27] As well as showcasing Indian arts and crafts, there would be 'authentic' Indian entertainments. 'A number of experienced nautch girls with attendant musicians, have been engaged, who will charm the ears of the unsophisticated

Briton with the strains of "Taza batazu nau ba nau", and delight their eyes with the dance peculiar to his country,' the *Times of India* announced. There would also be snake charmers, jugglers, wrestlers and other 'itinerant caterers of amusement familiar to residents in this country'. Every step was to be taken to ensure the performers were treated well. The promoters would cover cost of their passages. Their agent had entered into a bond to send them back to India when their contracts expired, the paper assured its readers.[28]

By the time Nazir's troupe sailed for London in September 1885, he had also assembled a theatrical troupe of twenty-five actors and actresses with a repertoire arranged to 'suit British tastes'. In total forty-two performers were brought to London. The native village, in the style of the 'durbar of Indian potentates', was renamed the 'India in London' display so as not to be confused with Liberty's 'Indian Village'. Newspaper reports described it as featuring 'a real Hindustanee nautch, Parsee gymnastics and wrestling, Mohammedan juggling, cup ringing and guitar playing, the gyrations of Tanjore dancing girls, and other diversions of the Far East'.[29] Visitors could also feast at a banquet presided over by a Parsi chef that included 'Fish a la Doobash', 'Mutton potatonised', 'Ducks onionised', and 'Fowl sweetenised'.[30] The venue's shops sold items such as gold-embroidery, fans, weavings, as well as items carved from ivory and wood.[31] Music at intervals was provided by an Anglo-Hungarian band.

As crowds thronged to the 'India in London' exhibit, Nazir's stage actors were rehearsing an ambitious three-part spectacular. The show featured the Hindustani opera *Saifus Suliman* or *Solomon's Sword*, the story of a ruined gambler who with the help of an itinerant musician, magic scimitar and an 'Asian Fairy', defeats the forces of evil. It was followed by an adaption of the American Negro minstrel play *The Fancy Ball,* featuring a troupe of nautch dancers and climaxing with a shrill falsetto rendition of 'God Save our Empress, God Save our Queen'. The programme concluded with an extract from the Sanskrit classic *Shakuntala* by Kalidasa. Aside from *The Fancy Ball,* the entire performance was in Hindustani. For the *London Evening Standard's* reviewer this was 'too large a dose for any audience, however good-natured and intelligent'.[32]

Despite the lukewarm reviews, Nazir's production was the first time that authentic Indian theatre had been staged in England. It was also the first time an Indian theatrical professional had taken a troupe of popular entertainers, including magicians, dancers and acrobats, abroad. Another of Nazir's innovations was using magicians in their traditional settings as well as on a modern stage. Part of the production at the Gaiety Theatre was incorporated into the 'India in London' exhibit and jugglers appeared in the magic-related sequences in *Suliman's Sword.* The experiment, however, lasted less than two months. On 18 February 1868, a magistrate at the Marlborough Street Police Court ordered the closure of Portland Hall on the grounds of safety because it did not comply with building regulations.

Coincidentally, on the same day as Nazir's players were packing their bags, a hearing south of the Thames was deciding the fate of another group of Indians. At the Wandsworth Police Court, several dozen jugglers and performers had gathered complaining that their contracts had been breached. The troupe was put together in the summer of 1885 after the management of the Albert Palace in Battersea Park asked London's leading department store, Liberty's, to set up an 'Indian Village'. Like Crystal Palace, the Albert Palace was an amusement park complete with souvenir stalls, reading and smoking rooms and kitchens capable of catering for 50,000 people. With a significant proportion of the store's merchandise imported from India, the 'Indian Village' was seen as an opportunity to generate publicity for Liberty's and to increase sales in its Oriental Antiques and Curios Department. By September 1885, the Albert Palace Association's agent, A. Bonner, had recruited forty-five Indians mainly from villages around Hyderabad. Under the terms of their contract, they were to receive seventy-five rupees a month for a six-month period with an option to extend for another six.[33] Bonner reportedly lured them with promises of an audience with the Queen and of further employment at the Colonial and Indian Exhibition, which was due to open in May 1886. He also promised that appreciative audiences would shower them with plenty of *baksheesh*. Those who took up his offer included silk spinners, sari weavers, embroiders, potters, furniture makers, engravers and carpet weavers. The entertainers comprised 'a dancing boy, a snake charmer and a juggler, a singing and dancing master, knife juggler, dancing girls and acrobats'. The intention was to create a 'living village of Indian artisans'.[34]

On 21 November 1885, both the *Graphic* and the *Illustrated London News* carried 'village' scenes. Corseted English women and men in top hats were shown exchanging greetings with turbaned Indians in homespun as they ambled down an avenue lined with potted palm trees and double-storeyed Indian houses. The village was divided into two sections: one for workers and the other for entertainers, with the latter group attracting 'a large number of spectators who were much interested in the exhibition of sleight-of-hand'.[35] *Vanity Fair* singled out Sayad Ussen Valad Sayad Irnam, a forty-year-old juggler from Hyderabad, for his 'exceedingly simple' but inexplicable feats, which included making a row of bottles disappear and cutting a piece of cotton into squares that were thrust up the 'well-made nose' of a unsuspecting member of audience before being pulled out as a length of 'red and yellow string longer than Mr Gladstone's manifesto'.[36]

As in the case of the Oriental Troupe a decade-and-half earlier, the sylvan scenes and cloying commentaries belied the true condition of the group. According to the *Indian Mirror*, the artisans and entertainers had been 'grossly deceived' by the recruiting agent, who had not given them the food, salary, housing and clothing specified in their contract. Their arrival also coincided with the coldest winter in thirty years.[37] When the hot-water pipes at Albert Palace froze, fires were lit to keep the performers warm. The sub-zero temperatures led to the death of thirty of the forty-two cobras and rock snakes belonging to snake-charmer, Sheikh Imam. To prevent humans in the group suffering the same fate, the Albert Palace Association was forced to supply overcoats, trousers, mufflers and boots to the artisans and entertainers, spoiling the spectacle for the English public. 'You cannot imagine how thoroughly a "billycock" can vulgarize the Asiatic type of head and face,' the *Indian Mirror* complained. The London correspondent for the *Times of India* agreed, commenting: 'It was rather odd to see a pair of jingling ankles over big hob-nailed boots.' The mismatched attire was not the only thing that jarred. Seeing the feats of the jugglers and conjurers was like 'witnessing a series of horrid tortures', the *Times* correspondent continued. As for the nautch dancing 'it was one of the most ungraceful things in the way of motion that I ever beheld'.[38]

Within a few months of their arrival it was clear that Liberty's Little India was going to be a big financial and publicity disaster. In late January 1886, the Albert Palace Association was in court for contravention of the Company's Act. On 18th February, an increasingly familiar scenario played itself out when twenty-seven 'villagers' descended on the Wandsworth Police Court demanding a hearing. According to a statement read out in the court, their contracts were valid until the end of April, but they were no longer being given food or money. The magistrate ruled he did not have power to intervene on the men's behalf and urged them to take the matter up with the Government. In London, a committee 'composed of a few English and Indian gentlemen' was set up to advise and assist the group and a relief fund was advertised in Bombay newspapers. 'They come back in a very helpless and miserable plight,' the *Times of India* editorialized on 18 March 1886, just ahead or their return. 'No one is in charge of them, and they are penniless as the result of their English adventure.' To prevent a repeat of what was being called the 'Indian Village Fiasco', the newspaper urged the Government of India 'to insist on a formal guarantee for the fulfilment of the contracts'.[39]

Unlike the plight of the Oriental Troupe, which had gone unreported in India, the case of the Indian Village received widespread publicity. The change was due to growing climate of nationalist discontent that had escalated with the annexation of Upper Burma in 1885 and the formation of the Indian National Congress. In India, the failure of the Indian Village triggered questions over why a supposedly civilized nation as Britain wanted to display human beings. 'There is no knowing where the mania for shows and exhibitions is to end in civilized society,' the *Hindoo Patriot* editorialized.[40]

The negative publicity surrounding the Liberty's exhibit could not have come at a worse time for the organizers of the Colonial and Indian Exhibition of 1886. The commission charged with planning the Exhibition was adamant in its desire to have 'a number of Indian artisans carrying on their various trades and callings'. The artisans would be displayed inside the courtyard of the venue's mock Indian palace on the occasion of Queen Victoria's Jubilee. A private shipping firm, Messrs S. King and Company, was hired to bring thirty-one 'skilled workmen' from India and to cover the cost of their 'transport, pay and maintenance'. In selecting the men, the organizing committee's priority was to include not only as many trades as possible, 'but such as were most picturesque, and most likely therefore to prove interesting to the public'.[41] The company subcontracted the recruitment of the artisans to Dr John William Tyler, the superintendent of the Agra Jail. Most of those recruited were inmates – the oldest being a 102-year-old potter named Bakshiram. Next to the palace was a faux Indian jungle featuring a stuffed tiger digging its claws into an elephant and other animals and reptiles. The tiger had been specially killed for the exhibition leading one writer to comment that this was 'no mere pasteboard and canvas affair such as one might see on the theatrical stage'.[42] Tyler's organizational skills were also singled out for commendation with the *Art Journal* stating, 'the public are indebted' for the success of the living display.[43]

Queen Victoria was so fascinated by Tyler's artisans that she invited three of them – Mahmud Hussein, the copper turner, Radha Bullub, a weaver, and Nazir Hussein, a poet and miniature painter, to her estate at Frogmore. 'Her majesty spent some time making water colour sketches of them in a tent in the garden, and afterwards regaled them with tea and fruit,' the *Dundee Evening Telegraph* reported. Hussein was then invited to play the sitar and 'sing the odes of Hindustan'.[44] On their return to India there was nothing but praise from members of the troupe. 'Every member of this company of artisans and other workmen, is full of praise as regards the treatment he received while in England. The mention of her Majesty's name is sufficient on his landing yesterday to make him clasp his hands as if in prayer and turn his eyes up to heaven.'[45]

The success of Tyler's troupe, however, was an aberration. When the members of the 'Indian Village' returned to Bombay, the *Indian Mirror* predicted that similar experiments 'will heat up few recruits in India'. In fact, the opposite was true. Three years later, an Australian named Charles Bastard – described by Calcutta's Deputy Commissioner of Police as a 'a collector of curiosities and manager of a skating rink' – went into partnership with his chief figure skater, an American named Henry Washburn and recruited a dozen Indian jugglers and show people. The 'Museum of Indian Curiosities' opened in Adelaide in June 1889. The *Evening Journal* reported such a large crowd attending the opening night that temporary platforms had to be erected.[46] The curiosities included a five-legged cow, weapons, musical instruments, shoes, trays, inlaid marble work, idols, toys, ornaments, armour and a brass model of the Golden Temple at

Group of jugglers and musicians, Nicholas and Curths, 1870. British Library.

Benares. The performers consisted of 'three pretty young women, said to be Queens of the late King of Oude, who sat in a canopied apartment smoking an Indian hookah'; Hunisraj, 'a chief from

Gwalior, who was also attired in expensive garments' and had a beard 'of extraordinary length'; the 'monkey boys', described as 'novel specimens of humanity'; and a contortionist who moved like a snake. There was also Painee Pindarrum, 'a juggler of high order' who demonstrated the cups and balls trick, produced fire from his mouth and spat out dozens of two-inch-long nails, and Galip Sahib who executed the Basket Trick with a young girl named Giddy.[47] The greatest curiosity was a fifteen-year-old boy from Benares named Murshy Samee who in addition to having a deformed body and legs, had a head thirty-eight-inches in circumference. Bastard put out a story that he had been forced to deposit a surety of £1000 with the 'Rajah of Bulpoar' for the safe return of his wives. According the press reports, the Royal Museum enjoyed steady patronage with the 'native queens' and the 'monkey boys' being particularly popular.

Within a few weeks of their arrival in Melbourne, however, police were called to investigate allegations of mistreatment. One of the jugglers allegedly bit the show's manager, Harry Friedman, after he tried to stop his allowance of two glasses of whiskey between evening performances. No charges were laid against Friedman, leading one newspaper to dismiss the allegations as having 'no existence outside the imagination of the malcontents'.[48] Things took a turn for the worse in late October when a juggler committed suicide. At a coroner's inquest into his death, Bastard blamed the suicide on the man's heavy drinking. Another member of the troupe, however, accused Bastard of threatening to imprison the juggler after a disturbance among the Indians a week earlier. The evidence was dismissed by the jury, which found alcoholism to have been the cause. During the course of the inquest, it emerged that the troupe was housed eight people to a room. One of the police inspectors recommended that instead of being exhibited, the 'monkey boys' should be put into an insane asylum.[49]

Minus one of their jugglers, the troupe resumed performances at the Grand Palace of Amusement, where they were billed alongside a twenty-two-inch high midget and Tikit Taro, 'the Marvellous Japanese Conjurer and Balancer'. But their return to the stage was short-lived. In developments similar to those that beset the Oriental Troupe in Norwich and members of the Indian Village in London, Bastard and Washburn were charged with embezzlement, leaving the Indians without a salary and contracts that were worthless. On 7 November 1889, the troupe staged what the local press described as a 'mutiny' and marched down Melbourne's main street to the District Court. According to the *Melbourne Herald,* members of the public stood aghast at the spectacle, particularly the 'monkey boys' who 'squealed and kicked and romped around like little puppy dogs' when they were refused entry into the court.[50] Eventually they were allowed to appear before the presiding magistrate and demanded their return passages to India now that their contracts had expired. Although the two men who had recruited them were clearly at fault, the judge showed little sympathy for the plight of the Indians, focusing instead on the potential inconvenience they posed. If individuals such as Bastard continued to indulge in the trade of show people: 'We shall soon have all the lunacy of the East out here, and consequently a great nuisance will be imposed upon the State,' he thundered, before giving Bastard until the following Monday to arrange for return passages.[51]

The passing of the deadline without a resolution brought matters to a head. Once again, the troupe marched down Melbourne's main street, taking up position in a yard adjacent to the court and refused to move. After the police arrested one of the men, the chief juggler started gesticulating wildly to the others. When the crowd grew to such an extent that the traffic was interrupted, the police locked all the Indians up on a charge of insulting behaviour. 'They resisted violently,' the *Argus* reported. 'The idiots, known as the Monkey Boys, fighting with teeth and nails.'[52] At the court appearance the following day, an interpreter explained to the judge that the 'Queens of Oude' were in fact low caste women from Madras and the 'monkey boys' were the offspring of a leprous mother. With no prospect of their contracts being honoured and the conduct of the case reflecting poorly on the governance and policing of the state, the Victorian government decided to repatriate the group at the cost of £11 per person. They arrived back in Madras on 31 December 1889.[53] It later emerged in the official police report on the case that the members of the troupe were too afraid to speak out against Bastard when police or doctors went to investigate the conditions they were living in. They were also forced to eat meat, even though it went against their religion, and they were often mistreated and beaten.[54]

A decade later the Melbourne 'mutiny' would be cited as a test case for whether Indian magicians and performers should be allowed to travel abroad for entertainment purposes. This time, however, the backer was not the manager of an ice rink or a railway contractor, but a highly successful barrister from Allahabad.

TEN

MOTILAL'S MAGICAL MENAGERIE

BOMBAY'S Elphinstone College, whose alumni include Coonvarji Sorabji Nazir, B. R. Ambedkar, the author of India's Constitution, and Bollywood's bad boy, Sanjay Dutt, is also the repository of the Maharashtra State Archives. Built in 1871 by the English architect James Trubshawe and financed by the Parsi philanthropist Sir Cowasjee Jehangeer, it is one of the finest examples of Gothic Revival east of Suez. Leading off the ornately carved galleries that face into the College's courtyard are dimly-lit rooms stacked with heavy leather-bound volumes containing files on everything from the East India Company plans to

Allahabad barrister and impresario Motilal Nehru. Wikimedia Commons.

combat piracy in the Gulf of Cambay, to the merger of India's princely states.

Buried in this bluestone labyrinth is a file entitled 'Ruling of the Govt of India regarding the Departure from Bombay of a Party of Indian Jugglers and Dancers for Service in Connection with the Exhibit in Paris'. Between the crumbling khaki-coloured covers tied together in rough hemp string, is the original of a letter dated 1 April 1900 from Motilal Nehru, to J. Walsh, the Protector of Emigrants in Bombay. 'I have just learnt that in order to send a party of Indians consisting of performers, musicians, acrobats and artisans to the ensuing Paris Exhibition it is necessary to obtain a permit from the Protector of Emigrants. As I am about to send such a party, I beg to state the necessary particulars for your information.'[1] The patriarch of South Asia's most powerful political dynasty had taken time out from his successful legal career to follow in the footsteps of the world's greatest showbiz entrepreneur, Phineas Taylor Barnum.

Marking 'a new stage in the forward march of contemporary civilization', the Exposition Universelle was the most ambitious world fair ever staged. More than 50 million visitors passed through the 108-acre site that spanned both banks of the Seine, a record that would not be broken until Montreal Expo in 1967. The Exposition aimed to present 'a picture of the world at the close of the nineteenth century with a minuteness and vividness never approached before'.[2] Visitors were transported to the site on the newly opened Metro and then transferred to a four-kilometre long 'moving sidewalk' that tracked around the grounds. At the Tour du Monde, panoramas and dioramas featured living displays of people from countries diverse as India,

Turkey and China, 'enacting the customs and habits of their daily life'. The official poster of the Indian court showed a procession of caparisoned elephants being led by turbaned warriors riding black stallions watched by men in dhotis and women in saris. Behind the procession is a building with white marble minarets and onion-shaped domes that looks like a cross between the Taj Mahal and a Rajput palace. 'All the world will go to Paris,' one journalist predicted ahead of the exhibition's opening on 14 April 1900, 'the exhibitors to show and sell their wares and win prizes, the general public to be amused'.[3]

Satisfying this insatiable thirst for amusements of the exotic variety was clearly the motivation for Nehru to assemble his menagerie of magicians, dancers and artists. He visited France twice during the 1890s and would have been aware of the success of the 1889 Paris Exhibition with its numerous ethnographic displays. Although stories that he sent his laundry to Paris for dry cleaning are apocryphal, Nehru was clearly an admirer of French culture, importing a model G Renault to Allahabad in 1902, and urging Jawaharlal, his son and independent India's first prime minister, to study the language while at Harrow. With millions of visitors from England and continental Europe expected to flock to the first world fair of the new century, there were profits to be made from showcasing India's wonder-workers.

Nehru displayed the same meticulous planning in sending the troupe to Paris as he did when preparing his briefs as a barrister at the Allahabad High Court. Attached to the file in the Maharashtra State Archives is a thirty-seven-page document laying out the memorandum and articles of association of the Societe des Grandes Attractions, a company formed in Paris 'to carry on the business of caterers for public amusements in France', as well as a range of other activities including the operation of hotels, restaurants, cafes and the production and distribution of wines and spirits. As Nehru elaborates in his letter, the £20,000, publicly listed company had acquired two sites adjacent to the exhibition ground and had also taken a contract to run certain shows in the Indian section. He had a £7000 stake in the company and had engaged about fifty to sixty persons to perform in Paris for an initial four-month contract, with an option to extend up to eight months. His nephew, Rai Bahadur Nehru, would be responsible for managing the group when it arrived. The letter ends with Nehru urging the Protector of Emigrants to grant 'the necessary permits and an early disposal of the matter'. Nehru also wrote a separate letter to Thomas Cook's agent in Bombay insisting 'there is no possible chance of any member of the party being let loose in Europe as a vagrant'. Nor could they be described as 'Indigent Natives'. 'Most of them are fairly well off and the salaries of some come up to 500 or 600 rupees a month, exclusive of board and lodging.'[4]

Nehru's straightforward tone belied the complexity of the case. Under the Emigration Act of 1883, the emigration of Indians was prohibited except to specified countries as manual labourers under special arrangements to ensure their proper treatment and safe return. These restrictions were tightened after an outbreak of the plague in Bombay in 1896, which spread rapidly to other parts of India and killed tens of thousands of people. In 1897, the Epidemic Diseases Act (No.3) was passed, giving the Government the power 'to prevent the carriage of epidemic disease to foreign countries by infected passengers

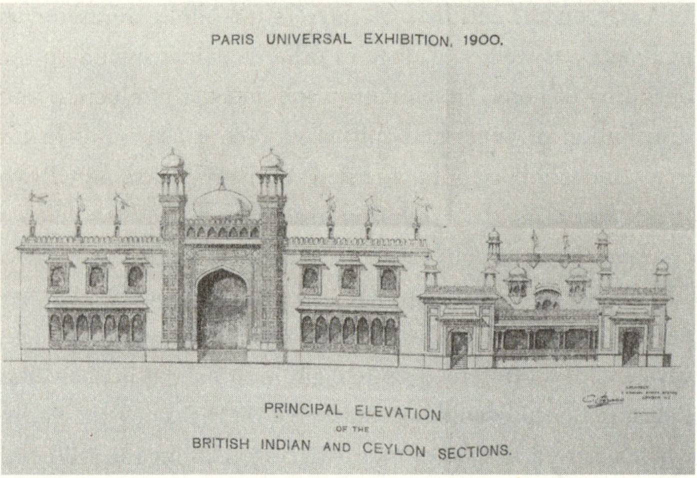

Plans for the British India and Ceylon sections of the Exposition Universalle, Paris, 1900. India Office Records, British Library.

from India'[5]. The Act led to a ban on all native residents leaving India through the Bombay Presidency, severely disrupting the supply of labourers, artisans and servants to work in colonies such as Uganda and Kenya. While pressure from mercantile groups led to a relaxing of the rules, provided the emigrants were subjected to vigorous health checks, travel to Europe and England of Indians was not allowed. Regardless of his guarantees, Nehru's jugglers, dancers and other performers were considered itinerants and therefore at a high risk of carrying the plague. Complicating the clearance of his request was an almost simultaneous application from Professor Deval's Great Indian Circus to take about sixty artists as well as elephants, lions and tigers for a month-long season in Egypt, before proceeding to the Paris Exhibition.

Both applications would be determined on whether performers such as magicians and circus artists could be classified as emigrants, i.e. manual labourers hired for specific tasks such as building railways and plantation work. If they could, the Plague Act would apply to them and they would be prevented from leaving. Exceptions were made for certain categories such as domestic servants employed under an oral or formal agreement. Conjurers, craftsmen, circus artists and other 'spectacular performers', who were being engaged in ever increasing numbers by the likes of Nehru, fell into a grey area. In what was one of the more bizarre cases to cross a Viceroy's desk, it would be left to Lord Curzon to rule on whether a jadoowallah's tricks constituted manual labour because they were executed by sleight of hand. For now, however, the government needed to make a decision based on facts before it. Nehru had to get his jugglers to Paris by 4th May, and time was running out.

Officials in Bombay, however, were in no mood to rush. There was division over whether Nehru's troupe and the Great Indian Circus should be treated any differently from the jugglers abandoned and then repatriated from Melbourne in 1889, who had come under the Emigration Act. Complicating matters was the more recent case of a troupe of jugglers from Burma who were ditched by their manager, forcing the Indian Office to pay for their costly repatriation. On 6th April, a few days after receiving Nehru's letter, the Protector of Emigrants in Bombay wrote a memorandum to the Government of India stating his view that the jugglers did come under the Emigration Act and their departure 'will be prevented unless Government permission is obtained'.[6] The Commissioner of Customs, however, took the opposite view, stating in a memorandum sent the following day, that 'jugglers and dancers are not "emigrants" within the meaning of the word as defined in the Emigration Act, XXI of 1883, seeing that the tricks and dances of these men can hardly be called "labour essentially manual" vide Government Resolution No 2782 of 26th June 1896.' The Commissioner also declared that the troupe did not 'come within the prohibition under the Epidemic Diseases Act, as the service is to be rendered in, and not out of Europe'.[7]

As the government equivocated over what to do about Nehru's ensemble, the Bombay representative for Thomas Cook wrote a hurried letter to the Assistant Secretary in the General Department on 10th April, asking him to treat the matter as a 'special case', because forty-one members of the party needed to leave Allahabad the following morning. If they failed to board their train, the ship they were booked on would sail without them. The request was passed on to J. Atkins, Secretary of the General Department, who weighed up various interpretations of the Emigration Act of 1883 and the Epidemic Diseases Act of 1896. In a lengthy handwritten memo, he noted that the Emigration Act of 1883 did not specify that emigration was banned to European countries. Nor did it apply to persons 'engaged for labour other than manual'. 'It is equally evident', the memo continued, 'that as the labour of jugglers and dancers is not (sleight-of-hand notwithstanding) what can reasonably be described as "manual labour", the prohibition under the Emigration Act does not apply.' Declaring there was no need to trouble the Government of India on what was a 'very clear question', he ordered the Commissioner of Customs to allow Nehru's 'jugglers and dancers' to leave for Paris.[8]

Five days later, on 15th April, the *SS Amphitrite* set sail for Trieste with Nehru's troupe on board. But their departure was not the end of the matter. In their rush to give their permission, Bombay neglected to collect any security from Nehru's representative to guarantee the party's return. Nor had local officials informed the Government of India of their decision. If they had, Nehru's troupe would not have been allowed to sail. Shortly after their departure, the Home Department refused permission for Professor Deval's circus to depart for Egypt under the provisions the Epidemic Diseases Act. The notoriety that would arise 'to any mishap connected with plague in the case of a circus troupe going to the Paris Exhibition', and the difficulty of managing sanitary arrangements for a travelling menagerie, were cited as the main reasons for the decision.[9] As far as the government was concerned, the same prohibition should have been applied to Nehru's company. 'The case seems to be on all fours with that of the Circus, and why the Bombay Government should refer to the Government of India before passing orders in one case and not in the other I cannot conceive,' Evan Maconochie, Under Secretary, Government of India (Revenue and Agricultural departments) complained on 3 May 1900. 'If these men have already embarked there is nothing to be done. But the Bombay Government should be given distinct instructions as to such cases in future.' The Home Department's F. Cowie called it 'a most unfortunate action' that 'stultifies beyond the possibility of any vindication our refusal to allow the circus to go to France'.[10] Amid the recriminations, Thomas Holderness, Secretary to the Revenue and Agricultural Department of the Government of India, pointed out that the terms 'emigrant' and 'labourer' as used in the notification, had never been properly defined. 'We have given the Bombay Government an interpretation of the terms for its own guidance. But the interpretation has not been publicly notified, and when we say we gave it, we had not in our minds the possibility of troupes of dancers, jugglers, circus attendants, and the like going to Europe.'[11]

Holderness's comments were an understatement. The demand for entertainers from India, Ceylon and Burma as well as other countries, was showing no signs of abating and had gone well beyond confines of international exhibitions, world fairs and ethnographic displays. Indian jugglers could be spotted at fair grounds, circuses, vaudeville shows, wax museums, velodromes and even beer gardens. In 1884, P. T. Barnum turned New York's Madison Square Garden into an Ethnographic Congress of Savage Tribes lumping together 'Hindoos, Syrians, and Siamese', with 'Cannibals, Oceanic Idolators, and Nautch dancing girls'.[12] The Congress won accolades from the press. 'As an educator, there has never been anything shown under canvas equal to it. It is, moreover, the only exhibit of the kind in the world. Wonderful jugglers from Hindustan, silver dancers from Ceylon, Cotta dwarfs from south India, Caribs from St Kitts, warriors from Samoa, giants from Zululand, Hindoo creoles from Trinidad ...'[13] The list went on and on. Three years later, Barnum offered his latest prize – the Hairy Family of Burmah, Mah-Phoon and Moung – who he insisted came 'not as freaks or monstrosities, but as pure, long-established types of the most weirdly, peculiar, distinct race of mankind of whom there is any trace or record'.[14] India also featured at the Columbian Exposition held in Chicago in 1893. Its twenty-seven million visitors feasted their eyes on 'Eastern primitive villages, Oriental and barbarian dances, Oriental jugglers, trained animals, ancient Greek portraits, a German museum, etc'.[15] In 1896, Barnum & Bailey's circus spectacular *Oriental India* crammed onto a single stage a plethora of stereotypical characters including snake charmers, sacred cows, Hindus praying and the 'famous dancing girls of Madras'.

The impetus to exhibit Indian magicians came from some unexpected sources. In 1895, Abdul Karim, Queen Victoria's Muslim munshi, and, to the consternation of much of her court, her closest confidante, accompanied the monarch on a visit to southern France. An entry in his diary records an encounter with a group of jugglers in Nice.

> Events, which we never thought or even dreamt of happening to us, cause us to wonder at the wonderful ways God makes use of in working out his purposes. This thought came to my mind as I considered the wonderful good fortune that happened to some Indian jugglers who chanced to be in Nice while Her Majesty was there. When Her Majesty came to hear of them she sent a request to have them brought before her to exhibit their tricks. The Queen was highly amused and delighted and the honour which was given to these poor jugglers must have made them happy for life.[16]

Karim wrote a testimonial for the jugglers and a few months later they found themselves performing alongside a hundred other magicians, dancers, acrobats and entertainers at the Empire of India Exhibition. Curated by the Hungarian impresario Imre Kiralfy, it was the most spectacular tribute to the glory and splendour of England's proudest possession ever staged. Wooden buildings from Poona were transported to London to recreate India at Earls Court. The official programme promised 'Hindu magicians and snake charmers ... in their weird and mystical performances. Hindu music, changing stones into money, burning the turban, thread and fire trick, the sacrificial act, the famous Basket Trick, playing with the deadly cobra, and many others.'[17] The centrepiece was a mock jungle inhabited with life-sized models of tigers, rhinoceroses, buffalos and monkeys. Specially imported camels and elephants carried visitors around the grounds on their backs, while children rode in bullock carts. A 'fine baboon', a live crocodile in a wooden tank, and a sacred six-legged cow, added to the surreal atmosphere. The exhibition included a curry house and twice daily three-hour long performances of the theatrical spectacular *India*, featuring 'a chorus of fanatical fakirs'. Music was provided by the bands of the Coldstream and Grenadier Guards. As winter closed in, Indian sailors were bribed to bring over fresh cobras on their boats to replace those dying of the cold. Tonnes of ghee were imported for cooking meals for the hundreds of artisans, performers and other Indian staff for the duration of the exhibition.

◈

THE provisioning of performers and animals for these grand spectacles was a finely tuned process that in the final decades of the nineteenth century was dominated by one family. German-born Carl Hagenbeck and half-brothers, John and Gustav, ran a multinational anthropomorphic trading empire spanning global

Hagenbeck's Exposition des Indies. Circus Museum.

trade routes that exhibited troupes from as far afield as Samoa and Somalia, the Siberian steppes and Tierra del Fuego. According to a reporter who visited the magnate's headquarters in Hamburg in 1902, the fishmonger's son-turned-millionaire had at any one time up to 6000 people 'en route through the most diverse parts of the world'.[18] Though the statement was an exaggeration, the German had a near monopoly on the international animal and show people trade. His highly choreographed displays reached their nadir in his revolutionary Tierpark in Stellingen near Hamburg, where animals were presented in what were meant to be their natural surroundings, alongside ethnographic displays, moving pictures and mechanical rides – a fictional story world with an exotic theme.[19] The mere mention of his name, Hagenbeck's biographer Eric Ames writes, 'conjured up a series of exoticized bodies, landscapes, and multi-sensory environments, even the audience's central position in the thick of things'.[20] Ames estimates that Hagenbeck was responsible for bringing a third of the more than three hundred ethnographic troupes that appeared in Germany between 1875 and 1914.[21] In 1898, *Carl Hagenbeck's India* was staged on Berlin's Kurfurstendamm, featuring more than sixty performers – all of them Tamils from Ceylon. Spectators were invited to stroll through an Indian village centred around Trishinapoli Square. Surrounding this plaza were plaster-cast Hindu and Buddhist temples and a towering statue of the elephant-headed god Ganesh. There was an Indian restaurant and a theatre that featured jugglers, acrobats, contortionists, *bayaderes*, as well as 'Mahbool Kahn and Asub Khan, the Indian wrestlers'. After watching a show, spectators could shop in 'Carl Hagenbeck's Indian Bazaar' for masks, statues and other souvenirs, before relaxing in 'Carl Hagenbeck's Ceylon Tea House'.[22]

Sourcing performers from Ceylon was done out of necessity rather than choice. The best jugglers were still found in and around Madras, but India's tough emigration laws meant they had to first travel to Colombo. While Carl was drumming up business in Europe and America, John and Gustav Hagenbeck were using Ceylon as a base for their activities in South and South East Asia. The presence of the two Germans became an increasing irritant for the Indian government as news of performers being mistreated or stranded abroad began filtering back to London. A confidential memo dated 1913 and prompted by the abandonment of more than a hundred Indian magicians and other performers at the Strangers' Home in London, stated that the Hagenbecks had been recruiting entertainers from Chetput on the outskirts of Madras since the late 1870s. They included animal trainers, conjurers, sword swallowers, fortune tellers, palm readers, tumblers, acrobats and animal trainers. Due to their frequent visits to Europe, most had acquired a smattering of various European languages and had a fair fluency in German. Nautch dancers were mainly sourced from Tanjore. Recruitment was done through a local Tamil physician named R. Krishnaswami. To avoid suspicion, the performers were booked to travel to Ceylon through the port of Tuticorin. Forced to repatriate the troupe stranded in London at a cost of more than £3000, the Government of India urged port authorities to be more vigilant to prevent illegal emigration of show people and, if they ever set foot on Indian soil, to press charges against the Hagenbecks and their associates. [23]

Aside from India and Ceylon, other British colonies found themselves caught up in what was fast becoming a major headache for governments and officials in both England and Europe. In March 1897, a troupe of twenty Burmese jugglers and performers were engaged in Rangoon to perform in Europe for six months. When their contracts expired, their employers told them they did not have the money to send them home. Some managed to pay their own passages, others had to rely on the charity of 'benevolently disposed persons'. In a report on the case prepared for the Home Department, the Chief Secretary to the Government of Burma, Edward Spence Symes, remarked that it was difficult to ascertain which of the three men involved in the recruitment of the troupe should be held responsible. He added that 'if any member of the troupe wishes to bring a civil action, the courts are open. This has been explained to them. It does not seem desirable that Government should interfere.' The publicity surrounding the case, Symes continued, would make it unlikely that Burmans would be induced to proceed to Europe 'without at least the assurance that they can return to Burma on the expiry of their engagements'. To guarantee against such regrettable incidents recurring, artistic troupes proceeding to Europe should have their contracts checked, and, if necessary, those travelling should be warned 'of the risks they are incurring'.[24]

In essence, Symes was maintaining the same line that the Government of India had been stubbornly adhering to since 1868, when it was faced with repatriating members of the Oriental Troupe. To expect that magicians recruited by unscrupulous agents would change their minds as they were boarding ships bound for England and Europe, was disingenuous. Even if the contracts were in order, there was little prospect of destitute strolling players appealing to the courts for redress if their managers ran into financial problems and were unable to pay them. Unless a sympathetic lawyer, the local Indian community, or a benevolent party came to their assistance, they could not afford the legal fees. Few, if any, had sufficient awareness of the workings of European legal systems to even ask for help.

In March 1899, an Englishman named Fairlie, who was involved in the recruitment of the earlier troupe of Burmese jugglers, travelled to Singapore. It is unclear whether his choice of destination was due to the adverse publicity he was receiving in Rangoon, or because he was afraid the Burmese authorities would be more vigilant. From among Singapore's large Indian community, Fairlie recruited fifty-nine artists, including jugglers, dancers and other entertainers. Four more jugglers were engaged en route to Europe in Ceylon. Although thirty-eight signed contracts with Fairlie, an administrative 'oversight' meant they were not warned of risks of being left destitute as they boarded their vessel. Another twenty-one left Singapore without any agreement at all. They arrived in Vienna on 1 May 1899, where they performed for four months before travelling to different cities in Germany. In November, they were asked to extend their contracts for ten months. By now, however, Fairlie had disappeared. Most of the troupe signed contracts with their new manager, a man named Drexler, but eighteen refused. The majority of the latter found their way to the Strangers' Home and were repatriated. The others continued performing for another four months until Drexler stopped paying their wages and also disappeared. The first time officials in London heard about them was when police in Brussels found forty-two destitute members of the troupe wandering the streets and sent them to Dover.

This time the cause of the show people abandoned by Fairlie and Drexler was taken up by one of the most formidable members of the English Parliament. Described as 'the most brilliant, inventive, and unpredictable politician in late Victorian England',[25] Joseph Chamberlain was a member of the Liberal Unionist party and half-brother of Neville Chamberlain. An arch-imperialist who sought to transform Britain's disparate colonies into a coherent military and trading imperial federation, he entered into a coalition with Salisbury's Conservatives after the 1895 election. He was instrumental in persuading Salisbury and his successor, Arthur Balfour, to pass a number of important social reforms that helped the Conservatives attract new working-class support. In 1895, Salisbury appointed Chamberlain Secretary of State for the Colonies. Although he had more pressing issues to deal with than the problem of what he termed 'Asiatics for exhibition purposes in Europe', he nevertheless set in motion important reforms that would have an impact on the future engagement of show people from India, Burma and Ceylon. Chamberlain lobbied for a ban on engaging artists from the colonies except under the most stringent conditions 'including substantial security for repatriation'. 'The importation of coloured persons into Europe for performing and exhibition purposes has led to much fraud and demoralisation as shown by various instances in which the assistance of this office have been bespoken on behalf of the natives,' he wrote to the Colonial Secretary of the Straits Settlements, J. A. Sweetenham. 'In my opinion, therefore, their engagement for the purposes in question should be so safeguarded by law as to render the recurrence of abuses impossible.'[26] The problem, he noted, was that the provisions of the Emigration Act did not apply to arrangements such as those entered into by Fairlie and others. This was because 'the men and women were not engaged to labour but as "artists" and the superintendent under the Indian Immigration Ordinance might also consider that they were not empowered to refuse to issue certificates under that ordinance to play-actors, jugglers & etc'.[27] In August 1900, Chamberlain wrote to the Secretary of State urging the government to urgently pass legislation to prevent more Indians 'engaging themselves to foreign adventurers'.[28]

Spurred on by the lobbying of Chamberlain, steps to amend the Emigration Act moved into high gear. The Home Department sent Curzon a list of previous cases of Indians being found destitute in England and its colonies. A total of thirteen cases were brought to the Viceroy's attention, including the Melbourne 'mutiny', Fairlie's Burmese jugglers and 'three Afghan Waziris' repatriated to Bannu 'on political grounds'.[29] An application from a consortium applying for permission to send a troupe of magicians and entertainers to the 1901 Glasgow exhibition, gave additional urgency to the need to clarify the status of 'spectacular performers'. On 31 October 1901, Curzon sent a memo to Hamilton, endorsing the need for an amendment to the Indian Emigration Act of 1883 to regulate the engagement of artisans and entertainers. Referring to the earlier incidents, he wrote: 'There seems reason to believe that such cases are not of infrequent occurrence and that their number may increase.' The engagement of skilled artisans by private employers for service out of India should be permitted, provided the Government can be 'assured of the considerate treatment of the employees and their repatriation on the termination of their engagement'. Similar consideration should apply to 'natives who have the offer of employment outside India in spectacular performances', Curzon continued. 'If the law is altered, as we now propose, it will be possible to engage skilled artisans as well as spectacular performers for service in any country ... with the previous sanction of the Local Government, and subject to such conditions as the Local Government may impose as to the terms of employment, the repatriation of the employees on the expiry of their agreement, and the periodical communication of information regarding their circumstances.'[30]

Entered into law the following year, the Indian Emigration (Amendment) Act, 1902 (No. 10) ruled that anyone wishing to engage artisans, entertainers including magicians, restaurant workers and certain types of domestic servants, had to 'apply for permission to the local Government, stating in his application certain specified particulars, and the person engaged must appear before, and be registered by, the Protector of Emigrants'.[31] For consortiums such as those put together by Nehru, the Amendment provided regulatory certainty. The mistreatment of show people from South Asia lessened, but was not eradicated completely.

◈

IRONICALLY, the greatest pressure to end the trade in Indian show people would come not from the Government, but from the Indian National Congress now led by Jawaharlal Nehru. On 14 November 1926, *The Tribune* in Lahore published a letter from Daulat Ram Dev, an Indian resident of Breslau in Germany, complaining about the 'Indian show' at Berlin Zoo. The spectacle was the brainchild of the flamboyant John Hagenbeck who took over the business following the death of Carl in 1913. Though he liked to pose in business suits and pince-nez glasses, John was a fearless hunter and animal catcher, who honed his skills killing rogue elephants in the jungles of Ceylon. Posters plastered around the city advertising 'Indians in the Zoo', had irked their fellow countrymen. In his missive, Dev said the human zoo 'throws dust in the eyes of the civilized world'. He accused Hagenbeck of making money at the expense of the 'innocent and ignorent [sic] classes of depressed countries along with his running show of wild animals'. From India, he recruited 'the poorest, lowest-classed darkest and ugliest Indians, who could perform and play the part of snake-conjurer, or charmer jugglers, buffoon etc'. He also alleged that more than one hundred Indians, including ten children aged from five to seven, were crammed together in a shed just fifteen-feet long and eight-feet high with twenty-five cabin-style beds. 'They must breath [sic] together the filthy and dirty respiration of each other as sheep in a hurdle. For their daily use, there are only two water-closets of Indian fashion and two aqueducts.' They were made to perform outside for three hours a day dressed as they would be in an Indian summer, despite the freezing Berlin winter. 'The more they play the part of buffoon, the more they are applauded,' Dev complained, adding that India had been insulted, made fun of and suffered for too long. 'We should give Mr Hagenbeck a bitter lesson through protest meetings all over India. Why does not this man dare to start a Japanese or

Chinese show? The answer is that these nations are living with full energy and strength and do not bear such insult.'[32]

Almost six decades after the outcry over the treatment of the Oriental Troupe in London, the British government was still reluctant to intervene to protect magicians, musicians, artists and other groups. This was despite an incident in 1912 when 112 'Cingalese' (in reality mainly South Indians), turned up in Hamburg after quitting the service of Gustav Hagenbeck. The performers had been made to sign contracts that were 'the most unbusiness-like documents possible', the British consul in Hamburg Walter Hearn complained, and were now seeking repatriation back to India. The contracts had 'no rate of wages, no dates of commencement or termination and [are] of not legal value'.[33] Gustav claimed he had lost £10,000 bringing the troupe to Germany owing to inclement weather. Its members were surviving by doing juggling tricks and selling trinkets.

Nor were they prepared to blame John Hagenbeck, despite once having ordered his prosecution for similar offences. This time the response had more to do with domestic Indian politics than welfare concerns. George Lyall, the British Consul in Berlin, blamed the Congress party for using the issue to stir up an anti-colonial agitation. 'No complaints of ill-treatment have been received at this consulate from any members of this troupe,' Lyall wrote in a memorandum to the Foreign Office in London on 20 December 1926.[34] Instead he was prepared to accept the word of Hagenbeck, who told him the source of the stories was British journalist Agnes Smedley, who was in close contact with members of the local Indian Students' Association and the journalist A. C. N. Nambiar. Smedley was married to the Indian revolutionary Virendranath Chattopadhyay, also known as Chatto. All three were close associates of Subash Chandra Bose, who would later split from Congress to form the Forward Bloc and become leader of the Indian National Army. At the time, Bose was also editor of *Forward*, and used its pages to denounce Hagenbeck. Indians were being kept and displayed 'as if they were a new species of quadrupeds'. Even watching them eat food was an attraction 'similar to the excitement [people] receive while watching lions and tigers being fed in their cages'.[35] Motilal Nehru's earlier contribution to the stereotyping of Indians and profiting from the trade in show people was conveniently swept under the carpet.

Hagenbeck told Lyall he had started libel proceedings against Smedley for alleging his ill-treatment and cruelty towards the Indians. 'His evidence is convincing, and agitators like Miss Smedley, Nambiar and other associates have only themselves to blame if Mr Hagenbeck secures orders of deportation against them from the German authorities,' Lyall commented. Meanwhile, Hagenbeck took on his detractors with a series of carefully choreographed articles in sympathetic newspapers. The troupe's manager H. D. H. Dharmadasa told the *Ceylon Observer* that while in Berlin the performers were accommodated in a hotel adjoining the show grounds. It was 'quite absurd to think we were housed with the animals', he countered. They received every comfort they wanted including beer and brandy, were taken to see bioscopes and theatres on Hagenbeck's account and earned between fifty to one hundred pounds each, not including tips. 'These are the bare facts,' Dharmadasa insisted.[36] On their return to Ceylon on 11 November 1926, one of the members of the troupe told the *Ceylon Morning Leader* that 'all they could do was invoke the blessings of God on Father Hagenbeck'. He had 'treated them like his own children, and did all he possibly could for their comfort and welfare'.[37]

Hagenbeck still had one hurdle to cross. He had been interned by the British when the war broke out, but had managed to escape and travel to Germany via Java and Italy. The Foreign Office was reluctant to lift an embargo on his return to Ceylon because of earlier cases of mistreatment of performers. The difficulties of running Tiergarten, replenishing its stock of animals and hiring show people as a consequence of the war, were made worse when the Government of Ceylon tightened rules governing the recruitment of theatrical, musical and spectacular performers in 1917. Although he was evading the rules using middlemen, false passports and getting officials at ports of embarkation to turn a blind eye, the Government of India was maintaining its stand as late as February 1927. In June of that year, however, Colombo decided to withdraw its objection to members of the Hagenbeck family entering Ceylon and allowed them to directly recruit performers for circuses and other shows. 'There has been no recurrence of the trouble experienced prior to the war with regard to the repatriation of performers engaged by the Hagenbeck family,' the Governor of Ceylon Herbert Stanley wrote on 21 November 1928. 'Allegations of ill-treatment have been made occasionally, but have not been substantiated.'[38]

The reprieve turned out to be of little consequence. After returning to Ceylon, Hagenbeck established the island's first Zoological Gardens at Dehiwala, an eleven-acre site he used as a collecting depot for wild animals destined for European zoos.

But his enterprise went bankrupt in the mid-1930s. He died in 1940 without seeing the devastation wrought on Tiergarten by Allied bombing during the Second World War. Public opinion towards 'humans zoos' and ethnographic displays was also changing. The turmoil in Europe in the lead up to the war meant fewer international exhibitions and fewer touring circuses. The demand for Indian magic, however, remained as strong as ever. By now tens of millions of people had passed through the turnstiles at international exhibitions and fairs in major cities in Europe, Britain and North America, and had watched dhoti-clad jugglers performing amazing feats of legerdemain, turbaned snake charmers coaxing their half-frozen cobras out of baskets and tawny-coloured gymnasts defying gravity. And if that was not enough to equate the land of Hindustan with all things magical, the wondrous tales and mystifying tricks brought back from India by Western wand wavers was making that association even stronger.

ELEVEN

THE FAKIR INVASION

IN the summer of 1849, the tiny village of Bonchurch on the Isle of Wight, witnessed an unusual spectacle. 'The Unparalleled Necromancer' Rhia Rhama Rhoos, educated cabalistically in the Orange Groves of Salamanca and the Ocean Caves of Alum Bay' was the most majestic magician ever been seen in this part of England. The Eastern conjurer's playbill was impressive. The Pyramid Wonder was bought at a cost of 5000 guineas from 'a Chinese Mandarin who died of grief immediately after parting with the secret'. The feat of transporting a lady's watch from inside a wooden box into the middle of a loaf of bread had taken ten years of study in the Plains of Tartary. Another nine years of seclusion in the mines of Russia was required to master the Leaping Card Wonder.

Charles Dickens delighted in stage dramas, ghost stories, dressing up and making magic. His sister Mary recalled *Twelfth Night* parties where he made children 'scream with laughter' at his tricks. In a letter to a friend in America, Dickens described producing a plum pudding from an empty saucepan 'held over a blazing fire kindled in Stanfield's hat without damaging the lining' and creating a live guinea pig from a box of bran.[1] The idea to smear his face with boot polish, don a turban and a costume of silken robes, came after seeing Ramo Samee perform in the interval of the stage adaptation of Nicholas Nickleby in 1837. Dickens had referred to the South Indian's juggling in *An Unsettled Neighbourhood*, where his local greengrocer on Great Twig Street could always be found 'practising Ramo Samee with three potatoes'.[2] The name Rhia Rhama Rhoos was a corruption of Khia Khan Khruse, who billed himself as 'The Chief of the Indian Jugglers' and was Samee's rival in the late 1810s and early 1820s. Unbeknown to Dickens, his real name was Juan Antonio. He was Portuguese.

Cultural cross-dressing spanned magical genres from the Near East to the Far East, but Indian memes were a perennial favourite. Caught off-guard by the success of jugglers like Samee, Western magicians competed with each other to outperform their subcontinental counterparts adopting names such as 'The Fakir of Ava', the 'Fakir of Oolu', 'The Fakir of Simla' and the 'Fakir of Jeypoor'. The trend prompted one writer to complain about the 'fakir invasion'. 'If there were any towns in India who were lucky enough to escape from these specialists, they must have been confined in Houdini's Chinese torture cell, probably the only place on earth where they would have been secure from confiscation. And every one of these admitted, and even openly declared, that he himself was the genuine, most exalted, most illustrious, most majestic, and the real and only honest-to-goodness actual greatest that ever lived.'[3]

Early attempts to capitalize on an image of India as a land where impossibilities seemed commonplace by imitating

Orientalist stereotypes in dress, stagecraft or repertoire were fairly crude. It was not uncommon for performers to present Chinese, Egyptian, Indian and even Japanese magic on the same night. One of the most bizarre examples of cultural confusion was the American ventriloquist, necromancer and spirit rapper Reverend Dr. Haskell, who in the late 1840s began calling himself the 'Great Oriental Necromancer and Mysterialist [sic], the Fakir of Shiva'. Haskell's shows promised 'the mysterious and unaccountable phenomena of the Chinese and East Indian Soothsayers' displayed in a 'gorgeous Enchanted Palace, gotten up at the expense of a princely fortune'.[4] His tricks included 'suspension in the air' and the 'great bottle feat', which he claimed he performed before Queen Victoria and the rulers of Russia and Spain. In Baltimore in 1853, he presented his 'original troupe of Chinese Jugglers, Acrobats, Contortionists and Wonderments'. The troupe consisted of forty-two performers billed as coming directly from the 'celestial empire' and being seen by 400,000 people. The first part of the programme consisted of 'Hindoo miracles' performed by the Chinese members of the troupe, none of which bore any resemblance to Indian tricks aside from 'Magic Balls', billed as an 'astonishing East India Rite' performed by a twelve-year-old Chinese boy named Ar Boie. This was followed by Chinese juggling and a musical performance by a troupe of American minstrels calling themselves the Ethiopian Brothers.[5] Haskell continued performing as the Fakir of Shiva until the late 1890s, despite having numerous run-ins with the law for fraud and theft.

Across the Atlantic, the Englishman Alfred Sylvester, alternated between the 'Eastern Mystic, the Fakir of Oolu' and 'Hadji Mahommed Salib and his beautiful entranced Persian Princess'.

Sylvester started performing in London in 1865, moved to America and then returned to England in the early 1870s. During his shows, he dressed in Middle Eastern costumes on a stage decorated to look like an Indian palace. One of his best-known illusions was a levitation feat called 'The Denizen of the Air, or the Last Link Severed'. Sylvester bought the apparatus from the French magician Jean-Eugene Robert-Houdin and then modified it. In Robert-Houdin's Ethereal Suspension, his assistant floated above the stage with only his elbow supported on a stick, a trick originally performed by Sheshal, 'the air Brahmin' in Madras in the late 1820s. Wearing a jewelled turban and shimmering maharajah's robe, the burly bearded Englishman began by putting his assistant in a mesmeric state and then used his wand to raise her until she lay suspended in the air with only her elbow resting on a wooden pole. This was pulled away leaving her supported by only the palm of his hand. Sylvester then walked off stage as she remained floating mysteriously in the air.

Playbill for the Fakir of Oolu (Alfred Sylvester). Flickr.

Other 'fakirs' were Indian in name only. Despite promising 'Hindoo Miracles, Asiatic Jugglery, Demonology, Mythology, and BRAMATICAL [sic] CHICANERY', there was nothing particularly Indian about the Fakir of Ava's performance or indeed about the magician himself. His real name was Isaiah Hughes, he came from Buffalo in New York state and his trademark acts included smashing a watch and making it reappear again as he fired a pistol in the air. Audiences were promised the 'Hindoo Cup Trick', but most of his acts comprised odd-sounding illusions that had no association with the East, such as 'The Express Laundry' and the 'Great African Box and Sack Feat'.[6]

In April 1865, Colonel Stodare, whose real name was Alfred Inglis, claimed to be the first Englishman to perform the Great Indian Basket Feat and the Mango Tree Trick, which he called Instantaneous Growth of Flower Trees. He told his audience he had received their secrets 'from the Far East' – despite having never been there. Stodare's basket, which resembled a picnic hamper on four legs, was just large enough to hold his female assistant. Dressed in a dinner suit, Stodare plunged his sword into the basket and then wiped off the blood on a white pocket-handkerchief as his victim begged for mercy. 'Ladies and gentlemen, I fear you imagine that I have hurt the lady who was the subject of this experiment,' he declared. 'Pray disabuse yourselves of such an idea. She had disobeyed me, and I therefore determined to punish her by giving her a little fright; but nothing more. The fact is, she had left the basket some time before I thrust the sword into it.' He then turned the basket over to confirm it was empty, before his assistant walked on the stage and bowed to thunderous applause.[7] Though crudely executed when compared with the jadoowallah's version, the *Daily News* called it 'unquestionably one of the most startling feats ever exhibited'.[8] Presented less than a decade after the Mutiny of 1857, audience members might have been forgiven for drawing analogies between the macabre nature of the Basket Trick and the violence inflicted on British citizens by rebellious sepoys.[9] Ever since J. Hobart Caunter's 1836 description of the ferocious, demonic juggler unleashing his fury on an innocent child trapped in a basket, descriptions of the trick in the popular press had played up its savagery. But for Stodare and others the act was aimed at debunking the rope tying and cabinet illusions of Spiritualists such as the brothers Ira and William Davenport – who claimed supernatural powers and were the most successful entertainers of their day – rather than making a political statement on the slaughter of innocents.

STODARE, Sylvester, Hughes and Haskell were able to get away with playing loosely with memes, costumes and oxymoronic names, because like them, the overwhelming majority of the public had never been to India and imagined it as a country where anything was possible. Perceptions of Indian magic and how it should be presented began to change as Western wizards began travelling to the subcontinent, drawn by a mixture of mystical appeal and mercantilism. India promised the keys to the most elusive of secrets – and the most lucrative of profits. A large cashed-up expatriate community, the growth of theatrical venues in major cities and an ever-expanding railway network, made it a desirable destination for all manner of mid-century popular entertainers including minstrels, musicians, burlesque companies, opera singers and balladeers. In 1858, John Henry Anderson, better known as the 'Wizard of the North', became the first magician to embark on a global tour that included the Near East, Australia and America. Carl Herrmann returned from India in 1860, claiming to have mastered 'many of the surprising feats of the marvellous Eastern jugglers'. Those attending his shows would be able to 'imagine themselves at Calcutta or Benares, as they witness the wonderful transformations, which they have, heretofore, only known by reading, or the description of some chance lecturer'.[10]

The opening of the Suez Canal in 1869, which halved the travel time between Europe and the subcontinent, and the commencement of regular mail and steamship services made touring easier and more profitable. Leading the muster of magicians was Robert Heller. Born William Henry Palmer in 1826 in Canterbury England, he abandoned a promising career as a concert pianist for magic after seeing a performance by Robert-Houdin. Heller styled himself as a renowned 'Wizard, Scientific Illusionist, Sorcerer, Magician, Prestidigitator, and Necromantic Musician', and promised 'Cyclogeal, Electic [sic], and Ecumenical Entertainments.'[11] Like Stodare, he presented the Basket Trick without ever seeing the genuine version. He billed it as 'A Man is put in a Basket, Assassinated, and Spirited away', making it sound more like a murder mystery than a piece of Oriental conjuring. Heller's first encounter with genuine Indian jadoo came in 1871, when his steamship broke a propeller shaft as it was about to dock in Madras. A boatload of hawkers and a juggler rowed out to the stricken ship to take advantage of a captive audience. The juggler's repertoire was fairly standard: making a mango tree grow from the deck, engaging in some snake charming and vanishing a pair of pigeons that later reappeared in different boxes. After the show was finished, Heller took one of the pigeons and to the horror of the jadoowallah ripped off its head and threw the still quivering carcass overboard. When the Indian was about to do the same to Heller, he pointed to the sky where the pigeon was circling unharmed.[12] Once on dry land, Heller's shows, which featured among other things India's first Punch and Judy performance, were immensely popular. Bombay's Parsi community demanded an exclusive season for their families 'to the exclusion of all Europeans'. The Grant Road Theatre, the city's largest venue, could not cope with the crowds.[13]

In 1878 'Heller's Wonders' opened in New York. His programme boasted of his performances before 'Emperors, Sultans, Kings, Presidents, Rajahs, Maharajahs, Baboos, Princes, Governors, Viceroys, Mandarins, Nobility, Priesthood and Public generally.' Audiences were promised 'The Wonders of the Oriental Fakirs, Jugglers & Conjurers Made Easy, or Orientalism Revealed.'[14] The show included an improved version of the 'Hindoo Basket Trick' and a Growth of Flowers illusion that borrowed heavily from the Mango Tree deception. The success of Heller's Wonders made him the most prominent magician in America, but his stay at the apex of his profession was brief. While performing in Philadelphia he was taken ill. Doctors diagnosed him as suffering from 'organic exhaustion'. He died two days later on 28 November 1878.

Heller was more concerned with capitalizing on his exotic adventures than with questioning whether Indian *jadoo* was living up to its reputation. But that was changing. Like two wizards preparing for a battle of wands, East and West were about to declare war over whose magic was the most authentic. One of the earliest attacks on India's thaumaturgic fraternity was an article entitled 'Indian Jugglers and Impostors' that appeared in *The Leisure Hour* in 1854. Published by the Religious Tract Society, the magazine was designed to counter the 'pernicious' morality of non-religious popular periodicals, whose 'sins' included devoting considerable space to sensational stories coming out of India about inexplicable feats of legerdemain. Determined to set the record straight, *The Leisure Hour's* anonymous correspondent blamed imposters for taking advantage of people's gullibility. Fortunately, 'the penetrating sagacity of educated Europeans has unmasked their villainy and exposed them to the derision and scorn of the more enlightened'. Two examples were cited. The first concerned the 'man that sat in the air', Apoosawmy Ragavah, also known as Sheshal, who floated above the ground with his hand resting on a wooden stick before a group of Europeans in Madras in 1830. The trick created a sensation until one Mr Conway proved it was done not by some mysterious force of magnetism, but by using a seat made of brass concealed beneath the Brahmin's flowing robes. The second example was the live burial of a 'faqueer' at Ludhiana. When the body was removed after ten months, there was no pulse or heartbeat. Only when his turned-back tongue was restored to its normal position and warm water was poured over the body, did the fakir come back to life. Yet even this 'most marvellous case of suspended animation' was a hoax, the author concluded, executed with some artifice that sustained the body's vitality during its 'long and arduous trial'. The two examples illustrated 'the subtle ingenuity of the Hindoos' and 'an ability that only wants leading in the right direction to constitute them most useful members of society'.[15]

The other source of scepticism came from within the Western conjuring community. Until the 1870s, what little information there was on Indian magic came either from descriptions of jugglers, 'fakirs', snake charmers and the like, published in newspapers, magazines and journals often accompanied by illustrations showing bizarre and even ghoulish acts. Now a new genre of travel literature and memoir writing was emerging as Western necromancers penned colourful accounts of their encounters with enchanters and adepts, khans and rajahs in strange and exotic lands. One the earliest examples of this genre was the part-diary, part-memoir, part-travelogue of Hugh Simmons Lynn.

Publicity photograph of Dr Lynn (H. S. Lynn). Alma Collection, State Library of Victoria.

A studio portrait of Lynn taken in the 1870s shows the English illusionist dressed in a waistcoat and tails with his left arm leaning on a pedestal and his right arm cupping his head. Severing his assistant's arms and legs before decapitating him was one of Lynn's favourite acts. Because his assistant was brought back in a perfect state of preservation, Lynn called his trick Palingenesia from the ancient Greek word for rebirth or regeneration. Twelve-year-old Ehrich Weiss was so impressed by seeing his performance in Milwaukee in 1886, he decided to become a magician, eventually pilfering Robert-Houdin's name to become Houdini.

Lynn became interested in Oriental magic in the early 1860s. The Bristol-born son of an English clergyman, he joined the royal navy while still in his teens, but quickly realized he was better at pulling rabbits from hats than hoisting sails. He gave his first magic show in Malta in 1862, and later toured Australia as an assistant to a conjuror named Shaw. He went on to tour the Far East, performing at the Great Canton Theatre at Shanghai, where the audience grew restive when he failed to decapitate himself on stage as shown on his posters. To make up for the omission, he offered to walk through the city the following day with his head tucked underneath his arm – which he did.[16] From Shanghai, he sailed to Japan, surviving an earthquake in Nagasaki that tore his hotel in two. In his book, *Travels and Adventures of Dr Lynn*, he boasted of appearing before the emperor of China at Peking, 'the Grand Llama [sic] of Tibet', two kings of Siam, the Dyaks of Borneo and the 'Khan of Crim' in Tartary – though there is little evidence to support his claims.[17] But he picked up enough Oriental feats to impress reviewers. 'Whatever the Hindoo jugglers or the Japanese wonder-workers could impart he has acquired, and his lissom fingers can accomplish. His programme is stored with Eastern novelties and his performance is the perfection of sleight-of-hand,' the *Royal Cornwall Gazette* enthused.[18] Lynn's loquaciousness earned him the moniker the 'talkee-talkee man'. 'From the moment he comes to the front with his wand, this plump magician keeps the attention of all in the room enchained; his restless eyes sparkle from side to side, his nimble tongue patters with the rapidity of a Wheatstone transmitter,' stammered one

London critic.[19] At the conclusion of each trick he would solemnly declare 'that's how it's done'. It became his catchphrase – though the audience 'will be no wiser for it'.[20]

In 1876, Lynn embarked on a tour of India whose 'miserably clad *jadoogars*', he wrote, were responsible for 'most of the best-known conjuring tricks of modern time'.[21] A few days after arriving in Madras, he came across a '*jadoogar*' who offered to put on a show if the Englishman reciprocated. Never one to let an opportunity pass, Lynn agreed. The Indian began by taking a sheet of paper, folding it into the shape of a tent and placing on the ground. Saying the words 'here is your bread', he gave the paper a twist and turned it into a half-pound cake. With another flourish of the paper he produced a child's hat. With a third, a miniature table. He then called out for his companion. When no one came, he started playing a strange sounding tune on an instrument resembling a 'wry-necked fife'. A vicious-looking cobra rose from the ground and began dancing to the tune. The jadoogar then asked: 'Shall I fetch a snake out of a river, or from the infernal regions, or out of a well or a mango tree, or out of a snake hole? Say which.' Before Lynn could answer, he extracted a hissing cobra from Lynn's coat pocket and made the two snakes dance together. For his final trick, the Indian began piling stones on the ground from his apparently empty hand with amazing rapidity. He then placed his turban over the stones and slowly raising it revealed a beautiful rose tree in full bloom. 'I could see by the satisfaction on the man's face that he thought he had acquitted himself well, and so indeed he had, for it must be remembered he had done all his tricks in the open air, squatting on his haunches on the bare ground,' Lynn would later recall.[22]

Now it was the Englishman's turn. Taking a sheet of paper, he folded it like a tent, a table and then, going one better than his Indian companion, into a cobra. Grabbing the flute, he made the snake dance before pulling another cobra out of the Indian's turban. He then produced a pile of stones and taking off his own hat made a rose bush bloom inside it. According to Lynn, his performance left the jadoogar 'flabbergasted and more than a little defeated'.[23] Graciously, he offered the man a job as his assistant and promised to take him to England – an offer he accepted. From Madras, Lynn travelled by ship to Calcutta and then by train to Benares, Allahabad, Agra, Delhi, Hyderabad and Bombay. So popular were his shows, fake tickets were being peddled by hawkers on the streets, probably the same ones, he mused, who sold tickets entitling the holders to meet the Prince of Wales, but at places the royal was not visiting.[24]

The subtext to Lynn's no doubt highly exaggerated accounts was that he had beaten the jadoogar on his own turf. What gave Indians the edge over their Occidental counterparts was their ability to perform squatting on the ground without a stage or any complicated mechanical props. There was more theatre than fact in Lynn's account, but his point was clear. No matter how crafty and audacious the jadoogar's feats, the modern Western illusionist was always going to be superior.

THE attacks on the skills of jadoowallahs and India's reputation as the home of magic intensified as more Western magicians returned home disappointed with what they found. For many, the mystic East turned out to be smelly, chaotic and disease-ridden. On the opening day of Carl Hertz's season at the Novelty Theatre in Bombay in January 1898, 121 people died from the plague. Though he cut his season short and had to submit himself to numerous medical examinations, the 'Black Death' had its upside. Theatres had been closed for the best part of two years, so all his shows were packed.[25]

The magician who had the greatest impact on how Indian magic was viewed in the West was Harry Kellar. The American learned the tricks of the trade from the Fakir of Ava, who picked him as his assistant from other hopefuls because his black and tan dog took a liking to the youth. He then worked with the Davenport Brothers, stole their secrets and earned a fortune imitating their shows in Mexico and South America, lost it all in a shipwreck and found himself in London in 1875. There he formed the 'Royal Illusionists' and after performing in the West Indies, North America, Australia and South East Asia, arrived in Calcutta in December 1877. As one of the first Western magicians to perform in India, his shows were enthusiastically received, with the *Indian Herald* declaring: 'Mr. Kellar in his illustrations of the high art of prestidigitation has never been surpassed.'[26] From Calcutta, Kellar and the Royal Illusionists travelled to Allahabad where they were kept awake at night by the wailing of jackals and hyenas. In Lucknow, Kellar's low caste assistant nearly caused a riot when his shadow fell upon a dish being eaten by a group of higher caste Hindus. The group went on to Delhi, Agra, Benares, Punjab and Bombay. He returned to India is 1882, bringing with him three automata: Psycho, Echo and Clio which could solve mathematical equations, draw portraits of celebrities and play 'Home Sweet Home', 'Yankee Doodle' and other tunes on a coronet.

Kellar's account of his travels, *A Magician's Tour: Up and Down and Round about the Earth,* was attributed to the pen of 'His Faithful Familiar, Satan Junior', but written by himself. Curious to see something of the marvellous tricks attributed to the jadoowallah, he 'witnessed everything of note in the juggling line the country afforded'. His conclusion: 'Apart from their skill as snake charmers, in the Basket Trick, and one or two other illusions, the ability of the entire fraternity of Indian jugglers is beneath contempt.'[27] Most of the wonders attributed to them 'have never existed anywhere outside of the imaginations of those who tell them'. Anyone who had claimed to see such impossible feats as 'throwing a ball of twine in the air to form a sort of Jack-and-the-bean-stalk', up which the juggler climbed out of sight, followed by a pistol shot from his companion which resulted in the climber's limbs falling from air only to be brought together to form a living, uninjured man, 'must have had their brains steeped in hasheesh'.[28]

A Magician's Tour, however, was not the last word from Kellar on the truth or otherwise of Indian conjuring. In January 1893, he published an article in the *North American Review* entitled 'High Caste Hindu Magic'. He signed himself as professor and claimed he had spent fifteen years in India and the Far East, neither of which was true. Kellar divided India's magicians into two groups. The first were 'low caste fakirs' that travelled in parties from three to six. 'They are arrayed in breech clouts and have an air of pitiable poverty and misery.' Their repertoire was fairly standard and included the sword, basket and mango tricks, the secrets of which they were happy to part with for just a couple of rupees. 'High caste fakirs' were only seen at great occasions such as the coronation of a Prince, the coming of age of a Nizam or the visit of a dignitary such as the Prince of Wales. They were 'very dignified men, of patriarchal appearance, with ascetic faces and long grey beards. ... quiet, suave and secretive, and appear to attach an almost religious significance to the manifestations of their power. There is nothing inherently improbable in the theory that they are initiated into a knowledge whose secrets have been successfully preserved for centuries.' There was no doubt in his mind that these high caste fakirs had succeeded in overcoming forces of nature which to normal people seemed insurmountable.[29]

Of the many feats Kellar observed, the two that baffled his deepest scrutiny 'and remained the inexplicable subject of my lasting wonder and admiration', were the levitation and transposition tricks. The levitation took place on the Maidan in Calcutta in the presence of none other than the Prince of Wales, numerous native rulers and dignitaries, and 50,000 spectators. An old 'fakir' began by burying three swords with their hilts in the ground with their needle-like points in the air. A younger magician then came forward and lay on the ground, becoming apparently rigid and lifeless after the older man passed his hands over him. A third conjurer then came forward and helped the man lift the body and balance it on the tips of the swords without penetrating the flesh. One-by-one, the swords were removed until the body floated in mid-air. As a murmur of admiration rippled through the crowd, the body was laid on the ground and restored back to life with a few passes of the master's hand.[30]

The second 'inexplicable' feat occurred in a dingy room in a Calcutta bazaar in the presence of a group of Europeans. Four 'fakirs' entered and sat down at the far end of the room where there were no doors or windows. The oldest took a chafing-dish and threw a white powder on its coals which gave out a fine semi-transparent vapour and a strong scent of tuberoses. He stood motionless in the middle as the others began a dance. Like whirling Dervishes, they spun faster and faster, their shapes becoming blurred. 'Suddenly, to our great astonishment, we became aware that there was only one form visible, that of the old man,' Kellar wrote. The old fakir then began the dance in reverse, this time reciting a monotonous chant 'which seemed to join with the vapours curling about the scene producing a condition of dreamy delight'. To Kellar it looked like he was throwing limbs from his body into the air, but when the dancing stopped he was the only performer visible. The others had disappeared. 'If this was hypnotism, so be it; but whether or not the existence of this charmed condition can be ascribed to hypnotic influences, I never felt my senses more completely at my command.'[31]

Strong on details, Kellar's eyewitness accounts must have sounded credible enough in 1890s America – except that the levitation trick never happened. During his tour of India in 1875–76, jugglers and snake charmers, dancers and acrobats entertained the Prince of Wales at various points of his journey. He was also accompanied by reporters, none of whom mentioned anything about levitating fakirs, which would have made front page news. The disappearing dervishes, if he did see them, were either the product of hypnotism or hashish wafting its vapours through the room.

The reasons for Kellar's contradictory statements – dismissing the entire corpus of Indian conjuring tricks as figments of the imagination, then describing deceptions he could not explain – are complex. Like Lynn, Kellar felt the need to prove the superiority of the Western prestidigitator, well drilled in the latest techniques of illusionism, over his tradition-bound, poverty-stricken Eastern counterpart. Both men were also reflecting the attitudes of missionaries and colonial officials who cited supposedly heathen necromantic practices as a reason for imposing Christian ideals and the norms of Western civilization on India's 'ignorant masses'. These attitudes served to justify Western imperialism and colonialism. Non-Western peoples were seen as benighted and superstitious, thus affirming, in Edward Said's phrase, 'that certain territories and people *require* and beseech domination'.[32]

Kellar could not afford to debunk Indian necromancy completely as it risked breaking the spell that attracted late Victorian-era audiences to his own magic shows – namely the public's association with the East as the place where the inexplicable still existed. 'Why Wait for a Yogi?,' one of his posters exclaimed, 'When KELLAR, The Incomparable Magician, is Winning New Laurels in the Marvels of the Exotic East, Transplanted, Beautified, and Illustrated in the Workaday West!'.[33] As Crispin Bates and Peter Lamont write: 'The idea that the feats of Indian jugglers were more mysterious than the events of the seance room, along with the additional mystery associated with distance and cultural difference, contributed to the growing view that India might be a place in which the magic no longer acceptable in a disenchanted West might yet still exist.'[34]

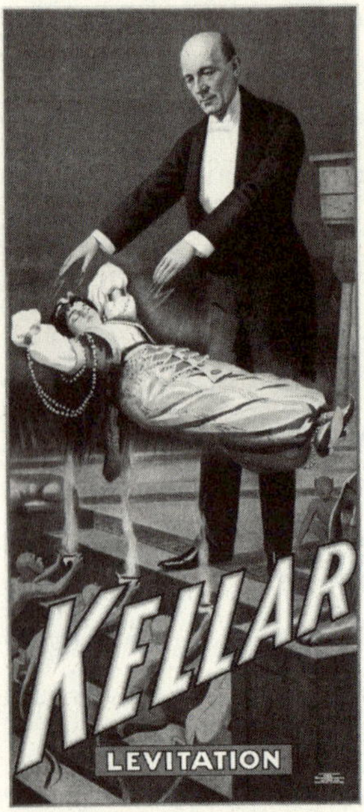

Poster for Harry Kellar's Levitation of Princess Karnac. Library of Congress.

The need to appropriate this mystery rather than dismiss it, became an integral part of Kellar's later work. On 17 January 1904 in Baltimore, he appeared on stage with The Levitation of Princess Karnac. Flyers described it as the most daring, bewildering and difficult illusion ever attempted. 'The dream in mid-air of the dainty Princess of Karnac surpasses the fabled feats of the ancient Egyptian sorcerers, nor can anything more magical be found in the pages of "The Thousand and One Nights" and it lends a resemblance to the miraculous tales of levitation that come out of India.'[35] Kellar told his audience that a version of the contrivance was shown to him by Koomra Sami, an Indian magician who made a small boy levitate several feet above the ground and passed a bamboo hoop around his body to prove there were no wires. Kellar offered Sami as much money as he wanted, but the Hindu would not part with its secret, claiming that if he did so 'the cycle within which he was permitted would be broken and he [would be] doomed to eternal punishment and much vexation, shame, failures and accidents during his remaining days upon earth'. Some three weeks later he saw Sami repeat the performance on the banks of the holy Ganges, 'and there I was able to penetrate the much-coveted secret. After much experiment, failures and at much cost, success crowned my efforts.'[36]

The real story behind Princess Karnac, widely acknowledged as a masterpiece of magical ingenuity and Kellar's greatest trick, had nothing to do with mystical revelations on the banks of India's most sacred river. The secret of how to make a body float in the air was stolen from John Nevil Maskelyne. The son of a saddle maker from Cheltenham, Maskelyne became the most important figure in the emergence of modern magic in England, dominating the conjuring scene for almost half a century. Working with George Alfred Cooke and later the 'society conjurer' David Devant, he turned Egyptian Hall on Piccadilly – a disused 'house of wonders' built in 1811 with an ornate facade featuring scarabs, sphinxes and hieroglyphics – into the leading venue for magical entertainment in England, hosting the world's leading mystifiers and introducing cutting edge effects.

Maskelyne incorporated multiple Indian themes into his elaborately staged productions, including his turbaned, whist-playing automaton, Psycho, and magical playlets such as *The Fakirs of Benares* (1884), *Modern Witchery* (1894), *The Soul's Master* (1895), *Le Miracle du Brahmine*, (1896), *The Entranced Fakir* (1901), *The Mascot Moth: An Indian Story* (1905), *The Magical Master* (1907) and *The Scarab* (1910). The rather contrived plot lines of most of these playlets were more than made up for by liberal doses of Eastern exoticism and spectacular illusions. Set on the stage of a travelling show, *The Entranced Fakir* featured Cooke as Dryanard Boo Sing, a fakir with a long white beard; the German Paul Valadon as Chin Chin Chew, a Chinese juggler; and Maskelyne as Dan'l Daw, an old showman. The highlight of the drama came when Boo Sing floated horizontally out of a coffin. The trick, done on a brightly lit stage far from any scenery or drapes, left 'magicians stumbling on the pavement of Piccadilly and blinking at each other in stunned silence. A man had been floating in the air, and there was simply nothing else to dissect,' the magic historian Jim Steinmeyer wrote.[37] Devant's playlet, *The Mascot Moth*, was set in the fictional town of Rajpur, where a British colonel engaged two Indian jugglers whose lives he saved to entertain his gambling nephew's fiancée and her mother. The moth's magical appearance and disappearance brings good fortune to the broke and hapless lieutenant, enabling him to wed.[38]

Despite relying on Eastern exoticism for his box office receipts, Maskelyne did more to tarnish the image of Indian magic than any other exponent of the necromantic arts. In his seminal essay, *Oriental Jugglery,* published in 1907, he blamed ignorant Westerners for idealizing 'vagabonds who are held in contempt, even by the most superstitious of their own creed'.[39] No subject ever embodied as wide a field of investigation as the records of the marvels of Indian jugglery, he continued. 'At the same time, there is no subject which, in so far as actual results are concerned, would be so very deficient in anything that may claim to be worthy of serious consideration, were it not for the alarming amount of misconception and falsehood to which it has given rise.'[40] The jugglers and snake charmers brought over by enterprising 'impresarios' who scoured the East through and through in search of marvels, seemed to lose their powers as soon as they left their native shores. 'Being deprived of their usual surroundings, stripped of the glamour of their associations, and brought into the clear cold light of matter-of-fact criticism, they prove to be the direst failures, the most transparent frauds, and, as the Americans say "don't draw a cent".'[41] A small substratum of fact combined with an untrained observer, a lapse of time and the corresponding lapse of memory, a little harmless exaggeration and the same amount of vanity had led to gross exaggeration. 'The snowball has started rolling. The molehill has become a mountain. The twig has become a tree. The insignificant trick has assumed the proportions of a mystery, the like of which man has never seen, nor may ever hope to see.' Maskelyne's advice: 'If, during your travels, you should ever witness any of the marvels of Oriental Jugglery, do not be led into the belief that in publishing a vivid description of what you have seen you will achieve immortality or even originality. It has all been done, and overdone, before.'[42]

THE debate over whether India and its magic were a twig or a tree had no impact on the numbers of magicians sailing for the subcontinent. By the beginning of the twentieth century, the steady stream of Western tricksters embarking on India-bound steamers had turned into a flood. Writing in 1904, the correspondent for the magic journal *Mahatma*, F. West Devine, complained of a glut of foreign performers crowding the country's theatres including the ventriloquist and change artist Dr Harley, Lazerne the Mystic, Hoffmeyer, the handcuff and rope tying master, Bradlaugh the Hypnotist, and the coin king, Alva the Great. That glut was about to take on a new and wondrous turn.

In October 1905, posters began appearing all over Calcutta showing a Mephistophelean-looking man with devil-like figures whispering in his ears. To Howard Thurston, India was the 'mecca of magic', the birthplace of the most wonderful illusions in the world and of mysteries that dated back thousands of years, some of which were still being performed by Mahatmas in the Himalayan mountains – or so he imagined. The American magician was six months into a round-the-world tour. He had performed before native chiefs in the Pacific islands, miners in the gold fields of Western Australia and expats in Manila. His best audiences, however, were in local theatres in Hong Kong and Shanghai. 'The Chinaman has as many wives as he can afford, and it is a common occurrence to sell thirty or forty of the best seats to one Chinaman for his family,' he told a writer from *The Sphinx* as he was about to board a Calcutta-bound ship in Rangoon.[43]

By going to India, Thurston was also determined to prove the superiority of scientific magic over primitivism or, as he put it, 'modern magic ... against the original masters of the ancient art of mysticism'.[44] It was an uneven contest. With sixteen assistants, two hundred pieces of luggage and thirty-two tonnes of equipment, Thurston's was the most ambitious magic show ever brought to the subcontinent. The jadoowallah, whose sum total of props could be carried in a couple of cloth bags, stood no chance. 'Many of them have no regular abode, but are provided for by whomsoever they may chance to ask for food – a doorway or stone pavement will answer for their bed,' Thurston observed. 'The natives of India call them teachers and seem to consider them with a certain respect and seldom refuse them assistance. They guard their secrets well and the son is taught by the father: and, from what I can learn, they never initiate a stranger or a person from another caste into the secrets of their art.'[45]

Thurston booked himself into Calcutta's Continental Hotel and hired twenty scouts to bring him every conjurer they could find. For the next ten days, he would lie in bed sipping coffee while watching their performances. The first wizard to arrive performed the Mango Tree trick accompanied by much beating of tom-toms, rattling of gourds and playing of flageolets while reciting weird incantations. After collecting sufficient baksheesh, a three-foot high mango tree laden with ripe mangoes had grown in his hotel room. Although the fruit was delicious, Thurston could see through the deceit and declared the trick 'a failure as far as magic was concerned'.[46]

On the third morning of his stay, it was the turn of a wizened old snake charmer. Patting his body to prove there was nothing concealed on his person, he asked Thurston for a towel. After dancing and playing his flute for a few minutes, he pointed under the bed crying out: 'Cobra-hai, cobra-hai, sahib!' Thurston looked but there was no snake. Then the magician called out again, waved the towel in the air and threw it on the ground. Raising it quickly he revealed a large hissing cobra. The snake lifted its head and started following the magician's musical gourd. Suddenly he grabbed the snake by the neck and held it above his head crying: 'Cobra-hai, Sahib!' 'I will never forget that strange scene,' Thurston later wrote in *My Life of Magic*. 'I had witnessed magic that mystified me.' He begged the snake-charmer to repeat his trick. Removing his yellow coat, the old man again patted down his body, started dancing and playing music. A throw of the towel produced another cobra from the same spot. When he did the trick a third time, Thurston offered him a gold English sovereign to reveal the secret. The snake charmer obliged. The cobras had been defanged. They were hidden inside small buttoned up canvas bags that were tied under his arms and at the back of his knees. The waving of the towel concealed the sleight of hand that allowed the snakes to be released without the audience knowing.

Overall, Thurston found the performances of Indian magicians disappointing. He was shocked to see one troupe present the same repertoire he saw them perform at the Chicago World Fair in 1893. Their sleight of hand was clever, their misdirection and patter were well timed, and many had a highly developed sense of showmanship, but 'nine-tenths of the tricks could be bought from any magic dealer in America or London', he complained. Indian juggling had 'taken on a European aspect. It is now the fashion in India to produce as many of the old small hand tricks and

Howard Thurston performing a levitation illusion. Wikimedia Commons.

small mechanical tricks as possible.'[47] Instead of seeing authentic Indian conjuring, he was being shown catalogues from leading magical dealers in Europe and America, and asked how the tricks they listed were done.

To express his gratitude to all those jadoowallahs that appeared before him, Thurston announced a special show at the 1400-seater Theatre Royal. The response was overwhelming, with the theatre filled to more than double its capacity. Looking like a Tatar chieftain, with his green-and-maroon-striped turban, a jacket embroidered in yellow and gold Chinese characters, high riding boots made of Moroccan leather, red jodhpurs and a maroon silk cummerbund, Thurston stepped on the stage to thunderous applause. The programme followed the same repertoire he had taken through the Pacific and Australasia and culminated in a levitation feat called Amazement. Coming second only to the Rope Trick in the hierarchy of legends, levitation was something usually ascribed to yogis or Tibetan monks – lending a truly mystical element to the show. On the stage, his wife and assistant Beatrice lay hypnotized on a couch. At his command, she rose slowly into the air to a height of six feet as he passed hoops around her body to prove there were no hidden wires. Members of the audience were invited on the stage to check for any concealed props, passing their hands over and under her body. 'To my astonishment, the magicians fell on their faces. There was a general murmur in the audience and I was told that they were declaring that I had supernatural powers.'[48] Unfortunately, there is no record of what the brightly attired jadoowallahs made of Thurston's mock Oriental costumes and scenery. The reviews of the rest of the season before a mostly European audience, however, were gushing. His sleight of hand was praised as being more astonishing than anything an Indian could accomplish; the levitation feat, Amazement, was more imaginative than the usual Indian legends. 'His name is heard at every street and house,' *The Sphinx* reported after his shows in Bombay.[49]

From Calcutta, Thurston went to Allahabad where he was told audience numbers might be low because it was cobra season. Theatre workers were issued with staffs in case they encountered the snakes. When Thurston's manager was cutting through the stage at the British Club to make a trapdoor, he discovered to his horror that the subfloor was swarming with the serpents. Boys with lights were employed to keep the cobras at bay and staff patrolled the grounds to kill any they came across. From Allahabad he continued travelling West to Bombay, before returning to Calcutta where he took a twelve-week lease at Classic Theatre on Beadon Street in the heart of the 'native' quarter. On the day of the season's opening, an angry crowd gathered in front of the theatre demanding it be closed down. There was a boycott of British goods and Thurston was accused of being an Englishman. To calm the protesters, Thurston assured them he was an American and told them he had given 1600 rupees from his box office receipts to victims of recent floods. It was only when explained that he was a great magician who could make people float in the air, make them pass from one place to another and cast spells that brought luck or misfortune, that the crowd was finally pacified. Thurston later declared the season to be the most successful of his world tour. Among the dignitaries who attended his shows were Rabindranath Tagore, who promised to find him a yogi who could levitate through the power of prayer, and the Amir of Afghanistan, who gave him a ring with a blue sapphire called 'The Light of the

Harem'. The Nizam of Hyderabad turned up with ninety-seven of his wives and tipped the American one thousand rupees. While in Calcutta, Thurston commissioned a massive circus tent that he used in Benares where there was no theatre large enough to accommodate his performances. His success in India did not go unnoticed. Writing in the *Conjurer's Monthly* Houdini reported: 'Rumour has it that Howard is making several fortunes in the Orient and has great prospects of making more money than any magician that has ever "gone the route" through India.' [50]

Thurston presented his stay on the subcontinent as an exercise in securing 'local material and ideas'.[51] He took out advertisements in all the leading Indian dailies offering a reward of $1000 to anyone who could perform genuine magic, including the fabled Rope Trick. 'I met many people who related strange and wonderful stories. In fact, the entire country was filled with reports of weird mysteries. But no one ever attempted to claim the reward.'[52] Accompanying him on his return to America was Bella Hassan, a jadoowallah he had employed in Bombay as his assistant. When a reporter in St Louis interviewed the pair, she described Hassan as 'picturesque if nothing else'. 'With a deep salaam and frequent gestures about the head he prayed in Hindoostance [sic].' Thurston told the reporter Hassan swore by the Prophet 'to be a good man always if Allah will send us good business and plenty of ruppess [sic].'[53] His signature trick was juggling a long bow that supported three wooden balls. As Hassan held the bow diagonally, pointed upward and spun his body in a circle, the balls climbed the bow in various puzzling configurations. Though he was the most skilful magician he had come across, Thurston was dismissive of his talents. 'We had to teach him half of his tricks; the best thing he did in his act was to wrap his turban around his head.'[54]

Thurston's condescending views of Indian magic did nothing to prevent him from exploiting its mystique or his fictionalizing his experiences to add a highly Orientalized aspect to his shows. In December 1920 at the Folly Theatre in Brooklyn, he presented a new version of Kellar's Levitation of Princess Karnac. Thurston told the audience he first saw the trick in the 'Temple of Love' in Allahabad.[55] To add spice to the show, he was helped by 'Abdul from Secundabad', who came on the stage wearing an embroidered robe, white turban and slippers with curled toes, and sat at the side of the stage chanting the nonsensical words '*surakabaja, surakabaja*' as the dainty princess soared above the stage.[56]

Over the next decade, Thurston expanded his Indian repertoire to include live burial, fire eating, the Basket Illusion and the Indian Rope Trick, which was speciously billed as being presented for 'the first time' out of India. The latter was his most challenging act. It required a generator to produce clouds of steam, a semi-transparent movie screen draped over the top of an archway to cover the end of the rope and curtains of black velvet to conceal the boy after he made his climb. As the steam cleared, a motion picture of the boy appeared on the movie screen, giving the impression he was still there. The movie would then flicker and stop and the boy would disappear. As an attempt to recreate the Rope Trick of legend, it fell well short. Few people watching, however, would have either known or cared. They trusted the Thurston mantra that anything was possible if it originated in India, while conveniently forgetting the magic maestro's own words: 'Never believe your own press.'[57]

TWELVE

FROM TURBANS TO TOP HATS

MAHARAJAH Mulkan Singh's elegant long hand is clear and deliberate, and he wastes no time in getting to the point. 'Dear Friend,' he begins, addressing William Jardine, the Political Agent at Nowgong in Bundelkhand. 'I presume the Government will arrange some entertainment for the occasion of H. H. the Amir of Kabul's visit to Agra in January. If so, I would like to offer the services of my court magician, Professor Ahmad.'

Professor Ahmad of Charkhari, Magic, *December 1904.*

The letter, dated 11 November 1906, is written on the official stationery of 'The Palace, Charkhari State, Central India' and bears a gold embossed seal on its top right-hand corner showing Hanuman and Lakshmi worshipping Vishnu. 'On the face of so many excellent testimonials which the Professor possesses from His Excellency the

Viceroy downwards, it would be superfluous to say any more about the skills he has acquired,' Mulkan Singh continues. For the benefit of the Amir and his nobles, Professor Ahmad will use Persian instead of English, 'something rare among native experts'. As to the terms of his engagement, none were needed. 'Professor Ahmad is a bona fide servant of the state. The Charkhari Darbar will gladly send him to Agra at its own expense and he will be proud to give his performance before his Royal Highness the Amir.' The response from Nowgong is swift. Professor Ahmad would be welcome and should report to the Durbar camp no later than 8th January.[1]

A town of tawny grey buildings and white-washed palaces set around a picturesque lake, Charkhari rarely came to the notice of the British, apart from the occasional outbreak of cholera and stray incidents of dacoity. The eleven-gun-salute state's loyalty during the Mutiny had earned Mulkan Singh a knighthood – an honour he wore with pride. A visitor to Charkhari in 1894 described him as a wise, prudent, energetic and hardworking ruler who was fond of his 'coach-and-six, which he guides with great precision round the corners and along the excellent and well-kept roads of his thriving state'. Primary education was compulsory and pupils at the boy's high school were taught English, Urdu, Hindi, Sanskrit and Persian. The Maharajah was particularly proud of Charkhari's 'modern' hospital with its twenty-four wards and six cells for lunatics 'who are never discharged unless they are criminal lunatics, in which case they are sent to jail'.[2]

Given his modern outlook it was natural that Mulkan Singh would want a 'modern' magician. Sporting a fan-like moustache that drooped over his lips, an oversized Fez and eyes that were meant to convey intense concentration, but instead looked startled and slightly sad, Professor Ahmad was 'modern' by the standards of the time. Born Mirza Ahmad Husain in 1869, he became interested in conjuring after discovering a Sovereign in a slice of Christmas pudding. 'This quickly led to his possessing an irresistible desire to pass other people's money into hot rolls, buns, &c., and their watches into cakes or loaves of bread.' The mania for presenting such 'bewildering surprises never left him'.[3]

The description of the professor's unorthodox introduction to the art of illusion was carried on the front page of the journal *Magic* in 1904. Billed as 'the only paper in the British Empire devoted solely to the interests of Magicians, Jugglers, Hand Shadowists, Ventriloquists, Lightning Cartoonists and Speciality Entertainers', it was edited by Ellis Stanyon. The magazine described Ahmad as a 'drawing-room magician … not prone to the flights of fancy associated with the fakir (i.e., *jaduwallah*), but excels in Western magic'. His performances had been well received by Lord Curzon and he carried some 400 testimonials from Indian princes and British officers. 'He is familiar with many Indian Jadoo tricks which are absolutely bewildering, and also buys the latest ideas in magic and illusions from England and America.' His first regular show was before the Lieutenant Governor of the North West Provinces in 1890.[4]

Unfortunately, no record exists of the professor's performance before Habibullah, the Afghan Amir, though we know from his publicity material that his repertoire would have included the Enchanted Mirror, Aerial Suspension, the Charmed Organ Pipes, the Marvellous Sphinx and the 'Jam-Jamshed' – all of which he claimed were his own invention. The presentation would have been part of the entertainment arranged for the state dinner in honour of the Amir on 11th January, which was attended by the Viceroy, Lord Hardinge, more than a dozen Indian princes and a host of notables. The dinner was preceded by a dazzling pyrotechnic display incorporating effects such as 'the Ariel Jugglery of Coloured Balls making a screen of shifting colour 300 feet long', a 'Weird White Waterfall forming a cascade of fire over 4500 square feet' and an 'Aladdin's Jewel Box'.[5]

Ahmad was not the only Indian magician to offer his services to the British. In 1902, Professor N. S. Swaminathan Sastriar, 'Royal Illusionist and Cabalistic Entertainer' from Trichinopoly, wrote to the Military Secretary of the Government of India expressing his desire to appear at the Coronation Durbar the following year. Sastriar boasted of appearing before 'His Majesty the Emperor of India, H. R. H. Prince Albert Victor, H. I. H. the Czar of Russia, Lord Elgin and Lord Curzon, Viceroys of India, Lord Havelock and Lord Ampthill, Governors of Madras, H. H. The Maharaja of Mysore, many other numerous Maharajas and distinguished nobles.' Attached to his letter was a sample programme. The four-part show included fourteen variations of the Cups and Balls trick, a magnetic parrot, 'Productions of Cobra Snakes' and the 'Indian Hand Cuffs & Rope Tying Mystery'. The finale was a triple yoga display. His application was rejected for reasons never stipulated.[6]

Just as comfortable performing at the courts of European potentates as they were in the durbar halls of India's princes, Ahmad and Sastriar represented a new class of Indian magicians. The 'flights of fancy of the fakir' had been replaced by highly polished shows featuring Western-style tricks, using the latest imported props. At a time when the mania for Oriental themes and dress was at its peak in Europe and America, Indian magicians were swapping their turbans for top hats, their sherwanis for starched collars. Magic was seen as something progressive, scientific and educational. It was a profession to be learned from books, not from the pavement-dwelling jadoowallah. Success was measured by testimonials from heads of state, invitations to tour overseas, publishing tricks in Western journals and membership of the prestigious International Brotherhood of Magicians. When Professor Ahmad sent *Magic* a circular printed in English outlining his repertoire, the editors seized on it as proof that the journal's efforts to popularize Western-style 'mystic art' was having 'far-reaching effects'.[7]

These new professionals clustered around magic societies such as the Wizard's Club, which was established in Calcutta in 1876, and the Friends' Necromantic Association, co-founded in the same city four years later by Professor S. C. Ghosh. An accomplished magician, Ghosh toured in England and France, appearing at Paris Exposition Internationale in 1900 before sell-out crowds. He later formed the Bengal Bioscope Company and incorporated cinematic effects in his shows. On the occasion of the Janmastami festival in August 1910, he staged a theatrical spectacular that blended black art with conjuring, a religious opera and a mythological drama at the Kohinoor Theatre on Beadon Street in Calcutta. The Friends' Necromantic Association changed its name to the Indian Magicians Club in 1935 and had over a hundred members.

For those aspiring to show their skills at cards or sleight-of-hand, there was no shortage of instructional material. By the mid-1870s, the shelves of booksellers W. Newman & Co. of

Calcutta groaned with titles such as *Hanky Panky: A Book of Conjuring Tricks* and *The Secret is Out: Or One Thousand Tricks in Drawing-Room or White Magic, with an Endless Varieties of Entertaining Experiments*. Both sold for two rupees and eight annas. The tobacconists and cheroot dealers, Barton and Co. of Bombay, were importing the booklet, *Conjuring Tricks, New and Amusing in Great Variety*, from Europe. Crudely produced magic chapbooks could be picked up on railway platforms for just a few annas.

Publications such as the *Wizards' Manual Mind Reading Conjuring & Magic Ventriloquism &c., &c* were aimed squarely at professionals. Published in Calcutta in 1901, the manual stressed the importance of keeping audience members guessing. 'If they do not know what to expect, they are less likely to discover the means by which you accomplish a mysterious result.' Rehearsing one's patter 'until it flows from the lips without hardly a thought on the part of the conjurer', was of utmost importance. If wearing a jacket, it was essential to make sure that 'instead of the small coat tail pockets, there are two large pockets on each side, with openings across the tops'. There were also instructions on how to build a wizard's table, the art of palming cards and coins and a method for producing fish and fire from a borrowed shawl. No Indian tricks were listed.[8]

To further distinguish themselves from the jadoowallah, many Indian magicians adopted titles such as 'Professor' and added strings of letters after their names. Nahar Perianan Alvaro, who was born in Surat in 1882 and took up magic at the age of thirteen in defiance of the wishes of his high-caste Brahmin-Kshatriya family, reinvented himself as 'Professor Alvaro, Psd. M.M.C.;

M.L.S.A.PS. (London & Nancy)'. Sporting a goatee and a carefully manicured moustache, its ends waxed into perpendicular needle-points, he took pride in being mistaken for the legendary American parlour magician Alexander Herrmann. Alvaro made his debut in the journal *Wizard* in 1907, which published a photograph of him wearing a top hat and full evening dress with three medals pinned to his chest. The photograph was accompanied by an explanation of the Magical Racket, where a tennis racket is used to pick out a card selected by a member of the audience.

Portrait of Professor Alvaro, Indian Magician, *vol. 2, 1933.*

Alvaro's attire did not go down well in his hometown, where the editor of Surat's English daily accused him of denying his heritage and 'accepting the status of a suntanned European whenever it was accorded him'.[9] A year later he reappeared in *Wizard* wearing full Oriental regalia. The transformation had more to do with competition from magicians such as Chung Ling Soo than with a rekindling of any kind of patriotism. Chung Ling Soo was the stage name of William Robinson. With his flowing silk robes, fake make-up, waist-length platted pigtail and East Asian repertoire, Robinson, an American, was so convincing he won the epithet of the 'Original Chinese Magician' over Ching Ling Foo, a real Chinaman, who for a brief period was the highest paid foreign performer in the United States. Robinson was not the first to recognize the appeal an Oriental stage persona had over audiences willing to suspend belief because of the apparent mysteriousness of the East, but he was the most successful at exploiting it. After making his stage debut in 1875, he underwent several incarnations starting with the Egyptian mystic 'Achmed Ben Ali', moving on to the 'East Indian Necromancer in Oriental Occultism, Nana Sahib', followed by the Turkish conjuror 'Abdul Khan', before finally settling on the 'Oriental Wonder Worker, Chung Ling Soo'.

Alvaro also found himself up against the oxymoronic Gustave Fasola, 'The Famous Indian Fakir and Continental Conjurer'. Fasola was an Englishman whose real name was Fergus Greenwood. His earliest tricks borrowed more from Chung Ling Soo's repertoire than anything subcontinental, but that didn't stop him from claiming to be 'the first Indian magician who ever made an enormous success in England'. His playbills featured a richly caparisoned elephant, with a turbaned mahout sitting astride a banner emblazoned with his Germanic-sounding name. Writing in *The Magician* in 1905, an unnamed correspondent remarked: 'Costumed with that rich magnificence, so characteristic of the country of rupees and rajahs, he presents an imposing study in colours, yet gazing at him – his innocent face and simple figure – you would never believe him capable of deception.'[10] The magic historian, David Price, took a more nuanced view. 'The reality did not quite measure up to the publicity. Fasola's photograph looks very much like an

Englishman dressed in a turban and robe. The only thing Indian about him or his show was his title, wardrobe and claims.'[11]

Across the Atlantic, the 'Hindoo Prince' and 'East Indian Sensation' Kar-mi was perfecting a routine where instead of swallowing a sword, he put a gun barrel down his throat. Aiming at his loin-cloth clad assistant across the stage, he fired the gun breaking a soda cracker on his head. His other signature acts included changing the sex of his female assistant, Selma, after placing her in an empty wooden cabinet, swallowing light bulbs and a two-foot-long table leg. Known for his flamboyant posters in which a dark visage stared out from beneath an over-sized turban, Kar-mi's real name was Joseph Bryant Hollingsworth. He was from Malden, Massachusetts and was originally known as the 'New England Yankee' for his work in Wild West shows. Like Robinson he performed in pantomime to avoid his real identity being revealed. By all accounts he was convincing. Writing after seeing one of his shows in San Franciso, Syril Dusenbery of the Pacific Coast Society of Magicians declared: 'When a man can make the local Hindoo colony believe he is an Indian Prince, he must be SOME magician and Prince Kar-Mi is.'[12] Hollingsworth was also the author of *The Spook Mystery and its Solution.*

Undeterred by the success of Chung Ling Soo and Fasola, Alvaro continued to tour overseas and contribute to Western magic journals. To bolster his credentials, he joined the growing chorus of Western magicians exposing the tricks of their Eastern counterparts. Writing in Will Goldstone's *The Magician Annual* of 1908–1909, he explained how a fakir could produce three coconuts and an endless variety of soft goods from his mouth using a special bag concealed between the folds of his dhoti, as well as the mechanics of cooking an omelette on a woman's head, 'a trick that causes endless excitement when performed', together with other common illusions.[13]

He travelled extensively during the 1920s, performing in Peking, Mombasa, Cape Town, the Ivory Coast and Casablanca, where he entertained French soldiers of the Foreign Legion. In August 1931, he was invited to Kabul to be the official magician to the Afghan King, Nadir Khan. Shortly after arriving in Kabul for the Independence Day celebrations, Alvaro met Ben James, a young lawyer from New York who had gone to Afghanistan on a whim, bribing his way across the border by offering the guard a tin of Gold Flake cigarettes. In his lively and entertaining memoir, *The Secret Kingdom,* James describes Alvaro as looking like Kaiser Wilhelm before he became an autocrat. 'The Doctor was proud of his resemblance and assured me that in Singapore in 1912 he had caused considerable commotion by being mistaken for the German Emperor on tour *incognito.*' Alvaro regaled James with tales of illusion-making at the palaces of Maharajahs. 'He knew the crotchety ones, the sensuous and the stingy ones. He narrated how one gift of roupees [sic] he had received as a tip for entertaining an Indian Prince's child, had established him in a suite at the Taj Mahal Hotel in Bombay. He built up a clientele of rich Parsees, who made fortunes in following the advice he was able to give them by reading their palms.'[14]

Alvaro arrived in Kabul with his 'stupendous, hypnotic, mystifying galaxy of the supernatural' show, which was billed as the main entertainment for the Independence Day event. But he had not counted on performing on a round stage encircled by a grizzly audience of Afghan tribals, a situation guaranteed 'to strike terror in the soul even of a royal magician', James contemplated. As Alvaro's confidence deserted him, 'the stern brave lines etched on his countenance through a lifetime suddenly vanished, leaving only a look of bewilderment and pain. … His belligerently debonair moustache seemed to wilt, the square erectness of his shoulders collapsed into a despondent stoop.' A young Afghan magician was brought on stage to complete the performance, followed by a Punch and Judy pantomime and mummers on stilts. The doughty tribesmen in the audience viewed the whole evening's show with hardly concealed contempt, James recorded. 'It was probably as well they had checked their guns at the door on the way in.'[15]

The Kabul catastrophe failed to put a dent in Alvaro's career. The winter of 1932 saw him performing the bullet catching trick in the Bombay suburb of Kabladevi. Audience members were invited 'to shoot him in the mouth at point-blank range with a muzzle loader and the flying bullet is caught between his teeth'. Reports of his show carried the obligatory testimonials, including from the Viceroy Lord Reading and the Countess of Reading. 'His is an exceptionally neat and clever original and most mystifying show of incomparable wonders,' one reviewer gushed.[16]

NOT all Indian magicians turned to the West in the search for success. In April 1901, Nathu Manchhachand was featured on the cover of *Magic*, the first time an Indian had been given such a profile in any Western journal. 'In Nathu Manchhachand we have an Eastern representative of the Mystic Art, not as practised

Nathu Manchhachand on the cover of Magic, *April 1901.*

by the Mahatmas of Thibet [sic], or by the Fakir who is supposed to be able to vanish himself by way of a rope thrown in the air, then to cause the rope to disappear in the same direction, or like absurd imaginations, but a representative of the art as practised by the magicians of the Western World,' the accompanying article stated.[17]

Manchhachand was pictured wearing a Marathi-style turban and a traditional *angadi* or shirt, holding a wand in one hand and an egg in the other. Born in the seaside town of Mahuva in Gujarat, he began learning the art of necromancy when he was a child. 'When I was about eighteen years old, I could perform before private meetings to the surprise of all and the mystification of not a few. At last I was emboldened to come before the public; and I succeeded, not indeed beyond my hope, but certainly beyond my expectations. I devoted myself to the *profession*, and gained a sort of reputation.'[18]

Manchhachand's emphasis on defining his calling a *profession* (the italics were in the original article) chimed well in the wider magical fraternity. Writing in *Mahatma* in 1902, the journal's Indian correspondent, Durlabh Kolyan, applauded those who adopted Western methods. 'While the art of magic has taken its birth in India, its development is due almost entirely to the fertile and imaginative minds of Western performers, and it is largely due to the willingness of artists such as Professor Manchhachand to accept these new ideas, that the residents of India are enabled to see and admire the wonderful effects made possible by later-day magic, and stimulated by his example and success, we see many native conjurers springing up all over the country who are most eager to adopt the latest ideas.'[19]

Kolyan's prediction proved accurate. When a hitherto largely unknown stuntman from New York's East Side who called himself Harry Houdini, stumped police at Scotland Yard by escaping from a pair of handcuffs in July 1900, Indian magicians were quick to follow his example. Within months they were wrapping themselves in straightjackets, chains and leg irons, jumping off bridges and being locked up in crates. English escape artist Jim Mokana, who toured India with the Royal Coronation Circus in 1904, reported that handcuff kings were 'springing up all over the country'. There was such a demand for the trick he was making good money giving private shows.[20] Among those inspired by Houdini was Ganapati Chakraborty, a Bengali Brahmin who started his career in the 1880s as a stuntman in Professor Bose's Great Bengal Circus. Chakraborty's most famous trick, the Illusion Box, went one step further than Houdini's version. After untying his ropes and removing his chains while locked in a wooden casket, he did the process in reverse. The trick was achieved 'with a speed and dash which have never been equalled by any other performer', India's most famous magician, P. C. Sorcar, would later write. Though Sorcar refers to him as the Father of Indian Magic, Charkraborty is barely known outside magic circles in his native Bengal, let alone the rest of India. 'He did not know English, but toured the seven seas with his brilliant magic shows and his own native tongue (patter) mixed up with broken English here and there, [was] appreciated by all.'[21]

Houdini travelled widely and borrowed memes and tricks from the subcontinent, but never went to India. One of his earliest appearances was at the World's Columbian Exposition in Chicago in 1893, where he donned dark make-up, a tattered white robe and worked as an 'authentic Hindu fakir', sitting cross-legged in front of the Algerian and Tunisian village.[22] While playing at a dime museum in Lynn, Massachusetts, he saw the 'Hindoo Needle Trick' being performed by 'Maxey, the Human Sewing Machine'. The trick, which was brought to England in the 1810s by Ramo Samee, involves threading sewing needles in the mouth and pulling them out in a single strand. It became such an integral part of Houdini's repertoire he claimed it as his invention and tried for years to stop other magicians from using it in their shows. Finally, in 1914, the National Vaudeville Artist's Arbitration Board ruled in his favour on the grounds that he had been doing it for so long it had become inseparably connected with his shows. It was the first and only Indian illusion to be protected by intellectual property rights.

Despite their skills, professional Indian magicians faced stiff competition from Western performers who dominated the theatrical circuit in cities such as Calcutta, Bombay, Poona and Madras. The dawn of the twentieth century saw India swamped with acts from England, Europe, America and Australia. Aside from illusionists, theatres were fully booked with dance and comedy routines, romances, operas, operettas, pantomime, minstrel shows, vaudeville and burlesque, ventriloquists and variety acts. Breaking into this circuit was difficult. European audiences still favoured shows by performers such as 'The Great Aldow', a white-faced clown who used electricity to light up his nose, a novelty at the time, and Hoffmeyer, whose handcuff and rope-tying tricks were going down well in Simla, Ranikhet and other Himalayan hill stations.

Manchhachand had to settle for displaying his card, coin and billiard ball tricks before Sayajirao, the Gaekwar of Baroda, and other notables, as well as appearing at smaller theatres catering for Indian audiences. The burgeoning number of amateurs taking to the stage was also having a detrimental effect on the craft. 'Magic is as dead as it could possibly be out here, chiefly owing to the number of "one man-shows" that travel through the country, faking up a few simple tricks and executing them in a clumsy manner, calling themselves kings, marvels, etc,' Frank West-Devine wrote from Calcutta for *Mahatma* in 1904. 'They sicken the people of the very mention of the word magic. I know of several towns in India where the theatre is refused to magicians on account of past frauds.' He was also quick to direct his anger at the jadoowallah. 'Another enemy of the art is the native conjurer who falls far below expectations, pesting [sic] travellers and exposing tricks for a couple of annas – although few of them are even worth that – yet withal, initiating the ignorant into the secrets of how simple a cause will give a great effect.'[23] An unnamed 'correspondent' for *The Wizard* writing from Gwalior in September 1906, echoed West-Devine's sentiments. 'Every school boy pretends to know more or less of magic in India. I have seen second-rate native performers give their shows for ten rupees per night.'[24]

India's evolution into a Mecca for overseas magicians worked to the advantage of both native conjurers and stage performers.

Touring shows often employed locals as stage-hands and assistants, with a lucky few accompanying their employers to the West. Other performers joined travelling circuses such as Harmston's, which made several passages through India in the late 1800s and early 1900s from its base on the west coast of America. The Bengali juggler and gymnast Pabu Kristo Lall Bysack travelled through the Indonesian archipelago, the Philippines, Japan and Siberia with Harmston's. 'He comes with a handsome fortune and a fine experience of life gained through his extensive travels,' the Bengali daily *Amrita Bazar Patrika* reported in 1896 on his return. More important, the paper noted, was the fact that throughout his travels he had 'tried to keep his nationality and religion as far as was practicable under the circumstances and he returns a Hindu – with all his true sentiments and beliefs.'[25]

The presence of magicians such as Thurston gave locals an opportunity to learn the latest tricks and stage effects. When the American was performing in Bombay in April 1907, Manchhachand travelled more than 500 miles from Junagadh in Gujarat to see his show and then reviewed it in *The Sphinx*. Thurston shared the secret of one of his best-known tricks, the Aga Levitation, with the Parsee magician and mind reader, Mino the Mystic. Born in Bombay in 1880, Mino Nowroji took up his calling after finding a collection of tricks from Bland & Co. of London among his dead uncle's effects. While at school he entertained his classmates during recess hours with tricks from *The Boy's Own Conjuring Book,* which his teachers gave him to improve his English.

When Thurston arrived in Calcutta, Mino watched closely as he executed his levitation trick, passing a hoop around his female assistant as she rose above the stage. Successive magicians used improvements in technology to refine the deception to the point where a person appeared to soar effortlessly around the stage. After the performance Mino met Thurston and suggested how the artifice could be improved. The two men became close friends and Thurston allowed him to adapt some of his other tricks to use in his shows. Mino also picked up numerous deceptions from Charles Bertram during the English magician's season in Bombay in 1899. By the time he was touring internationally, Mino's repertoire consisted of Japanese, Chinese and Egyptian acts, a handcuff and packing case mystery, a full black art act and sleights of hand that he executed dressed as a Pharaoh.[26] 'Try and be wide away from the old trodden path. Originality is the KEY of success,' he would later write. 'Do not copy your friends' programmes, but try to do something else.'[27]

The quest for originality and authenticity was challenging for Indian magicians. Not only were they competing against highly sophisticated and professionalized Western artists, 'Brand India' was being tarnished. Driven by the desire to prove the superiority of Western conjuring, wholesale exposes of the feats of traditional Indian wonder-workers were appearing in the popular press. In 1899 Bertram was interviewed for an article in *Strand Magazine* provocatively titled 'Are Indian Jugglers Humbugs?'. His answer was unequivocal: 'I have no hesitation in saying that, after seeing the performances of 176 conjurers, who were gathered together in various parts of the country by the different Rajahs before whom I performed during my last tour, there is not a single trick which Indians perform that European conjurers cannot do as well, and even better.' As for the Rope Trick, it was nothing but 'Moonshine'.

In case the point was lost on readers, the interview concluded by noting that Indian jugglers were so overcome with astonishment when witnessing Bertram's performances 'they frequently fell down on the ground before him and kissed his feet in token alike of admiration and acknowledgement of his superiority'.[28]

Bertram's arrogance reflected the uglier side of the East-West exchange in magical methodology, but it was by no means atypical. Professional Indian magicians touring in-country or travelling abroad, were forced to adopt an ever-wider range of genres. Including the token Oriental act as part of an Occidental show was no guarantee of success. Nor was donning a turban and adopting an exotic-sounding name. Finding a formula that appealed to audiences demanding ever more mystifying and complex tricks, without stripping the Indian-ness out of their shows would prove elusive – but not impossible.

◈

IN early October 1901, newspapers in London reported the appearance of a mysterious potentate known only as 'Prince Ranjit of Baluchistan'. Accompanied by a retinue of twenty-eight servants including cooks, pages, musicians and a dancing girl, the prince booked two dozen rooms in St Ermin's Hotel where he stayed for a fortnight 'in all the splendour of Oriental opulence'. 'He is a man of fine physique, dark skinned and handsome,' one newspaper reported. 'All his food was prepared in accordance with the strictest Oriental usages, by his own servants, who wore gorgeous robes and were nightly marshalled by a major domo for exercise in an adjoining park.'[29]

The prince's unannounced arrival did not escape the notice of the India Office, which cabled Simla for clarification as to his antecedents. The inquiry drew a blank. Meanwhile, a member of his party named Sakharam lodged a formal complaint alleging he was tricked by the prince's agent into leaving India on an unfulfilled promise of employment and wanted to go back. It was only after Ranjit paid his hotel bill in gold bullion, left for Liverpool and then sailed to Montreal on 26 October that the penny dropped. 'It seems that he holds the position of curry cook at a New York restaurant, and went to India to hire assistants,' William Curzon Wyllie, the political aide-de-camp to Lord Curzon noted after receiving advice from Scotland Yard. 'In England, Mr Ranjit played the part of a native prince, and found people only too ready to believe him.'[30] His real name, Curzon Wyllie discovered, was 'Joe Ranji Smile'. Despite claiming to have 'a family tree as endless as the rope the Hindu fakir throws into the air with no visible means of support', Smile would always deny he had deliberately set out to deceive anyone. His parents chose Prince as his first name, he later explained, because they thought it would 'look good on their young hopeful's visiting card'.[31] Smile, it transpired, was a corruption of Ishmael.

Smile's departure for North America was not the end of the matter. A few weeks later, nine Indians turned up at Victoria Station where a reporter from the *Daily Mail* spotted them 'in a state of destitution'. The paper's editor arranged for board and lodging and the following day took the men to the India Office in Whitehall. According to a statement from one of the group, Charles Ganglee, Smile asked him to recruit the men in Karachi and bring them to New York to work for him. Now they were begging the India Office to save them from 'disgrace and death'.[32]

The India Office showed little sympathy for Ganglee or his party and sent them to the Strangers' Home for Destitute Asiatics to await deportation. On 19th November, they were put on a ship bound for New York where Smile was due to arrive with the rest of his retinue, ready to use the inheritance he had claimed in Karachi to open a Manhattan curry house. Their appetites wetted by Smile's adventures in London, the American press was tracking his every movement. 'We shall now wait patiently for the printed and advertised invitations to visit the Oriental Prince's restaurant on Fifth Avenue and may smack our lips in delightful anticipation of the piquant curry and delicious rice that may be had there for a few dollars per plate,' quipped one reporter.[33]

Not surprisingly Smile turned out to be more of a con artist than a cook. His claims to have been a chef at Cecil's in London, to have invented the 'Omar Khayam Cocktail', and to have devised a range of special curries guaranteed to add lustre to the 'eyes, complexion and figure' of any woman who ate them, had about as much substance as a plate of boiled basmati rice. There was no restaurant and the majority of the almost three dozen Indians in his entourage suddenly found themselves facing a long winter with no shelter or means of support. One of those abandoned on the bitterly cold streets of Manhattan in 1901 was seventeen-year old Amar Nath Dutt.[34]

On the first floor of the Magic Circle, a century-old, members-only institution hidden behind a heavy blue door on Stephenson Way near London's Euston Station, hangs a full-length poster of Dutt as 'Linga Singh, The Hindoo Sorcerer'. The poster shows the corpulent, moustached Punjabi arrayed in a red-tasselled turban, topped with white plumage and a heavy maroon and gold robe worn over a blue silk sherwani. He is wrestling six cobras simultaneously, all the while remaining cool and composed. The scene comes from one of Dutt's signature acts, Sacred Living Fire Snakes, first presented in 1911.

Poster of Linga Singh (Amar Nath Dutt), Hindu Sorcerer. Collection of Nigel Dutt.

Dutt's journey from a fabulist prince's servant to the London stage was tempestuous. Over the next decade he was a frequent visitor at the Strangers' Home. He faced deportation, detention and was nearly killed while attending an anarchist-led May Day parade in Argentina. After cutting his ties with Smile, Dutt managed to find work as a cook for a lady who rented out her rooms to lodgers on Remsen Street in Queens, where he stood out for his 'colourful appearance and his fakir-like trickery'. Claiming to belong to an esoteric Buddhist cult, he entertained street kids by sitting on the steps of his brownstone building and disappearing in a cloud of cigarette smoke. 'He was there one second with his bright eyes and his red and white clothes, and the next second there was nothing but the smoke cloud,' the local paper reported. 'He tossed things in the air, which did not come down. Sometimes he would find things, tops, marbles, knives and the like in boys' mouths and ears'.[35]

In May 1902, Dutt and some of the other Indians abandoned by Smile decided to take the pseudo-prince to court for breach of contract. By doing so, however, they attracted the attention of the immigration authorities and were deported to England. His party was taken to the Strangers' Home where the India Office offered to pay for their passage home. Most took up the offer, but Dutt decided to return to New York arriving on Ellis Island in September 1902 with $30 in this pocket. He placed an ad in the local paper posing as a former employee of the Maharajah of Bikaner and offering to work as a curry cook for $35 a month. There is little information on his movements over the next few years aside from a British intelligence report stating that he worked for an electrical engineering firm and took up conjuring. His eventual repertoire suggests he was mentored by Prince Ishmael (no relation to Smile), an Indian juggler who worked the sideshows at Barnum and Bailey Circuses in the early 1900s. In 1905, Dutt was back in London and spent the next two years in and out of the Strangers' Home. In a letter to the India Office in July 1906, the Home noted that 'he was not a sea-faring man – he was a conjuror and acrobat – an adventurer who had tried various trades in America'. It applied for funds for his maintenance, but the request was turned down.[36]

Penniless and out of work, Dutt fell back on his conjuring skills, assembling a small troupe of jugglers and touring England and Europe. But his career was cut short in 1907, when he was recruited by India House, a London-based revolutionary group bent on the violent overthrow of British rule. His designated mission was to go to America to learn about guns and bomb-making. He joined the firearm manufacturing firm of Iver Johnson & Co. in New Haven, Connecticut, but was recalled to Paris after just one month for reasons unknown.

Led by the fiery Madam Cama, a Bombay-born Parsi who some of her followers believed was an incarnation of the goddess Kali, the Paris cell of the revolutionary movement had developed close links with Russian Communists and was under constant surveillance by British intelligence. 'The precise reason for this Parsi lady's extreme animosity towards the British Government is not known,' a confidential cable sent to London read. 'She is evidently a quarrelsome woman as she has been unable to live in harmony neither with her own husband in Bombay, nor with the small band of revolutionaries in Paris. She is not a person of conspicuous ability, but she makes up for this by the apparent strength of her convictions and the extravagance of her language.'[37]

Dutt's dealings with Madame Cama were anything but harmonious. When she ordered him to travel to India as an emissary, he refused, earning an expulsion from the cell. Believing he knew enough about the group's secrets, he attempted to blackmail one of its members, G. A. Bhawsar, a Bombay pearl merchant, for the sum of £40. Bhawsar called his bluff and Dutt was arrested by French police and spent six months in prison. On his release, he travelled to Argentina where he again worked as a magician. In 1909, he was marching in a May Day parade through the streets of Buenos Aires when police opened fire killing more than eighty people. As bullets whistled overhead, he dragged a French woman to safety. Her name was Charlotte Aubert and they married soon afterwards. Two years later, the couple returned to London where Dutt relaunched his magic career as 'Rambhuj, the Necromancer of the Himalayas'.[38]

By adopting the persona of Rambhuj, Dutt was playing an Orientalist card, not a nationalist one. The ex-revolutionary recognized a gap in the market. While jadoowallahs could be found by the dozens arrayed in their breech cloths and turbans, charming snakes and making mango trees grow out of the bare earth at world fairs and exhibitions, the curtain had yet to rise on an authentic Indian spectacle complete with sophisticated props, costumes and scenery. According to one reviewer, Dutt's first season at the Croydon Empire in August 1910 delivered just that:

> A dimly lit stage discloses a wild rocky scene with a cave entrance to the palace of mystic rites beyond. A weirdly clad attendant rushes on bearing a flaming torch, through the gateway of rocks, and (as the as the scene rises to the flies) fires at the magic altar beyond, illuminating a brilliant spectacular palace, resplendent in carved and gilded elephants with upraised trunks, supporting magnificent fretted arches of oriental character. A curtain conceals a raised dais at the back, which, drawn aside – without illusion – introduces Rambhuj seated in majesty with his suite grouped at his feet. Habited as a nautch girl, a lady assistant performs a few sinuous movements, while the setting is rearranged for the magician portion of the act.[39]

Over the next hour, Dutt paced the stage directing a contraption described as a cross between 'a sedan-chair and a *jin-ricksha*'. A fountain that symbolized the waters of the

Ganges spouted from a coconut shell into a series of urns. His assistants changed gender, vanished and reappeared from paper-covered boxes and cabinets. In the most spectacular scene of all, a maiden emerged unscathed after being burnt alive inside a cremation oven.

Yet for all its spectacle, the reviewer felt disappointed that someone billed as the 'greatest example of his country's wonder workers', had abandoned the 'fabled mysteries of the East' to seek 'favour with familiar Western effects'. 'This is almost to be regretted, as the field of true Indian magic is practically unoccupied today. With the excellent showmanship Rambhuj undoubtedly possesses he could at once leap to an enviable position up on British vaudeville stage had he presented an act comprising even a few colourable [sic] imitations of his native marvels.'[40]

Dutt's biggest drawback was his lack of experience. He had been living in the West for almost a decade, much of it spent dodging deportation orders or plotting the overthrow of the British Raj. On stage he was often mistaken for an Englishman playing the part of an Indian. In November 1911, he repackaged his show as 'Linga Singh, the Mysterious Hindoo Sorcerer'. The exotic stage settings were largely the same, but the number of Eastern marvels had multiplied and now included the Temple of Buddha, the Bride of the Ganges, the Sacred Living Fire Snakes, Indian Sands and his highly popular Burnt and Restored Turban. His chef d'oeuvre, however, was pulling a four-wheeled carriage across the stage using his hypnotic powers. Members of the audience were invited on the stage to witness the feat.[41] The show was better received, but the box office takings weren't enough to offset the cost of such a lavish production. He was losing money fast, and in April 1912 his mother-in-law had to bail him out with a loan of £500.

Off-stage there was as much drama as there was during his performances. In February 1912, a disgruntled employee fired two shots at him before his gun jammed. A few months later he was briefly jailed for fraud and then declared a bankrupt. In 1917, he joined the Indian Army Service Corps as a sepoy. When he returned to the stage in the early 1920s he added 'Has done his bit' under his stage name.

Over the next decade-and-a half, Dutt kept reworking his familiar – and at last successful – formula, blending Oriental and Western tricks against lavish Indian backdrops, on occasion making his entrance on an elephant that vanished. He also expanded his repertoire to include circus, variety, pantomime and cabaret. In 1929, he returned to Argentina where he met up with the illusionist Bamberg, who had adopted the stage name Fu Manchu after Sax Rohmer's famous thriller character. Dutt's last great act was suspending his assistant over a scimitar, which he performed at the Trocadero Restaurant in London within a few feet of diners. On 22 November 1937, he started feeling ill while performing at the Theatre Royal in West Bromwich. Ignoring his doctor's advice, he refused to cancel subsequent shows. A few days later, he collapsed in the middle of a performance and was taken to hospital. He died of pneumonia, complicated by diabetes on 26 November 1937 aged fifty-four, and was cremated with full Hindu ceremonies at Golders Green cemetery. His final request was that all his stage equipment be piled up and burned.[42]

Despite his multiple setbacks, Dutt became the most famous Indian illusionist to perform in the West since Ramo Samee a century earlier. Although he never achieved the same status as Chung Ling Soo, Harry Houdini or Howard Thurston, he set the bar for presenting Indian magic at a new high that would not be matched until P. C. Sorcar's shows in the 1950s. Thanks to Dutt, Alvaro, Manchhachand, Ghosh and others, the magic of South Asia could no longer be dismissed as something primitive or frozen in time. Having 'civilized' the conjurers of the subcontinent though a mixture of science and cultural imperialism, Western magicians began accepting their Eastern counterparts into their innermost circles. But there was still one example of legerdemain that the self-appointed guardians of this ancient art felt needed to be exposed. It was the most baffling and bizarre illusion ever to come from the East – the Indian Rope Trick.

THIRTEEN

'THE MOST FAMOUS TRICK NEVER PERFORMED'

> The old man brought out a ball of string, handed the end to Husayn [al-Hallaj], and threw the ball into the air: and it became an arch onto which he climbed; then he climbed down and said to Husayn: 'Is that what you ask for?' 'Yes,' he replied. 'That is only a tiny sampling of the knowledge of the masters,' the old man said. 'Go further, for the land is full of it.'[1]

In 905, the Sufi mystic, Mansur al-Hallaj, set out from Mecca in search of magic. We know he reached Kashmir because the ninth-century historian of mysticism, Sulami, recounts meeting him in the *Kitab al-uyum*. When Sulami asked where he was going, al-Hallaj answered: 'To India, to learn about white magic, in order to draw men to God, may He be praised and exalted, by this means.'

Of all the miracles he sought, it was the Rope Trick that he wanted to see first and foremost. In another version of his encounter with one of India's adepts, al-Hallaj meets an old woman who has a rope that is twisted and knotted 'like a veritable ladder'. She mutters some words and climbs up the rope, but instead of returning to earth she disappears.[2]

Poster for magicians Le Roy, Talma and Bosco and the Great Indian Rope Trick, c. 1912. Wikimedia Commons.

The Rope Trick is the greatest and most controversial of all the legends associated with Indian magic. 'There is simply no book on, or description of travels in India, wherein this experiment is not mentioned in some form or other,'[3] The *Linking Ring*, the official organ of the International Brotherhood of Magicians, declared in 1927. Versions have turned up in the *Jataka* stories written two and a half thousand years ago, the writings of the sixth-century Hindu philosopher Sankara, and the memoirs of the Mughal emperor Jahangir. No lesser authority than Field Marshall Earl Haig, hero of the Great War, vouched for its authenticity. Not only was it real, swore Helena Petrova Blavatsky, the founder of the Theosophical Society, it was proof of the mystical powers of the East.

The most remarkable of these accounts was left by the Moroccan adventurer, Ibn Battuta, in approximately 1350. While visiting the court of the great Chinese Amir, Qurtay, he saw a juggler perform the identical trick he had seen in India:

> That same night a certain juggler, one of the Qan's slaves, was there. The Amir said to him 'Show us some of your feats.' So he took a wooden ball with holes in which there were long leather thongs, and threw it into the air. It rose right out of our sight, for we were sitting in the middle of the palace court, during the season of intense heat. When nothing but a short piece of the cord remained in his hand, he ordered one of his apprentices to go up the rope, which he did until he too disappeared from our sight. The juggler called him three times without receiving any reply, so he took a knife in his hand, as if he were enraged, and climbed up the rope until he disappeared as well. The next thing was that he threw the boy's hand to the ground, and then threw down his foot, followed by his other hand, then his other foot, then his trunk, and finally his head. After that he came down himself puffing and blowing, with his clothes all smeared with blood, and kissed the ground in front of the Amir, saying something to him in Chinese. The Amir gave him some order, and thereupon he took the boy's limbs, placed them each touching the other and gave him a kick, and up he rose as sound as ever.[4]

So shocked was Battuta by what he saw, he suffered 'palpitation of the heart' and had to be given a potion for 'removing my distress'. The Amir's qadi, Afkhar ad-Din, who was sitting beside him tried to calm the Moroccan by saying, 'By God, there was no climbing or coming down or cutting up of limbs at all; the whole thing is just hocus-pocus.'[5]

Whether the rope feat was an Oriental *Jack and the Beanstalk* or just hocus pocus, it would become the most debated subject in corridors and meeting rooms of magic societies in the first decades of the twentieth century. To believe that a rope, a string, a tape or a chain, could be thrown in the air, remain upright and rigid enough to allow a person to climb up and disappear and for the person's cut up limbs to fall down and then be reassembled by a conjurer, was to be labelled a heretic by the guardians of conjuring orthodoxy. It was also controversial in al-Hallaj's time – and the punishment was severe. When the Sufi mystic returned to Baghdad, people believed 'he was waited on by *djinn* and many stories went the rounds concerning him'.[6] According to his biographer Louis Massignon, al-Hallaj never claimed he could perform miracles; instead he used juggler's tricks and innocent sleights of hand, to attract the crowd that he wanted 'to evangelize'.[7] His detractors, however, accused him of associating with Shi'ites and infidels. In 922, he was charged with blasphemy and executed. His body was burned and his remains thrown in the Tigris river to prevent his family and followers from giving him a proper Muslim burial.

It was not al-Hallaj, however, who first brought the Rope Trick to the attention of the West, nor the writings of Ibn Battuta, Marco Polo or Jahangir. These did not become widely available until the second half of the nineteenth century. References to the illusion started appearing in travellers' accounts two hundred years earlier. The English clergyman, the Rev. J. Ovington's *A Voyage to Surat in the Year 1689*, which purported to be an authentic and reliable account of the 'habits and towns of many men' included the following description: 'Among the Men, whose Imployment [sic] it is to divert Spectators with amazing Shows and Sights, some, they say, will take in their Hands a Clew of Thread, and throw it upwards in the Air till it all unravels, and then climbing up themselves by this tender Thread to the top of it, presently fall down piecemeal upon the Ground; and when all is dropt, unite again the parted Members.'[8] Edward Melton, an Anglo-Dutch seaman, claimed he witnessed the trick in 1670 in Batavia performed by a troupe of Chinese jugglers. As he watched the severed limbs of the man who had climbed the rope 'creep together', Melton exclaimed: 'Never in my life was I so astonished as when I beheld this wonderful performance, and I doubted now no longer that these misguided men did it by the help of the Devil. For it seems to me totally impossible that such things should be accomplished by natural means.'[9]

As the number of Europeans either living in or visiting India increased, so did eyewitness accounts of the marvel. In *Glimpses in the Twilight*, published in 1885, the Rev. Frederick George Lee, collated numerous accounts of Indian jugglery and magic described to him by churchmen. One of these describes a magician performing with a 'long, thin, silk rope':

> Taking it in his right hand, yet holding one end in his left, and with a vigorous shout and great bodily exertion, he threw it perpendicularly into the air. It fell. He threw it again. Each time it went higher, though it fell several times. All the while he kept muttering, gesticulating, whining, imploring, expostulating, crying. At length – warning the spectators, who were crowding upon him, to keep the circle around as wide and broad as at the outset – he gathered the rope once more into circular coils in his right hand, and with a supreme effort and a wild shriek, threw it up a great height toward the sky. He then all of a sudden pulled it with the greatest violence two or three times. It fell not,

> however, but on the contrary seemed tightly fastened. With a yell of triumph, half laughing and then shrieking, he at once climbed up the rope, first with one hand then with the other, his legs equally agitated and acting, he rose higher and higher, and then – actually vanished out of sight in the air.[10]

In August 1889, the *Times of India* published a story based on the testimony of Siddeshur Mitter who described a performance by a group of jugglers near Calcutta. According to Mitter, one of the jugglers climbed into a box that was carefully nailed up and bound with cords. After the usual 'weird spells and incantations', the box was broken open and found to be perfectly empty. The chief juggler explained that the man had gone to the heavens to fight the god Indra. 'In a few moments, he expressed anxiety at the man's continued absence in the aerial regions and said he would go up to see what was the matter.' A boy came with a long bamboo pole, which the magician climbed up until he disappeared, Mitter explained. 'Then fell on the ground before us the different members of a human body, all bloody – first one hand, then another, a foot, and so on until complete.' According to Mitter, the boy held up the pole again. This time, the main juggler reappeared telling the onlookers his friend had been killed by Indra before he could save him. The mangled remains were then placed in the box, which was sealed as before. 'Our wonder and astonishment reached their climax when, a few minutes later, on the box being opened again, the man jumped out perfectly hearty and unhurt.'[11]

Mitter's claims were reported in newspapers around the world but did not carry the same weight as those of Fred S. Ellmore, a

Yale graduate with an interest in photography, and his classmate and artist, George Lessing. On 8 August 1890, an article appeared in the *Chicago Tribune* about their encounter with a group of wonder-workers in India. They described a fakir who made a mango tree grow from a small seed placed in a bowl and then placed a baby under a blanket, slashed and cut it with a knife, before lifting the blanket to show there was nothing there. The final act was the Rope Trick. A ball of twine was tossed in the air, a boy climbed up and disappeared, as did the twine. Ellmore and Lessing, however, were ready for this. Ellmore secretly took photographs of the trick with his Kodak, while Lessing sketched the scene. It was only after the film was developed that the secret was revealed. When the photograph and the sketch were compared, there was no rope, no boy and no magician. 'Mr Fakir had simply hypnotized the entire crowd, but he couldn't hypnotize the camera,' the article's anonymous author triumphantly declared.[12]

Over the next weeks and months, the story reappeared in newspapers in America, England and Europe, prompting a flurry of speculation as to whether the trick existed. Letters started arriving at newspaper offices from people claiming to have seen it in India and insisting it was no hypnotic illusion. The only illusion, it turned out, was the story itself. Four months after going to print, *The Tribune* published a retraction admitting the article had been a hoax 'written for the purpose of presenting a theory in an entertaining form'. The key character's name, Fred S. Ellmore, a pun on 'sell more' newspapers, should have been a give-away, but no one, it seemed, got the joke.[13]

The retraction, however, did little to dampen the controversy. In its ham-fisted effort to boost circulation, *The Tribune* had unwittingly let the jinn out of the bottle, turning an obscure legend into a full-blown Oriental fantasy. The ingredients were all there. The trick had a provenance going back hundreds, if not thousands of years. There was more secrecy attached to its execution than any other feat of Eastern magic, and the supernatural imagery of a rope ascending heavenward and a fakir making bloodied limbs rain down from the sky, had an almost apocalyptic quality.

Believers in the trick fell into two broad categories: those who insisted it was real and accomplished by some force or supernatural power that only the most skilful adepts could master; and those who insisted it was real but executed using some kind of ingenious props. The deniers were broadly in agreement that the trick had never existed. What is certain is that by the turn of the century it had taken on a life of its own, crossing the boundary between miracle and marvel. Not to believe in it became synonymous with not believing in the peculiarly esoteric qualities of Indian magic. Equally, the existence of such belief was justification for the need to impose a system of rationality on the Indian masses that Western magicians and imperial overlords saw as their duty. 'The rope trick thereupon ceased to be what it was – a "trick", and became what it was not – a "miracle" – the Hindu's greatest claim to occult powers,' Arthur Train wrote four-and-a-half decades after *The Tribune* hoax when debate over the legend was still showing no signs of slowing down.[14]

One immediate effect of *The Tribune's* story was to elevate Indian jadoo to evermore extraordinary heights. From Benares, the *Daily Graphic* brought news of the 'Magnetic Lady'. For a couple of rupees, visitors could enter her temple and witness the 'wizened and shrivelled up' face, as small as a baby's, magnetically attract goats, cats, pigeons and snakes. When a youth came in, she passed her hand under his body, slowly raised him to a height of two feet, put him into a hypnotic trance and turned him sideways. When she repeated the levitation feat on the *Daily Graphic's* correspondent he reported feeling a sensation that resembled 'an intense discharge from an electric battery'.[15] In 1896, the occult journal *Borderland*, published a letter from the office of the Akhbar-i-am in Lahore concerning the 'wonders of Professor Jhingan'. A man of 'stout muscles, but delicate skeleton', the young professor could levitate, make his body so stiff that no hammer could hurt it or break his skull and erase his shadow. The same article carried an account of the Simla jeweller and diamond merchant, Alexander Malcolm Jacob. 'Those who know him aver to his mysteriousness,' *Borderland's* correspondent assured the journal's readers. Jacob could make a vine laden with ripe, black Hamburg grapes grow instantaneously from the end of a walking stick, create his own double and conjure up 'a storm of butterflies, so dense, that no object in the room or its walls or ceilings could be seen through'.[16]

THE Western magic fraternity was not going to let the mysterious, inexplicable and uncontrollable world of Indian magic with its disappearing ropes, magnetic witches and fruit-producing walking sticks go unchallenged. For John Nevil Maskelyne, the Rope Trick was an example of a writer with a fertile imagination evolving 'from his inner consciousness a romance embodying suppositional incidents and fictitious miracles. This, on being published, is seized upon with avidity by those in search of the marvellous, and repeated as a record of something that has actually occurred.'[17]

When not using a pen as their weapon against the Rope Trick, Western wizards used their wallets and their wands. After *The Tribune* story, no self-respecting necromancer could go to the subcontinent without posting a reward to see the deception performed, quizzing every jadoowallah about the legend, interrogating every prince who might have commissioned it, or scouring every Gangetic ghat and Himalayan grotto for evidence of the illusion or, at the very least, a credible eye-witness account. They came back divided between those who believed the trick existed and those adamant it was the biggest hoax in the history of magic.

Charles Bertram, who styled himself as 'Royal and Imperial Court Magician,' probed more thoroughly than most on his tour of India in 1899 and returned convinced the trick was a con. Bertram spent six months entertaining various rulers and dignitaries, including the Viceroy Lord Curzon and the Nizam of Hyderabad. In what was a rare honour, the Maharajah of Dholpur allowed him to perform for the Maharani and the women of the zenana, who arrived for his show resplendent in 'semi-European costume' and 'wearing a profusion of priceless jewels'. Although timid at first, they began to laugh and exhibit their 'intense wonderment' and 'childish delight' as his show progressed. Bertram later proclaimed it was the 'first time such a departure from the usual custom has been permitted'.[18] In Patiala, he also performed for the ladies of the zenana, though they remained in purdah, and coached the personal conjurer of Bhupinder Singh, the Maharajah. Singh procured jugglers from various parts of the country for Bertram's edification, giving him the opportunity to witness many tricks he could otherwise not have seen. [19] Yet, despite seeing hundreds of jugglers gathered together in various parts of the country by different rajahs, not a single one had observed the Rope Trick or could do it. 'I heard of men who had heard of others who had seen it, but I could get no direct evidence, and all that I could discover about it from the Indians themselves was voiced by one man, who said to me, in his curious English, "All in imagination, looking traveller tales. I've been all over India looking tricks; would I not have that if I could get it?"'[20] Bertram claimed he offered £500 to the first jadoowallah who could do the trick, but there were no takers. 'With this evidence, I think this wonderful feat may be numbered with the mysteries of Aladdin's Palace, Prince Ahmed's wonderful carpet, and a few other fancy tales enumerated in *Arabian Nights' Entertainments*.'[21] As for Indian jugglers in general, Bertram agreed with Kellar that the entire fraternity was 'beneath contempt'. 'Taking them as a body, I heartily concur in this view, and here place it unmistakably on record, that I consider the Hindoo Juggler a greatly over-rated personage, around whom a fictitious glory has been cast, for what purpose it is difficult to imagine.'[22]

Carl Hertz, who had travelled to India in 1898, presenting among other novelties the first moving pictures projected using a cinematograph, also searched in vain for the elusive illusion. 'I have gone off the beaten track and made expeditions to remote districts to try and see the trick performed, but was always unsuccessful,' he wrote in *A Modern Mystery Merchant*. This lack of success, however, did not prevent him from staging a version of the feat in 1916, or claiming that he was 'the only one to produce it with a near approach to the skill of the Hindu fakir'.[23] A full

Poster for Carl Hertz's version of the Indian Rope Trick, c. 1916. Wikimedia Commons.

page advertisement in *The Era* promised 'full light, no traps, glasses, mirrors or curtains'.[24] Hertz's show climbed to new heights of Oriental kitsch. 'A Purdee lady reclines on a divan, fanned by a Punkah Wallah and amused by a Nautch dancer. Then enters

Carl Hertz dressed as an Eastern despot. Dusky attendants rush about,' one reviewer cooed. Posters showed a bearded jadoowallah holding a rope as a scrawny-looking boy climbed into the clouds. Bare-chested natives bowed before the magician, while others held their hands in exclamation at the feat. In his performance, Hertz threw up a rope that rose to the top of the proscenium. Satisfied that it was strong enough, he directed a semi-naked boy to ascend. A cloth was suddenly thrown over the boy. When removed, he had disappeared. The rope dropped to the ground and next moment the same boy materialized in front of the stalls.[25]

Horace Goldin joined those offering a reward to anyone who could show him the trick. 'I played in many of the mysterious and romantic towns in India and never even heard the trick mentioned, though, naturally, the talk often ran on the subject of magic,' he wrote in his memoir, *It's Fun to be Fooled*.[26] Like Hertz, he attempted to replicate the legend on stage. Goldin told his audiences that during his Indian travels he met Yogi Caram Dumbila, a Hindu holy man who showed him, among other feats, how it was possible to hang upside down from a tree for days. 'It came to my knowledge that this yogi was a master of the Indian Rope Trick, which was performed as a sacred and secret religious rite, and I asked him to divulge the secret. For many days he refused, but at last he imparted the secret after I had sworn on oath not to perform it until he had passed away.' After waiting eighteen years for the yogi's passing, he was now ready to replicate the feat.[27] Goldin's story was so convincing many people believed he had indeed learned the secret. Deceiving audiences was remarkably easy, he later wrote. 'It is lucky that I have never had criminal instincts.'[28]

Another tactic employed to counter the reputation of India as the birthplace of magic, was to expose the secrets of the jadoowallah's craft. Maintaining secrecy was central to Occidental magic, but when it came to the Orient, anything was fair game. In March 1898, the illusionist and shadowist Clivette devoted an entire show at the Orpheum in Kansas City to lifting the veil on as many Indian routines as he could in the two-hour programme. 'I never knew a man who had any real understanding of magic to be fooled by one of those Hindoo, presto, change boys,' he scoffed. Articles written about jugglers were 'the outgrowth of a very vivid imagination combined with a desire to tell a remarkable story'. Added Clivette: 'The juggler does his best; the traveller does the rest.' The Rope Trick was no different than other standard deceptions – in fact, there was nothing particularly mysterious about it, he insisted. The performance always took place in an open courtyard. When the rope was thrown into the air, it fastened onto a hidden wire so it appeared to remain upright with no visible support. By employing the techniques of black art, the boy climbing up the rope passed behind a black painted screen making as if he had disappeared.[29]

Professor Hoffman, whose encyclopaedic *Modern Magic* (1876) was one of the most influential practical and theoretical textbooks on the magician's art, took exposure a step further when he penned an article in the November 1901 edition of *Chambers Journal* entitled 'Indian Conjuring Explained'. In the 'interests of truth and commonsense' Western conjurers had been visiting the East to scrutinize the performances of their competitors. 'The natural result has been that the alleged miracles are found to be perfectly easy of explanation, deriving, in fact, their prestige from the loose accounts which casual observers have given of them.'[30] Hoffmann then proceeded to clarify that the Hindu conjurer was actually 'a low-class Mohammedan'. Though their attire was limited to a turban and a loin cloth, there were ample opportunities to hide articles in their hair or the hollow of their armpits, 'enlarged by habitual use'. Various tricks including the Diving Duck, the Basket Trick and the Mango Trick were explained. As for the Rope Trick 'all that need be said is that no such thing ever happened'. The probable origin of the story was a curious balancing feat Indian jugglers did with a rope a few feet long. In that feat, a rope was thrown in the air and balanced vertically on the palm of the hand. This is achieved by years of practice and with the help of a wire running through the rope giving it some rigidity. 'The rest is but the embroidery added by successive narrators, reporting it from hearsay.'[31]

A more detailed exposé was published in a booklet by Hereward Carrington in 1913. Carrington, an American psychic investigator, set out to test 'how far we are entitled to assume that there is anything in them suggesting the supernormal, anything calling for explanations that necessitate the operation of laws "other than those known to Western science."'[32] Of all the illusions he examined, only the levitation and rope tricks defied those laws of science unless performed on a proper stage with the necessary equipment. As for the rope feat, he concluded that if ever witnessed by Europeans, 'it must have been the result of some sort of hallucination, possibly hypnotic, which the onlooker was experiencing at the time'.[33] Carrington also cited Richard Hodgson's investigation of Indian jugglery for the Society of Psychical Research, agreeing that if the deception had been performed at all, it was the work of hallucination.

One of the cases Hodgson investigated was Madame Blavatsky's knotty, or possibly nutty, encounter with the trick. The Melbourne-born spiritual investigator had little time for the Theosophical Society's founder who he famously described as 'one of the most accomplished and interesting imposters in history'.[34] Blavatsky had included a chapter entitled the 'Indian tape-climbing trick' in her two-volume classic, *Isis Unveiled,* even though she claimed to have witnessed it in Egypt using an eighteen-inch-wide contrivance. Dismissing the notion that such feats might be the result of trickery, she cited the French authority, Louis Jacolliot, who had 'not met, either in India or in Ceylon, a single European, even among the oldest residents, who has been able to indicate the means employed by those devotees for the production of these phenomena'.[35] Hodgson's conclusion was the exact opposite. 'The performance of all the "jugglers" whom I saw were unquestionably conjuring tricks, and I sought in vain for an eyewitness, European or native, of the famous rope exploit of which we have heard so much in travellers' tales.' Even Blavatsky's closest confidante, Colonel Olcott, had admitted to him he had never witnessed rope-climbing.[36]

In 1912, Maskelyne took another shot at the Rope Trick, while trying to take down Blavatsky and the Theosophical Society at the same time. *The Fraud of Modern Theosophy Exposed and the Miraculous Rope-Trick of the Indian Jugglers Explained* was meant to be final word on the 'pernicious influence' Indian mysticism had over people.[37] The reputations of both Blavatsky and the Rope Trick were the result, Maskelyne claimed, of the exaggerated accounts of easily deluded persons. He labelled Blavatsky as a 'gross, vulgar, sensual adventuress' who 'turned the scale at seventeen stone' and whose language was at times 'too bad for publication'.[38] Compared with his attack on Blavatsky, the Rope Trick got off lightly. If anything, Maskelyne toned down his earlier position that it was all a figment of the imagination. His explanation for the feat was based on a description given to him by a 'gentleman who had been stationed in India and had seen the trick on several occasions'. Its execution relied on two things: the construction of the rope, which was made up of small interlocking pieces of bamboo covered with a cloth that locked together to form a pole thirty-feet high; and the harsh sunlight, which left the audience blinded when they tried to see what happened to the boy climbing up the pole. All that was missing, he said, was the documentary evidence.[39] It would not be long in coming.

Version of the Rope Trick being performed at Kirkee, The Strand, *April 1919.*

◈

IN April 1919, the *Strand Magazine* announced it was publishing the first-ever photograph of the Rope Trick. It showed a juggler holding what appeared to be a rope that had risen about twenty feet into the air with boy balancing spread-eagled on the top. The photographer was not someone who could be readily accused of fakery. Lieutenant F. W. Holmes was a Victoria Cross recipient, an award he received for rescuing under fire a wounded comrade in the trenches of northern France in 1914. Accompanying his photograph was an explanation of how the trick was done.

> One day in May, 1917, I was standing on the veranda of my bungalow at Kirkee, near Poona, in the company of several other officers, when an old man and his boy came up to us, over the open ground, to give us his performance. He had no pole – a thing which would have been impossible of concealment. He began by unwinding from about his waist a long rope, which he threw upwards in the air, where it remained erect. The boy climbed to the top, where he balanced himself, as seen in the photograph, which I took at that moment. He then descended, and the conjurer, holding the pole with one hand, tapped it gently with the other, when it collapsed into rope-like flexibility, and he coiled it round his waist, as before. I offer no explanation. I simply relate what took place before our eyes.[40]

Holmes's description, but not the photograph, was first published in the *Daily Mail* on 28 January 1919. It immediately drew the attention of Lieutenant-Colonel Robert Elliot. A Cambridge graduate, Elliot went to India in 1893, where he did pioneering work in the field of ophthalmology. He was appointed the superintendent of the Government Ophthalmic Hospital in

Madras and then Professor of Ophthalmology in the Madras Medical College. While in Madras he became an expert on snakes and their venom, surviving a bite from a Russell viper as well as a mongoose. He also developed an interest in Indian magic. In 1904, he became the founder of the Madras Magic Circle and remained its president until his return to England in 1914. Over the next two decades, he wrote multiple papers including 'The Evidence for the Rope Trick,' 'Witchcraft,' 'On Immunity from Snake-Bite,' 'The Mongoose and the Cobra,' and 'The Adder'. An opponent of fraudulent spiritualism, Elliot was elected Chairman of the highly secretive Occult Committee of the Magic Circle in June 1919. In 1934, he published *The Myth of the Mystic East*. To Elliot the glory and strength of Western magic was the constant pressure to develop new ideas and methods, something the 'changeless East' was 'totally unconscious' of. 'The conjurer is doing today in the same way the same tricks his ancestors have done for many generations; he sees no need to change either his programme or his methods; the very suggestion that he should do so would shock him.'[41]

Elliot's reputation for remaining cool and level-headed when under pressure and his eye for detail, served him well when it came to testing Holmes's claims. When he examined the photograph taken at Kirkee with a magnifying glass, he found that the rope looked remarkably like a solid bamboo pole. He rang Holmes who not only agreed, but readily refuted his initial suggestion that it was a telescopic device. The photograph was of the pole-balancing trick, a centuries-old acrobatic feat involving a child balancing on the end of a long piece of bamboo. Jugglers had performed a variation of the feat in England as early as

1869, and it could be seen at almost any mela or on any maidan in India.

In February 1918, Sidney Clarke invited Holmes to a special meeting of the Magic Circle at Anderton's Hotel in Fleet Street to test his claims. Because it was the most prestigious society of magicians in the world, its verdict on controversy would be considered final. The theme of the gathering was 'The Great Indian Rope Trick – In Tradition and in Reality'. Members were urged to arrive early because of the unprecedented interest from the public and the press – and to wear evening dress in order 'to give a good impression and sustain the reputation of the Circle'.[42] The meeting began with Clarke, who edited the *Magic Circular* and was a believer in the hallucination theory, giving a history of what he called the 'the most illusive trick in the world' including descriptions by Battuta and Jahangir. Holmes produced his photographs and offered the explanation that the juggler had used a rigid rope or pole.[43] The hypnotism theory was backed by Chris van Bern, a member of the Inner Magic Circle, who described his experience of seeing an old fakir doing the trick in a Liverpool drawing room using a small monkey that clung to the rope 'like death, but declined to climb or to vanish'. Elliot then announced he was offering a reward of 200 guineas to anyone, whether they were from the East or not, who could do the trick to the satisfaction of the Magic Circle's Council. [44] As the *Times* summed up sarcastically, the magical assembly 'was unable to conjure up mystic carpets' necessary for reaching a consensus.[45]

In the May 1919 issue of *The Magic Circular,* Elliot pulled together the main findings of the Magic Circle meeting and traced the evolution of the trick from a pole balancing feat to the legend it had become. Once the stories of Battuta, Jahangir and others started to become widely known in the English-speaking world, traditional Indian jugglers found themselves under pressure to add a rope trick to their repertoire.

> [The juggler] knew that he could not make a rope self-supporting, let alone capable of bearing a climber, but he could and did convert his pole into the semblance of a rope. Instead of using a continuous pole, he cut it into short sections, and these he inserted into a sheath or covering, woven to resemble the outer strands of a rope. Such a contraption when coiled round a man's body would pass for a rope, but when uncoiled and held up becomes stiff, and when the lowest section is driven home and supported within the performer's waist-belt, the affair becomes fairly rigid and capable of supporting the boy. When the balancing is over, the bottom section is allowed to fall, the whole then become limp, and can be recoiled round the body.[46]

Elliot added that the secret of the apparatus was 'given away' by an Indian magician named Dugwar, who performed at the old Polytechnic in London in the 1870s. According to Dugwar, it was 'in uncoiling and getting the "rope" into position for the performance', that the skill of the juggler came to the fore. The 'throw into the air' was done with one hand, while the other was used for closing together the joints inside the cotton tube. 'The boy is light and agile, and the juggler is, of course, a first-class equilibrist.'[47]

Elliot's explanation of the trick and Holmes's admission came too late to prevent the rope-climbing story taking on a life of its own – yet again. Three decades after *The Tribune's* bombshell, the *Daily Mail* found itself in the middle of a media maelstrom. Shortly after Holmes's letter was published, F. G. Smith of Blockley wrote that he was part of a large audience that had seen an identical performance in Benares in the summer of 1896 and again in Delhi the following year. 'Beyond the fact that the trick was exactly as described by you, I am unable to offer any suggestion as the "cause", hypnotic or otherwise, but that which one has actually seen cannot possibly be an "hallucination".'[48]

Articles and letters from both sides of the debate flowed furiously. The deniers included General Sir Arthur Lytellton-Annesley, Commander of the Scottish Forces, who claimed he knew every part of India from Bengal in the east, Madras in the south, the Punjab in the west and Ladakh in the north. He enquired about the trick from numerous native princes, all of whom insisted it did not exist.[49] Sidney Arthur Vipan, a fluent speaker of Hindustani, who lived in India for fourteen years and interrogated magicians at the courts of the Maharajahs of Patiala, Kapurthala and Mysore, also drew a blank.[50] Those vouching for its authenticity included the Nawab of Murshidabad, Nusrat Ali Mirza, who wrote that he had witnessed the trick on board an English ship in Bombay harbour and at his father's court. He first saw it as a young boy hiding behind the curtains of his grandmother's room, where he could not have come under a hypnotic spell. A 'prominent Hindu' living in France named C. C. Sen, insisted he had seen it in Calcutta performed in the open as described by Ibn Battuta. He made his admission 'not as a stranger nor as a tourist, but as a Hindu'.[51] Another witness was a sergeant of the East Surreys Regiment stationed at Ferzapore, who wrote: 'We hadn't been there two days when an old Hindu entered camp one morning. He carried a little basket and a long rope, rather thick, was slung across his shoulder; two little boys accompanied him. We gave them a few coppers and the performance began.'[52] The *Daily Mail* also reprinted an 1898 account from the *Civil and Military Gazette* in Lahore that described it being staged before a large gathering of Europeans and Indians at a party given by a local Rajah.[53]

Stepping into the fray was Lionel Hugh Branson, another member of the Magic Circle, and like Elliot, an old India hand. Branson grew up in India and after graduating from Sandhurst was posted to Dinapur near Patna in 1899. He learned the art of conjuring from Professor Hoffman's *Modern Magic* and gave numerous performances in his spare time, including one at the palace of the Maharajah of Patiala for the Prince of Wales. '[I] discovered he was a keen amateur conjurer. I have a card bearing his signature that appeared whole once more, quite restored, after being torn to bits and burnt. It was appropriately the King of Hearts,' Branson wrote in his autobiography *A Lifetime of Deception*.[54] Until he was invalided out of the Indian Army in1922, he was regarded as its best magician and credited his 'conjurer's mind' for out-manoeuvring an ambush by Mahsud warriors while stationed in Waziristan.[55] Branson was present when Holmes displayed his now infamous photograph at the Magic Circle's meeting in January 1919. He told the gathering that he had offered a £300 reward, the equivalent of a year's pay to a sepoy, but no one had come forward to demonstrate the trick. In 1922, he published *Indian Conjuring*. The book's cover showed a semi-naked jadoowallah throwing a rope in the air with a young boy balancing on the end against a background of onion domes, chhatris and minarets. His reward offer was printed beneath his name. As well as sketches showing how common illusions such as the Basket Trick were done, *Indian Conjuring* featured photographs of his friend, Shah Mohammad. The eighty-seven-year-old told him his tricks had been passed down to his great grandfather from a friend in Lahore. The only change in 150 years had been the singing of 'Ta-ra-ra-boom-de-ay' between each act of jadoo. 'He seldom has any patter worth listening to and that which he uses consists usually of "Beggie, beggie, aow" or "Beggie beggie jaow". "Bun, two, three, four, five, white, bite, fight, kite." Amusing to a casual observer, but hopeless from an artist's point of view.'[56] His condescending tone continued in his put down of Indians attempting Western-style magic.

> They have purchased the necessary paraphernalia from London and have as much idea of using it to its best advantage as a crocodile has of arranging the flowers on a dinner table. Our Indian Jadoowallah usually gets himself into a very tight fitting third or fourth-hand evening dress on these occasions, to show, I presume, how European he is. The audience is more concerned with the possibility of its bursting and their having to leave the theatre for decency's sake, than they are of the feats he is attempting to imitate.[57]

Branson continued his tirade by taking on the Rope Trick. After twenty-three years spent in India, he had met 'innumerable people whose aunt's sister's cousin saw it done, but never have I had the pleasure of meeting anyone directly deceived by it'.[58]

Nor had there been takers for the various rewards offered for the trick, including his. It was not a case of hypnotism or any other deception, the trick performed outdoors, as described by Battuta and others, had simply never been performed.

◈

NO amount of rationalism, however, could lessen the appeal of the Rope Trick in the public's mind. Despite Branson's dismissal of their talents, audiences flocked to see the Indian magicians such as Manek Shah, the 'Genuine East Indian Necromancer direct from Bombay', who featured it in his George's Palace programme 'as performed at Delhi during the Darbar', alongside the Human Water Fountain Trick, The Gurkha's Gong and other 'wonderful feats'.[59] Manek Shah was followed by Englishman David Devant, who also claimed to be 'the first and only European Conjurer to attempt a reproduction of this fabulous feat of the famous Fakirs of India'.[60] By the 1920s, the number of magicians featuring the Rope Trick in their repertoire included Howard Thurston, Servais Le Roy, Cecil Lyle, Nicola and Harry Blackstone.

The fierce competition to present the trick turned to farce in 1924 when a Mr Bhumgara, the owner of the Indian Theatre at British Empire Exhibition in Wembley, announced he had 'a fakir who would do it for the first time on any stage'. Bhumgara had gone to India to find a rope-climbing magician. As usual, despite meeting hundreds of people who had heard of the feat, not a single one had seen it. Finally, a juggler came forward claiming he could do the trick. He refused to do a demonstration, but his conjuring was so good Bhumgara decided to bring him to

England on the condition that he would only get paid once he staged the feat. A special preview for the press, public and exhibition officials, however, ended up as a fiasco with the *Lancashire Evening Post* declaring that the only illusion on display 'would hardly have deceived a short-sighted centenarian'.[61] Things started to go wrong after the jadoowallah – a 'tall swarthy gent, with beard', wearing a black and gold turban, gold braided red tunic and sugar-bag blue pants, produced a ball of thin red twine and threw it over the backstage drop. After the usual hypnotic stunt, an assistant climbed up and vanished between the drop and a hanging batten. A second later what were obviously pieces of a dismembered dummy came raining down. A box was then lowered to the stage from which the assistant stepped out. 'Mr. Bhumgara … admitted that the show would not deceive a schoolboy, and a large number of people who had bought tickets for subsequent public performances received their money back.'[62] When plans were being drawn up for the Indian exhibition at the

Poster for the 1924 British Empire Exhibition, Wembley. Beinecke Rare Book and Manuscript Library, Yale University.

Chicago World Fair in 1933, the organizers insisted there would be 'Dancing Girls, Yogis who read minds, and men who do the Mango Trick', but 'no Rising Rope Trick in the fakir section of theatrical tent for there is no record of the rope ever having risen'.[63]

The persistence of the legend and steady arrival of reports from credible-sounding witnesses, including the commander of the British Expeditionary Force on the Western Front, Field Marshall Earl Haig, began to irk Elliot. The frustration clearly showed when he reached for inter-stellar metaphors in a letter to *The Spectator* on 9 March 1935. 'It is a belief that implies temporary suspension of the law that not merely determines the fall of the apple and the swing of the earth's vast oceans, but reaching far out into space enables us to weigh stars whose colossal distance can only be measured in light years.'[64] With the memory of the failure of the 1919 meeting to settle the matter once and for all still fresh in his mind, he announced an extraordinary meeting of the Magic Circle to be held on 30 April 1934 at the Oxford House Theatre on High Street, Marylebone. The meeting would be chaired by the President of the Magic Circle and a former Viceroy of India, the Rt. Hon. Lord Ampthill, together with a committee that included the Rt. Hon. The Lord Meston, KCSI, LLD (the former Governor of the United Provinces, Agra and Oude), Sir Michael O'Dwyer, GCIE, KCSI (the former Lieutenant-Governor of the Punjab) and an impressive armada of experts in various fields. This time Elliot was taking no chances. As one of those present later said, the aim was 'to kill the Rope Trick stone dead and give it a decent funeral'.[65]

At 8 p.m. sharp, Lord Ampthill declared the meeting open. It was once again left to Sidney Clarke to present a history of the legend. He was followed by Elliot, who forensically refuted recent claims by Haig and others. He also noted some of the more fanciful versions of the trick, including the experience of Colonel H. Cornes who witnessed it being done in a street so narrow the overhanging verandahs almost touched each other. The troupe of conjurers lit a fire that gave off dense smoke screening out the upper stories of the houses and provided plenty of cover for an accomplice to catch the rope when it was thrown up. Elliot ended his statement by repeating his position that he did not believe the Rope Trick ever had been done or would be done and laid down the following challenge: 'If anyone will come forward and perform the Indian Rope Trick before my Committee, we will give him 500 guineas. The rope must be thrown into the air and defy the force of gravity, whilst someone climbs up it and disappears.'[66]

After Elliot came several other 'experts', who noted it was strange that in the case of performances witnessed in places full of Europeans, no one could corroborate their accounts, nor were they reported in the local press. Dr Edwin Smith, ruled out hypnotism by pointing out that visual hallucinations could not be produced under the conditions that prevailed when the 'trick' was performed. Sir Francis Griffith, a former Inspector General of Police in India, blamed the power of suggestion – 'like the impressionable American lady of travel who said the most remarkable thing she had seen in all India was the sun setting behind the Aga Khan'.[67] Branson, O'Dwyer and others all spoke of their unsuccessful attempts during their residence in India to see the trick or to find anyone who could describe it at first-hand. Harry Price, Director of the National Laboratory of

Psychical Research, stated there was not one word of evidence in his collection of 12,000 volumes on conjuring. The lesson to be drawn from the controversy, the Magic Circle's vice-president, the psychic researcher Eric Dingwall concluded, was that such reputed marvels must be investigated scientifically. He closed the meeting with a hearty vote of thanks to Lord Ampthill and expressed the thanks of the Occult Committee for the large attendance.[68]

The verdict of what it termed the Grand Inquest was to relegate 'this ancient myth to the realm of the non-existent', the *Magic Circular* emphatically declared. The 'negative evidence' presented by a group of such distinguished men, with centuries of experience in India between them, 'was overwhelming, and it will be a bold man, or one careless of his reputation for veracity, who in future claims to have seen the most famous trick which has never been performed.'[69] It was not going to be so easy. What Dingwall, Elliot, Ampthill, Branson and the others hadn't counted on was the tenacity of a travelling Gypsy showman and his eleven-year-old son. Like the entombed fakir, the trick – and the controversy – was refusing to die.

FOURTEEN

A ROPE TRICK IN A SNOWSTORM, A FIRE WALK IN SURREY

ARTHUR Claude Derby knew how tough it was to be a travelling showman, living out of a Gypsy caravan with his wife Polly and their seven children, always on the move, always on the look out for the next lucky break. Born in Birmingham in 1888, he was the son of watchmaker and jeweller, but instead of following his father's trade, he joined the circus at the age of ten. In the 1930s, he started using the stage name 'Phantom', working the music halls and sideshows doing circus-style rope acts, card manipulation and ventriloquism. It was a hand-to-mouth existence. To sustain his family, he worked at various times as a cleaner for the railways, a mural painter, sign writer and a fitter and turner. When news reached him that the Magic Circle was offering a 500-guinea prize to the first person who could do the Indian Rope Trick, he saw an opportunity too good to miss.

The Magic Circle's offer had fired up the public's imagination, leading one newspaper to complain that the Rope Trick business was 'getting rather frayed'.[1] Old eyewitness reports were dredged up including one dating back to 1889, describing how an old juggler had performed the feat several times a day before hundreds of soldiers on the troopship *Malabar*.[2] Offers came flooding in from as far away as Pretoria where the South African-born, Indian juggler, Jaysirie Singh, insisted he could do the deception anywhere in the world with four or five barrels of sand, provided his expenses were paid.[3] Closer to home, a Professor Bofeys of Charlton Kinks, told the *Gloucestershire Echo* he had made a rope rise in the air two years earlier at a conference of the International Brotherhood of Magicians, but had refused the Magic Circle's challenge because it would cost more than £500 to stage the deception again.[4] One letter writer to the *Nottingham Evening Post* insisted the trick could be replicated using a radio picture projected from another planet. 'We know how the cinema can place before us impossible happenings – I can place many similar pictures (radio) before you which cannot possibly be challenged, and are without a shadow of a doubt from interplanetary service.'[5]

Dr Sir Alexander Cannon, KGCB, MD, DSc, PhD, DLitt, etc, etc, etc., a London psychiatrist and author of *The Invisible Influence* and *The Powers that Be,* not only claimed he had seen the trick, he promised to replicate it. Throwing caution to the wind, the Occult Committee allowed him to present his case. He introduced himself as a yogi, something that Robert Elliot was quick to refute. 'A Yogi is one who exists on what charity comes his way and all he possesses is a begging bowl and staff and just sufficient clothes to wear. Dr Cannon was wearing a beautiful cut suit and top hat.'[6] Cannon then listed his conditions. For a fee of £50,000 he would bring to England a group of yogis and a shipload of special sand. The feat would be performed in London's Albert Hall, which would have to be heated to tropical temperature. The Committee asked if he could give 'a banker's guarantee that the money plus the expenses would be returned in the event of failure. The reply was in the negative.'[7]

Less elaborate versions of the most marvellous illusion of the East were now a fixture at country fairs, garden parties and even Scout camps. It was the headline act in Indian magician Linga Singh's London line up, alongside 'an attractive company of nautch girls'. Horace Goldin featured the trick in a programme that also included 'The Prisoner of Cawnpore', where a man vanished into space after being fired from a cannon. The meme even found its way into a mustard ad. A clever copywriter had come up with the ditty: 'The rope trick is like indigestion; some people know that it exists, while others refused to believe in it.' The catch line was: 'It's nicer with Mustard – Coleman's Mustard.'[8] Newspaper cartoonists used it to lampoon politicians making phoney promises. Douglas Fairbanks filmed a stage version in his docu-drama, *Around the World in Eighty Days* (1932). But the challenge set by the Magic Circle was about to take a more serious turn.

◈

On a brisk November day at a traveller's camp in Devonport, a gaunt-looking, dark-skinned man and his son, both wearing voluminous red and yellow pants, embroidered jackets and sky-blue turbans, emerged from a caravan. In front of Reginald

Lewis, a photographer from the *Western Morning News,* and a small group of curious onlookers, the man spread an Oriental carpet on the roadway and stood in the centre with a long coil of rope in his hand and proceeded to swing it in the air like a lasso. He then sat on the rug with the rope coiled between his legs. Taking one end in his left hand, he started pushing it up with his right until it stood in the air at a height of about six feet. The man, his son and Lewis then drove to Roborough Downs on the edge of Dartmoor, where the feat was repeated in an open field, this time with the boy climbing the rope. On 22 November 1934, after satisfying himself they were genuine, the newspaper's editor published Lewis's photographs with a caption stating the performer was prepared to do the trick using any kind of rope before any public assembly in the city. The rope would also be passed around for examination. Using his skills as a fitter and turner, Derby, it seemed, had pulled off the impossible. The gypsy from Birmingham was now Karachi, the mysterious Indian fakir, his eldest son Cyril was now the rope-climbing Kyder.

While Elliot could afford to ignore claims linking the Rope Trick with pictures beamed from outer space, the photographs in the *Western Morning News* appeared to be even more authentic than those presented by Holmes a decade-and-a-half earlier. That was also the opinion of Richard Lambert, the founding editor of the BBC's fortnightly magazine, *The Listener.* On 5th December, the magazine published two of Lewis's photographs accompanied by a letter from Wilfred Willcocks of Newquay vouching for their authenticity. Lambert's decision to publish was sparked by his interest in magic and the supernatural – an interest that nearly jeopardized the public broadcaster's authority. In 1931, a poltergeist mongoose named Gef 'appeared' at a farmhouse belonging to the Irving family on the Isle of Man. Gef, who claimed he was born in India in 1852, turned out to be a highly intelligent 'animal'. The Irvings taught him to recognize bird and animal sounds, then nursery rhymes, and finally to speak. Gef in turn regaled them with stories rivalling the *Arabian Nights* in the fantastic improbabilities they contained.[9] When Lambert published an article about the mongoose in *The Listener*, a retired colonel, Sir Cecil Levita, alleged his obsession with the rodent was evidence he was 'off his head'. Lambert responded by bringing a slander suit, referred to as 'The Mongoose Case', against Levita. The BBC's chairman, a friend of the retired colonel, suggested to Lambert he drop the proceedings. He refused, won the case and received substantial damages. But the Chairman's intervention caused a major crisis, prompting the prime minister to launch a special board of inquiry into the matter.

Working with Lambert to investigate the mongoose phenomenon was Harry Price. Ghost hunter, psychic researcher, amateur conjurer and member of the Magic Circle, Price was also the Honorary Secretary of University of London's Council for Psychical Investigation (CPI). Unlike other members of the Magic Circle, he was prepared to accept the existence of supernatural forces, but only after conducting forensic, Sherlock Holmes-like probes. His exposés of fraudulent mediums included the 'spirit' photographer William Hope and Frederick Tansley Munnings, who claimed he could produce the 'spirit' voices of Julius Caesar, Dan Leno, Hawley Harvey Crippen and King Henry VIII. Eager to test Karachi's claims, Price and Lambert decided to invite him to London to give a demonstration

Karachi arrived at Price's office at London University on 31 December 1934, but instead of demonstrating the trick, he announced he needed at least four days to prepare the site. He also had to scour London to find a 'certain rare mineral' that had to be planted in the ground where the feat was to take place. The field needed to be large enough for him to work without being overlooked. Price had planned to use the Hampstead garden of the CPI's chairman, C. E. M. Joad, but at Karachi's insistence the site was moved to West Hampstead and the demonstration rescheduled for the following Monday, 7th January.[10]

As Price remarked later, West Hampstead was far removed from the Rope Trick's traditional mise-en-scene: 'Blinding sun, cerulean skies, scorching sands, a – very convenient – hazy horizon, with attendant palm trees and Sons of the Desert.'[11] On the appointed day, the sodden field was enveloped in cold drizzle, which turned to snow accompanied by a bitter nor'easter. Fortunately, there was a comfortable pub close by, the Nelson, where Price found Karachi and his son waiting at the bar. Aside from Price, those present included Lambert, Mary Adams of the BBC's talks department, J. W. Brown, General Manager of the British Film Institute, an official photographer and a crew from Gaumont-British Films. After a few drinks, the group moved outside where Karachi had planted his rug on a slight eminence to give the film crew the best possible shots. His warm up act consisted of balancing the rope horizontally on his hands and vertically on his chin as well as some clever sleight of hand with cards, but they were soon sodden with snow. After a few words of introduction from Price, the show began.

Karachi and his son Kyder (Cyril) perform the Rope Trick at West Hampstead. Harry Price Collection, Senate House Library.

Seated on a rug 'like a real fakir' with Kyder bare-footed by his side, Karachi threw a six-foot long rope to his audience, which was examined to see if it had been tampered with. It was placed under a piece of red cloth and on Karachi's command rose vertically in a series of jerky movements. A longer piece of loosely woven rope was then produced and examined before being placed under the cloth. Karachi made it rise into the air, though as Price noted, it was now tightly woven. 'When about eight feet of the rope had been paid out, Karachi commanded his son to climb up – which he did with considerable agility.[12]

Back at the Nelson, Karachi offered to tell Price how the deception was done. But Price stopped him saying he had already worked it out. As he explained to *The Listener's* readers, a metal pole had been fitted inside the loosely woven longer rope. A buried socket pipe would have been strong enough to support a long rod bearing Kyder's weight. The pole would have been in sections joined together like a fishing rod. 'I congratulated him upon his simulating the Rope Trick so cleverly and, with a little more showmanship, he could make a convincing spectacle. In the hands of Houdini, it would look like a miracle. But we were not grumbling. We have seen the Rope Trick – and in snowstorm!'[13]

Price's article in *The Listener*, accompanied by stills from footage shot by Gaumont-British films and Lambert's photographs, drew a sharp response from Karachi, who wrote to the magazine refuting the explanation of how the trick was done. 'I am delighted with Mr. Harry Price's guesses as to the principle used in my performance of the Indian Rope Trick. Kyder is also delighted at these guesses! I do not wish to be personal – I agree with respectability – but I must say that Kyder, although only eleven years old, knows more about the Indian Rope Trick than these scientists at present.' He added that he had learned the secret many years ago from a mortally wounded Gurkha soldier he was caring for during the Great War. The soldier's dying injunction was that he should not stage the trick in public for profit except when driven by necessity. 'It is for this reason, Sir, that the Trick has not been performed for so many years, but now the time has come when I find it necessary to demonstrate its reality and convince a sceptical world that the Secrets of the East have not entirely perished.' He then issued a direct challenge to Elliot and the Occult Committee of the Magic Circle. He would perform the first part of the trick where the rope is thrown upright and a boy climbs to the top under the following conditions: the 500 guinea reward would be lodged with a neutral party who would decide whether the performance was satisfactory; the rope would rise to a height of ten feet from where he was seated; Kyder would climb it and remain at the top for thirty seconds to be photographed; as long as it had a good grip, the rope could be supplied by any well-known manufacturer; the open place for performance would be chosen by the neutral party, but forty-eight hours was needed for preparation time. He ended his letter with an extraordinary claim: 'I will add that I am able to perform all my Rope Tricks on a table, which can be examined beforehand. This disposes off the suggestion of bamboo canes, telescopic rods, etc. Now, Sir, these are fair conditions, and if the Magic Circle is really seeking enlightenment it will accept my challenge, and this much-disputed tradition will become a reality.'[14]

Elliot's riposte was swift and uncompromising. Referring to Karachi by his real name, he wrote to *The Listener* dismissing any possibility of entertaining his offer as it did not meet the terms for doing the trick as stipulated by the Magic Circle at its 30 April 1934 meeting. 'So far from giving Mr Darby 200 guineas for this trick, we would not give him twenty pence for it. If he likes to challenge me I will tell your readers exactly how he does it.' The Magic Circle's motive was to put an end to 'the humbug that in the Rope Trick there is anything supernatural,' he continued. 'We have no intention of allowing Mr Darby or anyone else to alter our terms and so deflect us from our purpose.'[15]

As *The Listener's* letters pages suddenly found themselves on the front line of yet another battle over the authenticity of the rope feat, public opinion seemed to swing Karachi's way. In a letter to the magazine, Basil Holywell of Eastbourne asked why the Occult Committee was going to let a paltry 500 guineas stand in the way of finally getting to the truth. 'I am sure I speak in the name of many listeners when I say: Get on with it. Let us have your challenges, your denials, your articles, your photographs, your Karachis, your Magic Circles, brought together and tested at the bar of public evidence. Let the laws of gravity be defied by Karachi. Let the Magic Circle be squared.'[16] A fortnight later Hugh Morrison of Manchester accused London's conjurers of being too afraid to accept Karachi's challenge. 'But in common justice to the Plymouth showman, they should stifle their timidity and give him a chance. Should Karachi fail to win their award, Colonel Elliot and his friends can hold another meeting and kill the Rope Trick all over again.' Edward Pitt-Arkwright of Melton Mowbray agreed. Karachi had 'put a spoke into the Magic Circle, which, partly out of credulousness, and partly from apparent desire for publicity, has now got itself into the false position of first offering 500 guineas for the performance of a feat which it alleges to be impossible, and then running away from anyone who offers to demonstrate that it *is* possible.'[17]

But the Magic Circle refused to budge. Aside from Price, Karachi failed to get the support of the conjuring establishment and was instead met with ridicule – something that reflected the ingrained prejudice against Oriental mystifiers. Karachi might be a Birmingham-born Gypsy, but by appropriating the garb of an Indian showman and daring to take on the greatest illusion of its day, he had traversed a line that only professional Western prestidigitators were allowed to cross.

The failure to claim the prize, however, was no deterrent to the showman. Publicity brought success at the box office and the Rope Trick received top billing. He was now 'The Great Karachi', performing 'Under Royal Patronage'. On 26 September 1935, he wrote to Price offering to sell the trick for £50 and announced he had moved into a 'proper house' at Maradon Green near Birmingham.[18] Price congratulated him on purchasing a house, but declined to buy his secret, writing: 'If you ever have a more imposing method of doing the trick (I mean if Kyder could go up much higher), I should like to see it.' In his autobiography, *Confessions of a Ghost Hunter*, Price admitted that meeting Karachi had changed his mind about the Rope Trick never being done in its traditional form. 'The trick itself has been witnessed as a conjuring illusion, accounts of which have been distorted and exaggerated by credulous travellers who were completely ignorant of the deceptive methods employed by the intolerant Eastern magician,' he wrote.[19] Karachi continued to perform the trick, joining the Entertainments National Service Association, which provided much-needed diversions for British Troops during the Second World War. In 1947, he emigrated to Perth, Western Australia, and two years later advertised for 'a small boy, a monkey, or a cockatoo to climb the rope when he performs the Indian rope trick', now that his son was too heavy. He also played a back-hander to the Magic Circle, by announcing he would pay £500 to anyone who proved that the rope he used had any hidden apparatus.[20] He toured Australia until the early 1960s with a travelling tent show and painted his own placards showing an Oriental magician on a magic carpet and the rope rising like a giant cobra. Signage proclaimed him as King of Magicians and The Man Who Challenged the Magic Circle. He died in Perth on 17 July 1970, aged ninety-two.

With the Occult Committee's successful staring down of challenges by Karachi and others, the notion that Indian jugglers had access to 'counter-physical supernatural causation' and were somehow superior to Western conjurers had been put to rest. Scientific reason had triumphed over Orientalist fantasies. Modern magic, founded on the principals of rationality would now rule supreme over Eastern superstitions and the rot of Spiritualism – or so it seemed.

❖

ON a blisteringly hot, sand-blasted day in May 1935, the Orient liner *Orontes* sailed from Port Said for England. On board was a slim, strong-featured Kashmiri with luxuriant black hair that rolled back from his high forehead, dark deep-set eyes and a pencil-thin moustache. Kuda Bux was born in the village of Akhnur in Kashmir in 1905, to a landowning family who made their wealth from growing saffron. At the age of thirteen he left home and roamed through Burma, Ceylon and India to study magic, learning his skills from fire walkers and levitating yogis, he would later claim. In the early 1930s he moved to Bombay, changed his name to Professor K. B. Duke and worked the city's theatres and nightclubs as a blindfold artist.

Travelling on the same ship was Reginald Teague-Jones. Brought up and educated in St Petersburg, Teague-Jones was fluent in Hindustani, Russian, French and German. Unknown to anyone on board, Teague-Jones was travelling under an assumed name: Ronald Sinclair. The British government had ordered him to change his name to avoid being killed by a Soviet hit squad after he was implicated in the execution of twenty-six prominent Bolshevik prisoners in Baku by Socialist Revolutionaries. Joseph Stalin called him the 'agent of British imperialism'. Since 1917, he had worked at the Delhi Intelligence Bureau heading a section monitoring developments in the Persian Gulf. In 1922, he had driven across Persia in a Model A Ford pretending to be scouting for trading opportunities, while in fact spying on Soviet agents in the country. Teague-Jones was also fascinated by Indian jadoo: 'The whole thing is conducted with an air of great seriousness, despite a certain amount of talking and a great deal of very expressive hand waving and pantomime. Even though the performance may have been seen many times before, one is still impressed by the atmosphere of expectation, mystery and sincerity in the creation of which the Indian jadoowala [sic] is a past master,' Teague-Jones wrote in an unpublished manuscript on mysticism in India. 'He appears to be absorbed in the problem before him, and follows through each successive stage with apparent concentration, while his face registers in turn anxiety, expectation, then astonishment, culminating in relief and expectation. So convincing is the acting that an air of suspense and mystification is created in which the spectator finds himself voluntarily carried along.'[21]

Late one afternoon as the two men were relaxing on the sports deck, Bux suddenly picked up Teague-Jones's thick tweed sports coat that was lying at his feet and threw it over his head and shoulders. He then asked to borrow the book he was reading. 'He opened the book at random and read out a passage without hesitation or faltering. . . . He could see without his eyes anything that he could see with them.' He told Teague-Jones he developed this skill as a child by keeping his eyes focused, without blinking, for long periods on the blue portion of the flame of a burning candle.[22]

Shortly after arriving in London in June 1935, Bux took to the stage at the Trocadero nightclub as 'The Man With the X-Ray Eyes'. The reviews were enthusiastic. When Price heard he was in England, he invited the Kashmiri to his office. He found him a remarkable man with an engaging personality and an extraordinarily versatile magician. 'He will eat a bundle of hay if placed before him. He will consent to be buried alive (in an ordinary grave, with just a board over his face) for a limit of three hours. He will – apparently – stop his heart and pulse at request, and demonstrated this trick in my office. He will drink poison. He has performed the classic fire walk on many occasions, and can handle live coals.'[23]

The meeting at the CPI's London University headquarters on 10 July 1935 was attended by several of its members and *The Listener's* Lambert. Price came prepared with surgical bandages, adhesive tape, pads of cotton wool and a special tie-on mask composed of two thicknesses of heavy black cloth between which

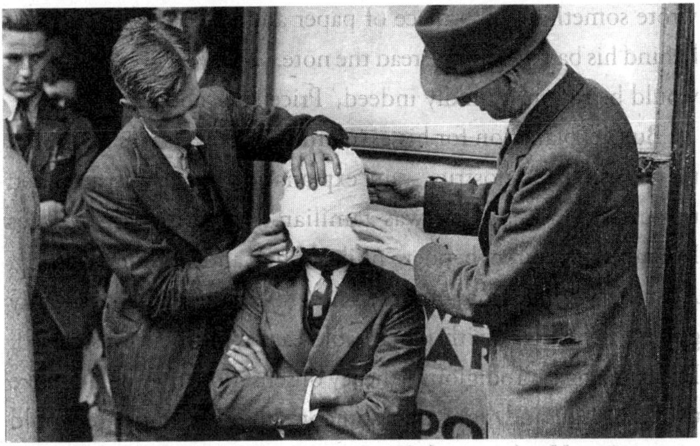

Kuda Bux being tested for his X-ray Eyes trick at the Council for Psychical Investigation, 1935. Harry Price Collection, Senate House Library.

was a layer of cotton wool. Bux had brought an almost identical set of bandaging materials in addition to a lump of fresh dough. Price commenced by taking the dough and squeezing a piece into each eye socket. The rest of the bandaging material was wrapped around his head until only his nostrils and mouth were left free. For his performance Bux sat at the seance room table facing the audience. He asked for a book to be placed before him. Price went to a bookshelf and chose a book. He opened it at random, laid it in front of Bux, put a finger on a paragraph and asked him to read it out loud. 'This he did at once ... There was no hesitation.' To exclude the possibility that the bandaging may not have been done properly, Price called for a qualified doctor to redo the blindfold. Placing his hand on his forehead, Bux sat in the same position and read whatever Price put in front of him 'with astonishing ease and accuracy'. Next, he was made to face sideways while Lambert wrote something on a piece of paper and placed it on the table behind his back. Again he read the note. 'To say we were surprised would be to put it mildly indeed,' Price later noted.[24]

Bux's explanation for his extraordinary powers was his ability to see using his nostrils – an explanation Price was prepared to partially accept. He was familiar with the work of Jules Romains, the French poet, philosopher and author of *Vision Extra-Retinienne*. Romain noted how somnambulists apparently guided themselves with remarkable ease with their eyes closed. By acquiring a 'prodigious delicacy of sensation' they could make use of a thousand signs that someone in a waking state would not notice. He theorized (quite incorrectly) that nasal mucosa was sensitive to light and to different coloured regions of the spectrum and an unknown organ of extra-retinal vision was located somewhere in the body. His theories are now discredited. Price also suspected Bux could somehow see down the side of his nose, though he could not satisfactorily explain how this was accomplished when lumps of dough were placed over his eyes. Bux would later quip: 'If I am blindfolded, I don't make mistakes. But if I close my eyes I make the same mistakes as other people – I collide with objects.'[25]

Bux's X-Ray Eyes feat was not the only skill Price wanted to test. For years, the psychic researcher had been fascinated by accounts of fire-walking from different parts of the world. In 1934, he placed an ad in the *Times* calling for amateur and professional fire walkers to perform the feat. As in the case of the Rope Trick there were hundreds of people claiming to have seen it, but no one prepared to do it. Price was determined to find out whether fire-walking was based on trickery, if walkers burned their feet, prepared them in any way, or developed callouses that made them immune to pain. Or was it all a question of 'faith'? Bux was about to provide the answers.

Price announced his fire walk experiment in *The Listener* on 7 August 1935 and called for volunteers. This time scores of people came forward including three young women and a fourteen-year-old boy. Bux promised that anyone who went hand-in-hand with him through the fire pit would be unharmed, prompting one letter writer to say she wanted to do it so her husband would 'respect and fear me and stop jeering at me'.[26] But Price was taking no chances. He announced volunteers would have to sign a statement acknowledging that the CPI would not be responsible for any injuries arising from the experiment. In the end, however, he decided against including outsiders. The event would be closed to the public. Aside from specially invited guests, including Lambert and a team of doctors and psychologists, only press reporters and television crews would be allowed to attend.

As Price soon realized, staging a fire walk required a good deal of organization. There was uncertainty about the size of the trench, the type of combustible material needed to fill it, and how to test Bux's mental and physical state, before and after the walk. A friend of Price's, Alex Dribbell of The Halt in Carshalton, Surrey, offered his garden for the experiment. After consulting several accounts of fire walks in India and elsewhere, it was decided the trench should be twenty-five feet long, three-feet wide, and twelve-inches deep. 'Two tons of oak logs, one ton of firewood, half a load of oak charcoal, ten gallons of paraffin, twenty-five copies of the *Times* – and a box of matches,' was all that was needed for Britain's first fire walk.[27] At 11.20 a.m. on

8 September 1935, Price set the pit on fire. Within an hour the heat was so intense it was impossible to go within three feet of the inferno. Bux arrived at noon wearing a long frock coat, braided black trousers and bright yellow shoes. At 12.55 p.m. he walked over to the pit, placed one of his bare feet on the glowing coals and declared it was ready. At one o'clock, a piece of paper was thrown on the coals and it ignited immediately. Satisfied that everything was going to plan, Price ordered a break for lunch and for everyone to reconvene at 2.30 p.m.

Before attempting the walk, Bux's feet were examined by a doctor who took several swabs. These were sent to a pathology lab and later found to be normal. His feet were washed to ensure no preparation or chemical had been used to make him immune

Kuda Bux's first fire walk in Surrey, 1935. Harry Price Collection, Senate House Library.

from burns and then photographed. To Price they appeared soft and not calloused. Before stepping into the trench, Bux carefully brushed away the ash from the red embers so there was no insulating layer between the feet and the fire. Hitching his pants above his ankles he walked across the glowing fire-pit not once, but four times. Yet Bux was not happy. The fire had burned down too much, in places almost to the ground. 'I must have thick fire to walk on', he told Price. After the final walk his feet were examined and photographed and were not affected in any way. There was not even a suspicion of a blister.[28]

After the demonstration, Digby Moynagh, the editor of *St Bartholomew's Hospital Journal,* who had been watching Bux, offered to repeat the walk. The doctors present advised him not to, as did the Kashmiri. Price, however, agreed, admitting it was 'necessary in the interests of science that someone should do the identical walk at the same time as Kuda Bux, with the same fire and under identical conditions'. Removing his shoes and socks, Moynagh, after a moment's hesitation, stepped boldly into the fire, walked two paces and jumped out, crying in pain. Half an hour later, he developed severe blisters on the soles of his feet and had to be seen by a nurse. 'He was somewhat badly burned, and felt the effects of his fire-walking adventure for some time afterwards,' Price would later recall.[29]

A photograph of Bux's triumphant walk graced the front cover of the 18th September issue of *The Listener*. Inside was Price's description of the event together with more photographs of every stage of the demonstration, including Moynagh's botched attempt. No one could be in any doubt – Bux had walked on fire. There was no trickery involved, his feet had not been specially prepared. There were only three explanations, Price concluded: That it was done by 'faith'; that the callosity of the skin was responsible for the absence of burning or pain, though this did not apply to Bux; and that a knack in placing the feet had prevented the burns. Price was also prepared to consider a fourth possibility: there was something special in the way the fire had been arranged. After all, Bux had been unhappy about the preparations. Together with other members of the CPI, he fixed 17th September for the next test. This time there would be twice the amount of wood and Bux would be able to inspect the trench as it was being filled. London's leading physiologists, biologists and psychologists would be present. 'With Bux's aid, we hope to solve a mystery which has puzzled the world for hundreds of years,' Price confidently declared.[30]

Footage shot by a BBC film crew of the second test shows Bux loitering on the lawn, smoking cigarettes as the last-minute preparations for the fire walk are made. The only change he insists on is for a platform to be constructed dividing the trench in two. His feet are examined and the temperature of his soles is taken. At precisely 3.14 p.m., Bux makes the first walk, taking four strides to reach from one end of the trench to the other in a time of 4.5 seconds. The temperature of the soles of his feet is measured and found to be 93° Fahrenheit, a fraction cooler than before the walk. They are unscathed. At 3.17 p.m., Bux again walks across the first part of the pit, but refuses to cross the second, saying there is 'something wrong with it'. After the second walk, the temperature of the main body of the fire is found to be 1400° Centigrade (2552° Fahrenheit), or high enough to melt steel. The surface of the fire is a white hot 430° Centigrade

(806° Fahrenheit). Bux then prepares to walk a third time; but this time he suddenly changes his mind. Price would later reveal that the instruments and the tests had unnerved him. Placing a thermometer in the pit had 'desecrated it'. 'Something inside me has broken,' he told him. 'I have lost my faith, and if I do it again, I shall burn myself.'[31]

For Price the sudden breakdown after the second walk indicated that 'faith' (or confidence) did play some part in the performance. 'I think that may be the secret of the fire walk. After that faith had "broken" within him, nothing would induce him to do the walk. He was not in a fit mental condition.' Otherwise the experiment was a success. 'We proved that the immunity from burns is not due to the callosity of the skin, as Kuda Bux has soft skin, which is not callous. We exploded the theory that ash acts as an insulator between feet and fire, as the wind and our rakes removed it all. We have proved that it is a fallacy that "anyone can do it". There was no proof that the feet were prepared in any way, and we were successful in providing an even hotter fire than is usual in India.' Price hypothesized that in Bux's case there was 'some obscure relationship between physical and mental forces, and this helps to make him immune from injury. I think he also works himself up into a kind of semi hypnotic state. [But] that state is easily disturbed.'[32] Edmund Henderson Hunt, a doctor who studied the Rafa'i fakirs of Hyderabad, had seen ceremonial fire walking in southern India and witnessed Bux's demonstration, concurred. He told the *Times* that the test was carried out under unusually severe conditions that would have deterred most fire walkers. 'The trench is shallower than is customary and with the high wind increasing the surface combustion and blowing away all the ash, the heat is far more intense and is transmitted without any insulation.'[33]

For the next few weeks, stories on Bux's fire walk accompanied by photographs appeared in newspapers all over Britain and around the world. As a writer in the *Guardian* noted, no other demonstration of this kind in England had produced more discussion. Bux's fire walk had nothing to do with the condition of his feet or hypnosis, the writer declared. 'There is some force at work of which science knows nothing.'[34] An editorial in the *Observer* compared it to the invention of the wireless, calling it a genuine 'miracle' – 'something to wonder at from the standpoint of ordinary experience and reasoning'. To the modern mind, Bux's accomplishment was 'not as an interruption of the laws of Nature', but 'a revealing hint of her un-probed inwardness. ... It is not the suspension of feeling, but the absence of any injury to feel that is the intriguing feature of the ordeal. Unless some better explanation emerges, a state of mind would appear to have influenced the behaviour of matter through channels of which we have no knowledge.'[35] The *Nursing Times* said it was not a question of mystery or magic. 'The young Indian's faith must have been strong indeed to survive the battery of scientific apparatus and the coldly critical attitudes of the audience.'[36]

Like the Rope Trick, the news of Bux's fire walk also prompted people to come forward claiming to have witnessed similar demonstrations. E. A. C. Stowell wrote to the *Listener* explaining how his son had walked on fire in Bombay. The event had been arranged by a 'fakir' who himself did not walk, but sat to one side and 'concentrated' as others performed the feat. Aside from his son who walked across the fire pit in his socks without scorching them, 'numerous natives' and a Parsee and his two children took part. 'In the end the fakir's powers appeared to be exhausted, and he cried out (in his own language) "Enough, enough". And the last walkers in the trench had their feet burnt.'[37]

Dr Charles Darling of London's Institute of Physics offered a more scientific explanation. Writing in *Nature*, he said the feat was just a variation of the fireside experiment when a hot cinder is picked up and returned it to the fire without the fingers getting burnt if the action was performed quickly. The average time of contact of Bux's foot on the coals was half a second on each step. Using a special thermometer on an apparatus that mimicked this action, Darling found that the temperature of the soles of the feet on each contact with the coals would have risen only 15 to 20°C, or not enough to cause blisters. 'Fire walking is really a gymnastic feat, and the agile way in which Kuda Bux walked across the fire compelled admiration, and would be difficult to imitate without much training,' he concluded.[38]

Bux's rejoinder, published in the *Listener*, where little else was being discussed, dismissed his explanation as insufficient. Darling and other so-called experts had clearly never witnessed the 'many mysteries to which only the East holds the key'. In their ignorance of such matters, 'they blare out statements that must sound absurd to those with even a vague conception of "Occultism" as practiced in parts of India'. Bux ended by saying he would like to see Darling attempt the walk himself. In the meantime, he was thinking of opening a yoga school and if Darling felt like paying a visit he would show him things he could not even attempt to explain.[39] As for Price, his conclusion was broadly in line with Darling's, but with the caveat that for the feat to succeed the performer needed absolute confidence. 'If he hesitates or flounders, he will be burnt.'[40]

For Bux, the longer the debate lasted, the better it was for his career. Twelve days after the fire walk, he was pictured in the *Sunday Graphic and Sunday News* riding a bicycle down a congested London street blindfolded as a policeman directed traffic. 'Blinded by applications of dough, cotton wool and bandages, he rode steadily along, obeying traffic signals and behaving more confidently than many a normal, seeing traveller,' ran the caption.[41] A fortnight later he told BBC radio he was preparing to demonstrate being bitten by poisonous snakes, buried alive, plunging his bare arm into a pot of boiling oil and lifting an eighty-pound weight with his eyelids. After watching from the sidelines, these claims were finally too much for Elliot of the Occult Committee. No abnormal powers were involved in any of Bux's tricks he insisted. Live burial could be faked, the evaporation of moisture from the arm provides a blanket of steam that protected it from the greater heat of the boiling oil, though he admitted he 'would be very sorry' for anyone who swallowed real poison. As for Bux, he could appear before the Committee at any time.[42]

Bux was in too much demand to test such trivialities. From the late 1930s until the 1950s, 'The Man with the X-Ray Eyes' became one of the most remarkable magic acts in the world. 'Kuda Bux is probably the greatest newspaper copy in show business today. And one of the few acts not explained readily by magicians,' A. L. Baldwin, the secretary of the International Brotherhood of Magicians, declared in 1955.[43] Bux would be lauded as 'The Wonder of the Century'; 'One of the most famous "Makers of

Magic" who ever came out of the East'; and the 'Eighth Wonder of the World.' When war broke out in Europe, he moved to America performing the fire walk at a building site near Rockefeller Plaza. In 1949, he appeared on the first episode of Robert L. Ripley's *Believe It Or Not* television show. Roald Dahl transformed him into all-seeing gambler Imhrat Khan in *The Wonderful Story of Henry Sugar.* Asked by a journalist in 1942, what his next challenge would be, Bux answered: 'Christ was the first man in the world to walk on water. I, Kuda Bux, will be the second. [I] have been making experiments, and my preparations are almost complete. Soon I shall be ready.'[44] Tragically – and ironically – 'the man with the X-ray eyes' developed glaucoma and was legally blind when he died in 1981.

FIFTEEN

THE MAHARAJAH OF MAGIC

AT 9.15 p.m. on 9 April 1956, the BBC's switchboard suddenly lit up with calls from hundreds of viewers convinced they had just witnessed a gruesome murder live on their television screens. A mysterious-looking Oriental magician had put a seventeen-year-old girl in a trance, laid her on a table and sliced her body in half with a massive buzz saw as if she were a slab of meat on a butcher's table. To prove there was no trickery involved, a large metal cleaver was pushed between the two parts of her body. It was meant to be the climatic finale to that evening's top-rated *Panorama* programme, but something appeared to have gone terribly wrong. When the magician rubbed his assistant's hands and tried to revive her, she did not respond. As he shook his head and covered her face with a black cloth, presenter Richard Dimbleby stepped in front of the camera and announced the programme was over. As the credits came up, the phone lines at the Lime Grove studios went into meltdown.

Breaking into the Western magic scene had been a struggle for P. C. Sorcar. His recent Paris season had been poorly attended and panned by the critics – at best, the reviews were 'short, salty and

Early poster for Sorcar's X-Ray Eyes and Mysteries of India. Collection of Saileswar Mukherjee.

a little sarcastic', one writer noted[1]. He had fallen out with fellow conjurers for his insatiable ego and for having the nerve to call himself 'The World's Greatest Magician'. He was accused of stealing most of his tricks from other illusionists and his blatant attempts at self-promotion had earned him nicknames such as 'P. C. Boxcar' and the 'princely parader'. To rub salt into his wounds, *The Stage*, the leading entertainment newspaper in England, mistakenly referred to him as a 'Pakistani illusionist'.[2] To the West Bengali it was all a conspiracy, tinged with a good deal of racism. This was a battle of East versus West, a tussle over whose magic was superior and who was the best performer to represent India to the world. There was room for only one 'Maharajah of Magic' and no-one was going to stand in his way.

For now, however, the forty three-year-old was staring at failure. London's Duke of York theatre was reserved for a three-week season, but bookings were patchy. His two-and-a-half-hour stage show featured dozens of performers, multiple set changes and tonnes of props and equipment. It was complex and expensive. It was too big to fail. The opportunity to appear on

Panorama was a coup – one that he was determined to exploit. The official explanation for the show's abrupt termination was that Sorcar's set ran overtime and the producers had no choice but to end the broadcast. Anyone who had followed his career knew better. Even his detractors admitted he was a master of timing. To leave his assistant, Dipty Dey, severed by a screeching razor-sharp steel blade, was the ultimate sleight of hand. Even the statement assuring viewers the girl was safe, broadcast on the late-night news bulletin, was staged. The story made the front-pages the following day, with headlines screaming 'GIRL CUT IN HALF – SHOCK ON TV' and 'SAWING SORCAR ALARMS VIEWERS'. His season at the Duke of York sold out. The *Evening News* critic, who covered the opening night, said: 'This man is one of the best (if not the very best) magicians we have seen.' As magic historian Milbourne Christopher later wrote, 'No magic show in British history ever received such fantastic publicity.'[3]

Sorcar was born Protul Chandra Sarkar on 23 February 1913 in the village of Ashekpur in the Tangail district of Bengal (now Bangladesh). At school, he excelled in maths – some say he was a prodigy – but his real calling was magic. When he was a boy he saw a performance by the Bengali magician Ganapati Chakraborty and became his student. After graduating with an honours degree in Mathematics from Calcutta University in 1933, he changed his name to Sorcar – it sounded like 'sorcerer' – and started performing in private homes, clubs, carnivals, circuses, public halls and theatres. He also started referring to himself as 'India's Greatest Magician', much to the chagrin of the Anglo-Indian illusionist Eddie Joseph, who was using the title already and was thirteen years his senior. Still a complete unknown outside a few cities in Bengal, Sorcar decided to go one better by calling himself 'The World's Greatest Magician' or 'TW'sGM' for short. Not even Howard Thurston, Harry Houdini or the world's other leading mystifiers had the gall to make such a claim. His boast would nearly lead to his undoing, but for now it worked wonders, with the local press applying it uncritically. Invitations for him to perform started to pour in from across the country.

In 1936, Sorcar packed his props into two large suitcases and with a couple of assistants toured through Malaya, China and Japan, but his chances of making his name on the European and American circuits were cut short by the outbreak of the war. The few Western magicians touring India in the early 1940s were mostly Americans employed by the United Services Organization to entertain Allied troops in Assam and Bengal. Realizing the road to success depended on garnering maximum publicity for himself, he started contributing to magic journals, giving talks on All India Radio, scooping up obscure awards and joining local and international magicians' societies. He also made a point of contacting as many of the USO entertainers as he could. One of those was John Platt, who had heard so much about Sorcar that he compared meeting him in Calcutta with finding Mahatma Gandhi. Platt was impressed by how much the Bengali knew about American magic. Two days later he went to see him perform. 'Again, I was surprised to find that Sorcar presented a show that consisted of many modern American and European effects, such as the Doll House, Square Circle, Phantom Tube, Buzz-Saw Illusion and a masterful demonstration of X-Ray Eyes.'[4]

Sorcar on the cover of The Sphinx, *July 1946.*

Sorcar's persistence paid off when, in July 1946, his photograph was published on the cover of *The Sphinx,* the official organ of the Society of American Magicians. With his slightly pudgy boyish face, cheeky grin, pencil-thin moustache and twinkling eyes, he looked like a genial jinn. Inside was a glowing testimonial from Jack Gwynne, another of the USO magicians he had tracked down and befriended in Assam. Gwynne attended one of his shows and was mesmerized by the beautiful stage settings and props, the mix of familiar and original tricks and the 'well-trained and smartly costumed crew of assistants'. Sorcar also performed his signature tongue-cutting trick, inviting the American on stage together with a local doctor to witness the feat. 'As far as I am concerned he cut a slice right off the end of the victim's tongue and in front of the doctor and myself, and healed it again in the space of a few minutes,' Gwynne wrote.[5]

Meanwhile, the *Linking Ring*, the journal of conjuring's peak body, the International Brotherhood of Magicians, ran a Sorcar 'press release' describing his appearance at Jodhpur Fort. 'Hundreds of gun salutes shook the air' as an assemblage of Indian princes arrived in silver-rimmed Rolls Royces and wearing courtly uniforms 'dripping with fabulously wealthy jewels', for a magic show that had all 'the pomp and ceremony of a distinguished State function'.[6] The story stated that Sorcar was the only magician listed in India's *Who's Who* and all the latest Year Books. Indeed, he was 'the only Indian Magician talked about – and in most favourable terms too – for he has played a prominent part in bringing Magic into the high esteem it now enjoys in India'. Although India was known around the world as the Land of Magic, 'its professors were mostly the uneducated folk and the untouchables, born and brought up to their job, who gained their native skill by practice and training with native masters. As a result, the art was dying – un-esteemed even in its own land.' Only recently had 'polished and educated performers' started studying magic seriously'. There were no prizes for guessing who was leading that renaissance. 'Among those who are reviving the old glory of Indian magic, Mr. P. C. Sorcar stands foremost.'[7]

IN May 1950, Sorcar made his maiden visit to the United States. Waiting at Chicago airport to meet him were Platt and Gwynne. The occasion was the combined convention of the International Brotherhood of Magicians and the Society of American Magicians, a mega event that brought together more than a thousand mystifiers under the one roof. Sorcar strolled into the Sherman Hotel's convention hall looking as if he had stepped out of the pages of the *Arabian Nights*. He wore his now trademark trickster's outfit: plumed turban with a diamond encrusted *sarpanch*, a heavily embroidered sherwani-style jacket, close fitting trousers and golden slippers with turned up toes.

Heads turned and press photographers made a beeline for the exotic Oriental who was telling anyone who cared to listen that he was a seventh-generation magician and had learned the art of conjuring while still an infant. Having hyped up the press and his fellow prestidigitators, he walked on the stage and presented his debut act, Eyeless Sight, where he read whatever was written on a blackboard with his eyes tightly bandaged. The world's greatest magicians were unimpressed. It was so poorly executed that the act's leading exponent, George Jason, left it out of his routine in deference to the Indian. There was worse to come. Midway through a performance by local magician, Matt Schulien, Sorcar shouted out that he had seen him palming a card. He then made a similar charge of cheating during a show by the highly respected close-up artist Slydini. Jaws dropped, recalled *Genii* editor Samuel Patrick Smith. 'This was not the way things were done in America. The waters parted, and on one side were Sorcar's sympathetic supporters; on the other were an equal number of disgruntled detractors.'[8]

Unfortunately for Sorcar, his detractors included Gene Gordon, co-founder of the I. B. M., who used his influential 'Without the Shuffle' column in *Genii* to cut the brash Bengali down to size.

> We don't blame you for wanting publicity by sending contributions to our journals of magic, but you should let your contributions prove how great you are and not spend so much space telling about yourself. It is all right to tell the public that they have a chance to see a great magic show, but you don't use the same technique on your brother magicians. You were around

> Blackstone a lot at the convention, Sorcar, and he has one of the finest magic shows the world has ever seen. Did you hear him telling people how great he or his show is, or do you read where he claims that in the magic magazines? He performs and lets the other fellow do his boosting. Can you blame us for wondering what kind of a guy you are when you went home and claimed that your act was selected as the best of 1032 magicians from all parts of the world? All you did was an eyeless vision act, and any magician over here who would perform it with the blackboard down near the floor would be ridiculed. ... Just take a tip and let us do your boasting for you and you'll be a popular guy over here. We like you, anyway, but we'll like you a great deal more if you just be your own sweet self and quit trying to impress us.[9]

With the publication of Gordon's missive, the gloves were off. The next to point his wand at Sorcar was the Englishman Robert Harbin. 'With good publicity, judicious use of aeroplanes to get you there first, good front-of-the-house showmanship, you have been a financial success,' he wrote in an open letter to Sorcar published in the weekly *Abracadabra*. His advice: Now that the Eastern public was convinced that you are The World's Greatest Magician, leave it at that. '*Please* do not try to convince your brother magicians as well; they will be justifiably angry and dismiss you as a conceited little magician.' Harbin also took issue with Indians imitating Western tricks. He had spent a year in India and had seen magicians doing some first-class illusions, but Western-style magicians did not impress him because 'they were using a medium unsuitable for their particular style'. Behind the beautiful stage settings, Sorcar was a disappointment, Harbin concluded. 'Trick for trick you cannot compare yourself with the Masters: Lafayette, Goldin, Dante, Thurston, Blackstone, Carter, Chefalo, etc.,' he wrote, citing the names of the twentieth century's leading exponents of the magical arts.[10]

Not one to let such accusations remain unanswered, Sorcar wrote to *Abracadabra* in what would be the opening round of a series of exchanges. Whereas his Buzz-Saw Illusion was so realistic it made people faint, Harbin's set-up was so clunky he could have concealed an elephant inside it, Sorcar sneered. Since the best magic in the world was from India and he was the best Indian magician, he was within his rights to call himself the world's greatest. He ended his letter by thanking Harbin for complimenting him on being such a good businessman. 'I have performed on the very stage where most of the other masters you listed appeared, and my box-office record shows that I had the highest sale in the last fifty years, exceeding other magicians' sales by several tens of thousands.'[11] Harbin responded by accusing Sorcar of 'consummate conceit'. His advice: 'Make your title Sorcar the Great and let the rest of the world decide.'[12] Sorcar's riposte was a series of full page ads. The first featured a quote from the magazine's editor, Charles Goodliffe, saying: 'Sorcar is just about the most astute showman since Houdini,' together with head-shots of himself and of the American escapologist. The second showed him photographed with Blackstone and the Dutchman Okito Bamberg with the caption: 'Each of them is the greatest Magician of the continent they come from. Is it a mere coincidence or historical repetition?' A third contained quotes from prominent magicians, including one taken out of context that seemed like Harbin was praising Sorcar. Another boasted that more than thirty people had fainted watching his show in Singapore. The statistic was repeated in a further ad together with the (unsubstantiated) claim that he had twice won the 'Nobel Prize of Magic', awarded by *The Sphinx*. Almost a dozen ads were published over a six-month period emblazoned with similar platitudes.

Westerners weren't the only ones smarting at TW'sGM. His claims to greatness were not shared by all members of India's necromantic fraternity. In 1947, Eddie Joseph, then Vice President of the Society of Indian Magicians, started publishing a journal called *Magical Digest*. One of its early issues carried an article highly critical of Sorcar titled 'Pricking the Bubble', by the magazine's publisher, Fram D. Nasikvala. Sorcar's reputation as a magician was entirely of his own making and developed through his writings, Nasikvala claimed. He also accused the Bengali of adapting the tricks of other magicians and claiming them as his own.[13] Sorcar hit back writing a letter to *Genii* accusing Joseph of using his journal for the sole purpose of smearing his name. Calling him an amateur, he charged his rival with being driven by jealousy. 'Naturally I am winning everywhere. This has motivated his envy evermore.'[14] As for Joseph, he couldn't understand what the fuss was all about. 'He has always been at me although I have not met him for the past six years. … He has always extolled my work and … wants to buy all my books and tricks. This will prove that there is something wrong with the guy.'[15]

The bickering reflected a simmering East-West divide in Indian magic, with conjurers clustered around Bombay seeing themselves as being more cosmopolitan in their outlook than their contemporaries in Calcutta. A further crack appeared when

Sorcar set up his own Ring, or chapter, of the I. B. M. in 1949, and named it after himself in competition with the existing Calcutta Ring. His opponents claimed it was stacked with his supporters and 'designed, developed and operated purely as a publicity stunt'.[16] Sorcar wasn't having a bar of it. 'India,' he said during a speech to his Ring, 'is the proverbial home of magic and occultism. Modern Western fakirs, with their improved scientific knowledge and advanced mechanics, have made vast strides. India must follow the trend of modern magic. This I.B.M. Ring in Calcutta will be the Suez or Panama Canal between the magic of the two hemispheres.'[17]

In reality, India's magicians stood no chance against the Sorcar juggernaut. By the early 1950s he was President of the Indian Magicians Club and the Indian Magic Expansion Board. His publicity strategy was so effective it would later become a casebook study of how magicians should market themselves. He employed a team of assistants, mostly relatives, who typed individual letters on his brightly printed stationery to magic magazines, societies, magicians and newspapers in India and around the world. News clippings of him cycling blindfolded through the streets of Paris, meeting Lord and Lady Mountbatten, being handcuffed to a railway line in China as a train bore down, were stuffed into folders along with his lavishly printed programmes and posters. 'Sorcar is the most consistent publiciteer in my files, with his theatre throwaways, magazine articles, printed publicity and souvenir programmes, and press releases – all of which arrive in the news or in the mail with amazing regularity.' wrote Jack Lamonte in *The Magic Wand*, 'Sorcar's printed matter is always first class and as an illusionist with a big show he must have impressive memos, brochures, posters and programmes with a lavish lay-out to match. Accordingly, I must admit that the letterhead used by Sorcar is one of the most attractive I have seen, a multi-coloured lithographed design and picture which is indeed worthy of the bill matter "World's Greatest Magician".' The Indian had set a new bar for self-promotion. Lamonte urged aspiring magicians to take a leaf out of his book. The mantra was: be consistent, avoid anything cheap, carelessly written or poorly printed.[18]

Writing in the *Linking Ring*, John Booth remarked that he had 'never seen any performing magician's business set up on so methodical and elaborate a plan'. His Ballygunge headquarters in Calcutta consisted of two stucco buildings facing each other across a narrow court. He lived in one with his wife and five children. The other housed his office and a workshop, as well as a large storage area where dozens of large crates containing illusions, sets and other equipment could be loaded straight onto to railroad wagons waiting on the track that ran behind the building. 'There is an almost Teutonic zeal for system, dozens of filing boxes, scrapbooks, and cabinets, all classified. He even has a printed book listing the contents, in detail, of some seventy crates, not only to help his assistants but to facilitate the passage of his equipment through customs when he crosses national borders.'[19]

Sorcar's elaborate filing system kept tabs on magicians and writers around the world. Reviewers who dared to be critical of TW'sGM were excised from his mailing list. 'Time was when my postman used to collapse on the front porch, loaded down with the latest Sorcar publicity send-outs. Then I made a few ridiculous remarks regarding his full-page ads in the *Linking Ring*, claiming to be the "World's Greatest Magician",' quipped George

Johnstone in *The New Tops*. 'My ego was bruised as I was under the assumption that I was the "World's Greatest". I stated that his claim was as ridiculous as Sophia Loren complaining that Twiggy had stretched her sweater . . . That did it!!' Mailing his material to magicians around the world must cost a fortune, Johnstone mused. 'I think twice before mailing out plain black and white photo cards . . . So, due to financial reasons I am relinquishing the throne to The Great Sorcar. But to salve my impoverished pride, I am now changing my billing . . . "The Not-So Great Johnstone, the Man Who Taught Sorcar".'[20]

Taking the approach that any publicity was good publicity, Sorcar wrote an extraordinary letter to *Genii* in June 1955, attacking the 'false and malicious lies' of his detractors, and calling on Americans to stand up for him in the same way they stood up for 'justice, truth and democracy'.[21] It also compared his box office earnings with those of other magicians in the same venues in Bangkok, Singapore and Bombay. His receipts were anything from two-to-eight times that of other shows. Making such claims was risky. Competing on the Asian circuit was one thing. Succeeding in Europe and America, as he was about to find out, was going to be a whole lot harder.

On 15 November 1955, Sorcar opened at the Théâtre de l'Étoile in Paris. It was his first foray on the Western stage since his unspectacular appearance in Chicago five years earlier. This time he had an entirely new show called *In-dra-jal*, which was translated as *The Magic of India*. Two years in the making, it redefined what Western audiences expected from an Indian magician. With more personnel, more variety, and more equipment than anyone else touring at the time, Sorcar was clearly out to prove his critics wrong. While unashamedly plugging every Eastern cliché, it presented what was essentially a programme of Western numbers. It was a slick production, with immaculately painted backdrops, an orchestra, numerous costume changes, sophisticated lighting and a well-oiled production team that ensured the show's frenetic pace never flagged. Dressed in a devil's costume, Sorcar walked on to a stage cluttered with tables, props, assistants and odd pieces of scenery. Over the next two-and-a-half hours, flowers turned into darts, alarm clocks into beer bottles, a pitcher poured endless quantities of water, chickens, pigeons and fish appeared as if out of thin air. After the interval came the Shanghai Mystery, the vivisection of two clowns dressed as Laurel and Hardy, Crushing a Lady and the Temple of Benares, followed by a series of Egyptian tricks. The most elaborate number was named Confusion at the Airdrome, where Sorcar tried to find his missing assistant using a series of false cabinets made to look like telephone booths and pieces of luggage. It featured Indians dressed as customs officers, a fake airplane and a man in an ape suit. The show's second half also included his blindfold act and the always dramatic Buzz-Saw Illusion. Previewing the show, the critic Frank Joglar warned that success would depend on whether the staging was good enough for public to be fooled into thinking they were seeing new illusions.[22] Initial reviews were disappointing. 'The show's melange of what seems Western magic, plus some exotic "fakirism", gave it a familiar air,' wrote *Variety*. 'There are enough offbeat aspects to make this interesting, for magic shows always have appeal, but presentation is somewhat unregulated and the cumulative effect is not outstanding. More pacing and selection might make this magical batch, which is now a hash, into a more vibrant affair.'[23] Instead of modifying his act, Sorcar's publicity machine began bombarding the local press with photographs, stories and cartoons. By the end of December, the campaign was beginning to pay off. A review in the *International Herald Tribune* called his show 'attractive and fascinating … beautifully costumed and filled with the exotic dazzle and din of the East'.[24] As audience numbers increased, the show's run was extended by several weeks.

The turning point in Sorcar's career was undoubtedly his sensational appearance on the *Panorama* programme. Although television was still in its infancy, he was astute enough to exploit its potential. No other magician had used the medium so successfully. Once dismissed as an exotic upstart, he was now being taken seriously, no matter how much his actual talents as a magician appeared to be wanting. Writing in *Tops*, American conjurer Tommy Windsor remarked:

> Sorcar is doing more to help keep magic alive, and keep it in the public eye, than anyone I know of. So let's have no more talk about Sorcar being not so hot, etc. Anyone who can get that kind of publicity in big papers all around the world wherever he plays … and get rave reviews about his show like the ones I read, deserves your support. … I don't see anyone in THIS COUNTRY that's getting that kind of publicity … nor playing big theatres and doing big business with a show that big.[25]

Sorcar soared above other magicians for his flamboyance, his stage effects and his chutzpah. He had taken Indian magic where it had never gone before, presenting Western-style tricks in elaborate Oriental settings with a flair that left his rivals looking flat-footed.

At a time when much of the world still equated Indian magic with the Rope Trick, he left the act out of his shows. While acts such as Water of India, the Shanghai Mystery and the Temple of Benares gave his programme an Oriental veneer, his routines were Eastern in name only. Aside from the tongue-cutting trick, the only things that were Indian were the costumes, stage settings and music. Theatres would be false-fronted to look like the Taj Mahal, hired circus elephants raised their painted trunks to welcome audiences as they arrived. Inside an Indian orchestra struck up an eerie sounding tune, as dancers attired in exotic outfits flitted around the stage ahead of Sorcar's theatrical entrance. Stripped of their Eastern trappings, most of his presentations looked suspiciously like they were borrowed from existing programmes. Even his triumphant Buzz Saw was a variation of Sawing a Lady in Half, first presented in public by the British Magician P. T. Selbit in 1921. In the highly competitive world of big-star magic, Sorcar's tactics were dangerous. For all the glamour and publicity, he was still a small fish in a very big pond – and guilty of two very serious sins. One was his indomitable ego. The other was being an Indian encroaching on what had always been a predominantly white Anglo-Saxon domain. Ramo Samee got away with it because he never presented himself as anything other than an Indian juggler. Linga Singh stuck to mainly Oriental tricks, while Kuda Bux's fire-walking and X-ray feats were novelties at the time. Sorcar's defence was that 'typical Indian magic' was unsuitable for the Western stage. His magic must be 'Western magic dressed up with Indian costumes, scenery and music'.[26]

Kalanag (Helmut Ewald Schreiber), Hitler's favourite magician. Collection of Saileswar Mukherjee.

PLUMP, balding and bespectacled, Kalanag, whose real name was Helmut Ewald Schreiber, was Adolph Hitler's favourite magician. He performed for Luftwaffe troops in Lapland and Blitzkrieg divisions in France. When the American Third Army captured Munich in the closing days of the war, he played for General Patten and somehow convinced a Hamburg court he had never been a member of the Nazi Party. He borrowed his stage name from the black snake *kala nag*, in Rudyard Kipling's *Jungle Book* tales. With his wife Gloria de Vos, hailed as the most beautiful woman in magic, he took his *Sim Sala Bim* show around the Continent and to England, where it was enthusiastically received despite the German's connection with the country that nearly bombed most of its neighbours out of existence. Like Sorcar, his success was due in no small part to his judicious use of publicity material and promotional stunts. In what would be dubbed 'The Battle of the Titans' by editors of magic journals who watched the spat unfold with a certain amount of glee, Kalanag accused the Bengali of systematically stealing his effects and deliberately sitting through show after show to learn how they were done. Launching his own Blitzkrieg, the German circulated an eight-page, mimeo-graphed document to editors, calling his rival a 'conceited self-admiring Oriental', who ignored the roughest preliminary conditions of a theatre performance.[27] To back up his claims, Kalanag included French press reviews of Sorcar's Paris shows and used words and photographs to detail how nine out Sorcar's nineteen tricks had been stolen from him. The reviews were damning. Instead of his highly touted 'Wonders of India', Sorcar was accused of using tricks bought off the shelf in magic stores. *France Soir* compared him to 'an automaton' and called him a 'Stakanovist of magic', referring to the Soviet labour hero. The list of tricks allegedly stolen from the German included Water of India, where water from a *lota* is poured out in an endless stream, the Kalanag Vanishing Auto, the Four Ace Trick and the Surgeon's Operation for Sawing – the infamous Buzz-Saw Illusion that became Sorcar's signature trick. 'This is no tempest in a teapot,' a columnist in *New Phoenix* wrote. 'Kalanag has one of the biggest shows on earth today, and is a man of determination. As long as Sorcar stayed in India, he was all right, but now he is moving into Kalanag territory, and if as stated, he has half the tricks of the Kalanag show (whether done well or not), it will still hurt.'[28]

The German's demand that Sorcar be banned from performing in Europe, however, was a step too far. The wounds of the war had not healed entirely. Writing in the February 1956 issue of *Hugard's Magic Monthly*, Arthur LeRoy reminded 'Herr Helmut' that he had appropriated an Oriental nom de plume and tried to hide his nationality by pretending to be 'Charles Edouard' from Switzerland. Furthermore, he had lifted the name of his show from the routine of Danish magician, Harry Jansen, better known as Dante. LeRoy then forensically tore apart Kalanag's attack, identifying where he had borrowed or stolen each of the tricks in question. His version of the Buzz Saw Trick, for example, was done by the magician Richardi in 1932, and was still being performed by his son. As LeRoy pointed out there was no such thing as originality in magic circles any more. Every 'new' trick had its precursors. Thanking the German for his monograph and photographs, he wrote: 'I'm convinced of only one thing: the photos prove that Sorcar has an exotic, sensuous appeal and seems to be theatre worthy. I think a good manager could sell him here in the U.S. if only on an exotic pitch.'[29]

Sorcar followed his British season with a sell-out tour of New Zealand and Australia, and then travelled to America, timing his arrival to appear on NBC's *Festival of Magic* show. Screened nationally on 27 May 1957, the ninety-minute programme had an estimated audience of 33 million viewers. The brainchild of the magician and historian Milbourne Christopher, it featured conjurers from around the world. Sorcar presented his Buzz-Saw Illusion, claiming it cost $15,000 for his fifteen-minute slot. This time he restored his young female assistant in deference to Christopher, who told him that American audiences liked 'happy endings'. 'For suspense, Sorcar took all the honours,' the *Chicago Daily Tribune* gloated. 'With the murderous looking buzz saw in full view of the audience, he cut a woman in half. No boxes, no draperies, just a woman and a saw. It was a masterpiece of illusion, magic, or what have you. This looked like the real thing.'[30] The praise however was far from unanimous. Writing in the *Linking Ring*, Don Tanner panned Sorcar for doing a 'strictly mechanical act presented in a strictly mechanical way.'[31] The NBC programme was his second television appearance in less than a week. On 22nd May, he drove a bicycle through New York's Times Square at noon while blindfolded, his plumed turban rising majestically out of the thick blindfold covering his face. Coverage of the stunt was broadcast that night.

Christopher would become one of Sorcar's closest friends, his most vocal champion and the first to dub him the 'Maharajah of Magic'.

> [T]he world at large knew Indian Magic as something a traveler had seen in a sultry, crowded street. In all of the fabled land of mystery there was not one illusionist with credit of an established international full evening show. Sorcar dreamed of the spectacles of Thurston and Dante and strove to establish magic as a cherished part of India's cultural life. Prodigious study, experimentation and an unrelenting drive to succeed brought him to the fore. Woven in the rich tapestry his current productions are not only baffling illusions, but authentic Indian art, costume and ritual as well.[32]

More hagiography came from Booth, who credited the Bengali with arriving like a beacon of light when Indian magic had plunged into its darkest night. 'The brilliant heritage was there,' he wrote, 'but the art [of magic] had sunk into dormancy, associated with mediocrity and parochialism. One might say that India, one of the world's largest nations and oldest civilizations, was waiting quietly and hopefully for a long overdue giant to appear who could release the springs of creativity and bring the conjuring art back into full flower.'[33] Sorcar was that giant, Booth continued.

He cast aside conventional costumes and arrangements. Instead of a tuxedo he 'donned the rich robes of an Indian prince. The legends and arts of his own country provided settings and themes for the best magic that the world could offer.'[34] Booth compared Sorcar with the Frenchman Jean-Eugene Robert-Houdin, widely acknowledged as the founder of the modern magic tradition and the greatest prestidigitator of the mid-nineteenth century. Like Robert-Houdin, Sorcar marked a clean break with the past and lifted the art of conjuring from its traditional trappings, raising its status to that of other art forms.[35]

In 1964, India's president accorded Sorcar the ultimate accolade, the Padma Shri, the country's highest honour. In some quarters his greatness was being equated with that of Mahatma Gandhi. Such comparisons silenced all but a few brave critics. In any case he was rarely in the one place long enough for would-be detractors to arm themselves. His world tours were taking him from Moscow to Melbourne, Tehran to Tanganyika. Reports of the monthly meetings of the Sorcar Circle of the I. B. M., faithfully recorded in the society's mouthpiece, the *Linking Ring*, read like Soviet-era propaganda. His name was always prefixed with the word 'Great', his shows were always sold out, his box office receipts a record, the reviewers effusive in their praise, as if he were the only Indian magician capable of such wonders. He wasn't.

Born Danpat Rai Gogia in the Multan district of what is now Pakistan in 1910, Gogia Pasha fooled the world and his fellow mages by pretending to be an Egyptian for most of his career. A qualified doctor, he gave up the medical profession after watching a performance by the British magician and inventor Owen Clark in Blackpool, England in the late 1920s. After the show, Pasha went up to Clark and suggested how to improve some of his tricks. The Englishman made him his apprentice and when he died in 1929, left him his equipment. Pasha grew a goatee, giving him a slightly wicked look, donned a turban and a set of shimmering robes that hovered over his rotund frame, and was nicknamed the Gilly Gilly man, after the Egyptian slang for magic. His shows combined comedy, comment and humorous patter with tricks, and incorporated dancers between sets. His signature acts included Cups and Balls, producing live chickens from his mouth and a levitation feat where his assistant was placed upon the points of three swords, two of which were removed, leaving only one under her neck to support her. He toured extensively throughout Europe, Asia and Australia. While in Germany he presented a coin act called The Man with the Hundred Million Dollars to Hitler, who reportedly enjoyed it so much he jokingly asked him to become the Reich's treasurer.[36] He also worked in film, appearing in features such as the Tamil action thriller *Minnalkodi* (*Bolt of Lightning*, 1937), starring Rukmini who played a dacoit. After the war – and probably in response to Sorcar – he began calling himself the 'World Renowned Egyptian Master of Magic'. In 1953, he was elected president of the Indian Magicians' Club and three years later was the headline act at the 1956 I. B. M. Convention in Miami, Florida. His programme was an amalgam of Western and Oriental tricks and included X-Ray Eyes, Tongue Cutting, Noah's Ark, Flying Ranee, Cigarettes and Cards, the Cabinet of Dr. Albini, King Pharaoh's Dream, Wonders of the Pyramids, the Haunted Hotel and the Basket of Death.[37] According to a report on the Convention, his Miser's Dream, done in 'Gilly Gilly style', 'produced a multitude of silver balls and a string of flags of almost all nations from his mouth'. He also severed strings that suspended swinging balls using a bow and arrow.[38] Besides making magic, Pasha was known for his culinary skills, cooking 'delicious meals in Persian and Indian style utilizing rare curries and spices' to anyone who visited him at his home in Dehradun.[39] Unlike Sorcar he let his magic do the talking, a trait not lost on Gene Gordon who called him 'a Hindu with a sense of humour and the ability to mix with the gang and be a regular fellow instead of a princely parader. Gogia was a real showman and sold his stuff well.'[40]

In the galaxy of Indian magic, Pasha and Sorcar occupied different orbits, rarely crossing paths. Perhaps not to draw attention to the fact that the Punjabi was the pioneer of some of his stage effects, TW'sGM rarely referred to his rival, who he erroneously believed was Kashmiri, even though in the late fifties he was getting consistently better reviews. The same was not the case for many Bengalis, who found themselves smothered by the smooth-talking magical Maharajah. The magician K. Lal told the American author Lee Siegel that Sorcar had allegedly bribed a member of his crew with 10,000 rupees to sabotage his sawing a lady-in-half routine. When Lal realized what had happened, the saw's motor was already running. Determined that the show must go on, but terrified that it might be too late to save both his assistant and members of the audience from being mortally wounded by a runaway saw, he inserted one of his fingers into the hole where the nut had been removed, leaving it bloodied and cut to the bone. Another of Lal's stories described Sorcar booking a hall in Bangalore to stage a rival show just as his was about to open. Lal also listed a number of innovations his better-resourced rival had allegedly stolen, including using music in a magic show, dressing his troupe in a variety of costumes and employing electric lights. He also claimed to have been the first Indian magician to pose as a Maharajah.[41] Over in Bombay, the cosmopolitan city's conjuring community was largely unaffected by the Sorcar effect. Eddie Joseph, nicknamed the 'Bombay Baffler', nurtured a vibrant circle that counted Hindus, Muslims, Parsis and Anglo-Indians as its members. The leading figures included Hamid Sayani, Jehangir (Jean) Bhownagari, Homi Mehta and Rutton Bharucha, who performed as Chung Ling Soo. The city also benefited from being the first port of call for magicians coming to India from England, Europe and America.

There is no doubt that Sorcar inspired a generation of Indians to take up the art of magic, though many cloned his manners and techniques. Devkumar, 'The Greatest Wizard of the East,' dressed in Sorcar-style clothes and called his show 'Miracles of India'. Praised in the press as the 'Greatest Talent in the World of Magic', his two-and-a-half-hour show featured thirty items including Materialising a Duck, The Man with the Extra Eyes, Skull Takes Hot Tea and How Netaji Disappeared from India (billed as his own magical interpretation) – a reference to the mystery surrounding the fate of the Indian National Army leader, Subhash Chandra Bose. Others who tried to emulate brand Sorcar included The Great Hasmook, the 'World's Master Magician', whose Magiana show featured routines such as Smokers Dream and Going by Boeing. Then there was L. K. Roy, another 'World's Master Magician'; Kiran Kumar, the 'World's Marvellous Magician'; the Great Hakasa, who boasted on being 'the only

Bose, the magician, modelled his Indrajal show on Sorcar's. Collection of Saileswar Mukherjee.

magician who has toured maximum number of times with full show and a big team in foreign countries'; and Bose, who also called his show *Indrajal.*

◈

ON 23 December 1970, ignoring the advice of his doctor who warned him he was not well enough to travel, Sorcar flew to Japan for the sixth time. The fifty-seven-year-old reportedly told his doctor, 'I must go. If I die, I must die while performing.'[42] Even by the frenetic schedule of previous tours, this one tipped the scales. Thirty tonnes of equipment had been shipped by sea for the four-month programme of sixty performances. The weather was extremely cold. Sorcar was exhausted and suffering from a heart condition. On 6 January 1971, he performed *Ind-ra-jal* in the city of Shibetsu on the island of Hokkaido. As he left the stage he suffered a massive and fatal heart attack. Sorcar's body was taken to a Buddhist monastery and placed on an altar decorated with flowers, as mourners and monks joined in prayers for his departed soul. The Japanese government offered to give him a funeral 'benefiting a great magician of the Orient', but in accordance with Sorcar's written instructions, his body was returned to India and taken to the family home for an overnight vigil. The next day thousands of people lined the streets that ran from the house to the cremation ground – an outpouring of grief that would not be repeated until the death of Mother Teresa a quarter of a century later.

Sorcar's passing prompted copious eulogies from his peers. Frances Marshall wrote that the world had lost one of 'magic's stoutest and most ardent supporters':

> Sorcar was 'great' the way that Buffalo Bill was great, the way that Barnum was, the way that Orson Welles is. All these men had the same thing – absolute faith in themselves and their own convictions. They ignored criticism; they expended no time trying to convince people they knew what they were doing. They first went ahead and did it, and the bigger and more bizarre the idea, the more they pushed ahead. Sorcar believed he was a great magician and he spent his life acting and living like one.[43]

As the respected magic historian David Price noted, Sorcar had arrived on the magic scene just as India needed a great native-born master to take on the big names in the West. Thanks to him,

'Indian magic had come of age, magically speaking, and would have to be reckoned with by magicians around the globe'.[44]

Sorcar's legacy is complex one. As a showman, he excelled in his craft and was a master of self-promotion – something that rankled Western magicians, who tended to look down on their Indian counterparts as amateurs, while conveniently forgetting their own sins. As Sid Lorraine pointed out in 1951, 'even if his ego is one of the biggest in the business, magicians should be the last ones to point a finger of derision at him for this feature'.[45] Ego was everything in the highly competitive world of big stage magic – and there was nothing shy about Sorcar. By elevating himself to such heights, however, he all but ensured that other innovators such as Ramo Samee, Linga Singh, Ganapati Chakraborty and Gogia Pasha, would be largely overlooked in the country of their birth. Despite being a prodigious writer, publishing letters, articles and descriptions of magic tricks in magazines and journals around the world, he added only slightly to our knowledge of the history Indian jadoo and its exponents. For Sorcar, India was always the 'Home of Magic' and owed its eminence to wonders worked by its ancient occultists. On the difference between Eastern and Western traditions, he wrote that the magic of the East was psychological, 'based on Yogic principles of faith controlling the will-power and abstraction', whereas the West's 'was purely based on medicinal and mechanical devices'. He saw himself as an inventor of a new style of magic that bridged this gap. He called it 'Anglo-Indian Magic', an amalgam of Indian street, European and American stage techniques. As more and more 'educated' Indians explored these ancient roots and adopted them to the modern day, the Golden Age of Indian Magic was imminent.[46]

Sorcar was also a product of his time. He exploited new mediums such as radio and television, carefully nurtured influential contacts in the Western magical fraternity and learned quickly what battles were not worth fighting. There was greatness there – in larger doses than any Indian magician had ever achieved when measured by the number of countries he visited, shows performed, publicity generated and news articles produced. He was an innovator rather than an inventor, taking existing ideas and routines and transforming them into dazzling Oriental extravaganzas. He challenged how the world saw Indian magic and proved that a man born in a small Bengali village could compete with the international giants of the craft. His most enduring legacy is the pride that most Indians feel when they remember him. More than anything, more than all the controversy over who really was the world's greatest, Sorcar loved being a magician and giving his audiences what he believed they wanted and deserved.

EPILOGUE

EARLY in Sandip Ray's 1983 film *Phatik Chand*, twelve-year-old Bablu finds himself at the Ochterlony Monument at the northern end of Calcutta's Maidan. Bablu, played by Rajib Ganguly, is the son of a wealthy businessman who has been kidnapped by four goons. Their getaway car crashes, killing two of them. Bablu is thrown out of the car and knocked unconscious. When he wakes up, he has lost his memory. He walks to a railway station where he is helped by a man who introduces himself as 'Harun Al Rashid. The Caliph of Baghdad. King of Jugglers.' Harun, played by Kamu Mukherjee, finds Bablu, who now calls himself Phatik, a job as a waiter in a chai shop, and the impoverished entertainer and the pampered son of an upper caste family, form a strong bond. One day he takes Bablu to watch him perform. Every Sunday, the green space around the minaret-like monument, turns into an open-air fair ground. When Harun and Bablu arrive, green parrots are picking out cards and handing them to fortune tellers, *qalandars* wrestle bears, quack doctors dispense dried roots and animal bones, and performing monkeys dance in fancy dress. A man balances upside-down, his head buried in the dirt. A child performs acrobatics on the end of a twenty-foot high pole. Harun finds a vacant corner of the park and goes through his paces, keeping a top spinning on the end of a stick that is balanced on his chin, then juggling four brass balls and repeating the feat using fire sticks. Bablu is so mesmerized he forgets that he is there to collect money from the crowd. He doesn't have to. So impressed are the onlookers that Harun is showered with coins.

Almost every Bengali I spoke to over a certain age, recalled seeing jadoowallahs performing beneath the Ochterlony Monument and in suburban parks. Classical musician and collector, Somit Das Gupta, remembers how in the 1960s *madaris*, as they were referred to, would wait outside his school and do impromptu shows. So great was the demand for elaborate props from showmen such as P. C. Sorcar and K. Lal, it created a cottage industry of what Das Gupta calls 'stage gadget makers'. 'There were coffin makers, mostly eighth- or ninth-generation Portuguese Goans, who had their workshops in Lal Bazaar, and were particularly good at making wooden props for circuses and magic shows,' he says. 'Even panel beaters kept their car workshops going on Sundays to fulfil orders for magic contraptions.' Das Gupta, whose collection of sarods, sitars, sursingars and veenas fills every available space in his Calcutta flat, blames the decline of the magic arts and classical music on the breakdown of the patronage system. Zamindars and petty rajahs once employed personal musicians, court painters and conjurers. When the Communist government introduced land reform in 1955, they lost their main source of income and could no longer maintain these artists. Even stilt walkers who were employed to patrol the fields at night, using their height advantage to spot cattle thieves, found themselves out of a job. Those that could, moved to big cities such as Calcutta.

While researching this book, I looked in vain for the street magicians and strolling players that were a common sight when I first visited the city in the late 1970s. Outside the Indian Museum, an enterprising young boy had loosened part of the pavement and buried his head in the dirt. Slack rope artists performed stunts in the laneway next to my Sudder Street hotel, snake charmers stopped office workers in their tracks in busy Dalhousie Square, and in Alipurduar, in the far north of West Bengal, I saw the Basket Trick. Today the ancestors of the Bengali jugglers who enthralled Jahangir, rarely venture into this over-crowded metropolis.

Traces of Bengal's magical heritage can still be found for those prepared to look. Satyajit Ray, the doyen of Bengali cinema, was also a prolific writer whose output included thirty-five short stories featuring the master sleuth, Feluda. Magic appears in several of these detective mysteries, including *Indrajal Rahasya* (*The Magical Mystery*) and *Nayan Rahasya* (*The Eye Mystery*). Ray wrote *Phatik Chand* in 1983 and it was adapted to cinema by his son, Sandip. According to his biographer, Andrew Robinson, Ray's passion for magic started after seeing a Bengali conjurer perform at a wedding in his uncle's house. The conjurer gave a pack of cards to a person in the audience and borrowed a stick from another. Pointing at the pack with the stick, the magician called out 'Ace of Spades!' The card slipped out of the pack, flew to the end of the stick and remained there. Ray encountered the magician a few days later near his house and asked him to teach him some tricks, which he did. 'Manik [Ray] never set eyes on the man again; so thrilled had he been to meet him, he forgot to take his address.'[1]

Cinema and conjuring have been closely connected in India. The country's first feature film, the 1913 epic *Raja Harishchandra* by Dadasaheb Phalke, featured a palace that granted its owner every wish. Like the pioneer of cinema, the Frenchman Georges Méliès, Phalke was a trained magician. While studying art in Baroda, he met an itinerant German illusionist and became his assistant before presenting his own shows as 'Professor Kelpha'. Phalke went on to produce and direct more than a hundred films, most of them mythological dramas, using special effects to bring the maya of the gods to the screen. Magic and fantasy dominated the Indian cinema until the 1930s with films like *Bulbul-e-Paristan* (*Nightingale in Fairyland*) and *Aladdin aur Jadui Fanas* (*Aladdin and His Magical Lamp*). On 31 December 1932, the *Bombay Chronicle* reported that police were lathi charging crowds demanding tickets to see the film *Maya Machhindra* (*The Illusion of Machhindra*) at the Krishna cinema. The 'first Indian perfect

Poster for the Homi Wadia movie Aladdin and His Wonderful Lamp. *Priya Paul Collection.*

talkie' was a 'stupendous mystery', the paper's reviewer gushed. 'Miraculous happenings are enlivened by the sprinklings of comedian hits. Songs and acting leave no room for suggestion.'[2] The first Western box office hit in India, Douglas Fairbanks' *Thief of Baghdad*, featured the Rope Trick and a magic carpet suspended by six piano wires that flew over a fantasy city of domes and minarets. In 1952, Homi Wadia staged a major hit with his version of the Aladdin story, *Aladdin aur Jadui Chirag* in which a jinn flies through the air carrying the hero's palace. In trying to find a cure for blandness, today's Bollywood directors seem more interested in finding exotic foreign locations, than in looking for inspiration in India's rich magical heritage.

At the book bazaar on College Street next to Calcutta University, I was lucky enough to pick up an old edition of one of P. C. Sorcar's books on conjuring tricks in Bengali. Today, P. C. Sorcar Jr is keeping his legacy alive. His father's chief stage assistant, he stayed on to complete the season in Japan, rather than attend his father's funeral. I met him in his TW'sGM's former office opposite the family home in Ballygunge. He had just come back from a tour of Assam with his daughter Maneka, one of India's leading female magicians. A giant painting of Sorcar Sr, garlanded with fresh marigolds every day, dominates the room. The pair has inherited his Teutonic zeal for organization. Shelves are crammed with neatly arranged magic books and journals. Display cases groan with prizes and memorabilia. Brand Sorcar is still going strong, but at a reduced pace. Sorcar Jr who titles himself 'The Living Legend of Indian Magic' has kept the core of his father's *In-dra-jal* show intact, although he is also known for acts such as vanishing the ten-bogey Amritsar Express after it arrived at Howrah Station in July 1992. Assam was a box office success, but he was disappointed at not finding evidence to support its claim to being 'the land of magic'. 'We went there in search of magic, in search of those people if ever they exist, but I couldn't find anybody alive,' the soft-spoken Sorcar Jr said. 'Even where there are still pockets of traditional magicians, they won't open up,' added Maneka. 'If they have to work in a factory or as a taxi driver, they feel a sense of shame that they are no longer in their profession.'

The same air of despondency greeted me when in 2016 I visited Shadipur Depot, a West Delhi slum set up in the late 1960s that takes its name from an adjacent bus garage. It was often referred to as Kathputli colony, or the Puppeteers' Colony, because it contained the largest concentration of street performers in India. Immortalized as the 'Magician's Ghetto' in Salman Rushdie's *Midnight's Children,* Shadipur always had a precarious existence. In its early years it was demolished and rebuilt a number of times. In 1976, the thumbprints and signatures of the colony's 'puppeteers, singers, balladeers, jhula-wallahs, animal trainers, jugglers, acrobats, magicians, toymakers, wood-carvers, peep-show-wallahs and street entertainers' appeared on a petition pleading for recognition and help. 'We remain scattered and forgotten, wandering from place to place and living wherever we can pitch a ragged tent and place three stones to mark our hearth,' it stated.[3] A year later, a flamboyant young designer and the founder of Delhi's first discotheque, Rajeev Sethi, stepped in and helped the signatories form a cooperative known as the Society of Neglected and Forgotten Artists. Thanks to Sethi and his co-workers, the colony's jadoowallahs, katputliwallahs and other artists found themselves as kurta- and sari-clad cultural ambassadors performing at festivals of India in Washington, New York and London. A roster was set up to ensure no family or community was singled out for favouritism when opportunities arose at home or abroad. Shadipur would be home to some of India's most famous street magicians including Ishamuddin, who did a version of the Rope Trick in 1995 that made front-page news all over India.

You knew you had arrived at Shadipur by the mounds of uncollected rotting refuse piled up on both side of the entrance to the colony. And also by the sounds – an almost constant refrain of drumming that occasionally burst into a crazed crescendo. Once inside the slum, things were much cleaner except for suspicious looking black sludge that trickled down the middle of the unpaved laneways. What little running water there was, came from a few communal taps. Sanitation was almost non-existent. My guide and interpreter, Mohammad Ayaz from Sethi's Asian Heritage Foundation, seemed to know almost everyone. I was taken meet Iqbal, son of the late Chand Pasha, legendary hypnotist and conjurer from Andhra Pradesh. Pasha, who died in 2015, was famous for playing tunes on an ordinary trumpet just by placing it against his neck. Between engagements, he was employed by the government to spread the message of family planning, producing half a dozen babies out of an empty box after putting a male and a female doll inside, but none when a condom went in with the dolls.[4] These days Iqbal increases HIV awareness by demonstrating a trick that uses two ropes, one red and one white. Knots magically disappear or move from one rope to another, before the ropes themselves change colour. There's no better way to hold a crowd's attention and his patter about the dangers of unprotected sex does the rest. For his next trick, he took a folded piece of cardboard and transformed it into dozens of different shapes – a policeman's hat, an umbrella, a video camera, a lotus flower and so on.

Later, I met Rehman Shah who had just returned from doing a show outside a nearby metro station. He knows the local cops who normally turn a blind eye to his breach of the Bombay Prevention of Beggary Act (1959) in exchange for a hundred-rupee bribe. The Beggary Act (which was extended to New Delhi in 1960) continues to bedevil anyone who dares to mount a puppet show or an acrobatic display on the capital's streets. Determined to rid the city of the 'social menace' of begging

Cartoon highlighting the plight of show people in New Delhi, Sudhir Dar. Asian Heritage Foundation Library.

ahead of the 2000 Commonwealth Games, the government formed teams to round up beggars and deployed mobile courts to prosecute them. The act's very loose definition of beggar and vagrant reflects its colonial antecedents and includes members of nomadic communities such as magicians, singers, dancers, acrobats and fortune tellers as well as people who earn their living by selling medicinal herbs, tools baskets, mats, brooms and so on.[5] Qalandars and their performing bears largely disappeared off the streets in the early 1990s after Maneka Gandhi, the environment minister in the Congress government, introduced a ban on keeping the animals in captivity. Many turned to puppeteering instead. Snake charming, prohibited under the Wildlife (Protection) Act 1972, has also gone into decline. In November 2004, hundreds of snake charmers threatened to release their serpents in the Orissa State Assembly because their traditional means of livelihood was under threat.

On some days, Shah is lucky to earn what he has to give out in bribes, leaving him with nothing to buy food for his family. It's a massive fall from grace. His ancestors started performing magic in the days of the Mughals and once were feted by the royal courts of Rajasthan. After serving syrupy milk tea and salty biscuits, he ran through a few routines including the Egg Bag trick and the always stomach-churning spectacle of spitting out a series of large brass balls from his mouth. Although it is getting harder to work as a street magician, he is grooming his sixteen-year-old son, Junaid, to follow his profession. It takes about fourteen years to learn the jadowallah's craft. But these days, being streetwise is just as important as being a good performer. 'He has to be old enough to face the police, some criminals are there, the *sharabi* (drunk people) and some other communities. He has to have enough experience to manage those things,' Shah explains.

Shadipur Depot's existence was always unstable. In 2009, the Delhi Development Authority announced a public-private partnership with the Raheja group to redevelop the site. The artists' colony was to be replaced by the capital's highest residential tower and a shopping mall. Those who opted to relocate would be assigned new accommodation in high-rise flats on the periphery of the development, an outcome that critics said would destroy the slum's cohesion and spell the end of its artistic traditions. Rajeev Sethi wanted the site retained as a model colony for street artists complete with an auditorium and museum. As the legality of demolishing the slum and evicting its tenants languished before the courts, some residents moved to alternative accommodation at two sites, one of them 30km away. On 30 October 2017, those remaining were startled by the sound of bulldozers and the sight of hundreds of lathi-wielding police ordering them to vacate their dwellings. By the day's end, half the slum had been demolished. 'We are artists. We perform and entertain people and they kicked us out of our own house. Is this democracy? This is absolute injustice,' complained dhol and harmonium player Pappu Bhatt.[6]

Despite the odds steadily shortening on the survival of other communities of street performers, Sethi is surprisingly optimistic about the future of their craft. 'In the past such communities proved to be wonderfully adaptable,' he says, citing the example of the thirteenth-century Sufi saint, Bu Ali Shah Qalandar of Panipat, who created the qalandars to go out and spread his teachings. 'They had to learn how to tell his story, to sing it and to keep the narrative alive for audiences over many days and nights.

The only difference is that in those days it was interpersonal, today it is all done in the mass media.'

Looking back over more than forty years of work with India's street performers, folk artists and crafts people, Sethi warns against underestimating the basic human need to be wonderstruck, to be entertained and to search for originality – the very formula that creates and sustains magic in its broadest sense. 'I don't think this is going to be the end of it,' he says after disagreeing with my suggestion that we're both rather old-fashioned when it comes to regretting the erosion of traditional art forms. 'They won't disappear. There will be a reaction. It will come in a different way. That need to sit across and to engage with one another ... is finding new ways of expression. I'm still an optimist. The will to survive is what is at the heart of the creative urge.'

ACKNOWLEDGEMENTS

The genesis of this book was a chance remark at a dinner party in Sydney about an Australian magician who took to the stage mimicking a Chinese conjurer in the early 1900s. It turned out the trickster in question was in fact the American William Robinson, who adopted the name Chung Ling Soo and would go down in history for being the unfortunate victim of a bullet-catching trick that went tragically wrong. Intrigued by what motivated magicians to partake in such cultural cross-dressing (let alone risky behaviour), I soon discovered that oxymoronic 'Hindu fakirs' from as far afield as Buffalo in New York state and Plymouth in England once vied to outdo each other in over-the-top, orientalized magic shows, complete with jewel-encrusted turbans and curly toed shoes. The popularity of this genre peaked just as the first Indian mystifiers trained in Western magic made tentative appearances before audiences in England, America and continental Europe fitted out in top hats and tailored dinner jackets. I found this juxtaposition intriguing and realized that there had been very little scholarship on how

India's wonder-workers had influenced what was arguably the leading genre of popular culture at the time.

I am immensely grateful to Associate Professor Kama Maclean of the University of New South Wales, who helped coalesce a set of disparate thoughts into a coherent proposal for a PhD thesis. This work takes a much broader and more anecdotal look at the story of Indian magic than the transnational history focus of my doctorate. The book's completion would not have been possible without the support of the Faculty of Arts and Social Sciences at UNSW and an Australian Government Research Training Program Scholarship. I would also like to acknowledge the helpful inputs of my co-supervisor Emeritus Professor Stephen Muecke. Thanks are also due to Amitabh Mattoo, Vinod Mirchandani, Roomana Hukil and the staff at the Australia India Institute in New Delhi where I enjoyed a stimulating one-month fellowship that focused on links between Australian and Indian magicians during the colonial period.

With funding from the Australia India Council at the Department of Foreign Affairs and Trade in Canberra and Tata Literature Live in Bombay, I presented a troupe of Australian magicians to Indian audiences in November 2016, thereby reviving a century-and-a-half-old legacy of conjuring exchanges and allowing me to pick up much useful material on the contemporary magic scene. Adam Mada, Lucas Itrawan and Ash Hodgkinson let their amazing tricks do all the talking and Jo Dyer was an excellent producer. Anil Dharker and the Tata Literature Live team earned our enduring praise. Thank you Quasar Thakore Padamsee, Toral Shah and Vivek Rao. One of the highlights was a show in honour of the late magician Hamid Sayani at the Royal

Bombay Yacht Club on what would have been his 90th birthday. For that unforgettable experience (and for introducing me to the delights of Parsi Dairy Kulfi) I will be forever indebted to Ayesha and Aadore Sayani and Janine Bharucha. I am grateful to Cressida Lewis and Aliya Elariss at the Australian Consulate in Bombay and to Hema Rance, Aman Kaur, Shekhar Nambiar and Sandra O'Malley at the Australian High Commission in New Delhi for organizing that tour. Mhelly Bhumgara and Raj Kumar, convenors of the Society of Indian Magicians in Bombay and New Delhi respectively, organized the interactions with local magicians that made it so worthwhile. Particular thanks must go to the magicians of Kathputli Colony (Shadipur Depot, since demolished to make way for a shopping mall), especially Junaid and Rehman Shah, Mohamed Iqbal and Chand Pasha. Thanks also to members of Raj Kumar's troupe from Ghaziabad who are named in the introduction to the book.

For all the pressures of putting together a manuscript like this with its overly ambitious brief and seemingly impossible deadlines, I must admit it was a delight to work on. I had touched on the subject of Indian magic and the occult in my previous book, *The Mysterious Mr Jacob: Diamond Merchant, Magician and Spy*, but had little idea of the richness of the subject matter. For their patience and support, I would like to thank three of the most talented publishers I have ever worked with, Teesta Guha Sarkar and Sushmita Chatterjee of Pan Macmillan India and Michael Dwyer of Hurst in the UK. I must include in this list Diya Kar Hazra who originally commissioned the work for Pan Macmillan. Lee Siegel, whose *Net of Magic* was an inspiration, was exceedingly generous in his comments on, and praise for, an early draft of this manuscript. William Dalrymple was an enthusiastic, morale-boosting supporter of the project and alerted me to some valuable material.

Staff at the following archives were instrumental in helping me weave together the threads of this narrative. In India: the Alkazi Collection of Photography, the Library of the Asian Heritage Foundation, the Nehru Memorial Museum and Library, the National Archives of India, the Maharashtra State Archives in Bombay and the National Library of India. In the UK: the Asian and African Studies Collections at the British Library, Senate House Library at London University, the South Asian Studies Library at the University of Cambridge and the Magic Circle Library. In the US, the Conjuring Arts Research Center, the New York Public Library, the Rare Books and Manuscripts section at the Library of Congress, and the Valentine Museum, Richmond, Virginia. Finally, in Australia I'd like to thank the staff at the State Libraries of New South Wales and Victoria as well as the National Library.

It is impossible to list individually each act of generosity, encouragement, hospitality and advice I received in writing this book, but that does not lessen the appreciation I feel. In alphabetical order my thanks go to Juhee Ahmed, Rahaab Allana, Mark Allon, Sagnik Atarthi, Sunil Badami, Rana Bandyopadhyay, Shreya Banerjee, Jonathon Barlow, Pablo Bartholomew, Bindu Batra, Kaushik Bhaduri, Sidharth Bhatia, Maina Bhagat, Kaizad, Zenia and Mhelly Bhumgara, Raaja Bhasin, Kent Blackmore, Arun Bonerjee, Akshay Chavan, Gerson and Uma da Cunha, Toni Chapman, Jennifer Chowdhury, Ronnie Chhibber, Savitri Chowdhury, Sam Dalal, Nigel Dutt, Jo Dyer, Indira and Renuka

Dhanrajgir, Anil Dharker, Rosalyn D'Mello, Betsy Emmanuel, Naresh Fernandez, Karl Fischer, Sarah Gandee, Anirban Ghosh, Samir Kumar Ghosh, Preeti Gill, Benjamin Gilmour, Kevin Greenbank, Somit Das Gupta, Zafar Hai, Mala Hashmi, Sanjoy Hazarika, Mohamed Iqbal, Sharon Irani, Anita Jacob, Madhu Jain, Priya Kapoor, Kelly Kerney, Pramod Kumar KG, Peter Lane, Jim Masselos, Art and Ruth Max, Mini Menon, Chris Mikul, Sarbajit Mitra, David Nabo, Aman Nath, Chand Pasha, Priya Paul, Aman and Christine Rai, Hema Rance, Rani Ray, Saileswar Mukherjee, Vijay Sai, Santimoy, Deepthi Sasidharan, Rajeev Sethi, Sunil Sethi, Ishan Shivakumar, Luke Slattery, Maneka Sorcar and P. C. Sorcar Jr, Susan Stronge, Lakshmi Subramanian, Rishi Suri, Emma Tarlo, Geoff Tibbs, Safina and Patricia Uberoi, Hari Vasudevan, Deni Vidal, Sunayana Wadhawan, Anne and Belinda Wright and the Magic Circle's Terry Wright. Finally, and most importantly, I would like to thank my wife, Niki, and children, Adele, Alexander, Jonathon and Nicolas, for their patience, perseverance and praise when it was most needed.

NOTES

Introduction: 'So Wonderfully Strange'

1. *Memoirs of the Emperor Jahangueir*, trans. by David Price (London: John Murray, 1829), p. 6.
2. Ibid., p. 14.
3. Ibid., p. 121.
4. Ibid., p. 96.
5. Ibid., p. 96.
6. Ibid., pp. 96–97.
7. Ibid., p. 97.
8. Ibid., pp. 98–102.
9. Ibid., pp. 99–103.
10. Ibid., p. 104.
11. Ibid., p. 99.
12. Ibid., p. 102.
13. Milbourne Christopher, *Panorama of Magic* (New York: Dover Press, 1962), p. 52.
14. See Lee Siegel, *Net of Magic: Wonders and Deceptions in India* (New Delhi: Harper Collins, 2000); Peter Lamont, *The Rise of the Indian Rope Trick: The Biography of a Legend* (London: Little, Brown, 2004); and Chris Goto-Jones *Conjuring Asia: Magic, Orientalism and the Making of the Modern World* (Cambridge: Cambridge University Press, 2016). John Keel's *Jadoo* (London: W. H. Allen, 1958), is a marvelously entertaining romp in search of the

Rope Trick. Other scholarship on Indian magic includes Sarah Dadswell, 'Jugglers, Fakirs, and Jaduwallahs: Indian Magicians and the British Stage', *New Theatre Quarterly*, vol. 23, no 1, 2007, pp. 3–24; and Crispin Bates and Peter Lamont, 'Conjuring Images of India in Nineteenth-Century Britain', *Social History*, vol. 32, no. 3, 2007, pp. 308–324. The only biography of an Indian magician is Samir Kumar Ghosh's *Jadusamrat Ganapati o Bangalir Jaducharcha* (Kolkata: Saptarshi Prakashan, 2016), on the early twentieth century Bengali magician and strongman Ganapati Chakraborty. The writings of P. C. Sorcar will be considered in a later chapter.

15. John Nevil Maskelyne and David Devant, *Our Magic: The Art and Theory of Magic* (New York: E. P. Dutton & Co., 1911), p. 34.
16. Francesca Coppa, Lawrence Hass, and James Peck, *Performing Magic on the Western Stage: From the Eighteenth Century to the Present* (New York: Palgrave Macmillan, 2008), p.8. Most works on the theory of magic look at it in relation to religion, ritual and belief. However, there are some excellent appraisals of stage magic including Coppa, et.al., just cited; Michael Mangan, *Performing Dark Arts: A Cultural History of Conjuring* (Bristol: Intellect, 2007); Todd Landman, 'Framing Performance Magic: The Role of Contract, Discourse and Effect', *Journal of Performance Magic*, vol. 1, no. 1, 2013, pp. 47–68; Graham Jones, *Trade of the Tricks, Inside the Magician's Craft* (Berkeley, University of California Press, 2011); and Sophie Lachapelle, 'From the Stage to the Laboratory: Magicians, Psychologists, and the Science of Illusion', *Journal of the History of the Behavioral Sciences*, vol. 44, no. 4, 2008, pp. 319–334.
17. Edmund Leach, *Social Anthropology* (Oxford: Oxford University Press, 1982), p. 133.
18. Ibid, p. 235.
19. Jan van Baal, *Symbols for Communication: An Introduction to the Anthropological Study of Religion* (Assen: Van Gorcum, 1971), p. 55.
20. Michael Muhammad Knight, *Magic in Islam* (New York: Tarcher Perigee, 2016), p. 16.
21. Simon During takes a similar approach with regard to what he calls Western 'secular magic' using the concept of 'the magic assemblage'. For During, a magic assemblage encompasses 'the motley of shows in the public spaces where magic was performed: theatres, farms, streets, taverns, and so on'. In addition to conjuring, it includes a vast range of amusements

such as magic lantern shows, early film, juggling, ventriloquism, animal shows, fortune telling and even joy rides. See Simon During, *Modern Enchantments: The Cultural Power of Secular Magic* (Cambridge: Harvard University Press, 2002), pp. 66ff.

22. Joseph C. Berland, *No Five Fingers are Alike: Cognitive Amplifiers in Social Context* (Cambridge: Harvard University Press, 1982), p. 103.
23. 'Are Indian Jugglers Humbugs? The Opinion of an Expert. An Interview with Mr Charles Bertram', *The Strand Magazine*, vol. 18, December 1899, p. 657.

Chapter 1: Of Levitating Brahmins and Prophesizing Apes

1. *Herodotus*, trans. by William Beloe, vol. 2 (London: H. Colburn & R. Bentley, 1830), p. 86.
2. Ibid., pp. 88–89.
3. Rudolf Wittkower, 'Marvels of the East. A Study in the History of Monsters', *Journal of the Warburg and Courtauld Institutes*, vol. 5 (1942), pp. 160–61.
4. John Watson McCrindle, *Ancient India as described by Ktesias the Knidian* (Calcutta: Thacker & Spink, 1882), pp. 8–9.
5. Ibid., pp. 15–16.
6. Matthew Dickie, *Magic and Magicians in the Greco-Roman World* (London: Routledge, 2001), pp. 111–12.
7. *The Invasion of India by Alexander the Great as Described by Arrian, Q. Curtius, Diodoros, Plutarch and Justin*, trans. by John Watson M'Crindle (London: A. Constable & Co., 1896), p. 387.
8. Maria Dzielska, *Apollonius of Tyana in Legend and History* (Rome: L'Erma, 1986), p. 76.
9. Vincent A. Smith, 'The Indian Travels of Apollonius of Tyana', *Zeitschrift der Deutschen Morgenländischen Gesellschaft*, vol. 68, no. 2 (1914), p. 340.
10. Osmond de Beauvoir Priaulx, *The Indian Travels of Apollonius of Tyana, and the Indian Embassies to Rome* (London: Quaritch, 1873), p. 31.
11. Philostratus, *The Life of Apollonius of Tyana*, trans. by E. C. Conybeare (Harvard: Harvard University Press, 1960), pp. 190–91

12. Ibid., p. 257.
13. Ibid., p. 255
14. Ibid., pp. 257–59.
15. Priaulx (1873), p. 52.
16. Ibid., p. 44.
17. Osmond de Beauvoir Priaulx, 'The Indian Travels of Apollonius of Tyana', *The Journal of the Royal Asiatic Society of Great Britain and Ireland*, vol. 17, 1860, p.105.
18. Cited in Peter J. Ucko and Timothy Champion (eds), *The Wisdom of Egypt: Changing Visions Through the Ages* (London: Cavendish, 2003), pp. 92–93.
19. Dickie, *Magic and Magicians*, pp. 300–02.
20. E. H. Warmington, *The Commerce between the Roman Empire and India* (Cambridge: Cambridge University Press, 1928), p. 154.
21. Dickie, pp. 308–09
22. *The Satires of Juvenal,* trans. by James Sinclair (Edinburgh: James Sawers, 1815), p. 70.
23. D. P. Chattopadhaya, *India and China: Twenty Centuries of Civilization, Interaction and Vibrations* (New Delhi: Motilal Banarsidass, 2005), pp. 284–5.
24. Ibid., 288–291.
25. Tansen Sen, *Buddhism, Diplomacy, and Trade: The Realignment of Sino-Indian Relations, 600–1400* (Honolulu: University of Hawaii Press, 2003), p. 100.
26. Ibid., pp. 46–7.
27. Sally Hovey Wriggins, *The Silk Road Journey with Xuanzang* (Boulder: Westview Press, 2004), p. 94.
28. M. Aurel Stein, *On Alexander's Track to the Indus* (Cambridge: Cambridge University Press, 2015), p. 15.
29. Charles Orzech, Henrik Sørensen and Richard Payne (eds), *Esoteric Buddhism and the Tantras in East Asia,* Leiden: Brill, 2011, p. 297.
30. Abu Zayd al-Sirafi, *Two Arabic Travel Books: Accounts of China and India, and Mission to the Volga* (New York: New York University Press, 2014), p. 117.
31. Ibid., p. 57.
32. *The Book of the Marvels of India,* trans. by L. Marcel Devik (London: George Routledge & Sons, 1928), p. 89

33. Ibid., p. 143.
34. Ibid., p. 90.
35. John Elverskog, *Buddhism and Islam on the Silk Road,* (Philadelphia: University of Pennsylvania Press, 2010), p. 68.
36. Henry Yule (ed.), *The Book of Ser Marco Polo, the Venetian: Concerning the Kingdoms and Marvels of the East,* vol. 1 (London: John Murray, 1874), p. 292.
37. Ibid., p. 292.
38. Ibid., p 171.
39. Ibid., p. 83.
40. Ibid., p. 307.
41. Cited in A. D. Khan, *A History of the Sadarat in Medieval India: Pre-Mughal Period* (New Delhi: Idarah-i Adabiyat-i Delli, 1988), p. 223.
42. Ibn Battuta, *The Travels of Ibn Battuta: In the Near East, Asia and Africa, 1325–1354,* trans. by Rev. Samuel Lee (New York: Dover, 2004), p. 162.
43. Cited in Carl W. Ernst, *Refractions of Islam in India: Situating Sufism and Yoga* (New Delhi: Sage, 2016), p. 358.
44. Ying-Yai Sheng-Lan, *The Overall Survey of the Ocean's Shores (1433),* trans. by Feng Ch`eng-Chun (Cambridge: Hakluyt Society, 1970), pp. 164–65.
45. Cited in Jorge Flores, 'Distant Wonders: The Strange and the Marvelous between Mughal India and Habsburg Iberia in the Early Seventeenth Century', *Comparative Studies in Society and History,* vol. 49, no. 3, 2007, p. 560.
46. Niccolao Manucci, *Storia do Mogor,* trans. by William Irvine, vol. 2 (London: John Murray, 1907), pp. 134–35.
47. Manucci, *Storia do Mogor,* vol. 3, p. 201.
48. Francois Bernier, *Travels in the Mogul Empire, A.D. 1656–1668,* trans. by Archibald Constable (Oxford: Humphrey Midford, 1916), p. 321.
49. 'A True Relation without all Exception, of Strange and Admirable Accidents, which Lately Happened in the Kingdome of the Great Magor, or, Magull, who is the Greatest Monarch of the Indies', *The Harleian Miscellany,* vol. 3 (London: Robert Dutton, 1809), p. 423.
50. Ibid., pp. 423–24.
51. Richard Folz, *Mughal India and Central Asia* (Oxford: Oxford University Press, 1998), p. 108.

52. Ibid., p. 120.
53. 'A True Relation', p. 424.
54. Edward Terry, *A Voyage to East-India* (London: J. Wilkie, 1877), pp. 385–86.

Chapter 2: Casting Indra's Net

1. Teun Goudriaan, *Maya Divine and Human* (Delhi: Motilal Banarsidass, 1978), p. 213.
2. Heinrich Zimmer, *Philosophies of India* (Princeton: Princeton University Press, 1951), p. 76.
3. Kenneth G. Zysk, *Asceticism and Healing in Ancient India: Medicine in the Buddhist Monastery* (Delhi: Motilal Banarsidass, 1998), p. 13.
4. Mircea Eliade, *A History of Religious Ideas, Vol. 1, From the Stone Age to the Eleusinian Mysteries* (Chicago: University of Chicago Press, 1978), p. 236.
5. Dominik Wujastyk, 'An Alchemical Ghost: The Rasaratnakara by Nâgârjuna', *Ambix*, vol. 31, no. 2, 1984, p. 74.
6. Laurie L. Patton, *Bringing the Gods to Mind: Mantra and Ritual in Early Indian Sacrifice* (Berkeley: University of California Press, 2005), p. 19
7. Arthur Berriedale Keith, *The Religion and Philosophy of the Veda and Upanishads*, part 1 (Delhi: Motilal Banarsidass, 1998), p. 311.
8. D. A. Pai, *Monograph on the Religious Sects in India among the Hindus* (Bombay: The Times Press, 1928), p. 2.
9. Moriz Winternitz, *A History of Indian Literature*, vol. 1 (Delhi: Motilal Banarsidass, 1996), p. 110.
10. N. J. Shende, *Religion and Philosophy of the Atharvaveda* (Poona: Aryabhushan Press, 1952), p. 118.
11. Edward Hopkins, *Religions of India* (Boston: Ginn & Co., 1895), p. 153.
12. Margaret Stutley, *Ancient Indian Magic and Folklore* (Delhi: Motilal Banarsidass, 1980), p. 27.
13. Shende, *Religion and Philosophy of the Atharvaveda*, p. 71.
14. Rajaram Narayan Saletore, *Indian Witchcraft* (New Delhi: Abhinav, 1981), p. 2.
15. Zimmer, *Philosophies of India*, p. 19, n. 11.

16. William Wilkins, *Modern Hinduism: An Account of the Religion and Life of the Hindus in Northern India* (Calcutta: Thacker, Spink & Co., 1900), p. 411.
17. Goudriaan, *Maya Divine and Human*, p. 211.
18. W. N. Brown, 'Vyaghramari, or the Lady Tiger-Killer: A Study of the Motif of Bluff in Hindu Fiction', *The American Journal of Philology*, vol. 62 (1921), pp. 126–27.
19. Zimmer, p. 123.
20. Wendy Doniger, *The Hindus: An Alternative History* (Oxford: Oxford University Press, 2009), p. 516.
21. Cited in Jeaneane D. Fowler, *Perspectives of Reality: An Introduction to the Philosophy of Hinduism* (Sussex: Sussex Academic Press, 2002), p. 250.
22. Abraham Eraly, *The First Spring: The Golden Age of India* (New Delhi: Viking, 2011), p. 546.
23. Ibid., p. 111.
24. *Select Specimens of the Theatre of the Hindus*, vol. 2, trans. by Horace Hayman Wilson (London: Turner & Co., 1871), pp. 307–08.
25. Virginia Saunders, 'Magic in the Sanskrit Drama', *Journal of the American Oriental Society*, vol. 45, (1925), pp. 112–13.
26. *The Ocean of Story: Being C. H. Tawney's translation of Somadeva's Katha Sarit Sagara*, vol. 1 (London: Chas. J. Sawyer, 1924), p. xxxi.
27. Ibid., p. xxxi.
28. Ibid., p. 22.
29. Ibid., pp. 22–23
30. Ibid., pp. 204–05.
31. Susanne Mrozic, 'Materializations of Virtue: Buddhist Discourses on Bodies', in Ellen T. Armour and Susan M. St. Ville (eds), *Bodily Citations: Religion and Judith Butler* (New York: Columbia University Press, 2006), p. 31.
32. See John S. Strong's discussion in *Miracles, Mango Trees, and Ladders from Heaven: Reflections on the Tale of Prince Kāla at Śrāvastī and the Buddha's Descent from Trayastrimsa*, Paper presented at the ISEAS/EFEO 2009 Kyoto Lectures Series, pp. 4–6.
33. Ibid., p. 7.
34. *The Ocean of Story*, p. 153.
35. Arthur Llewellyn Basham, *History and Doctrines of the Ajivikas, a Vanished Indian Religion* (Delhi: Motilal Banarsidass, 1951), p. 61.

36. Ibid., p. 6.
37. Piotr Balcerowicz, *Early Asceticism in India: Ajivikism and Jainism* (New York: Routledge, 2016), p. 55.
38. Cited in Ibid., p. 63.
39. Ibid., p. 66.
40. Jagdish Chandra Jain, *Life in Ancient India: As Depicted in the Jain Canon and Commentaries, 6th Century BC to 17th Century AD* (New Delhi: Munshiram Manoharlal, 1984), pp. 262–63.
41. Ibid., pp. 267–70.
42. R. C. C. Fynes, *Lives of Jain Elders*, canto 12, verses 311–224.
43. John E. Cort, 'A Fifteenth Century Digamber Jain Mystic', in Peter Flügel (ed), *Studies in Jaina History and Culture: Disputes and Dialogues* (London: Routledge, 2006), p. 274.
44. Phyllis Granoff, 'Scholars and Wonder-Workers: Some Remarks on the Role of the Supernatural in Philosophical Contests in Vedanta Hagiographies', *Journal of the American Oriental Society*, vol. 105, No. 3, 1985, p. 460.
45. Ibid., p. 465.
46. Lal Mani Joshi, *Studies in the Buddhistic Culture of India During the 7th and 8th Centuries A.D.* (Delhi: Motilal Banarsidass, 1987), p. 236.
47. Monier Monier-Williams, *Hinduism* (New York: Pott, Young & Co., 1878), p. 129.
48. Cited in Joshi, *Studies in the Buddhistic Culture of India*, p. 120.
49. Cited in Ibid., p. 296.
50. Patton Burchett, *Bhakti Religion and Tantric Magic in Mughal India*, PhD dissertation, Columbia University (2012), p. 132.
51. Ronald Davidson, *Indian Esoteric Buddhism* (New Delhi: Motilal Banarsidass, 2004), p. 234.
52. Mircea Eliade, *Yoga: Immortality and Freedom* (Princeton: Princeton University Press, 2009), p. 88n.
53. Praphulla Chandra Ray, *History of Hindu Chemistry*, vol. 1 (Oxford: Williams and Norgate, 1902), p. ii.
54. David Gordon White, *The Alchemical Body: Siddha Traditions in Medieval India* (Chicago: University of Chicago Press, 1996), p. 53.
55. Ibid. pp. 54–55.
56. *Alberuni's India*, trans. by Edward C. Sachau, vol. 1 (London: Trubner, 1888), p. 193.

57. Ibid., pp. 191–92.
58. Ibid., p. 189.
59. Cited in White, *Alchemical Bodies*, p. 67.
60. Ibid., p. 68.
61. Wujastyk, 'An Alchemical Ghost', p. 71.
62. Ibid., pp. 73–74.

Chapter 3: The Lovers of Jinns

1. Hans H. Wellisch, *The First Arab Bibliography: Fihrist al-'Ulum* (Chicago, University of Illinois, Occasional Paper, no. 175, 1986), p. 8.
2. *Fihrist of al-Nadim: A Tenth-Century Survey of Muslim Culture*, trans. by Bayard Dodge, vol. 1 (New York: Columbia University Press, 1970), pp. 1–2.
3. *Fihrist of al-Nadim*, vol. 2, p. 723
4. Ibid., p. 725.
5. Ibid., p. 726.
6. Ibid., p. 733.
7. Ibid., p. 732.
8. John Elverskog, *Buddhism and Islam on the Silk Road* (Philadelphia: University of Pennsylvania Press, 2010), pp. 60–61.
9. *Fihrist*, vol. 2, pp. 826–27.
10. Carl W. Ernst, 'Being Careful with the Goddess: Yoginis in Persian and Arabic Texts', in Pallabi Chakrabarty and Scott Kugle (eds), *Performing Ecstasy: The Poetics and Politics of Religion in India* (Delhi: Manohar, 2009), p. 191.
11. *The Travels of Pietro della Valle in India*, vol. 1, trans. by G. Havers (London: Hakluyt Society, 1892), p. 106.
12. Carl W. Ernst, *Refractions of Islam in India: Situating Sufism and Yoga* (New Delhi: Sage, 2016), p. 291.
13. Ibid., p. 391.
14. Ernst, 'Being Careful with the Goddess', p. 196.
15. Ibid., p. 199.
16. Ibid., p. 195.

17. Ali Anooshahr, 'Shirazi Scholars and the Political Culture of the Sixteenth-Century Indo-Persian World', *Indian Economic Social History Review,* vol. 51, no. 33, 2014, p. 340.
18. William Dalrymple, 'The Renaissance of the Sultans', *The New York Review of Books*, 25 June 2015.
19. Emma J. Flatt, 'The Authorship and Significance of the Nujum al-'ulum: A Sixteenth-Century Astrological Encyclopedia from Bijapur', *Journal of the American Oriental Society*, vol. 131, no. 2, 2011, p. 240.
20. Emma J. Flatt, 'Spices, Smells and Spells: The Use of Olfactory Substances in the Conjuring of Spirits', *South Asian Studies*, vol. 32, no.1, 2016, p. 14.
21. Ibid., p. 9.
22. William Crooke, *An Introduction to the Popular Religion and Folklore of Northern India* (Allahabad: Government Press, 1894), p. 166.
23. A. S. Tritton 'Spirits and Demons in Arabia', *Journal of the Royal Asiatic Society*, vol. 66 no. 4, 1934, pp. 717–18.
24. Mary Frere, *Old Deccan Days; or, Hindoo Fairy Legends, Current in Southern India* (London: John Murray, 1868), pp. xii–xiii.
25. Ibid., p. xiii.
26. Michael W. Dols, *Majnun: The Madman in Medieval Islamic Society* (Oxford Scholarship Online, 2011), p. 214.
27. Tritton, pp. 716–77.
28. James Forbes, *Oriental Memoirs*, vol. 2 (London: White, Cochrane & Co., 1813), p. 370.
29. E. A. Leslie Moore, 'Indian Superstitions', *Journal of the Royal Society of Arts*, vol. 59, February 1911, p. 369.
30. Ibid., p. 378.
31. *North Indian Notes and Queries,* vol. 2, 1902, p. 117.
32. William Crooke, Pandit Ram Gharib Chaube, *Folktales from Northern India* (Santa Barbara: ABC-CLIO, 2002), p. 293.
33. Horace Arthur Rose, *A Glossary of the Tribes and Castes of the Punjab and North-West Frontier Province 1911,* vol. 1 (New Delhi: Nirmal, 1997), p. 561.
34. A. Azfar Moin, *The Millennial Sovereign: Sacred Kingship and Sainthood in Islam* (New York: Colombia University Press, 2012), p. 65.
35. Ibid., 67.

36. Bamber Gascoigne, *The Great Mughals* (New Delhi: Time Books International, 1987), p. 47.
37. Rachel Parikh, 'Yoga under the Mughals: From Practice to Paintings', *South Asian Studies*, vol. 31, no. 2, 2015, p. 226.
38. Audrey Truschke, *Culture of Encounters: Sanskrit at the Mughal Court* (New Delhi: Allen Lane, 2016), p. 121.
39. Gascoigne, *The Great Mughals*, p. 100.
40. Ibid., pp. 252–53.
41. Doniger, *The Hindus*, p. 532.
42. Harbans Mukhia, *The Mughals of India* (Malden: Blackwell, 2004), p. 168.
43. Abu al-Fazl 'Allami, *The Ain i Akbar,* trans. by Henry Blochmann, vol. 1 (Calcutta: Asiatic Society of Bengal, 1873), pp. 164–65.
44. Ibid., pp. 200–01.
45. Henry Miers Elliot and John Dawson (eds), *History of India as told by its Own Historians*, vol. 5 (London: Turner & Co., 1873), p. 538.
46. Cited in Sir William Foster, *Early Travels in India, 1583–1619* (Oxford: Oxford University Press, 1921), pp. 276–77.
47. Edward Terry, *A Voyage to East-India* (London: J. Wilkie, 1877), p. 253.
48. *The Tuzuk-i-Jahangiri; or, Memoirs of Jahangir,* trans by Alexander Rogers (London: Royal Asiatic Society, 1909), p. 412.
49. Ibid., p. 143.
50. Waldemar Hansen, *The Peacock Throne: The Drama of Mogul India* (New Delhi: Motilal Baransidass, 1996), pp. 156–7.
51. Iftikhar Ahmad Ghauri, *War of Succession Between the Sons of Shah Jehan 1657–1658* (Lahore: Publishers United, 1964), p. 36.
52. Hansen, *The Peacock Throne*, p. 158.
53. Niccolao Manucci, *Storia do Mogor*, trans. by William Irvine, vol. 2 (London: John Murray, 1907), p. 168.
54. Elliott and Dawson, *History of India*, vol. 7, p. 295.
55. Manucci, *Storia do Mogor*, vol. 2, p. 168
56. Ibid., p. 8.
57. See for instance Katherine Butler Brown, 'Did Aurangzeb Ban Music? Questions for the Historiography of His Reign', *Modern Asian Studies*, vol. 41, no. 1, 2007, pp. 77–120.
58. Cited in Jafar Sharif, *Islam in India or the Qanun-i-Islam*, trans. by G. A. Herlocks (London: Oxford University Press, 1921), p. 218.

Chapter 4: In the Court of the Kings

1. Abraham Eraly, *The Age of Wrath: A History of the Delhi Sultanate* (New Delhi: Penguin Viking, 2014), p. 351.
2. S. H. Askari, 'Khusrau's Works as Sources of Social History', in *Amir Khusrau* (New Delhi: Publications Division, 1975), p. 145.
3. Eraly, p. 351.
4. Khunwar Ashraf, 'Life and Conditions of the People of Hindustan (1200–1550 A.D.)', *Journal of the Asiatic Society of Bengal*, vol. 1, no. 2, 1935, pp. 305–07.
5. Surinder Singh and Ishwar Dayal Gaur (eds), *Popular Literature and Pre-Modern Societies in South Asia* (Delhi: Dorling Kindersley, 2008), pp. 317–18.
6. *Arthashastra*, trans. by R. Shamasastry (Bangalore: Government Press, 1915), p. 178
7. Ibid., p. 28–29.
8. Ibid., p. 564.
9. Ram Sharan Sharma, *Aspects of Political Ideas and Institutions in Ancient India* (Delhi: Motilal Banarsidass, 1959), p. 257.
10. Dipakranjan Das, *Economic History of the Deccan: From the First to the Sixth Century AD*. (Delhi: Munshiram Manoharlal, 1969), pp. 90–91.
11. Anil Baran Ganguly, *Fine Arts in Ancient India* (New Delhi: Abhinav, 1972), pp. 141–142.
12. Dharmendra Kumar Gupta, *Society and Culture in the Time of Dandin* (Delhi: Meharchand Lachhmandas, 1972), p. 490.
13. Ibid., p. 277.
14. Ibid., p. 236.
15. Maurice Bloomfield, 'The Art of Stealing in Hindu Fiction', *The American Journal of Philology*, vol. 44, no. 2, 1923, p. 118.
16. V. Raghavan, *Yantras, or Mechanical Contrivances in Ancient India* (Bangalore: Indian Institute of Culture, 1952), pp. 16–17.
17. Manohar Laxman Varadpande, *History of the Indian Theatre*, vol. 2 (New Delhi: Abhinav, 1987), p. 68.
18. Raghavan, pp.9–10.
19. Ibid., pp. 18–19.
20. M. K. Dhar, *Royal Life in Ancient India* (Delhi: Durga Publications, 1991), p. 19.

21. P. Arundhati, *Royal Life in Manasollasa* (New Delhi: Sundeep Prakashan, 1994), pp. 157–176.
22. Ibid., p. 146.
23. Ibid., p. 20.
24. Cited in Muzaffar Alam and Sanjay Subrahmanyam, *Indo-Persian Travels in the Age of Discoveries, 1400–1800* (Cambridge: Cambridge University Press, 2007), p. 61.
25. Richard Henry Major, *India in the Fifteenth Century* (London: Hakylut Society, 1857), p. 79.
26. Ibid., p. 96.
27. Ibid., p. 87.
28. Ibid., p. 88.
29. Anna Libera Dallapiccola, *King, Court and Capital: An Anthology of Kannada Literary Sources from the Vijayanagara Period* (New Delhi: Manohar, 2003), p. 52.
30. Ibid., p. 129.
31. A. Afzar Moin, 'Peering through the Cracks in the Baburnama: The Textured Lives of Mughal Sovereigns', *The Indian Economic & Social History Review*, vol. 49, no. 4, 2017, p. 512.
32. Musharraf Ali Farooqi, 'Hoshruba: The Land and the Tilism', *Pakistaniaat: A Journal of Pakistan Studies*, vol. 1, no. 2, 2009, p. 154.
33. Ibid., p. 152.
34. Ibid., pp. 154–55.
35. Varadpande, *History of the Indian Theatre*, p. 140.
36. Ibid., p.136.
37. *The Travels of Peter Mundy in Europe and Asia*, vol. 2 (London: Hakluyt Society,1914), p. 255.
38. Ibid., p. 254.
39. Francisco Pelsaert, *Jahangir's India, The Remonstrantie of Francisco Pelsaert*, trans. by W. H. Moreland (Cambridge: W. Heffer & Sons, 1925), p. 72.
40. Jean de Thévenot, *The Travels of Monsieur de Thévenot into the Levant*, vol. 3, trans. by Archibald Lovell (London: H. Clark, 1687), p. 77.
41. Ibid., p. 78.
42. Bernier, *Travels in the Mogul Empire*, pp. 243–44.
43. Ibid., p. 192.
44. Ibid., p. 192.

45. *The Travels of the Abbe Carré in India and the Near East (1672–1674)* (London: Hakluyt Society, 1947), p. 300.
46. Ibid., p. 265.
47. Jean Rousselet, *India and its Native Princes*, trans. by Charles Buckle (London: Bickers, 1882), pp. 463–64.
48. Ibid., p. 466.
49. Olive Risley Seward (ed.), *William H. Seward's Travels Around the World* (New York: D. Appleton & Co., 1876), p. 462.
50. Ibid., p. 463.
51. Ibid., p. 470.
52. Henry Steel Olcott, *People from the Other World* (Harford: American Publishing Company, 1875), p. 332.

Chapter 5: A Bed of Nails

1. Siegel, *Net of Magic*, p. 4.
2. Cited in V. A. Narain, *Jonathan Duncan and Varanasi* (Calcutta: Mukhopadhyay, 1959), p. 177.
3. Samuel Turner, *An Account of an Embassy to the Court of the Teshoo Lama in Tibet* (London, Bulmer & Co., 1800) p. 271.
4. 'The Travels of Pran-Puri, A Hindu who Travelled over India, Persia and Parts of Russia', *The European Magazine and London Review*, vol. 57, 1810, p. 351.
5. Jonathan Duncan, 'An Account of Two Fakeers, with their Portraits', *Asiatick Researches*, vol. 5, 1799, p. 50.
6. 'The Travels of Pran-Puri', p. 264.
7. Ibid., p. 346.
8. Ibid., p. 348.
9. Bernier, *Travels in the Mogul Empire*, pp. 243–44.
10. D. A. Pai, *Monograph on the Religious Sects in India among the Hindus* (Bombay: The Times Press, 1928), p. 77.
11. Jean Baptiste Tavernier, *Travels in India*, trans. by John Phillips (Calcutta: Bangabasi, 1905), p. 396.
12. Bernier, *Travels in the Mogul Empire*, pp. 243–4.
13. Cited in Ram Kumar Chaube, *India as Told by the Muslims* (Varanasi: Prithvi Prakashan, 1969), pp. 200–01.

14. John Campbell Oman, *The Mystics, Ascetics, and Saints of India* (London: T. F. Unwin, 1905), p. 66.
15. Ibid., p. 50.
16. Ibid., p 66.
17. Ibid., pp. 66–67.
18. Ibid., pp. 61–62
19. Cited in David Gordon White, *Sinister Yogis* (Chicago: Chicago University Press, 2009), p. 24.
20. 'A Study in Apparent Death', *Scribner's*, vol. 21, December 1880, p. 250.
21. Ibid., p. 250.
22. Ibid., p. 251.
23. 'Burying Alive', *The Asiatic Journal*, vol. XXII, January-April 1837, pp. 85–86.
24. Alexander Hamilton, *A New Account of the East Indies*, vol. 1 (London: C. Hitch, 1744), pp. 155–56.
25. Bram Stoker, *Dracula* (London: Penguin, 2003), p. 205.
26. *The Spectator*, 28 May 1926.
27. *The New York Times*, 19 February 1950.
28. Olive Crofton, *They Also Serve* (unpublished manuscript), Crofton Papers, University of Cambridge, n.d.
29. Ibid., p. 152.
30. Ibid., pp. 152–53.
31. Ibid., pp. 153–54.
32. Sharif, *Islam in India*, pp. 290–291.
33. Ibid., p. 291.
34. Edmund Henderson Hunt, 'The Rafai Fakeers of Hyderabad', *Man*, vol. 32, February 1932, p. 46.
35. Jack Devlin, 'Skewering', *Magic Circular*, vol. 46, no. 2, 1951, p. 217.
36. David Richardson, 'An Account of the Bazeegurs, a Sect Commonly Denominated *Nuts*', *Asiatick Researches*, vol. 7 (1803), p. 465.
37. Sharif, *Islam in India*, pp. 195–96.
38. Ibid., pp. 289–90.
39. Ibid., p. 291.
40. Malik Mohamed, *The Foundations of the Composite Culture in India* (Delhi: Aakar, 2007), p. 97.

41. 'Competition and Co-existence: Indo-Islamic Interaction in Medieval North India', *Itinerario*, vol. 13, no. 1, 1989, pp. 37–60.
42. Patton Burchett, 'My Miracle Trumps Your Magic: Encounters with Yogis in Sufi and Bhakti Hagiographical Literature', in Knut A. Jacobsen (ed.), *Yoga Powers: Extraordinary Capacities Attained Through Meditation and Concentration* (Leiden: Brill, 2011), p. 355.
43. Ibn Khaldun, *The Muqaddimah: An Introduction to History*, trans. by Franz Rosenthal, vol. 3 (New York: Bollinger Foundation, 1958), p. 167.
44. Ibid., p. 168.
45. Carl W. Ernst, 'Situating Sufism and Yoga', *Journal of the Royal Asiatic Society*, vol. 15, no. 1, 2005, p. 23.
46. Jaya Madhavan, *Kabir: The Weaver-Poet* (Chennai: Tulika, 2004), pp. 59–60.
47. Charles Swynnerton, *Romantic Tales from the Panjab with Indian Nights' Entertainment* (London: Archibald Constable & Co, 1908), p. 51.
48. David Gordon White, 'Ashes to Nectar: Death and Regeneration among the Rasa Siddhas and Nath Siddhas', in Liz Wilson (ed.), *The Living and the Dead: Social Dimensions of Death in South Asian Religions* (Albany: State University of New York Press, 2003), pp. 21–22.

Chapter 6: The Juggler's Child

1. IOR, 'Question of the future maintenance and disposal of a 9–year-old European girl found with a troop of itinerant jugglers near Hingoli in Hyderabad state,' L/PS/6/497, Coll 86/9: July 1858 – January 1859.
2. Ibid.
3. Ibid.
4. *Madras Times*, 6 August 1858.
5. Mathew Sherring, *Hindu Tribes and Castes, as Represented in Benares*, vol.1 (Calcutta: Thacker Spink & Co., 1872), p. 380.
6. James Stevenson, 'Some Account of the Phansigars, or Gang-robbers, and of the Shudgarshids, or Tribe of Jugglers', *The Journal of the Royal Asiatic Society of Great Britain and Ireland*, vol. 1, no. 2, 1834, p. 283.
7. 'Indian Gypsies', *Allens Indian Mail,* 7 June 1870, pp. 530–31.
8. Jean-Antoine Dubois, *Hindu Manners, Customs and Ceremonies* (Oxford: Clarendon Press, 1906), pp. 76–77.
9. Richardson, 'An Account of the Bazeeghurs', p. 464.

10. James Forbes, *Oriental Memoirs*, vol. 3 (London: White Cochrane & Co., 1813), p. 253.
11. Sherring, *Hindu Tribes and Castes*, vol. 1, pp. 387–89.
12. Ibid., 390.
13. William Sleeman, *The Thugs or Phansigars of India* (Philadelphia: Carey & Hart, 1839), p. 83.
14. William Sleeman, *A Report on the System of Megpunnaism* (Serampore: Serampore Press, 1839), p. 11.
15. Cited in Martine van Woerkens, *The Strangled Traveler: Colonial Imaginings and the Thugs of India* (Chicago: University of Chicago Press, 1995), p. 102.
16. Fanny Parks, *Wanderings of a Pilgrim*, vol. 2 (London: Pelham Richardson, 1850), pp. 452–53.
17. 'Kanjars in Upper India', *Calcutta Review*, vol. 77, no.154, 1883, p. 432.
18. 'Indian Gypsies', pp. 530–31.
19. R. V. Russell, *The Tribes and Castes of the Central Provinces*, vol. 4 (London: Macmillan & Co., 1916), p. 285.
20. Denzil Ibbetson, *Panjab Castes* (Lahore: Government Press, 1916), p. 285.
21. A. C. L. Carlleyle, 'Report of Tours in Gorakhpur, Saran and Ghazipur in 1877–78–79 and 80', *Archaeological Survey of India*, vol. 22, 1885, p. 67.
22. Cited in Mark Brown, *Penal Power and Colonial Rule* (New York: Routledge, 2014), p.144.
23. IOR, 'Criminal Tribes: Papers relating to various tribes, including Bauriahs, Sansiyas, and Minas, particularly in the Punjab, Madras and Sind; 1856–1905 and 1921–1947', Mss. Eur. F 161/157.
24. Captain E. C. Cox, The Successors of the Thugs in India, *The Police Journal*, vol. 1, no. 2, 1928, p. 230.
25. IOR, 'Forms of Crime (Some Peculiar to India)', Part I, 1861/1900, Mss. Eur. F 161/154, Box 7/1.
26. M. Kennedy, *The Criminal Classes in India* (Delhi: Mittal, 1985), pp. 333–34.
27. Cited in Brown, p. 84.
28. Ibid.
29. Woerkens, *The Strangled Traveler*, p. 39.
30. Andrew J. Major, 'State and Criminal Tribes in Colonial Punjab: Surveillance, Control and Reclamation of the 'Dangerous Classes', *Modern Asian Studies*, vol. 33, no. 3 (1999), p. 658.

31. Cited in Brown, *Penal Power*, p. 84.
32. Frederick Booth-Tucker, *Muktifauj: Or Forty Years with the Salvation Army in India and Ceylon* (London: Marshall Brothers, 1900), p. 204.
33. Cited in Brown, *Penal Power*, p. 180
34. William Crooke, 'The Head-dress of the Banjara Women', *Journal of the Bihar and Orissa Research Society*, vol. 4, no. 3, 1918, p. 247.
35. Cited in Brown, *Penal Power*, p. 160.
36. James Mill, *The History of British India*, vol. 1 (London: Baldwin, Craddock and Joy, 1817), pp. 320–21.
37. K. S. MacDonald, 'Magic, Sorcery, Astrology and Kindred Superstitions', reprinted from the *Indian Evangelical Review*, October 1902 (Calcutta: The Calcutta Christian Tract and Book Society, n.d.), p. 80.
38. Monier Monier-Williams, *Brahmanism and Hinduism* (New York: Macmillan, 1891), p. 201.
39. Ibid., p. 202.
40. Ibid., pp. 202–03.
41. R. E. Enthoven, *The Folklore of Bombay* (Oxford: Clarendon Press, 1924), p. 237.
42. Ibid., p. 241.
43. Dhirendra Nath Majumdar, *The Fortunes of the Primitive Tribes* (Lucknow: Universal Publishers, 1944), p. 96.
44. Enthoven, *The Folklore of Bombay*, p. 238.
45. Stephen Fuchs, *Children of Hari: A Study of the Nimar Balahis in the Central Provinces of India* (Vienna: Verlag Herold, 1950), p. 274.
46. Ibid. p. 274.
47. Ibid., pp. 272–73.
48. Ibid., p. 284.
49. Christoph von Furer Haimendorf, *Tribal Populations and Cultures of the Subcontinent* (Lieden-Koln: E. J. Brill, 1985), p. 46.
50. Verrier Elwin, 'A Note on the Theory and Symbolism of Dreams among the Baiga', *British Journal of Medical Psychology*, vol. 16, nos. 3–4, 1937, p. 237.
51. Verrier Elwin, *The Baiga* (London: John Murray, 1939), p. 343ff.
52. R. Montgomery Martin, *History of the Possessions of the Honorable East India Company*, vol. 2 (London: Whittaker & Co., 1837), p. 253.
53. Ibid., pp. 258–59.
54. Ibid., pp. 251–52.

55. Ibid., p. 253.
56. Ibid., p. 257.
57. R. N. Salatore, *Indian Witchcraft* (New Delhi: Abhinav, 1981), pp. 6–7.
58. C. A. Bayly, 'Knowing the Country: Empire and Information in India', *Modern Asian Studies*, vol. 27, no. 1, 1993, pp. 5–6.
59. Cited in Ibid., p. 6.
60. Manucci, *Storio do Mogor*, vol. 2, p. 213.
61. Bayly, 'Knowing the Country', pp. 13–14.
62. Ariel Glucklich, *The Sense of Adharma* (New York, London: Oxford University Press, 1994), p. 190.
63. Maurice Bloomfield, 'The Art of Stealing in Hindu Fiction', *The American Journal of Philology*, vol. 44, No. 2, 1923, p. 119.
64. Helen M. Johnson, 'Rauhineya's Adventures', *Studies in Honor of Maurice Bloomfield* (New Haven: Yale University Press, 1920), pp. 159ff.
65. Ibid., pp. 165–66.
66. Bloomfield, 'The Art of Stealing', p. 118.
67. Alessandro Passi, 'Perverted Dharma? Ethics of Thievery in the Dharmacauryarasayana', *Journal of Indian Philosophy*, vol. 33, no. 4, 2005, p. 516.

Chapter 7: Tricks of the Trade

1. Krishnanath Raghunathji, *Bombay Beggars and Criers* (Bombay: Government Press, 1892), n.p.
2. Ibid., n.p.
3. Ibid., p.1.
4. Ibid., p. 25.
5. Ibid., p. 22.
6. Ibid., pp. 35–36.
7. Ibid., p. 32.
8. Ibid., pp. 37–40.
9. Ibid., pp. 40–41.
10. Ibid., p. 66.
11. Ibid., pp. 76–77.
12. Ibid., p. 110.

13. Ibid., p. 63.
14. Ibid., p. 54.
15. Ibid., pp. 114–15.
16. Ibid., pp. 111–12.
17. *Govind Narayan's Mumbai, An Urban Biography from 1863,* trans. by Murali Ranganathan (London: Anthem Press, 2008), p. 259.
18. *The Western Times,* 21 January 1876.
19. IOR, *The Indian Rope Trick,* Mss. Eur. F 370/1409.
20. *Liverpool Mercury,* 2 July 1862.
21. *The Manchester Times,* 18 June 1851.
22. Emily Eden, *Letters from India,* vol. 1 (London: Richard Bentley & Son, 1872), p. 193.
23. John Mulholland, *Quicker than the Eye: The Magic and Magicians of the World* (Indianapolis: The Bobbs-Merrill, c1932), pp. 98–99.
24. J. Hobart Caunter, *The Cadet and Other Poems,* vol. 1 (London: Robert Jennings, 1814), p. viii.
25. J. Hobart Caunter, *The Oriental Annual: Or, Scenes in India* (London: E. Churton, 1836), pp. 22–23.
26. Ibid., pp. 26–27.
27. Ibid., pp. 24–25.
28. *The Western Times,* 21 January 1876.
29. Robert Elliot, *The Myth of the Mystic East* (London: Wm. Blackwood & Sons, 1934), pp. 122–23.
30. Caunter, *The Oriental Annual,* p. 140.
31. Ibid, pp. 142ff.
32. Ibid., pp. 164–65.
33. Ibid., p. 165.
34. Ibid., pp. 166 69.
35. Jean-Baptiste Tavernier, *Travels in India,* trans. by V. Ball, vol.1 (London: Macmillan & Co., 1889), p. 55.
36. *The Times of India,* 1 October 1881.
37. Henry Yule and A. C. Burnell, *Hobson-Jobson: A Glossary of Colloquial Anglo-Indian Words and Phrases, and of Kindred Terms, Etymological, Historical, Geographical and Discursive* (London: John Murray, 1903), p. 556.
38. *Pall Mall Gazette,* 15 February 1889.
39. *The Edinburgh Literary Journal,* 18 December 1830, pp. 373–74.

40. Thomas Frost, *Lives of the Conjurors* (London: Chatto & Windus, 1881), pp. 207–08.
41. 'The Air Brahmin', *Saturday Magazine*, no. 4, 28 July 1832, p. 28.
42. *Madras Mail*, 8 October 1884.
43. *Madras Mail*, 21 October 1884.
44. Louis Jacolliot, *Occult Science in India,* trans. by Willard Felt (New York: John W. Lovell), p. 235.
45. Ibid., pp. 237–38.
46. Yule, *The Book of Ser Marco Polo*, vol. 2, pp. 267–68.
47. James Johnson, *An Account of a Voyage to India, China &c.* (London: Richard Phillips, 1806), pp. 325–26.
48. John Splinter Stavorinus, *Voyages to the East-Indies,* trans. by Samuel Hull Wilcocke, vol. 1 (London: G. G. & J. Robinson, 1798), pp. 436–37.
49. Ibid., p. 136.
50. Ibid., p. 135.
51. Crooke, *An Introduction to the Popular Religion*, p. 135.
52. Gopal Pannikar, *Malabar and its Folk* (Madras: G. A. Natesan & Co., 1900), pp. 59–60.
53. James Forbes, *Oriental Memoirs,* vol. 2 (London: White, Cochrane & Co., 1813), pp. 385–6.
54. Monier Monier-Williams, *Brahmanism and Hinduism* (New York: Macmillan & Co., 1891), p. 325.
55. Cited in Jean Philippe Vogel, *Indian Serpent-lore: Or, The Nagas in Hindu Legend and Art* (London: Arthur Probsthain, 1926), p. 1.
56. *The Natural History of Reptiles and Serpents* (Dublin: J. Jones, 1821), pp. 130–31.
57. William Adam, *Report on the State of Education in Bengal* (Calcutta: Bengal Military Orphan Press, 1835), pp. 76–77.
58. Crooke, *An Introduction to the Popular Religion*, p. 123.
59. Miriam Robertson, *The Kalbelias of Rajasthan: Jogi Nath Snake Charmers. An Ethnography of Indian Non-Pastoral Nomads,* PhD thesis, London School of Economics and Political Science, 1987, pp. 108–09.
60. Ibid., p. 128.
61. *Saturday Magazine,* 23 May 1894.
62. Edgar Thurston, *Omens and Superstitions of Southern India* (New York: McBride, Nast & Co., 1912), p 95.

Chapter 8: Crossing the *Kala Pani*

1. *Hereford Journal*, 22 November 1809.
2. Ibid.
3. Robert Grenville-Wallace, *Forty Years in the World; or, Sketches and Tales of a Soldier's Life*, vol. 2 (London: Geo B. Whittaker, 1825), pp. 4–6.
4. Emma Roberts, *Scenes and Characteristics of Hindostan, with Sketches of Anglo-Indian Society*, vol. 1 (London: W.H. Allen, 1835), pp. 317–18.
5. 'Narrative of a Tour through Bengal, Bahar and Oudh to Agra, Delhi', *The Monthly Magazine*, vol. 28 (1810), pp. 372-73.
6. Johnson, *An Account of a Voyage*, pp.106–07.
7. Ibid., p. 107.
8. Delme Radcliffe, 'The Sportsman all the World Over', *The Sportsman*, vol. 6, no. 6, 1842, pp. 513.
9. *The Bristol Mirror*, 24 July 1813.
10. *The Times*, July 27, 1813.
11. *The Bristol Mirror*, 24 July 1813.
12. 'The Hindoo Jugglers', *The Repository of Arts, Literature, Commerce, Manufactures, Fashions, and Politics*, vol. 10, July 1813, p. 230.
13. 'Indian Jugglers', *The Satirist or Monthly Meteor*, no. 13, 1 August 1813, pp. 97–104.
14. Ibid.
15. *Description of the Performance of those Superior Indian Jugglers Lately Arrived from Seringapatam, etc.*, (London: T. Wood, n.d.), pp. 1–12.
16. Radcliffe, p. 513.
17. *Boston Intelligencer*, 11 September 1819.
18. Cited in http://www.swordswallow.com/halloffame.php.
19. *Alexandria Gazette & Daily Advertiser*, 2 February 1818.
20. *Boston Commercial Gazette*, 5 October 1818.
21. *Alexandria Gazette & Daily Advertiser*, 2 February 1818.
22. *City Gazette and Daily Advertiser*, 3 February 1818.
23. *Boston Commercial Gazette*, 5 October 1818.
24. Charles Pecor, *The Magician on the American Stage: 1752-1874*, PhD Thesis, University of Georgia (1976), p. 135.
25. Cited in John Wale, 'Indian Jugglers: Hazlitt, Romantic Orientalism and the Difference of View', in Tim Fulford and Peter Kitson, *Romanticism*

and Colonialism, Writing and Empire 1780–1830 (Cambridge: Cambridge University Press), p. 209.

26. *The Bristol Mirror*, 9 June 1821.
27. Cited in Harry Houdini, 'Unknown Facts Concerning Robert Houdin', *The Conjurors' Magazine*, vol. 1, no. 3 (November 1906), p. 26.
28. HPC, Playbill, 1820, 'Theatre-Royal Chester for the Benefit of Khia Khan Khruse', HPF/5A/1.
29. *The Hampshire Chronicle*, 29 June 1818.
30. *The London Gazette*, 23 July 1822.
31. Richard Knill, 'An Indian Juggler', *Evangelical Magazine and Missionary Chronicle*, vol. 16, 1838, p. 190.
32. *Königliches Hof und Nationaltheater*, 1824, n.d., n.p.
33. *Morgenblatt*, vol. 18, 27 May 1824, p. 508.
34. *Poulson's American Daily Advertiser*, 23 January 1818.
35. *The Morning Post*, 13 August 1822.
36. William Edwin Adams, *Memoirs of a Social Atom*, vol. 1 (London: Hutchinson & Co., 1903), p. 95.
37. Henry Mayhew, *London Labour and the London Poor*, vol. 3 (London: Griffin, Bohn and Company, 1861), p.107.
38. Evanion Collection, British Library, playbill no. 817, 1833.
39. *Morning Advertiser*, 26 October 1835.
40. *Vauxhall Papers*, no. 11, 11 August 1814.
41. *Bell's Life in London*, 25 August 1850.
42. *Bell's Life in London and Sporting Chronicle*, 1 September 1850.
43. *Reynolds' Newspaper*, 12 November 1871.
44. Bates and Lamont, 'Conjuring images of India', p. 310.
45. Cited in *The New Monthly Magazine*, vol. 7, no. 53, February 1871, p. 53.
46. *Figaro in London*, vol. 3, no. 155, 22 November 1834, p. 185.
47. William Hazlitt, 'The Indian Jugglers,' in P. P. Howe (ed.), *The Complete Works of William Hazlitt*, vol. 8 (London: J. M. Dent and Sons, 1931), pp. 77–78.
48. *Newcastle Guardian and Tyne Mercury*, 27 November 1852.
49. *The Tripod, or, New Satirist*, no. 18, 1 January 1814, pp. 16–17.
50. Wilkie Collins, *The Moonstone* (New York: Harper Brothers, 1868), p. 45.
51. Ibid., p. 100.
52. George A. Henty, *Rujub, the Juggler* (Chicago: M. A. Donohue & Co., 1910), pp. 17–18.

53. The Battle of Chillianwala was fought in January 1849 during the Second Anglo-Sikh War.
54. Henty, *Rujub, the Juggler*, p. 20.
55. HPC, Playbill, 1823, HPC 5A/1.
56. *The Chester Chronicle,* 16 May 1817.
57. *London Star,* 14 August 1818.
58. *Imperial Weekly Gazette and Westminster Journal,* 22 August 1818.
59. *Alexandria Gazette,* 1 August 1826.
60. NYPL, Blitz Playbill, Magic Scrapbooks, T-Mss 2011-31 S.
61. Mayhew, *London Labour*, p. 105.
62. Ibid., p. 105.
63. Ibid., p. 104.
64. Ibid., pp. 106–07.
65. Ibid., p. 106.

Chapter 9: Spell-casters in the Strangers' Home

1. IOR, 'R. M. Hughes to Under Secretary of State', 12 August 1868, Case of Natives of India in Distress in England, L/P/J/2/47.
2. *The Era*, 23 February 1868.
3. Cited in the *Norfolk Chronicle,* 20 June 1868.
4. *The Norfolk Chronicle*, 20 June 1868.
5. *The Sunday Times*, 2 April 1868.
6. *Pall Mall Gazette*, 25 March 1868.
7. *The Times*, 14 April 1868.
8. *The Norfolk News*, 11 July 1868.
9. *The Norfolk Chronicle*, 18 July 1868.
10. *The Norfolk News*, 18 July 1868.
11. Ibid.
12. *The Norfolk Chronicle,* 18 July 1868.
13. Paul Greenhalgh, *The Modern Ideal: The Rise and Collapse of Idealism in the Visual Arts* (London: V&A Publications, 2005), p. 119.
14. Ibid., p. 60.
15. Cited in Joseph Salter, *The Asiatic in England: Sketches of Sixteen Years' Work Among Orientals* (London: Seeley, Jackson and Halliday, 1873), n.p.
16. Ibid., p. 114.

17. IOR, 'Hughes to Northcote', 12 August 1868, Case of natives of India in distress in England, L/P/J/2/47.
18. IOR, 'Memorandum', 4 September 1868: Case of natives of India in distress in England, L/P/J/2/47.
19. IOR, 'Northcote Memorandum', 13 August 1868, Case of natives of India in distress in England, L/P/J/2/47.
20. IOR, 'Memorandum', 4 September 1868: Case of natives of India in distress in England, L/P/J/2/47.
21. Ibid.
22. IOR, 'Hughes to Northcote', 15 September 1868, Case of natives of India in distress in England, L/P/J/2/47.
23. IOR, 'Abdoolah to Northcote', 19 January 1869, Case of natives of India in distress in England, L/P/J/2/47.
24. Cited in *Journal of the Royal Society of Arts*, vol. 134, no. 5353 (1985), p. 55.
25. Eugene Rimmel, *Recollections of the Paris Exhibition of 1867* (London: Chapman & Hall, 1868), p. 238.
26. *The Morning Post*, 23 December 1885.
27. *Tamworth Herald*, 11 July 1885.
28. *The Times of India*, 14 July 1885.
29. *The Morning Post*, 23 December 1885.
30. Ibid.
31. *St James's Gazette*, 23 December 1885.
32. *London Evening Standard*, 21 December 1885.
33. *The Times of India*, 6 April 1886.
34. Alison Adburgham, *Liberty's: A Biography of a Shop* (London: George Allen & Unwin, 1975), pp. 59–60.
35. *The Illustrated London News*, 21 November 1885.
36. Cited in the *Dundee Evening Telegraph*, 30 November 1885.
37. Saloni Mathur, 'Living Ethnological Exhibits: The Case of 1886', *Cultural Anthropology*, vol. 15, no. 4, 2000, pp. 503–04.
38. *The Times of India*, 2 January 1886.
39. *The Times of India*, 18 March 1886
40. Cited in Mathur, p. 504
41. Cited in Ibid, p. 505.
42. *Freeman's Journal*, 23 April 1886.

43. Cited in Mathur, p. 506.
44. *Dundee Evening Telegraph*, 21 July 1886.
45. *The Times of India*, 26 October 1886.
46. *The Evening Journal* (Adelaide), 11 June 1889.
47. *South Australian Register*, 10 June 1889.
48. *The Age*, 15 August 1889.
49. *The Age*, 25 October 1889.
50. Cited in *The Evening Journal*, 8 November 1889.
51. *The Lorgnette*, 9 November 1889.
52. *The Argus*, 12 November 1889.
53. Ibid.
54. NAI, 'Regarding certain natives of Madras who were conveyed by a Mr Roberts from India to Australia', Revenue & Agriculture (Emigration), 21 April 1890, Proceedings nos. 19–22.

Chapter 10: Motilal's Magical Menagerie

1. MSA, 'Letter from Mr Motilal Nehru', General Department, 1900, no. 86.
2. Cited in Alexander Geppert, *Fleeting Cities: Imperial Expositions in Fin-de-Siècle Europe* (New York: Palgrave Macmillan, 2010), p. 65.
3. Cited in Ibid., p. 65.
4. MSA, 'Nehru to Thomas Cook, 2 April 1900', Ruling of the Govt of India, no. 86.
5. Cited in Sandhya L. Polu, *Infectious Disease in India, 1892–1940: Policy-Making and the Perception of Risk* (London: Palgrave Macmillan, 2012), p. 43.
6. NAI, 'Memorandum by the Protector of Emigrants Bombay', 6 April 1900, Revenue and Agriculture (Emigration), May 1900, Proceedings, nos. 20–27.
7. NAI, 'Memorandum by the Commissioner of Customs, Bombay', 7 April 1900, Revenue and Agriculture (Emigration), May 1900, Proceedings, nos. 20–27.
8. MSA, 'Note by Secretary, General Department', Ruling of the Govt of India, General Department, 1900, no. 86.

9. NAI, Letter from F. Cowie, 25 April 1900, 'Native jugglers, dancers and circus attendants', Revenue and Agriculture (Emigration), May 1900, nos. 20–27.
10. NAI, Maconochie, 3 May 1900, 'Bill to further amend the Indian Emigration Act, 1883', Revenue and Agriculture (Emigration), April 1902, nos. 1–4.
11. NAI, Letter from T. W. Holderness Home Department, 17 May 1900, 'Native jugglers, dancers and circus attendants', Revenue and Agriculture (Emigration), May 1900, nos. 20–27.
12. Cited in Bernth Lindfors, *Early African Entertainments Abroad: From the Hottentot Venus to Africa's First Olympians* (Madison: University of Wisconsin Press, 2014), p. 175.
13. Cited in Ernest Albrecht, *From Barnum & Bailey to Feld: The Creative Evolution of the Greatest Show on Earth* (Jefferson: Macfarlane & Co., 2014), p. 43.
14. Bluford Adams, '"A Stupendous Mirror of Departed Empires": The Barnum Hippodromes and Circuses, 1874–1891', *American Literary History*, vol. 8, no. 1, (1996), p. 47.
15. W. H. Holmes, 'The World's Fair Congress of Anthropology', *American Anthropologist*, vol. 6, 1893, p. 434.
16. Cited in *The Telegraph*, 26 February 2011.
17. *Reading Mercury*, 22 December 1895.
18. Cited in Eric Ames, *Carl Hagenbeck's Empire of Entertainment* (Seattle: University of Washington Press, 2008), p. 12.
19. Ibid., p. 3.
20. Ibid., p. 4.
21. Ibid., p. 65.
22. Ibid., p. 117.
23. IOR, 'R. F. Austin to chief secretary to the Government of Madras, 3 February 1913', Repatriation of a troupe of Indians and Singalese from Germany, L/PJ/6/1213.
24. IOR, 'Joseph Chamberlain MP to the J. A. Swettenham, Officer Administrating the Government of the Straits Settlement, 25 April 1890', Engagement of Asiatics to perform as artists in Europe, L/PJ/6 545.
25. John O'Sullivan, 'Joseph Chamberlain, Theresa May's New Lodestar', *The Spectator*, 16 July 2016.
26. IOR, 'Engagement of Asiatics to perform as artists in Europe', L/PJ/6.

27. Ibid., 'Swettenham to Chamberlain', 28 June 1900.
28. Ibid.
29. NAI, 'Proposed Amendment to the Indian Emigration Act of 1883 so as to provide for artisans and performers', Home, Public, Part B, Nov 1901, no. 177.
30. IOR, Curzon to Hamilton, 31 October 1901, 'Engagement of Asiatics to perform as artists in Europe', L/PJ/6.
31. Indian Emigration (Amendment) Act, 1902 (No. 10), *Journal of the Society of Comparative Legislation*, vol. 5, no. 2, 1904, pp. 336–7.
32. *The Tribune*, 14 November 1926.
33. IOR, 'Letter from Consul General Hearn, 3 December 1912', Repatriation of a troupe of Indians and Singalese from Germany, L/PJ/6/1213.
34. NAI, 'Memorandum re travelling Indian showmen engaged by Mr John Hagenbeck, Berlin, G. Lyall, Consul British Consulate, Berlin, December 20 1926', Home Political, F 50 KW 1927.
35. *Forward*, 4 August 1944.
36. *Indian Daily Mail*, 8 October 1926.
37. *The Ceylon Morning Leader*, 11 November 1926.
38. NAI, 'Recruitment of skilled workers for circus troupes of Messrs Carl Hagenbeck and others in Germany', Home Political 1929, 133.

Chapter 11: The Fakir Invasion

1. Mary Dickens, *Charles Dickens* (London: Cassell, 1889), p. 92.
2. Charles Dickens, *Miscellaneous Contributions: to 'Household Words', 'All the Year Round' &c.* (London: Gresham, 1912), p. 263.
3. Kit Clarke, 'The Story of the Gift Shows', *M. U. M.*, vol. 7, no. 58, January 1918, p. 6.
4. *Milwaukee Daily Sentinel*, 22 May 1852.
5. LOC, *The Fakir of Siva's Original Troupe of Chinese Jugglers!*, Thr. A6, Box 1, no. 1 Theatre Playbills Collection Oversize.
6. David Price, *Magic: A Pictorial History of Conjurers in the Theater* (New York: Cornwall Books, 1985), p. 142.
7. Professor Hoffman, *Conjuring Tricks with Dominoes, Dice, Balls, Hats, etc.* (Philadelphia: David Mackay, 1902 c.a.), p 106.
8. *Daily News*, 18 April 1865.

9. For a discussion of the Mutiny motif see Karen Beckman, *Vanishing Women: Magic, Film and Feminism* (Durham: Duke University Press, 2003), pp. 35–47.
10. Cited in Pecor, *The Magician on the American Stage*, p. 369.
11. Ibid., p. 327.
12. *Terre Haute Saturday Evening Ledger*, 15 March 1879.
13. Robert Heller, *His Doings* (Glasgow: Hay Lisbet, 1875), p. 31.
14. LOC, *Houdini Scrapbook*, no. 10.
15. 'Indian Impostors and Jugglers', *Leisure Hour*, vol. 2 (1854), pp. 791–94.
16. Geoffrey Lamb, *Victorian Magic* (London and Boston: Routledge & K. Paul, 1976), p. 90.
17. H. S. Lynn, *Travels and Adventures of Dr Lynn* (London: Published by the author, 1882), p.16.
18. *The Royal Cornwall Gazette, Falmouth Packet, and General Advertiser*, 15 September 1865.
19. Lamb, p. 93.
20. *The Era*, 21 September 1873.
21. *Lynn*, p. 56
22. Ibid., p. 57.
23. Ibid., p. 58.
24. Ibid., pp. 67–68.
25. *Launceston Examiner*, 12 March 1898.
26. Harry Kellar, *A Magician's Tour: Up and Down and Round about the Earth* (Chicago: Donohue, Henneberry & Co., 1891), p. 94.
27. Ibid., p. 114.
28. Ibid., p. 115.
29. Harry Kellar, 'High Caste Indian Magic', *The North American Review*, vol. 156, no. 434, 1893, pp. 76–77.
30. Ibid., pp 78–79.
31. Ibid., pp. 81–83.
32. Edward Said, *Orientalism* (London: Penguin, 1974), p. 9 (emphasis in the original).
33. Michael Jay Claxton, *The Conjurer Unmasked: Literary and Theatrical Magicians, 1840–1925*, PhD thesis, University of North Carolina (2003), p. 186.
34. Bates and Lamont, 'Conjuring Images of India', p. 318.

35. Henry Ridgely Evans, *The Old and the New Magic* (Chicago: Open Court Publishing Company, 1906), p. 252.
36. *The Linking Ring*, vol.16, no. 7, September 1936, pp. 546–47.
37. Jim Steinmeyer, *Hiding the Elephant: How Magicians Invented the Impossible and Learned to Disappear* (London: Arrow Books, 2003), p. 165.
38. Claxton, *The Conjurer Unmasked*, p. 112.
39. John Nevil Maskelyne, 'Oriental Jugglery,' in Lionel Weatherly, *The Supernatural?* (Bristol: J. W. Arrowsmith, 1891), p. 180.
40. Ibid., p. 153.
41. Ibid., p. 157.
42. Ibid., p. 180.
43. *The Sphinx*, vol. 5, no. 9, November 1906, p. 99.
44. *The Magician Monthly*, vol. 3, no. 20, April 1907, p. 53.
45. *The Sphinx*, vol. 6, no. 3, May 1907, p. 3.
46. Howard Thurston, *My Life of Magic* (Philadelphia: Dorrance & Co., 1929), pp. 189–91.
47. Ibid., p.188.
48. Ibid., p. 192.
49. *The Sphinx*, vol. 6, no. 2, April 1907, p. 3.
50. Jim Steinmeyer, *The Last Greatest Magician in the World: Howard Thurston Versus Houdini & the Battles of the American Wizards* (New York: Penguin, 2011), p. 145.
51. *The Wizard*, vol. 2, no.17, January 1907, p. 266.
52. 'Nothing up My Sleeve', *Colliers*, 8 June 1929, p. 18.
53. *The Times* (Louisville), 11 November 1908.
54. Steinmeyer, *The Last Greatest Magician in the World*, pp. 155–56.
55. Ibid., p. 10.
56. Ibid., p. 11.
57. Cited in Benjamin Robinson, 'Indian Magic', *The Linking Ring*, vol. 62, no. 12, December 1982, p. 43.

Chapter 12: From Turbans to Top Hats

1. NAI, 'Durbar: Visit of H. H. the Amir of Kabul to Agra,' Bundelkhand Agency, no. 417, 1906.
2. *The Times of India*, 15 March 1894.

3. *Magic*, vol. 5, no. 3, December 1904, p. 1.
4. Ibid., p. 1.
5. IOR, 'Viceroy's state visit to Agra 1907 attended by the Amir of Afghanistan,' Mss. Eur. F 122/12.
6. NAI, 'Professor N.S. Swaminathan Sastriar's desire to be employed as an entertainer in and conjuring at the Delhi Darbar,' Foreign Internal B, September 1902, no. 64.
7. *Magic*, vol. 1, no. 12, September 1901, p. 102.
8. *Wizard's Manual Mind Reading Conjuring & Magic Ventriloquism &c., &c*, (Calcutta: Messrs Y. Paul & Co., 1901), p. 2ff.
9. Ben James, *The Secret Kingdom, An Afghan Journey*, (New York: Reynal and Hitchcock, 1934), p. 167.
10. *The Magician*, vol. 1, no. 9, 21 August 1905, p. 99.
11. Price, *Magic*, p. 506.
12. *The Eagle Magician*, vol. 1, no. 6, 1916, p. 17.
13. Alvaro, 'Indian Tricks', *The Magician Annual 1908–09*, pp. 51–52.
14. James, *The Secret Kingdom*, pp. 165–166.
15. Ibid., p 174.
16. *The Bombay Chronicle*, 24 December 1932.
17. *Magic*, vol. 1, no. 7, April 1901, p. 1.
18. Ibid., p. 1.
19. *Mahatma*, vol. 5, January 1902, p. 496.
20. *The Magician*, vol. 1, 20 February 1905, p. 29.
21. P. C. Sorcar, 'India takes up Western Magic,' *The Sphinx*, vol. 46, no. 11, 10 January 1948, p. 548.
22. Jim Steinmeyer, *The Last Greatest Magician in the World* (New York: Penguin, 2011), p. 8.
23. *Mahatma*, vol. 8, no 2, August 1904, p. 20.
24. *The Wizard*, vol. 2, no. 14, November 1906, p. 10.
25. *Amrita Bazar Patrika*, 9 August 1896.
26. *The Linking Ring*, vol. 10, no. 4, June 1940, p. 320.
27. *Indian Magician*, vol. 2, no. 3, April 1933, p. 1.
28. 'Are Indian Jugglers Humbugs?', *The Strand Magazine*, pp. 657–64.
29. *Poverty Bay Herald*, 6 December 1901.
30. IOR, 'Copy of police report, dated 25 October 1901,' l/PJ/6, 1901 (2076).
31. *Philadelphia Inquirer*, 23 June 1905.

32. IOR, 'Statement of Charles Ganglee, dated 18 November 1901,' l/PJ/6, 1901 (2076).
33. *Printers' Ink*, vol. 37, 1901, p. 40.
34. I am indebted to A. N. Dutt's grandson, Nigel Dutt, for much of the biographical information on the period from 1901 to 1910.
35. *The Brooklyn Daily Eagle*, 23 May 1902.
36. Nigel Dutt, *Linga Singh alias Amar Nath Dutt*, unpublished manuscript.
37. *Indian Agitators Abroad.* Compiled in the Criminal Intelligence Office, Simla, November 1911, p. 28.
38. Prabha Chopra and P. N. Chopra, *Indian Freedom Fighters Abroad: Secret British Intelligence Report* (New Delhi: Criterion, 1988), p. 54.
39. *The Demon Telegraph*, no. 70, June-August 1943, p. 4.
40. Ibid.
41. *The Sphinx*, vol. 11, no. 2, April 1912, p. 5.
42. Price, *Magic*, p. 511.

Chapter 13: 'The Most Famous Trick Never Performed'

1. Cited in Louis Massignon, *The Passion of Al-Hallaj: Mystic and Martyr of Islam* (Paris: Gallimard, 1973) p. 97.
2. Ibid., p. 96.
3. P. Scheldon, 'The Indian Rope Trick', *The Linking Ring*, vol. 6, no. 6, August 1927, p. 479.
4. Ibn Battuta, *Travels in Asia and Africa, 1325–1354,* trans. by H. A. R. Gibbo (Oxon: Routledge Curzon, 2005), pp. 296–97.
5. Ibid., p. 297
6. Massignon, *The Passion of Al-Hallaj*, p. 97.
7. Ibid., p. 97.
8. Rev. J. Ovington, *A Voyage to Surat in the Year 1689* (London: Jacob Thomson, 1690), p. 258.
9. Henry Yule (ed.), *The Book of Ser Marco Polo, the Venetian: Concerning the Kingdoms and Marvels of the East*, vol. 2 (London: John Murray, 1874), pp. 281–82.
10. Rev. Frederick George Lee, *Glimpses in the Twilight; Being Various Notes, Records, and Examples of the Supernatural* (London: W. Blackwood, 1885), pp. 371–72.

11. *The Times of India,* 26 August 1889.
12. The story of the hoax is masterfully retold in Lamont, *The Rise of the Indian Rope Trick*, pp. 80–82.
13. Ibid., pp. 83–84.
14. Arthur Train, 'The World's Most Famous Trick', *Scribner's Magazine*, August 1936, p. 106.
15. *The Times of India*, 18 December 1891.
16. 'A Professor of Hindoo Magic. Or, the Wonders of Professor Jhingan and Mr Jacob of Simla', *Borderland*, vol. 1, 1897, pp. 181–82.
17. Lionel Weatherly and John Nevil Maskelyne, *The Supernatural?* (Bristol: J. W. Arrowsmith, 1917), p. 160.
18. Charles Bertram, *Isn't it Wonderful* (London: Swan Sonnenschein & Co., 1896), pp. 65–67.
19. Charles Bertram, *A Magician in Many Lands* (London: George Routledge & Sons, 1911) pp. 35–37.
20. 'Are Indian Jugglers Humbug?', *The Strand Magazine*, December 1899, p. 657.
21. Bertram, *A Magician in Many Lands*, p. 108.
22. Ibid., p. 99.
23. Carl Hertz, *A Modern Mystery Merchant* (London: Hutchinson & Co., 1924), p. 167.
24. *The Era*, 16 August 1916.
25. Hertz, *A Modern Mystery Merchant*, p. 167.
26. Horace Goldin, *It's Fun to be Fooled* (London: S. Paul & Co., 1937), n.p.
27. Ibid., n.p.
28. Ibid., n.p.
29. *The Kansas City Times*, 20 March 1898.
30. Professor Hoffman, 'Indian Conjuring Explained', *Chambers Journal*, vol. 87, 26 October 1901, p. 758.
31. Ibid., pp. 759–60.
32. Hereward Carrington, *Hindu Magic* (London: The Annals of Psychical Science, 1909), p. 49.
33. Ibid., p. 46.
34. A. T. Baird, *Richard Hodgson: The Story of a Psychical Researcher and His Times* (London: Psychic Press, 1949), p. 10.

35. Helena Petrova Blavatsky, *Isis Unveiled*, vol. 2 (New York, J. W. Bouton, 1877), p. 104.
36. Richard Hodgson, 'Indian Magic and the Testimony of Conjurers', *Proceedings of the Society for Psychical Research*, no. 9, 1884, p. 363.
37. John Nevil Maskelyne, *The Fraud of Modern Theosophy Exposed and the Miraculous Rope-Trick of the Indian Jugglers Explained* (London: George Routledge & Sons, 1912), p. 11.
38. Ibid., p. 61.
39. Ibid., p. 23.
40. *The Strand Magazine*, vol. 57, April 1919, p. 309.
41. Robert Elliot, *The Myth of the Mystic East* (London: Wm. Blackwood & Sons), 1934, p. 54.
42. *Magic Circular*, 13, 150, March 1919, pp. 85–7.
43. *Leeds Mercury*, 8 February 1919.
44. *Sheffield Evening Telegraph*, 6 February 1919.
45. *The Times*, 6 February 1919.
46. Robert Elliot, 'The Great Indian Rope Trick: In Tradition and Reality', *Magic Circular*, vol. 13, no. 152, May 1913, p. 128.
47. Ibid., p. 129.
48. Cited in *The Strand Magazine*, vol. 57, April 1919, p. 311.
49. *Daily Mail*, 6 February 1919.
50. *Daily Mail*, 7 February 1919.
51. *Daily Mail*, 13 February 1919.
52. *Daily Mail*, 10 January 1919.
53. *Daily Mail*, 27 January 1919.
54. Lionel Branson, *A Life Time of Deception* (London: Robert Hale, 1953), p. 151.
55. Ibid., pp. 36–37.
56. Lionel Branson, *Indian Conjuring* (London: George Routledge & Sons, 1922), pp. 10–11.
57. Ibid., p. 11.
58. Ibid., p. 80.
59. *Biggleswade Chronicle*, 21 May 1915.
60. *Daily Record*, 25 October 1916.
61. *Lancashire Evening Post*, 9 September 1924.
62. *Daily Mail*, 9 September 1924.

63. *The Sphinx*, vol. 31 No. 7, September 1932, p. 275.
64. *The Spectator*, 9 March 1934.
65. Harry Price, 'I Have Seen the Indian Rope Trick', *The Listener*, 16 January 1935, p. 98.
66. 'Exit – The Indian Rope Trick', *Magic Circular*, vol. 28, no. 320, June 1934, pp. 136–138.
67. *The Hindu*, 13 May 1934.
68. 'Exit – The Indian Rope Trick', p. 138.
69. Ibid., p. 136.

Chapter 14: A Rope Trick in a Snow Storm, a Fire Walk in Surrey

1. *The Tatler*, 27 June 1934.
2. *Western Morning News*, 29 November 1934.
3. *The Belfast News-Letter*, 13 July 1934.
4. *Gloucestershire Echo*, 3 May 1934.
5. *The Nottingham Evening Post*, 15 June 1934.
6. Ibid.
7. Lamont, *The Rise of the Indian Rope Trick*, p.130.
8. *The Sydney Morning Herald*, 5 March 1936.
9. Harry Price, *Confessions of a Ghost-Hunter* (London: Putnam, 1936), pp. 89–90.
10. Ibid., p. 347.
11. Ibid., pp. 347–48.
12. Ibid., p. 349.
13. Harry Price, 'The Indian Rope Trick', *The Listener* 16 January 1935, p.100
14. 'Karachi Challenges the Magic Circle', *The Listener*, 30 January 1935.
15. 'The Magic Circle and Karachi's Challenge', *The Listener*, 6 February 1935.
16. 'The Indian Rope Trick', *The Listener*, 6 February 1935.
17. 'The Magic Circle and Karachi's Challenge', *The Listener*, 20 February 1935.
18. HPC, HPD/2/30.
19. Price, *Confessions*, p. 354.
20. *The Daily News*, 22 January 1949.
21. IOR: Ronald Sinclair, *Magic and Mysticism* (unpublished manuscript), Mss. Eur., C313/27.
22. Ibid.

23. Price, *Confessions*, p. 314.
24. Ibid., pp. 315–316.
25. John Booth, 'The Genius of Kuda Bux, Blindfold Expert', *The Linking Ring*, vol. 60, no. 11, November 1980, p. 59.
26. *The People*, 15 September 1935.
27. Harry Price, 'Walking through Fire', *The Listener*, 18 September 1935.
28. Price, *Confessions*, p. 369.
29. Ibid., pp 369–70.
30. *The Times of India*, 24 August 1935.
31. Price, *Confessions*, p. 375.
32. Ibid., p 377.
33. *The Times*, London, 18 September 1935.
34. *The Guardian*, 27 September 1935.
35. 'A Strange Ordeal', *The Observer*, 22 September 1935.
36. *The Nursing Times*, 28 September 1935.
37. *The Listener*, 6 November 1935.
38. Charles Darling, 'Fire-walking', *The Nature*, no. 136, 1935, p 521.
39. *The Listener*, 20 November 1935.
40. Harry Price, *Search for Truth, My Life for Psychical Research* (London: Collins, 1942), p. 188.
41. *Sunday Graphic and Sunday News*, 29 September 1935.
42. *The Morning Post*, 15 October 1935.
43. *The Linking Ring*, vol. 35, no. 2, April 1955, p. 123.
44. *Larne Times*, 5 November 1942.

Chapter 15: The Maharajah of Magic

1. Frank Joglar, 'Backstage', *Hugard's Magic Monthly*, vol. 13, December 1955, p. 76.
2. *The Stage*, 12 April 1956.
3. Milbourne Christopher, *The Illustrated History of Magic* (London: Robert Hale & Co., 1975), p. 409.
4. 'Sorcar, Best in India!' *Tops*, vol. 12, February 1947, pp. 4–5.
5. Jack Gwynne, 'P. C. Sorcar, Indian Magician', *The Sphinx*, vol. 45, no. 5, July 1946, p. 4.
6. Ibid.

7. 'Sorcar – Great Indian Magician', *Linking Ring*, vol. 26, no. 4, June 1946, p. 22.
8. Samuel Patrick Smith, 'P. C. Sorcar, 1913–1971', *The Linking Ring*, vol. 89, no. 10, October 2009, p. 54.
9. Gene Gordon, 'Without the Shuffle', *Genii*, vol. 15, no. 8, April 1951, p. 24.
10. *Abracadabra*, vol. 14, no. 363, 10 January 1953, p. 304.
11. *Abracadabra*, vol. 15, no. 471, 7 March 1953, p. 128.
12. *Abracadabra*, vol. 15, no. 472, 14 March 1953, p. 123
13. *The Conjurors' Magazine*, vol. 3, no. 10, December 1947, p. 81.
14. *Genii*, vol. 15, no. 7, March 1951, p. 292.
15. *Genii*, vol. 15, no. 10, June 1951, p. 414.
16. *Genii*, vol. 16, no. 4, December 1951, p. 36.
17. *The Linking Ring*, vol. 33, no. 8, October 1953, p. 111.
18. Jack Lamonte, 'Publicity a la Sorcar', *The Magic Wand*, vol. 42, no. 240, December 1953, p. 224.
19. 'John Booth Returns to India', *The Linking Ring*, vol. 33, no. 8, October 1953, pp. 21–22.
20. *The New Tops*, vol. 8, April 1968, p. 11.
21. *Genii*, vol. 19, no. 10, June 1955, p. 4
22. Frank Joglar, 'Backstage', *Hugard's Magic Monthly*, vol. 13, no. 3, October 1955, p. 350.
23. Cited in Joglar, 'Backstage', *Hugard's Magic Monthly*, vol. 13, no. 5, December 1955, p. 76.
24. Cited in *Abracadabra*, vol. 21, no. 521, 21 January 1956, p. 4.
25. Tommy Windsor, 'Merchandising Magic', *Tops*, vol. 21, June 1956, p. 23.
26. *Abracadabra*, vol. 20, no. 54, 3 December 1955, p. 305.
27. Arthur LeRoy, 'Kalanag, King of Comedy', *Hugard's Magic Monthly*, vol. 13, no. 9, February 1956, pp. 392.
28. *New Phoenix*, n.d., p. 147.
29. LeRoy, 'Kalanag', pp. 392–94.
30. *The Chicago Daily Tribune*, 28 May 1957.
31. Don Tanner, 'Don Tanner Reviews TV Festival of Magic', *The Linking Ring*, vol. 37, no. 5, July 1957, p. 36.
32. *TW'sGM – The Great Sorcar (A photographic monograph on his 50th birthday)*, http://www.pcsorcarmagician.com/books.htm
33. John Booth, *Wonders of Magic* (Los Alamitos: Ridgeway, 1986), p. 131.

34. Ibid., p. 133.
35. Ibid., pp. 135–37.
36. *The Linking Ring*, vol. 34, no. 2, April 1954, p. 39.
37. Delilah Harrow, 'Gogia Pasha of Derradun, India', *The Linking Ring*, vol. 36, no. 3, May 1956, p. 39.
38. *Abracadabra*, vol. 21, no. 545, 7 July 1956, p. 491.
39. Harrow, 'Gogia Pasha', p. 39.
40. Gordon, 'Without the Shuffle', *Genii*, vol. 21, no. 2, October 1956, p. 67.
41. Siegel, *Net of Magic*, pp. 374–75.
42. Price, *Magic*, p. 537.
43. Frances Marshall, 'Farewell to the Prince of Magic', *Abracadabra,* vol. 51, no. 1313, 2 January 1971, p. 211.
44. Price, *Magic*, p. 536.
45. 'Sid Lorraine's Chatter', *Tops,* vol. 16, November 1951, p. 17.
46. P. C. Sorcar, 'India takes up Western Magic', *The Sphinx*, vol. 46, no. 11, 10 January 1948, p. 358.

Epilogue

1. Andrew Robinson, *Satyajit Ray: The Inner Eye: The Biography of a Master Film-Maker* (London, I. B. Tauris, 2004), p. 36.
2. *The Bombay Chronicle*, 31 December 1932.
3. Untitled facsimile, Library of the Asian Heritage Foundation, New Delhi.
4. Siegel, *Net of Magic*, p. 39.
5. Meena Radhakrishna, 'Laws of Metamorphosis: From Nomad to Offender', in Kalpana Kannabiran and Ranbir Singh (eds), *Challenging the Rule(s) of Law: Colonialism, Criminology and Human Rights in India* (New Delhi: Sage Publications India, 2008), p. 20.
6. Cited in https://www.thequint.com/photos/humans-of-kathputli-colony-demolition, accessed 4 November 2017.

SELECT BIBLIOGRAPHY

Adburgham, Alison, *Liberty's: A Biography of a Shop* (London: George Allen & Unwin, 1979).

Alberuni's India, trans. by Edward C. Sachau, vol. 1 (London: Trubner, 1888).

Allami, Abu Fazl, *The Ain-i-Akbar*, trans. by Henry Blochmann, vol. 1 (Calcutta: Asiatic Society of Bengal, 1873).

Ames, Eric, *Carl Hagenbeck's Empire of Entertainment* (Seattle: University of Washington Press, 2008).

'Are Indian Jugglers Humbugs? The Opinion of an Expert. An Interview with Mr Charles Bertram,' *The Strand Magazine*, vol. 18, December 1899, pp. 657–64.

Arthashastra, trans. by R. Shamasastry (Bangalore: Government Press, 1915).

Arundhati, P., *Royal Life in Manasollasa* (New Delhi: Sundeep Prakashan, 1994).

'A True Relation without all Exception, of Strange and Admirable Accidents, which Lately Happened in the Kingdome of the Great Magor, or, Magull, who is the Greatest Monarch of the Indies', *The Harleian Miscellany*, vol. 3, 1809, pp. 421–27.

Basham, Arthur Llewellyn, *History and Doctrines of the Ajivikas, a Vanished Indian Religion* (Delhi: Motilal Banarsidass, 1951).

Battuta, Ibn, *The Travels of Ibn Battuta: in the Near East, Asia and Africa, 1325–1354*, trans. by Rev. Samuel Lee (New York: Dover, 2004).

Bernier, François, *Travels in the Mogul Empire*, vol. 2, trans. by Irving Brock (London: William Pickering, 1826).

Bertram, Charles, *A Magician in Many Lands* (London: George Routledge & Sons, 1911).

——— *Isn't it Wonderful?* (London: Swan Sonnenschein & Co., 1896).

Branson, Lionel, *A Life Time of Deception* (London: Robert Hale, 1953).

——— *Indian Conjuring* (London: George Routledge & Sons, 1922).

Brown, Mark, *Penal Power and Colonial Rule* (New York: Routledge, 2014)

Carrington, Hereward, *Hindu Magic* (London: The Annals of Psychical Science, 1909).

Caunter, J. Hobart, *The Oriental Annual: Or, Scenes in India* (London: E. Churton, 1836).

Christopher, Milbourne, *Panorama of Magic* (New York: Dover, 1962).

——— *The Illustrated History of Magic* (London: Robert Hale & Co., 1975).

Collins, Wilkie, *The Moonstone* (New York: Harper Brothers, 1868).

Crofton, Olive, *They Also Serve* (unpublished manuscript), Crofton Papers, University of Cambridge, n.d.

Crooke, William, *An Introduction to the Popular Religion and Folklore of Northern India* (Allahabad: Government Press, 1894).

Dadswell, Sarah, 'Jugglers, Fakirs, and Jaduwallahs: Indian Magicians and the British stage', *New Theatre Quarterly*, vol. 23, no. 1, 2007, pp. 3–24.

Dallapiccola, Anna Libera, *King, Court and Capital: An Anthology of Kannada Literary Sources from the Vijayanagara Period* (New Delhi: Manohar, 2003).

Description of the Performance of those Superior Indian Jugglers lately arrived from Seringapatam, etc., (London, printed by T. Wood, n.d).

Dhar, M. K., *Royal Life in Ancient India* (Delhi: Durga Publications, 1991).

Dickie, Matthew, *Magic and Magicians in the Greco-Roman World* (London: Routledge, 2001).

Doniger, Wendy, *The Hindus: An Alternative History* (Oxford: Oxford University Press, 2009).

Duncan, Jonathan, 'An Account of Two Fakeers, With Their Portraits', *Asiatick Researches*, vol. 5, 1799, pp. 37–52.

During, Simon, *Modern Enchantments: The Cultural Power of Secular Magic* (Cambridge and London: Harvard University Press, 2002).

Dutt, Nigel, *Linga Singh alias Amar Nath Dutt*, unpublished manuscript, n.d.

Elliot, Henry Miers and John Dawson (eds.), *History of India as Told by its Own Historians*, vol. 5 (London: Turner & Co., 1873).

Elliot, Robert, 'The Great Indian Rope Trick: In Tradition and Reality', *Magic Circular*, vol. 13, no. 152, May 1913, pp. 125–30.

——— *The Myth of the Mystic East* (London: Wm. Blackwood & Sons, 1934).

Enthoven, Reginald Edward, *The Folklore of Bombay* (Oxford: Clarendon Press, 1924).

Ernst, Carl W., 'Being Careful with the Goddess: Yoginis in Persian and Arabic Texts', in Pallabi Chakrabarty and Scott Kugle (eds.), *Performing Ecstasy: The Poetics and Politics of Religion in India* (Delhi: Manohar, 2009).

——— *Refractions of Islam in India: Situating Sufism and Yoga* (New Delhi: Sage, 2016).

Farooqi, Musharraf Ali, 'Hoshruba: The Land and the Tilism', *Pakistaniaat: A Journal of Pakistan Studies*, vol. 1, no. 2, 2009, pp. 150–71.

Fihrist of al-Nadim: A Tenth-Century Survey of Muslim Culture, trans. by Bayard Dodge, vol. 1 (New York: Columbia University Press, 1970).

Flatt, Emma J., 'The Authorship and Significance of the Nujum al-'ulum: A Sixteenth-Century Astrological Encyclopedia from Bijapur', *Journal of the American Oriental Society*, vol. 131, no. 2, 2011, pp. 223–44.

Forbes, James, *Oriental Memoirs*, vols. 2 & 3, (London: White, Cochrane & Co., 1813).

Fuchs, Stephen, *Children of Hari: A Study of the Nimar Balahis in the Central Provinces of India* (Vienna: Verlag Herold, 1950).

Goldin, Horace, *It's Fun to be Fooled* (London: S. Paul & Co., 1937).

Goto-Jones, Chris, *Conjuring Asia: Magic, Orientalism and the Making of the Modern World* (Cambridge: Cambridge University Press, 2016).

Goudriaan, Teun, *Maya Divine and Human* (Delhi: Motilal Banarsidass, 1978).

Govind Narayan's Mumbai, An Urban Biography from 1863, trans. by Murali Ranganathan (London: Anthem Press, 2008).

Granoff, Phyllis, 'Scholars and Wonder-Workers: Some Remarks on the Role of the Supernatural in Philosophical Contests in Vedanta Hagiographies', *Journal of the American Oriental Society*, vol. 105, no. 3, 1985, pp. 459–67.

Gupta, Dharmendra Kumar, *Society and Culture in the Time of Dandin* (Delhi: Meharchand Lachhmandas, 1972).

Harrow, Delilah, 'Gogia Pasha of Derradun, India', *The Linking Ring*, vol. 36, no. 3, May 1956, p.39.

Heller, Robert, *His Doings* (Glasgow: Hay Lisbet, 1875).

Henty, George A., *Rujub, the Juggler* (Chicago: M. A. Donohue & Co., 1910).

Herrmann, Alexander, 'The Art of Magic', *The North American Review*, vol. 153, no. 416, July 1891, pp. 92–8.

Hertz, Carl, *A Modern Mystery Merchant* (London: Hutchison & Co., 1924).

Hunt, Edmund Henderson, 'The Rafai Fakeers of Hyderabad', *Man*, vol. 32, February 1932, p. 46.

Jacolliot, Louis, *Occult Science in India*, trans. by Willard Felt (New York: John W. Lovell, 1884).

James, Ben, *The Secret Kingdom: An Afghan Journey* (New York: Reynal and Hitchcock, 1934).

Jones, Graham, *Trade of the Tricks, Inside the Magician's Craft* (Berkeley, University of California Press, 2011).

Joshi, Lal Mani, *Studies in the Buddhistic Culture of India During the 7th and 8th Centuries AD* (Delhi: Motilal Banarsidass, 1987).

Kellar, Harry, *A Magician's Tour Up and Down and Round About the Earth* (Chicago: R. R. Donnelly & Sons, 1886).

——— 'High Caste Indian Magic', *North American Review*, vol. 156, no. 434, 1893, pp. 75–86.

Knight, Michael Muhammad, *Magic in Islam* (New York: Tarcher Perigee, 2016).

Lamont, Peter, *The Indian Rope Trick: The Biography of a Legend* (London: Little Brown, 2004).

Lamont, Peter and Crispin Bates, 'Conjuring Images of India in Nineteenth-Century Britain', *Social History*, vol. 32, no. 3, 2007, pp. 308–24.

Lynn, H. S., *Travels and Adventures of Dr Lynn* (London: published by the author, 1882).

Manucci, Niccolao, *Storia do Mogor*, trans. by William Irvine, vols. 2 and 3 (London, John Murray, 1907).

Marshall, Frances, 'Farewell to the Prince of Magic', *Abracadabra*, vol. 51, no. 1313, 2 January 1971, pp. 194–95, 198.

Massignon, Louis, *The Passion of Al-Hallaj: Mystic and Martyr of Islam* (Paris: Gallimard, 1973).

Maskelyne, John Nevil, *The Fraud of Modern Theosophy Exposed and the Miraculous Rope-Trick of the Indian Jugglers Explained* (London: George Routledge & Sons, 1912).

Mathur, Saloni, 'Living Ethnological Exhibits: The Case of 1886', *Cultural Anthropology*, vol. 15, no. 4, 2000, pp. 492–524.

Mayhew, Henry, *London Labour and the London Poor: A Cyclopaedia of the Condition and Earnings of Those that will Work, Those that cannot Work, and Those that will not Work*, vol. 3 (London: Griffin, Bohn and Company 1861).

Memoirs of the Emperor Jahangueir, trans. by David Price (London: John Murray, 1829).

Moin, A. Azfar, *The Millennial Sovereign: Sacred Kingship and Sainthood in Islam* (New York: Colombia University Press, 2012).

Monier-Williams, Monier, *Brahmanism and Hinduism* (New York: Macmillan & Co., 1891).

——— *Hinduism* (New York: Pott, Young & Co., 1878).

Mulholland, John, *Quicker than the Eye: The Magic and Magicians of the World*, (Indianapolis: The Bobbs-Merrill, 1932).

Narain, V. A., *Jonathan Duncan and Varanasi* (Calcutta: Mukhopadhyay, 1959).

Oman, John Campbell, *The Mystics, Ascetics, and Saints of India* (London: T. F. Unwin, 1905).

Pai, D. A., *Monograph on the Religious Sects in India among the Hindus* (Bombay: The Times Press, 1928).

Pelsaert, Francisco, *Jahangir's India, The Remonstrantie of Francisco Pelsaert*, trans. by W. H. Moreland (Cambridge: W. Heffer & Sons, 1925).

Philostratus, *The Life of Apollonius of Tyana*, trans. by E. C. Conybeare (Harvard: Harvard University Press, 1960).

Price, David, *Magic: A Pictorial History*, (New York: Cornwall Books, 1985).

Price, Harry, *Confessions of a Ghost-Hunter* (London: Putnam, 1936).

Raghunathji, Krishnanath, *Bombay Beggars and Criers* (Bombay: Government Press, 1892).

Roberts, Emma, *Scenes and Characteristics of Hindostan, with Sketches of Anglo-Indian Society*, vol. 1 (London: W. H. Allen, 1835).

Robertson, Miriam, *The Kalbelias of Rajasthan: Jogi Nath Snake Charmers. An Ethnography of Indian Non-Pastoral Nomads*, PhD thesis, London School of Economics and Political Science, 1987.

Rousselet, Jean, *India and its Native Princes*, trans. by Charles Buckle, (London: Bickers, 1882).

Russell, Robert Vane, *The Tribes and Castes of the Central Provinces*, vol. 4 (London: Macmillan & Co., 1916),

Salter, Joseph, *The Asiatic in England; Sketches of Sixteen Years' Work Among Orientals*, (London: Seeley, Jackson and Halliday, 1873).

Sharif, Jafar, *Islam in India or the Qanun-i-Islam*, trans. by G. A. Herlocks (London: Oxford University Press, 1921).

Shende, N. J., *Religion and Philosophy of the Atharvaveda* (Poona: Aryabhushan Press, 1952).

Sherring, Mathew, *Hindu Tribes and Castes, as Represented in Benares*, vol.1 (Calcutta: Thacker Spink & Co., 1872).

Siegel, Lee, *Net of Magic: Wonders and Deceptions in India* (New Delhi: Harper Collins, 2000).

Sirafi, Abu Zayd al-, *Two Arabic Travel Books: Accounts of China and India, and Mission to the Volga* (New York: New York University Press, 2014).

Sleemann, William, *The Thugs or Phansigars of India* (Philadelphia: Carey & Hart, 1839).

Smith, Samuel Patrick, 'P. C. Sorcar, 1913–1971', *The Linking Ring*, vol. 89, no. 10, October 2009, pp. 54–56.

Sorcar, P. C., *Sorcar on Magic, Reminiscences and Selected Tricks* (Calcutta: Indrajal Publications, 1960).

——— 'India takes up Western Magic', *The Sphinx*, vol. 46, no. 11, 10 January 1948, pp. 348, 358.

Steinmeyer, Jim, *The Last Greatest Magician in the World: Howard Thurston versus Houdini & the Battles of the American Wizards* (New York: Jeremy P. Tarcher/Penguin, 2011).

Strong, John S., *Miracles, Mango Trees, and Ladders from Heaven: Reflections on the Tale of Prince Kala at Sravastī and the Buddha's Descent from Trayastrimsa*, Paper presented at the ISEAS/EFEO 2009 Kyoto Lectures Series.

Stutley, Margaret, *Ancient Indian Magic and Folklore*, (Delhi: Motilal Banarsidass, 1980).

Tavernier, Jean Baptiste, *Travels in India*, trans. by John Phillips (Calcutta: Bangabasi, 1905).

——— *Travels in India*, trans. by V. Ball, vol.1 (London: Macmillan & Co., 1889).

The Book of the Marvels of India, trans. by L. Marcel Devik (London: George Routledge & Sons, 1928).

The Natural History of Reptiles and Serpents (Dublin: J. Jones, 1821).

The Ocean of Story: Being C. H. Tawney's translation of Somadeva's Katha Sarit Sagara, vol. 1 (London: Chas. J. Sawyer, 1924).

The Travels of Pietro della Valle in India, vol. 1, trans. by G. Havers (London: Hakluyt Society, 1892).

'The Travels of Pran-Puri, A Hindu who Travelled over India, Persia and Parts of Russia', *The European Magazine and London Review*, vol. 57, 1810, pp 262–72.

Thévenot, Jean de, *The Travels of Monsieur de Thévenot into the Levant*, vol. 3, trans. by Archibald Lovell (London: H. Clark, 1687).

Thurston, Howard, *My Life of Magic*, (Philadelphia: Dorrance & Co., 1929).

Train, Arthur, 'The World's Most Famous Trick', *Scribner's Magazine*, August 1936, pp. 104–09.

Tritton, Arthur Stanley, 'Spirits and Demons in Arabia', *Journal of the Royal Asiatic Society*, vol., 66 no. 4 (1934).

TW'sGM – The Great Sorcar (A Photographic Monograph on his 50th birthday), http://www.pcsorcarmagician.com/books.php.

Varma, Rai Sahib H. L., *The Indian Rope Trick* (Ambikapur: State Press, 1942).

Vogel, Jean Philippe, *Indian Serpent-lore: Or, The Nagas in Hindu Legend and Art* (London: Arthur Probsthain, 1926).

Wellisch, Hans H., *The First Arab Bibliography: Fihrist al-'Ulum* (Chicago, University of Illinois, Occasional Paper, no. 175, 1986).

White, David Gordon, *Sinister Yogis* (Chicago: Chicago University Press, 2009).

——— *The Alchemical Body: Siddha Traditions in Medieval India* (Chicago: University of Chicago Press, 1996).

Weatherly, Lionel and John Nevil Maskelyne, *The Supernatural?* (Bristol: J. W. Arrowsmith, 1917).

Yule, Henry (ed.), *The Book of Ser Marco Polo, the Venetian: Concerning the Kingdoms and Marvels of the East*, vol. 1 (London: John Murray, 1874).

Zimmer, Heinrich, *Philosophies of India* (Princeton: Princeton University Press, 1951).

INDEX